Alaska's
Lost Frontier

**Life in the days of
homesteads, dog teams,
and sailboat fisheries**

Denton Rickey Moore

Illustrated

TO Bob & Family,
Hope you enjoy this book
Harry Moore   Son of D.R. Moore

Other books by this author:
Gentlemen Never Sail to Weather, (two editions)
    Prospector Press, 1993
Law and the Juvenile,
    Iowa Crime Commission, 1969

This book was published by:
Prospector Press
Post Office Box 1289
Moore Haven, Florida 33471
Tel. (813) 946-3212   FAX (813) 946-3628

Printing history:
Advance printing—September, 1994
Second printing—January, 1995

Publisher's Cataloging in Publication
(Prepared by Quality Books Inc.)

Moore, Denton R., 1926–
        Alaska's Lost Frontier : life in the days of homesteads, dog teams, and sailboat fisheries / Denton R. Moore.
            p. cm.
            Includes index.
            Preassigned LCCN; 94–067836
            ISBN: Hardcover 0-9628828-9-5   Paper cover 0-9628828-8-7

        1. Moore, Denton R., 1926– 2. Alaska—Biography. I. Title.

F909.M66 1995   917.9804'4'092
                             QBI94-1522

Cover photo is of Eskimo fishermen in Bristol Bay sailboat, 1947
Cover design by: Ken Alford of Arts & Graphs, Clewiston, Florida
MANUFACTURED IN THE UNITED STATES OF AMERICA

Table of Contents

Chapter   *Page Number*

Illustrations

Maps:

Other:

Photos:

Except where noted, all photos by the author

Southwestern Alaska
(including Lake Iliamna and Bristol Bay)

The map depicts the corner of Southwestern Alaska where the events described in this book occurred. The sheer immensity of Alaska's size becomes apparent when the reader realizes that this map, covering only a fragment of Alaska's area, depicts about 30,000 square miles, an area only slightly smaller than South Carolina, but with less than 4,000 year-around inhabitants. The terrain is rugged and mountainous. Elevations range from sea level to 11,000 foot mountains, including several live volcanos. It's a tough country.

Map drawn by Captain Jim Hogan

Aleknagik

Wood River

Nushagak River

Kvichak Riv

Dillingham

Government hospital

Levelock

Clarks Point

Taught school

Ekuk

Dogteam trail

Nakeen

Portage Creek

Naknek King Salmon road

Naknek

King Salmon

South Naknek

Nushagak Bay

Kvichak Bay

Naknek River

For greater detail
see page 16

Bristol Bay

For greater detail
see page 244

Bering Sea

Alaska

N

Lake Clark

Port Alsworth

Nondalton   Six Mile Lake
NEWHALEN ROAD
            Roadhouse
            Mountain
                                    ILIAMNA
                                    PORTAGE
                        Pedro Bay
            Roadhouse
                                Pile Bay   Carl William's place
Newhalen   LANDED HORSES
                            Poor Lake
                    Nondalton River
                                        Moose Lake
                        Copper River
                    Iliamna Winter Dogteam Trail
                                MOORE HOMESTEAD
Newhalen   Kokhanok Lake
Lake Iliamna   Kokhanok
                            Kokhanok River
                    Kokhanok
        DEW Line station   Augustine

                                        Kamishak Bay   Cook Inlet

Igiugig
                        Aleutian Mountain Range

e Creek   KUKAKLEK
                LAKE

Nonvianuk Lake   Kulik Lake

Kulik camp site

                        Alaska

ek   LAKE

                Area of Detail

Peninsula

Preface and Acknowledgement

This book is at once an historical account of the 1950s—the Statehood Decade—in Southwestern Alaska, and a family memoir, written in the hope that my children, whose formative years were spent in a tiny log cabin in the Alaskan wilderness, will not forget their roots.

Our experience reflected the self-reliant lifestyle common to many Americans a century earlier. But it was also significantly different. Unlike our forbears, we were surrounded by a dynamic society making enormous political, economic, social, and technological advances. Ultimately, we too obtained radios, chainsaws, gas powered boats, and penicillin. With statehood, we achieved political self-determination.

The story begins in 1947. It describes the social and economic climate then prevailing; the tuberculosis epidemic that was raging among the Eskimo people, and the archaic sailboat fishery in Bristol Bay. It documents the benign neglect of the Federal government, and how the fishermen shifted from a social system based on peonage to a rising generation of small independent businessmen-fishermen.

Nearly half a century has elapsed since this story begins. Many of the people described have passed on. Yet, they are immortal because they will live forever in our memories.

I especially wish to acknowledge my indebtedness to Captain Jim Hogan, whose carefully drawn maps grace these pages, and whose kind introduction sets the stage for what follows. I am also indebted to Ken Alford for his inspired cover design.

As in most of my endeavors, this project would have been impossible without the steadfast encouragement, proofreading skills, and willingness to cut the grass, that sets my loving wife, Velda, apart. My thanks to her and to everyone involved in this project.

Denton Rickey Moore
Moore Haven, Florida

Introduction

I was surprised when Denny Moore asked me to write this introduction; after all, I have never lived in Alaska. But I have known him for nearly 20 years, and I was familiar with his unusual history.

Denny was one of those wounded veterans who retreated at the end of World War II into the anonymity of Alaska's vastness, there to recover from war's hideous traumas. He did more than recover. He learned to cope with his battlefield disability so well that he became a leader among the fishermen.

He first describes his experiences as a school teacher in a tiny cannery village on the Bering Sea coast. He had several disadvantages, not the least of which was the fact that his formal education had ended at the 10th grade. As he dryly remarks, his only qualification for the job was his availability.

During their two-year stint in the village, he and his wife, Jan, came face to face with a veritable epidemic of tuberculosis. He faced down a murderous Eskimo, learned to drive a dog team, and helped his wife, a registered nurse, perform emergency medical miracles.

The middle part of the book takes the reader into Alaska's coastal interior where he and Jan (and six head of horses) dug in for the winter. They (but, unfortunately, not the horses) survived that first winter; then, step by step, in what is the most gripping saga of gritty personal achievement I can imagine, the Moores pulled themselves up by their bootstraps.

They endured incredible privation and hardship. Yet his good humor never abandons him as he instructs the reader in a proven method for removing porcupine quills from a dog team, reveals his recipe for potato whiskey, and how to rid a cabin of a horde of shrews.

Throughout the book, he describes his part in what one Scandinavian fisherman has termed the "toughest fishery in Alaska," the Bristol Bay sailboat gillnet salmon fishery that routinely killed as many as 20 to 30 fishermen every year.

At great cost to himself and his growing family, Denny played a vital role in reversing ruinous federal fishery management policies, and in leading local Indian and Eskimo fishermen from a state of near peonage with the gigantic food corporations that dominated the fishery to prosperity as independent fishermen.

The last part of the book describes his life in Naknek, where he consolidated the economic gains made by local fishermen, and established two newspapers. He tells about Long John's funeral in a way that is reminiscent of *The Burial of Sam McGee,* written nearly 100 years earlier.

Indeed, much of this book reminded me of Robert Service and Jack London. The life he describes is not different from the world they knew. Even the hardships of the trail are similar.

Denny is a master storyteller. Those who read *Gentlemen Never Sail to Weather,* his account of a long downwind sail that accidentally turned into a circumnavigation; a book that became a **Book-of-the-Month Club** selection, will know they are in for a treat when they begin to read *Alaska's Lost Frontier.*

Captain Jim Hogan
Solomon, Maryland

This book is for my children—

  Even if it was only
  A log cabin,
  It is important to know
  Your beginnings

An Alaskan Honeymoon

*I*t was a tense and scary moment as we listened to our enraged pilot scream at the ground agent over the roar of his idling engines, "If I get this crate to Anchorage, I'm going to red-tag every God damn thing on her! *And if I can't get her into the air by the time I get this far down the field, I'm going to swing her into the hut and take you with me!"*

One reason why they install doors between the passenger compartment and the flight deck on commercial airplanes became instantly and painfully clear. While foiling air hijackers may have something to do with it, there's another, possibly more important, reason. Like patients in an operating room, there are some things passengers are better off not hearing or knowing about. An intimate, heartfelt, and completely candid conversation between the pilot and ground crew is one of them.

Jan, my bride of only three months, and I nervously sat, strapped to our seats next to four other uneasy passengers, staring at a pile of greasy machinery lashed to the floor in front of us. I couldn't help but wonder at the peculiar and ironic result of my self-imposed penury as I watched the drama before my startled eyes.

By choosing to fly on Alaska Airline's war surplus DC-4 instead of Pan-Am's more luxurious

DC–6, we had saved $40—not an inconsiderable sum in 1947—but I already knew the "saving" was purely illusionary. Quite simply, we had been had.

Alaska Airlines was not then the sleek international carrier it would later become. Indeed, in 1947, Alaska Airlines was not even certified to fly the Seattle/Anchorage route, and was operating merely as a "non-scheduled" carrier flying freight and a few poverty-stricken passengers between the two cities in war weary, four-engine, transport planes.

At first, the $40 differential had seemed like found money. We were young. It didn't matter that instead of the tastefully decorated passenger cabin of a modern and speedy DC-6, we would be seated in the tail of a much slower DC-4, facing a pile of air freight. Or that here, instead of a printed menu, the cabin service would consist of a box lunch containing a cheese sandwich and a cup of stale coffee poured from a thermos bottle.

What we *hadn't* expected—the inevitable result of our naivete—was that as a non-scheduled carrier, Alaska Airlines was under no compulsion to go anywhere until they were good and ready, meaning until the cargo bay was full.

When we had reported to the Alaska Airline hut at Seattle's Boeing Field at the appointed time three days earlier, the agent had sadly shaken his head as we walked in the door. "I'm sorry," he had said, "the plane isn't ready. Come back tomorrow." We believed him. We had left our luggage in his care, and called a cab. The driver recommended a hotel in downtown Seattle, and for the first time in our brief married lives, I registered Mr. and Mrs. D. R. Moore into a hotel—this was 1947, remember—without luggage.

I'm sure the room clerk leered as he handed me the key—this being the sort of hotel that bellhops had abandoned shortly after the first World War. "Enjoy your stay," he said with what I thought was a lewd emphasis on the word *"enjoy."*

The next day, when we returned to the airfield, the ticket agent had shaken his head. "You should have phoned," he said righteously. "I could have saved you the trip out here. The plane's ready, but the weather in Anchorage isn't good."

In my innocence, I still believed him. On the third morning, the agent had greeted us with a smile. "This is the day," he said cheerfully as we walked through the door. "We'll be leaving in about an hour."

As I later reflected on that brief conversation, not without bitterness, I thought he should have added, *This will give you time to settle your affairs and get your papers in order.*

We were ushered aboard the plane and found that six lonely seats had been set up in the rear of the cabin behind a mound of crates, boxes and machinery lashed to the cabin floor with wide nylon straps. Uneasily, eyes averted, we nodded to our fellow passengers as we sat in the remaining seats and fastened our seat belts.

Because this aircraft was a freighter, there was no door between the main cabin and the cockpit. By craning our necks and peering over the mound of cargo, we had a perfect view of the flight deck.

The pilot started his engines. He released his brakes. We lumbered the length of Boeing Field. He spun the aircraft around. Standing on the brakes, he advanced the throttles on each engine, one at a time, testing their magnetos. So far, so good. Then, after a pause, he released the brakes. But instead of opening his throttles as I expected, we trundled the length of the field back to the airline hut.

When we arrived, he shut off his engines. Then, sliding his window open, he yelled down to the inquiring ground agent, "I want the clock fixed and these other instruments checked!"

Oh, oh.

There was a long delay while the agent summoned an instrument mechanic. Morale among the passengers, never high, noticeably began to sag. I found I was studiously avoiding eye contact with my fellow passengers. Jan and I exchanged more uneasy looks as, out the window, we saw the pilot walk out on the wings with a long stick in his hands. He was sounding his fuel tanks.

The stewardess motioned to us. "I think we're supposed to get off," she said apologetically. She released the latch to the cargo door as a step stand was pushed into place.

Walking down the steps, I overheard the pilot say to the agent, " **. . . and I want another 200 gallons of gas!**"

The agent protested: "But you're already overweight."

The pilot then uttered the ultimate blasphemy for a non-sched pilot. "Then take off some freight," he suggested, grinning a 50-mission grin at the worried man.

Helplessly, the agent summoned a tank truck, and while the mechanic tinkered in the cockpit, the pilot and truck driver added fuel. I thought about that fuel truck later, when, from a former Alaska Airlines bush pilot, I heard the probably apocryphal story about Alaska Airlines bush passengers being compelled to chip in to pay for the gas needed for their flight because Standard Oil refused to extend further credit to the fledgling airline.

When we climbed back into the aircraft, I wondered if we were making an awful mistake. I knew it would be pointless to ask for a refund, and that we couldn't afford to abandon our tickets; yet a moment later, after listening to the pilot's diatribe, had I been given the chance, I'd have been off that plane like a shot, dragging Jan behind me.

The other passengers probably felt as I did. I'm sure we all held our breath as, after again reaching the opposite end of the field, and after again testing his magnetos, the pilot pulled his throttles wide open and released the brakes.

Even in 1947, Boeing Field was only marginally suitable for commercial traffic. An already short runway was further abbreviated because heavily laden planes with poor climbing ability were forced prematurely into the air to avoid the upper floors of the buildings looming above a thicket of power lines at the end of the field.

The runway was paved with cement. As the wheels rolled over the evenly spaced pressure breaks, I was distressingly reminded of the rhythmic a–clickety–clack, a–clickety–clack of a train moving at a constant speed over the rails.

I'm sure it was only our collective will that lifted that airplane off the field at the last possible moment. In calm weather, when heavier planes like our overloaded DC–4 became airborne, they sometimes mushed through the air across the width of downtown Seattle in a virtual stall.

Our pilot gradually forced the plane's nose down, and we began picking up the sort of speed you might associate with a tired old DC-4.

After I tired of watching the left wing tip vibrate and wobble as if bidding Seattle farewell, I began to reflect on the peculiar and unforeseen circumstances that had led to my new career as a village schoolteacher.

While thousands of young men and women were preparing in the early autumn of 1947 to take up new teaching responsibilities in our nation's public schools, I doubt that any had been employed under such bizarre circumstances or were as ill prepared as I.

My *only* qualification for the post was my availability. My formal education, for all practical purposes, had ended in the 10th grade. While in the service, I had taken high school correspondence courses from the Armed Forces Institute and later, high school courses at the YMCA, but my crowning academic achievement to that point was having successfully taken the General Equivalency examination while I was still in the service.

I grew up during the Depression and entered the job

market in 1941, when I was 15. On December 7, 1941, the day that defined my generation, I was at work at a Union Oil gas station in Bremerton, Washington. When I was old enough, I joined the Marine Corps.

My military career was both short and undistinguished. After graduating from scout-sniper school, I was sent to Hawaii where I joined the 5th Division as a company scout.

I was wounded twice, and spent six months convalescing in Navy hospitals. Two weeks before I received my medical discharge because of the paralyzing shrapnel wound in my right leg, I was promoted to Private First Class.

In the spring of 1946, six months out of the service, I had gone to a cannery in Southeastern Alaska as a salmon trap watchman. At the end of the season, I had a chance to work my way south as a crew member on a cannery tender.

Foolishly believing I had acquired sufficient seaman's skills during that three-day voyage to qualify as a tugboat deck-hand, and ignoring the heavy steel leg brace I was obliged to wear, I talked my way into a deckhand's job with Puget Sound Tug and Barge Co. That career lasted only three months before I landed in the hospital again.

There, I met a cadet nurse named Jan Edwards, who was nearing the end of her training. She was my first real girl friend. After I was discharged from the hospital, we began dating, and we were married the following May on the eve of my departure for my second season in Alaska. I was a week shy of my 21st birthday.

This time, my destination was a cannery in Bristol Bay, on the Bering Sea coast immediately north of the Alaska Peninsula. I had been hired as a tallyman, a job requiring neither skill nor experience. Tallymen counted the salmon as the fishermen pitched them one at a time out of the boats into the fish barge.

Instead of traveling in ship's steerage as I had done the

previous year, I was flown with other cannery employees to Naknek Air Force Base (soon to be renamed King Salmon). There, we boarded small planes, and were flown to our respective canneries.

After we took off in our small plane, I saw at a glance that this country was very different from Southeastern Alaska. There, you saw spectacular mountains covered by magnificent stands of virgin timber and thousands of islands great and small, rising from great depths, sheltering secret passages and hidden anchorages.

By contrast, the view here was of unrelieved and drab Arctic tundra, seemingly devoid of life. It was barren, and almost frighteningly alien. It was treeless except for sporadic lines of brush marking low swales. Here and there were irregular pock–like ponds of stagnant water looking much like craters on the moon.

The author in 1945
before earning his first stripe

Minutes later, we flew over the 17–mile wide Kvichak River estuary, and there, for the first time, I saw the navigational labyrinth created by the power of 25 foot tides flowing over innumerable and ceaselessly shifting sandbars, channels and mud flats.

It was a fearful thing to see. Massive whorls, eddies and ripples marked the many tidal currents, where the otherwise smooth face of the dirty, opaque, river water was compelled by the power of the tides and unseen obstructions to reveal its true force and character.

7

Suddenly, we were again over the alien tundra. After flying nearly half an hour more, the pilot swooped low over an isolated cluster of faded red buildings huddled on the shore of yet another wide expanse of dirty water. This time he circled, and turning into the wind, gently floated his ungainly plane down to the water's surface. At the last moment, he caused the plane to flare as a teal might before he allowed his craft to enter the water.

As soon as we touched down, he advanced his throttles, and we taxied to the beach. His wheels were down and locked moments before we felt them touch the gravel, and with a sudden burst of energy, the plane, now as awkward and ungainly as before she had been graceful, lurched from the water. He spun her around and closed his throttles.

"This is Clarks Point," he said into the sudden quiet, "and that," pointing out the window,"is the Nushagak River. Stay in your seats until I open the door." He forced his crowded way down the aisle, pushing between men with weathered faces and callused hands. In a moment I heard the cabin door open. One by one, in their turn, his motley collection of passengers stood, and bending nearly double, walked back to the door at the rear of the compartment.

The pilot was rooting in the baggage compartment, handing down seabags, barracks bags, suitcases, and miniature, brightly decorated wooden trunks, that were claimed by men with a distinctly Mediterranean appearance and accent. *What's this?* I asked myself. *Who are these guys?*

Many, I later learned, were Sicilian fishermen. Several were foreign born, raised in the sailing fisheries of the Mediterranean. The little trunks accompanying them were filled with bottles of wine on the northern journey, and would be filled with leadlines, butter, tins of coffee, or anything that took their owner's fancy on the return trip to the states.

The bookkeeper's assistant came down to the beach to

greet us and to lead us to the office. I hoisted my seabag on my shoulder and followed the crowd up the coarse gravel beach, over a low bank covered with sea grass, to a dirt road paralleling the beach. We followed it to the cannery, a cluster of large, mostly two-story, buildings clad and roofed with rusty corrugated iron, covered with dull, flaking red paint.

As we approached the cannery, we passed a high wooden water tower supporting a large wooden tank on the right. Directly across the road from it, our guide pointed to the superintendent's residence, a prim white frame cottage overlooking the estuary, as incongruous among those grim red and gray buildings as a poodle among sled dogs.

We walked past a tiny house, not much larger than a doll's house on the left, and stepped across the twin rails of a marine railway, where barges, tugs and other large pieces of floating equipment were stored during the winter. I later learned that those tracks defined the boundary between cannery property and the village. On the cannery side of the tracks, we came first to a gray bungalow, the winter watchman's house, who was responsible for the cannery when the superintendent was away.

The next building on the left, also painted gray, was the combined office/store. Here, we crowded into the office and paused to fill out the necessary papers and be formally entered on the employee roster.

Then I was directed to the tallyman's quarters, a large room that contained a dozen recessed bunks built into the wall, in the machinist's bunkhouse.

Three young men seated on benches around a scarred old table in the middle of the room, eyed me as I came through the door. "Is this the tallyman's room?" I asked.

One of the three said, "Sure is. You must be the new man. Come on in, and help yourself." He waved his hand expansively toward the bunks.

I looked around the barren, undecorated, room and selected a bunk in the corner containing a rolled mattress, folded
sheets and a blanket, and tossed my luggage on it. Then I
turned back to the group sitting at the table and introduced
myself. "I'm Denny Moore," I said, offering my hand to the
nearest man, a young fellow about my age.

We all shook hands and they invited me to join them. I
was glad to find new friends so easily in such strange, not to
say alien, surroundings. It was nearly dinner time, and they
had just come in from their day's work.

I was assigned to help paint and otherwise prepare the tally
scow* for launching. The marine railway, where the scow was
stored, was next to the winterman's house. The winterman
served as the cannery's winter watchman and he doubled as
an outside foreman supervising the pre- and post seasonal
cannery work that bracketed the short but very intense
fishing season that began on June 25 and ended July 25.

This winterman, Henry Shade, was then in his fifties. He
had lived in western Alaska since just after the first World
War, working as a fur trapper and commercial fisherman
until he was appointed to his present job. Already slightly
stooped, his compact and solid torso was almost always clad
in neatly pressed gabardine trousers and a Filson jacket, or
in severe weather, a heavy down parka.

Henry's features like his body, were solid, reflecting his
German ancestry. His eyebrows were very heavy, but his
habitual expression was a pleasant one of amused and
quizzical surprise.

---

*As used here, the term "scow" means a flat bottomed, shallow draft,
vessel with living accommodations aboard. The tally scows were an exception,
but most scows also carry cargo. Some scows are self-propelled. Barges have a
similar hull configuration, but are limited to the carriage of cargo and are
not self-propelled.

Henry was a master in the fine art of indirection. Not until he succeeded did I realize that what I had foolishly assumed to be a tribute to the desirability of my company was really a desperate attempt on his part to recruit a schoolteacher, partly as a civic gesture, but also because he had three school age children. He saw in the tallymen a pool of young men of college age who could read and therefore were qualified to serve at least temporarily as schoolteachers. Henry's previous experience with Territorial schoolteachers had not left him with high expectations.

We were barely past the nodding stage when, to my surprise, Henry invited me to his home to meet his family. I'm sure he also invited the other tallymen, although nothing was said by the others, and not wanting to appear as if I were currying favor, I also kept my visits quiet.

The only women at Clark's Point were Henry's wife, Mary, her sister-in-law, a dozen housewives in the village, and assorted female children. For the most part, they kept out of sight. There was virtually no fraternization between cannery people and village folks, just as there was almost no fraternization between tallymen and the fishermen.

Mary was an attractive woman in early middle age. In many respects, as I later learned, Mary's Eskimo mother had left her with a powerful legacy of Yupik culture. Their children were typical American youngsters.

They quickly discovered I was a newlywed. Equally important, Henry also found that I had no job waiting for me in Seattle. Gently but with great insistence, he urged me to apply to the Territorial Department of Education for the position of village schoolteacher, a post for which there were no other candidates.

I was amused rather than hopeful. Considering my lack of qualifications, my tongue was firmly in my cheek when I submitted my application. However, Henry must have written

11

a powerful recommendation, because scarcely three weeks later, much to my great surprise, I received a telegram from the Department of Education in Juneau offering me the post of teacher at an annual salary of $3,240.

It was not then possible to make telephone calls to the states from western Alaska, so I sent a wire to Jan, who was spending the summer with my mother, outlining the offer and asking if she was willing to come to Alaska.

She replied almost immediately. "Sounds great! Love, Jan."

At the end of the season, I had returned to Seattle and with Jan, scurried around Seattle accumulating and packing rudimentary household furniture and supplies, frantically hurrying because the "Fall" ship—the last ship of the season—would not accept freight after the first week of August, and was to leave Seattle ten days later.

We had only my summer wages and Jan's slender savings to work with and about 10 days to accumulate and pack our selections, knowing that if we overlooked something that was too big to ship by parcel post, we'd have to wait until the first ship in the spring for it.

We met the deadlines, stayed within our budget, and now, finally on our way, we could relax for the first time in days. The plane was flying, and death was no longer imminent. Jan and I idly watched the tall buildings in downtown Seattle pass under our airplane's wing. However, not until we were over Elliot Bay with its miniature ships and tugs did we fully let our weight down, and begin to speculate about the life that lay ahead.

Clarks Point

As late as 1947, Anchorage was still enjoying a wartime economy, and hotel rooms were scarce. However, on our arrival in Alaska, a friendly and sympathetic young corporal in the reception area at Elmendorf Air Force Base quickly telephoned around and found a room for us in the old wooden Parson's Hotel on 3rd Avenue, after which he also called a cab.

It was raining that evening. Our sense of strangeness and alienation was increased by the long and confusing taxi ride into the city, and the brief glimpses of town lights we had through rain streaked cab windows. We reached the hotel, and struggled into the lobby with our luggage, registered, and wearily climbed the stairs to our room.

Mrs. Parsons and Jan spent the next morning getting acquainted, while I went to the Alaska Airlines office to arrange for the next leg of our flight to Bristol Bay. Luckily, traffic between Anchorage and Naknek was brisk. The following morning we were driven to Merrill Field, a small airport much closer to town than the Air Force Base. This time we boarded a twin engine DC-3 for a flight that took nearly three hours.

By noon, we were standing on a graveled landing strip at the Naknek Air Base. Although I had seen this field before, I looked at it now with new eyes.

As a new resident, I now had a proprietary interest in the place. However, apart from a row of rusting Quonset huts at the parking ramp, and others scattered over the tundra, there wasn't much to see.

We walked into the operations hut where we identified our baggage and shook hands with the pilot who would fly the last leg of our journey. He ushered us into a battered jeep and drove down a rutted dirt road to the river where an ancient five-place Bellanca Travelaire on floats (pontoons), also part of the fledgling Alaska Airlines fleet, awaited us.

There were four passengers. A young Eskimo couple returning from a shopping spree in Anchorage had arrived on the same flight. They were going to Dillingham. While the pilot loaded our bags, he explained that he and his wife lived in Dillingham—the largest town in the Bay area—14 miles east and across the Nushagak River from Clarks Point. He invited us to visit whenever we were in town.

At first, I thought he was merely being friendly; later, I realized that he, and nearly everyone else we met, were entirely sincere when they offered hospitality. That's the way things were.

Jan, the Eskimo woman, and I sat in the rear seats, while her husband and the pilot sat up front. Neither Jan nor I had ridden in a float plane before, and while I can't speak for Jan, I must say I enjoyed the enormous sense of power from the big rotary engine as the pilot opened his throttle and began his takeoff run.

As our planes had successively grown smaller and older, they had also lost speed. It took an hour to fly the 90 air miles from the air base to Dillingham. The terrain seemed familiar to me, but it was new and alien to Jan. She kept her nose pressed to the window, eagerly absorbing many first impressions of her new home.

I tried to imagine how she was seeing it. I could see a

superficial similarity to her native dun colored hills in eastern Montana. Even the small ponds that dotted the tundra had their counterpart along the Yellowstone River. And here, as there, brush and stunted trees grew in gullies and other areas protected from the wind.

Suddenly, we flew low over a tiny collection of miscellaneous buildings huddled on the river bank without seeming order. This was our first glimpse of Dillingham. I particularly noticed the Standard Oil logo painted on a tank near the water. After landing on the river, we taxied to the beach.

The tide was out. After we landed in the river, but before we reached the gravel beach, the plane shuddered to a stop on the submerged beginnings of a long mud flat. Only our pilot was wearing rubber boots.

I was surprised and impressed to see him offer his back first to the young man who had been seated next to him, then to the wife. He struggled bravely through the ankle-deep mud, carrying his passengers and their luggage to dry ground. Later, I discovered this courtesy was universally extended by nearly all bush pilots so their passengers would not need to get their feet wet.

He pushed his plane into the water, and soon we were back in the air. Minutes later, we circled the Clarks Point cannery and village, preparing to land at our new home.

I knew what to expect, but as we banked steeply over the village, Jan saw her new home for the first time. She saw a score of tiny cabins and their outbuildings strung along a quarter mile of dirt road on a narrow strip of dry ground closely paralleling the gravel beach. The eastern end of the road was lost in a maze of cannery buildings. The western end of the road ended abruptly against a steep brushy ridge standing perpendicular to the river. The ridge formed a towering cliff overlooking the river. Later, we would learn that as the river gnawed at the base of the ridge, and the

15

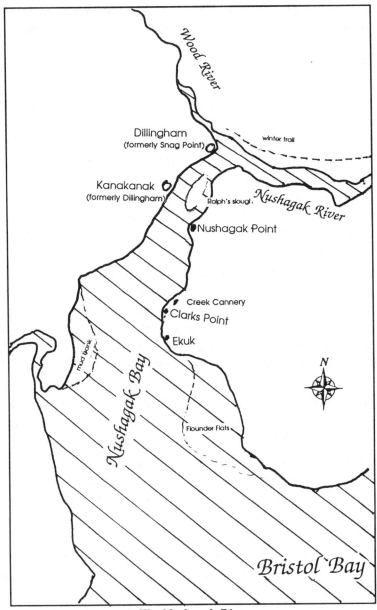

The Nushagak River
—Map drawn by Capt. Jim Hogan

permafrost thawed, occasionally, mastodon bones and other fossils would appear in the clay face of the cliff.

The ridge ran almost straight back from the river, looping toward the southeast. Between it and the narrow row of buildings along the road that comprised the village, was a large muskeg swamp with intricately connected ponds and marshy grasses.

The plane gently floated down to the river, and we distinctly heard over the roar of the engine, the intermittent hiss of the floats skimming the wavelets as the plane settled into the water.

The beach gravel at Clarks Point extended unbroken from the grass covered berm at the top of the beach, a foot or two higher than the road behind it, down a gentle slope for nearly a hundred yards to the water's edge.

With a sure hand on the throttle, the pilot delicately nudged his floats up to the gravel, then motioned us to descend to the float. We easily jumped ashore, and I held the wing's strut while the pilot carried our luggage to the dry gravel. We shook hands again, and waved goodby as he pushed his plane out into the stream. When it was pointed away from the beach, he started his engine. Lugging our suitcases, we struggled up the gravel bank to the dirt road.

Almost all the houses in the village were like the one next to the school; two or three room tar paper or iron clad shacks, roofed with rusty corrugated iron and featuring prominent stove pipe chimneys. Each was surrounded by various outbuildings, including caches, the inevitable out-house, and fish racks. Each cabin also had its share of oil drums and tarp-covered sleds.

The schoolhouse was a larger version of the other build-ings, constructed by the same carpenters, and of the same materials. Instead of tarpaper, however, the building was partly clad with siding and shingles that obviously had been

17

salvaged from old cannery buildings. It also was partly covered with corrugated iron. The school outbuildings included a corrugated iron-clad cache on four stilts, and a large two-hole outhouse. A shaky swing and a flag pole completed the school's outdoor furnishings.

Standing on the road in front of the school looking west, we saw several nondescript houses lining the shore side of the road. Fish racks and sheds stood between the road and the beach on the water side. The road ended abruptly at the foot of a steep hill rising about 100 feet into the air, which became a bluff where it towered over the beach.

From the beach, the hill extended in a long curving ridge in a southeasterly direction. It gradually lost its identity in a jumble of irregular hills on the southeastern horizon. The swamp we had seen from the air was composed of shallow ponds and shaky, spongy, vegetation.

The western ridge in winter
(Note dog team in background)

Looking south across the swamp, the foot of the ridge seemed to be about a half mile away.

We put our suitcases in the school's windbreak, and began walking east toward the cannery in the autumn sunshine. As we strolled along the road, we passed a dozen small buildings on the shore side of the road, and an odd assortment of smaller buildings, smoke houses, fish racks, and other outbuildings on the river side.

The smoke racks were heavily laden with drying salmon. The rich, pungent odor of alder smoke and drying salmon was strong in our nostrils.

Fish rack loaded with drying red salmon

I felt very self-conscious, muttering greetings to the people we met, and acknowledging the children's shy smiles and shining black eyes with smiles of my own. Sled dogs, chained near each cabin, apathetically watched us walk by.

While I had spent the summer here, I thought that now, from Jan's perspective, things must seem strange and very alien. But if Jan had misgivings, she never said so. Instead, she smiled at the children, studied the dog teams, and looked at the racks of drying salmon hanging over smoldering smudge fires.

I pointed the various landmarks out to her as we walked along the road. The ground on both sides of the road between the buildings and sheds was covered by thick, luxuriant grass. As we approached the cannery, I saw that the marine ways were loaded with barges, tenders, boats, and in the back near the winch house, off on a side track, rested *Tally Scow II*, my home during the summer just past, but she was more interested in the tiny hospital/dispensary.

The walks seemed strangely deserted now that the fishermen, cannery workers, carpenters, and bookkeepers had

gone south for the winter. We found Henry Shade directing
a crew of local men dismantling the dock extension.

The school and related outbuildings

Seeing us, he motioned to his assistant (and brother-in-law),
Emil Eglund, then turned to us.

"Well, well, well," he said smiling broadly, walking toward
us, hand outstretched, "I see you made it back from Outside." At first, I was mildly annoyed that he seemed surprised, but on reflection, I realized he had no way of knowing that I would return.

I introduced Jan, and explained that we had just arrived.
Henry nodded. "I saw the plane," he said. "Let's go up to the
house, and have coffee."

We followed his stocky figure along the plank sidewalk past
the store/office, and the cannery hospital, to the winterman's
house. He performed the introductions, and Mary promptly
invited us to "sit down for coffee."

The two women struck up an instant friendship. The

schoolteacher's apartment was theoretically furnished, but in a limited way. Mary quickly offered, and Jan accepted, the loan of furniture and household equipment that we might need until the fall ship arrived.

Henry gave me a key to the padlock securing the schoolhouse door. While Jan and Mary were packing necessary kitchen gear, linens, and other basic needs in boxes, young Henry, Jr. went for the truck. When the last box was filled, we carried them out to the truck, and Henry drove the truck down to the school.

It was already getting dark when we unlocked the door and Henry showed me how to light the Coleman lantern. We quickly unloaded the boxes while Henry showed Jan how to light the oil cook stove in the tiny kitchen. Mary had invited us to return for supper, but we declined. I was tired, and I think neither of us wanted to share the magic of our first night in our own home.

The next morning, standing on the cannery dock, we could see the snowcapped Tikchik mountains rising several thousand feet across the four-mile expanse of the swift flowing, dirt colored, Nushagak River.

Creek cannery, then nearly abandoned, was about three miles upriver, across Combine Slough. The indistinct mass of two abandoned canneries five miles beyond Creek cannery, at Nushagak Point, was faintly visible. We couldn't see the government hospital at Kanakanak across the river from Nushagak Point, but we knew it was there.

I also knew that the still operating Pacific American Fisheries (PAF) cannery lay beyond Kanakanak, and beyond that, two nearly abandoned canneries were in the village of Dillingham.

Downriver from Clarks, on the western side of the bluff, the Libby, McNeil, Libby cannery at Ekuk was three miles away. Like Clarks, the Ekuk cannery was fully operational.

21

The beach east of our cannery was strewn with rusting boilers and broken bits of abandoned tenders and other debris associated with the rotting carcasses of old fashioned steam powered vessels. This was the burial ground for worn out and discarded floating equipment, and the crematorium for worn out and rotten fishing boats.

That spring, when I had arrived at the cannery, I had felt something closely akin to culture shock. The minute I stepped from that airplane, I knew I had stumbled onto something different from anything I had imagined existed under the American flag.

That early realization was reinforced when I had stood in line in the office with my fellow passengers signing the payroll. It was obvious from the way the fishermen behaved toward the bored clerk standing behind the counter, and he toward them, that the informal congeniality of cannery life in Southeastern Alaska had not followed the industry to this alien and isolated corner of Alaska. When I learned more about Bristol Bay, I began to understood why.

Before Alaska became a state, salmon canneries in Southeastern Alaska obtained most of their fish from fish traps operated mostly by college boys and young veterans like me. The canneries in Bristol Bay, however, relied on hard-bitten professional fishermen, many of them, like the gray haired old man standing in front of me, immigrants from Sicily where they had learned their trade—fishing under sail—in the sunny Mediterranean.

I was in the company of the last of a vanishing breed of men capable of operating those dangerous little two-man sailing gillnetters in what one Scandinavian fisherman has described as "the toughest fishery in Alaska."

While easy nepotism supplied superintendents in the more civilized Southeastern Alaskan canneries, that role in Bristol Bay was deemed far too tough for someone's favorite nephew. Traditionally, superintendents for Bristol Bay canneries had been recruited from the ranks of retired sea captains, preferably men who had served aboard company sailing vessels and steamers. Only men with that background were deemed hard enough to maintain the discipline required to successfully catch and pack salmon in the harsh environment and isolated surroundings of Bristol Bay.

Consequently, the social structure in Bristol Bay canneries was both formal and rigid. A stern social order similar to that aboard ship had evolved and was rigidly observed, even though the cannery ships, and with them the pool of seasoned disciplinarians, had disappeared at the beginning of the second World War.

Fisherman, especially old timers like the man I had seen in the store, seldom spoke to the superintendent unless they were first spoken to, and many of the older men still removed their hats when confronted by the "Old Man."

At the bottom of the pyramid, the cannery workers—mostly Filipinos—lived segregated lives in their bunkhouse with their own cooks and mess. The tradesmen—the carpenters, machinists, blacksmiths, plumbers, and electricians, the clerical staff—and the tallymen (who occupied a niche roughly equivalent to that of a midshipman aboard an 18th century man-of-war) had their own bunkhouse and ate the same food as the fishermen, but in a separate room.

Like the mates on a ship, the bosses—the fish boss, the net boss, the cannery foreman, the doctor, the beach boss, and the bookkeeper—had a separate mess and never broke bread with their juniors.

At the top of this hierarchy was the cannery superintendent who, following square-rigger tradition, ate in solitary splendor, attended only by a man-servant.

Early on, as I walked around the cannery trying to get my bearings, I wandered into a warehouse where I saw scores of identical 28 foot, double-ended hulls resting on their blocks, still in winter storage, drab in last year's faded and chipped blue paint. I knew nothing of sailing, but eyeing those little open boats, I felt a thrill of nervous apprehension.

Over the years that followed, I would come to know a dozen or more men who went overboard, or more likely, who went into the water when their boats capsized. Without exception, they perished. Sometimes a horrified fisherman would discover a body in his net, but most often the bodies were never recovered.

This carnage was indirectly mandated by the US Fish and Wildlife Service which remained opposed, until 1951, to the use of any mechanical power in those boats more sophisticated than a pair of oars, on the ground that the greater range and increased efficiency of power boats would further deplete the salmon resource.

Cynics sometimes pointed out that the continuing sailboat requirement conferred a substantial monopolistic advantage on the salmon canners already in business; those who owned the sailboats. Moreover, since Senator Wesley Jones of Washington State had taken care that the *Act for the Protection of Seamen*, which bears his name, did not apply in the Territory of Alaska, sailboats were extraordinarily cheap to operate, because the canneries had no need to worry about such irritating technicalities as insurance or workman's compensation.

Commercial fisheries are sometimes romanticized as a last bastion of rugged individualism; of free enterprise based on a pure struggle between man and the elements. A blend of Kipling and Hemingway; of *Captains Courageous* and *The Old Man of the Sea.*

In a sense, that perception fit the Bristol Bay fishery except that Bristol Bay fishermen were then immune to economic risks. They were all company employees. The boats, nets, and related gear belonged to the canneries which, in turn, were wholly owned subsidiaries of major international food corporations like *Libby, McNeil and Libby, Del Monte,* and *A&P.* The only thing the fishermen risked was their lives.

Alaska Packer's Clarks Point <N> cannery, 1947

Most were hired in Seattle or San Francisco. Before the war, they had manned company ships sailing from San Francisco, but by the time I arrived on the scene, they were flown to Alaska by the companies which hired them. They were paid on a piecework basis, based on their seasonal catch of salmon. As I soon discovered, there was much tension between resident and non-resident fishermen. Even among the non-residents, there was considerable stress among the various ethnic groups.

In general, fishing, like farming, is an inherited trade. Most of the younger non-resident fishermen were sons or nephews, and although as a rule they were native born, in the bunkhouse, following their elders, they quickly reverted to their

European roots. The Sicilians clung together. Norwegians avoided the Italians, and the gloomy Finns stayed away from them both. None would have much to do with the residents.

Sometimes it worked the other way. I remember when Shorty Wilson from Levelock, spent the summer in a tent rather than share a bunkhouse with Italian fishermen.

I had learned over the summer that those complicated bunkhouse relationships mirrored other, more basic, differences between this odd little corner of the world and the society to which I was accustomed.

For example, even something as basic to our legal system as land ownership was, in Bristol Bay, something of a mystery. After my appointment as schoolteacher, I had taken a closer look at the village.

There were three institutional landowners in Bristol Bay. The federal government owned everything in sight except land that had been granted to the Russian Orthodox Church of North America, or sold to the salmon canning companies. But it was never entirely clear who, apart from the federal government, owned which parcel.

The church claims derived from Czarist Russia and the 1867 Treaty of Cession. With rare exceptions, those titles were not recorded except in church records, and nobody seemed to know which coastal villages were on church ground and which were not. Although Clarks Point had a consecrated Russian Orthodox graveyard, the nearest church was five miles away at Nushagak Point.

The cannery claims were almost as nebulous. To discourage potential competition, using Civil War soldier's script, the earliest cannery operators had purchased every potential cannery site in Bristol Bay.

The villager's concept of land ownership was different. The village was without metes or bounds. Each house was separated from its neighbor by a reasonable distance based solely on the mutual agreement of the first owner and his new neighbor.

Verner Wilson, an aging Norwegian, and his young Eskimo bride, Nancy, lived nearest to the cannery in a small, neatly trimmed, and painted house on the left side of the rutted road. His shop, in a glittering aluminum clad building, was on the river side of the road.

Next to Verner were five modest, almost decrepid, three and four room tarpaper cabins on both sides of the road. Each was surrounded by smaller buildings, the cache, an outhouse, a fish rack, and a dog yard where three to seven molting, fly and mosquito plagued, sled dogs were chained.

Those houses were occupied by Eskimos, mostly from Eek River and Togiak, and a lone Filipino bachelor, whose name we never knew, but who was called "Black Joe" by the school children. He was obviously fading away, and in our ignorance, we thought he was dying of tertiary syphilis. It could have been syphilis, but I'm now inclined to think he died of tuberculosis, a far more common fate.

The town cemetery was next. Clarks Point was well equipped with cemeteries. There was the cannery cemetery for employees and the few drowned fishermen whose remains had been recovered. Then, there was the town cemetery that occupied the 200 feet or so between Black Joe's place and the next two dwellings. Last, a consecrated cemetery was located near the top of the ridge west of the village.

Later, when I came to know the people, I was always mildly surprised that superstitious Mickey Lopez would have chosen to build next to the graveyard. But two smaller tar paper covered cabins, both with dogs chained nearby, housed the two expatriate Filipino brothers (and former cannery workers), their Eskimo wives, and large families. Both cabins were attended by more elaborate outbuildings than the Eskimo homes at the beginning of the road. The next building was the community center, where the school children would stage their Christmas program, and where we would enjoy frequent box socials and weekly dances.

George Romanos, otherwise and popularly known as "George the Greek," owned the much larger home next to the community center. He lived there with his Eskimo wife, Annie, and three children (and their inevitable dog team, of course). Unlike the others, George had built his house on a raised foundation.

The schoolhouse with its outbuildings, was about halfway between the cannery and the bluff. Next to us was an Eskimo family with an unlikely English name, the Roberts. Beyond them were several additional cabins sheltering Filipino/ Eskimo families and their children. In all, some 85 people lived year around in Clarks Point.

However, the school served a much wider area. Every morning before freeze-up, two boatloads of kids, one from Ekuk (the Libby cannery three miles down river), and one carrying three children from Creek cannery in the opposite direction, would arrive shortly before I rang the morning school bell. After freeze-up, during most of the winter except in the most dangerous weather, those same children would arrive in the dark by dog sleds; two sleds from Ekuk, and one from Creek cannery. The Ekuk boats and sleds were driven by two 11 year olds, while Harry, a 14 year old, drove his father's equipment from Creek cannery.

When the fall ship arrived, we discovered that the Department of Education had furnished two new oil space heaters for the classroom. Henry Shade, as the school's patron saint, promptly found 50 empty oil drums which were loaded aboard Emil Sorensen's little power scow for the 14-mile trip up to Dillingham.

Years earlier, the great steam boilers in the cannery had

been fired with coal. When the cannery converted to oil burners, an enormous pile of sacked coal remained. Over the years, local residents and the school had continued to use coal for cooking and as a winter fuel. After Standard Oil built the tank farm at Dillingham, and diesel became available to anyone able to pay for it, coal-fired heaters and stoves were gradually converted to oil. At last, the Territorial Department of Education decided to convert to oil.

It was almost the first of September. Realizing we wouldn't have a later chance to get to the store in Dillingham before freeze-up, Jan and I rode upriver to the Standard Oil dock in Dillingham with Emil Sorenson aboard his barge.

Dillingham, which we had briefly glimpsed a month earlier, was a quiet little cannery community located where the Wood River joined the Nushagak River. Originally called Snag Point, it was, according to Mary Shade, Martin Olson's desire to open a liquor store in Snag Point that prompted the village's name change to Dillingham.

The original Dillingham, now known as Kanakanak, was a government town. The Bureau of Indian Affairs (BIA) had built the hospital and school. The jail, commissioner's office and the Reindeer Service were located there. It was also the site of the only post office on the western shore of the Nushagak River.

The non-government people naturally chose to live near the expanding community of Snag Point. By the time World War II broke out, Snag Point had a tank farm, three stores, a hotel (which some claimed was built from US Reindeer Service lumber), a bar, and movies once a week. It also had a large Territorial school.

Dillingham, on the other hand, had withered. It had only the post office, hospital, and BIA school. Only government people lived in Dillingham. And who could blame them? There can't be anything duller than a government town.

Meanwhile, Martin Olson, a small businessman in Snag Point, had opened a little liquor store in a lean-to attached to his cabin. Business was good (the liquor business is *always* good in Alaska) and he was hard pressed to keep up with demand. Faced with the seasonal shipping schedules, he desperately needed more room for his inventory. But since there was a war on, he was unable to buy the needed building materials.

As luck would have it, the Dillingham postmaster died. Seeing his opportunity, Olson immediately bid for the job, not because he wanted to become a postmaster, but because he wanted to build a post office. In due course, he was appointed postmaster and received the priorities which enabled him to buy the needed lumber. He put up a building with two entrances and a sturdy partition running through the middle of it. One doorway proudly bore the legend US POST OFFICE, DILLINGHAM, ALASKA. The other doorway bore a smaller sign announcing OLSON'S LIQUOR STORE.

Naturally, there was grumbling by the government people in what used to be Dillingham, but which now reverted to its original Yupik name of Kanakanak, when they discovered that their post office had migrated four miles east over a bumpy and often impassable road that was little more than a dog team trail. But these complaints were inconsequential compared to the joy of the folks in Snag Point who now had a post office in their midst. It didn't even matter that it had a peculiar name. You can get used to anything; even becoming the namesake of a dead minor politician.

After we climbed the steps to the Lowe Trading Company store and hesitantly pushed open the door, we were greeted by a delightfully warm and friendly woman, Peggy Bradford, who then ran the store. Somehow, she already knew we were the new schoolteachers at Clarks Point. Recognizing our cheechaco (newcomer) status, she immediately began indoctrinating Jan into the mysteries of the annual grubstake.

While she and Jan began drawing up a monumental shopping list, Peggy realized that our finances would not be equal to the strain of the $1,000 investment necessary to buy our winter outfit, and she said right up front, "Don't worry too much about the total cost; you can pay me by the month if you want to."

Armed with that generous offer, Jan and I began ordering a case of this and a case of that and three cases of something else; plus three 100 pound sacks of flour and two 100 pound sacks of sugar. It wasn't long before we began to attract a crowd. Other women began to offer suggestions, and almost before we knew it, enough cases and sacks had accumulated to stock a small store. Someone, possibly with schoolteacher experience, pointed out that a single case of toilet paper (100 rolls) would scarcely be adequate for our needs and those of 20 to 30 students for nine months.

Jan didn't drink coffee at all, and I drank it only sparingly, but someone else suggested that our consumption probably would increase dramatically because of the climate and because coffee was the standard social beverage. Another case of coffee was added to the growing pile. When we were through, we had a great pile of cases and sacks, and were $1,500 in debt to the gracious Mrs. Bradford. Emil's crew loaded our purchases on his barge.

We spent a delightful evening with Maxine, one of Mrs. Bradford's clerks, a young widow whose husband had been killed in an airplane accident. We gratefully accepted her offer of hospitality, and spent the night on her couch.

The next morning, we left Dillingham on Emil's barge, and returned to Clarks Point. Emil timed his arrival with high tide, and he beached his barge directly in front of the schoolhouse. Stout planks were laid from the vessel's bow to the beach, and one by one, our precious drums of diesel oil were rolled down the impromptu gangplank to the beach and then rolled up the beach to the berm, and stood on end, out of reach of the tides. Then our groceries were carried ashore and piled neatly on the ground by the nearest corner of the schoolhouse.

Jan and I were learning. We sorted the boxes and sacks into two piles: The cases of vegetables, mayonnaise, catsup, tuna, and tomato juice went inside the building. Coffee, flour, sugar, and toilet paper; things cold weather wouldn't harm, went into the cache.

Even after making that initial sort, the huge cornucopia in the middle of our tiny apartment was daunting. We threw out the wooden boxes on which the bed rested, substituting pillars of cases of canned milk, tomatoes, tuna fish, and beans. Other cases were piled in corners where we hoped they would be both accessible and out of the way.

Our groceries were not the only abundance we faced. I was astonished on the first day of school, as children trooped into the schoolroom, followed by a second and even a third wave, to discover I lacked sufficient desks.

True, some children were older than the legally mandated 16, and several came from outlying villages and were boarding with relatives in the community, but when the dust settled, I found I had enrolled 44 youngsters in 8 grades.

Moreover, of my 15 first graders, nearly half couldn't speak English. Today, I suppose the politically correct thing would be for the teacher to take a crash course in Yupik and to make every effort to preserve that culture. The children would have approved that approach. They did their best to teach me to speak Yupik so as to save themselves the bother of learning English.

Clarks Point was a long way from my bosses in Juneau, and I had to rely on my common sense in situations like this. I reasoned that although English has its shortcomings, people wishing to navigate in the English-speaking world of jobs, bank accounts, insurance policies, and Social Security, needed the English language. I have never seen a traffic sign or insurance contract printed in Yupik.

Therefore, I made a rule. I ordained that henceforth, only English was to be spoken on the playground and in the classroom. I wouldn't say I achieved an enormous success. The fact that over a span of 50 years, I have retained a basic Yupik vocabulary of a half dozen phrases and a handful of nouns and verbs is a testimony to the perseverance of little Anuska and her sister, Anisha, and the other youngsters who patiently coached me in their tongue.

Those kids were almost too smart. They seemed to catch on to their preprimers remarkably well, especially when you consider that they didn't speak the language. Two youngsters—little Anuska was one—breezed through those little books with no difficulty at all—and managed to avoid learning anything except how to please their teacher.

They had remarkable retentive powers and were clever enough to associate the distinctive shapes of the letters with specific sounds. They had learned how, without the slightest comprehension, to mimic the noises I made. As soon as I realized I was training parrots instead of teaching children, I begged old Sears catalogs in the village, and put those kids to work with scissors and a paste pot, at the same time, reinforcing the rule that only English be spoken on the playground and in school. They quickly began to pick up the language, and by the year's end had gained sufficient ability in English, and beginning reading, so I was able to move them into the second grade with a clear conscience.

That winter, when the northeasterly winds were blowing, I'd almost always find a small snow drift in the middle aisle in the morning. The old-fashioned ink wells in the children's desks occasionally remain frozen for a week at a time.

In that weather, every hour or so, I would have the children stand and do calisthenics. Those youngsters who were obviously suffering from the cold, especially the little ones, were sent into our room, where Jan thawed them with hot cocoa.

I arranged the seating so the youngest children were seated nearest the stoves. This was sensible, but it had its drawbacks. Standing over those seated children, helping them decipher what Dick and Jane, Spot and Father, were up to ("See Spot. See Spot run. See Spot run, run, run!") I sometimes thought I would gag at the stench of the rancid seal oil their mothers used as hair dressing.

I faced other problems that most teachers would never encounter. Then, no high schools existed in Bristol Bay. A very small minority—one or two youngsters every ten years or so—might be selected to attend the Sheldon Jackson boarding high school in Sitka, 2,000 miles away. Others might have an opportunity to live with relatives in more urban surroundings. But for most kids, the eighth grade was the end of their academic career.

There were then two parallel educational systems serving rural Alaska. The Interior Department's Bureau of Indian Affairs (BIA) operated rural schools throughout Alaska. BIA teachers were expected to provide medical and social services in addition to educating the young.

The Territory had quite a different philosophy. Their view was that teachers were to teach, leaving first aid and welfare applications to others. This dichotomy had an unfortunate, but perhaps inevitable, result.

Regarding BIA paternalism as a poor preparation for nonreservation life, the authors of the Territorial school curriculum had, I think, overreacted by stressing academic studies without apparent purpose for that time or place.

Most people in a modern society receive much continuing education from newspapers, magazines, radio, television, and so forth throughout their lives. However, for at least ninety percent of the school population in rural Alaska in 1947, eighth grade education was terminal education in the fullest and most final sense of the term. Not only were there no high schools or colleges, there were no newspapers.

Other than the Armed Forces Radio Service (AFRS) offering headline news to those in the village who had battery-operated radios, we lived quite apart from the main stream. It seemed foolish, therefore, to waste a student's last year in school fretting about esoteric topics such as gerunds and participles. I could see merit in teaching beginning algebra and elementary geometry but I perceived it my responsibility to modify the curriculum, and instead of emphasizing English sentence structure, I spent much of that time concentrating on practical economics; on topics such as how to deal with banks and obtain banking services, what insurance was and how to obtain it, the importance of Social Security, and how to file tax returns.

I was also concerned because the children had no comprehension of a world larger than the tiny one of Bristol Bay. Momentous events occurred in Europe in 1949. Reasoning that my students were more familiar with air transportation than most stateside pupils, I seized the moment by developing a special math-geography-social studies curriculum based on the then topical and dramatic Berlin air lift.

For example, for the fourth graders, I devised simple arithmetic problems. . .if one DC-3 can carry three tons of coal. . . and more complicated problems for the fifth and sixth graders. At the seventh and eighth grade levels, we calculated a heat budget for Berlin, and considered the political and social implications of American foreign policy.

However, I don't want to leave a false impression. I had my share of disciplinary problems. But mine was an unusual situation because several students were boys 18 and 19 years old, scarcely a year or two younger than I.

I wasn't obliged to teach anyone over the age of 16, but I welcomed the older boys because my educational experience so closely paralleled theirs. Still, disciplining a nineteen-year old is different than controlling a nine-year old. I always had the option of expulsion, but I needed a less Draconian sanction.

Early in the school year, as part of our relatively unstructured civics class (which was directed primarily at the older grades, but to which the younger students also contributed), we had jointly established a code of classroom behavior, which included specific sanctions for certain deviant acts. Those sanctions included such punishments as a specific number of hours spent scrubbing the floor or washing windows; useful jobs that needed doing. I carefully avoided using extra academic assignments as punishment.

But what to do about those high-spirited older boys? Aided by my experience in the Marine Corps, I hit on it. You'd be surprised how fast a student body of 44 can fill an outhouse pit. We desperately needed a new one. Bingo. I had my middle-of-the road sanction. Every delict committed by an older boy carried a penalty of not less than two and not more than six hours of after-school digging for the new outhouse.

Immediately after school, my "chain gang," as the punishment detail became known in the village, would tend to clown around, and show off for the girls, as boys will do everywhere, as they gathered their tools and began digging. But their audience quickly became chilled and left. My miscreants then were left alone, unhappily chipping through frozen earth by the light of a kerosene barn lantern.

Each shift made progress, but the earth froze again overnight, so the boys were constantly working with frozen dirt. The boys always had the alternative of quitting school if they found my Marine discipline too tough, but none did.

I dismissed the first four grades at 2:30. Friday afternoons, after the little ones, except those waiting for a dog team driver, had been sent home, the students put their books away, and we spent the next hour and a half discussing any topic they cared to raise. There were no restrictions or limitations. All was grist for our mill, except gossip. Thus, while we freely discussed alcoholism and its consequences, including the then approved treatment for delirium tremens, (where else were they to learn it?), I was unwilling to point to specific people, illustrating the effect of excessive booze.

The questions raised by the students sometimes surprised me. For instance, one 16-year old asked, "Denny, is there really such a thing as a devil?"

How do you answer a question like that? Theology has never been my strongest suit. I told her (and the class) that there was no definitive answer to that question. It was a matter of faith. Some folks believed, others didn't. She wasn't going to let me weasel out of it that easily.

"What do you think?" she insisted.

I was trapped. Those kids knew my shaky credentials. The only thing I had going with them was the acknowledged fact that since I was older and had traveled further, I knew more about life than they did, and that I was willing to share that knowledge honestly and candidly. As far as I was concerned, it didn't even matter that they called me by my first name.

Knowing I was among true believers of the Russian Orthodox theology tempered by a rich Yupik mythology, I said, "As a matter of personal philosophy, because I think heaven and hell are conditions of our own making here on earth, I think that devils, whether you mean "moosemen" or other *chagiuk,* are imaginary."

The kids smiled knowingly. I'm sure every one of them believed in *chagiuk.* Nothing I said was likely to change that. On the other hand, nobody was offended because I had expressed my views, except possibly Father Endahl, the Jesuit missionary in Dillingham, who suggested, after I related the incident to him, that I might be better advised to refer such questions to him in the future.

Although we couldn't have guessed it at the time, before the next decade was out, Father Endahl was to play an enormous role in changing the course of my life.

On another Friday afternoon, that same girl asked another tough question. "How do you keep from having babies?"

Although I know he would like to have fielded that question as well, I didn't think Father Endahl was the appropriate expert. Here, I took the coward's way out. I referred the girls to Jan for instruction in birth control, while I wrestled with the boys over the same issue. Jan, in the meanwhile, had developed her own extracurricular after hours activity, teaching rudimentary home economics to girls who would never see a high school home economics class. She taught them to preserve fish in tin cans (Sears used to sell empty tin cans for home canning), to take proper care of babies, and why chocolate bars and potato chips do not constitute a balanced meal.

It was a good, solid, program. I wanted to test the efficacy of my philosophy, so I faithfully followed the instructions on the envelope guarding the Territory-wide year-end examinations. I'm proud to say that my eighth graders placed very well in competition with their peers throughout Alaska.

I enjoyed teaching. If the Territory hadn't decided to build a new school at Clarks Point in the summer of '49, installing flushing toilets, running water, and electric lights—amenities certain to attract qualified teachers—I might be there yet. There was plenty to do.

Most importantly, however, we were confronted with a terrifying public health problem. As part of her cadet nurse's training, Jan had worked for several months in a tuberculosis sanitarium where she had learned to recognize that excessive fatigue, afternoon sweats, and a foul breath could be symptomatic of active tuberculosis.

Day after day, she had watched several of my students, especially the four orphan children whose parents had died of TB, break into sweats, and for no apparent reason, become drowsy and confused almost every afternoon. She questioned their guardians, Henry and Mary Shade.

"Yes," Henry said with a sigh, "I wouldn't be surprised if those kids had a touch of TB in 'em."

The children, Billy, Vincent, Jacinto, and Aurora, ranging in age from six to 16, lived in the tiny doll house across the road from the Shade residence. Henry looked after them, making sure they had fuel oil, food, clothing, and other necessities, spending far in excess of the pittance he received from the Social Security Administration for their maintenance. But Henry, like most Alaskans, was like that: Generous almost to a fault.

Because the children's mother had been an Eskimo, they were BIA beneficiaries. Therefore, Jan quickly began negotiating over the cannery radio with the head nurse at the Kanakanak hospital, to have them X-rayed. What had originally seemed a simple, straightforward proposition quickly became complicated. Every evening, Jan found herself trudging through the snow up the road to the cannery radio shack where she joined Henry to plead with the head nurse during the evening radio schedule. This went on for months.

Jan is nothing if not persistent. When she learned that the BIA doctor, based 350 miles away in Bethel, would be visiting Kanakanak in a week's time, on his routine semi-annual visit, she literally squeezed a promise from the head nurse to X-ray 14 children. The woman insisted that was all the film she had on hand.

We arranged for a bush pilot to ferry the children and Jan, acting as their chaperon, to Dillingham and to bring them home the following day. That little expedition cost the taxpayers nothing. It cost the impoverished Moore family $350, or slightly more than 10% of my annual wage. But it was worth it, because lives were saved.

Jan selected the 14 children she thought were the sickest, including a six year old waif from Togiak with the unlikely English name (for an Eskimo boy) of Johnny Miller, and the four orphan children. She escorted them to the hospital. I shudder to think how many of the remaining 30 pupils also may have had active tuberculosis.

It was two weeks before the X-rays were read. **Tragically, all but one of the 14 children had active tuberculosis!** Jacinto, the 14 year old orphan, was the only exception, and he had an encapsulated lesion. His sister and brothers were infected. The little Eskimo waif from Togiak with the unlikely English name was also seriously ill with the disease.

As recently as 1947, there was no chemotherapy for tuberculosis. The only treatment then available was bed rest. Obviously, that was a long term proposition, with very uncertain results, and the Bureau of Indian Affairs facilities were absolutely crammed, with a long waiting list. I've since thought that might explain why the nurse at the hospital was so reluctant to X-ray the kids. She knew that positive diagnoses would merely add to their frustrating backlog of untreated cases. But they didn't know Jan.

She and I went to the doll house where Henry Shade met us with the children. Jan laid it out. "Aurora," she said, "I have terrible news. You, Billy, and Vincent are sick with the same disease that killed your mother and father."

She paused, then went on, "But you don't have to die, too. There's a good chance you can save your lives, but it won't be easy." She went on to tell them that they would have to stay in bed, and that Jacinto would have to do all the cooking, cleaning up, and laundry.

The younger children didn't fully comprehend what Jan was saying, but Aurora and Jacinto received the tragic news with poise and dignity far beyond their years. Aurora, the titular head of the little orphan group, at 16, was already a mature young woman.

"You'll have to keep the other kids out of here," I added to Jacinto, "and above all, you'll have to keep your little brothers quiet and in bed." In return, since they were all enrolled in the school, I promised to come every evening to give the bedridden youngsters their lessons. It's not that they were such eager scholars, although Vincent was an extraordinarily bright lad, but since this was before the days of television, I knew it would break the monotony of their days.

Aurora survived and I understand, today is a grandmother, but this story does not have a happy ending. Billy and Vincent died. I'm not sure what became of Jacinto.

The Blancaflor children—the four orphans—and Johnny Miller were especially poignant cases because they were so vulnerable. Little Johnny Miller became our problem. We simply could not ignore his situation.

Generally, Eskimos dote on children. Any child fortunate enough to be born into an Eskimo village acquires as many parents as there are adults in the village. It's not uncommon for children to be handed back and forth, or even for children to choose more compatible adults as parents when they are big enough to wander out of doors.

Unfortunately, the people looking after Johnny were an exception. He was not well treated. Taking one of my older students as an interpreter, I called on his foster parents, and tried to explain Johnny's problem to them. Both lungs were infected, and he needed immediate care.

Poverty and squalor are quite different things. The hut where he lived was dirty. I saw Johnny's bed. It was a pile of filthy rags in the windbreak, and according to Mary Shade, he was fed whatever was left over from the evening meal. The father was an older Eskimo who had distanced himself from his young family, and who was something of an outcast for reasons I never knew. His young wife was busy with twin babies and had nothing to give Johnny.

Unfortunately, my English or my interpreter's Yupik or both were unequal to the task. I could see it was hopeless. I hated the alternative, but it didn't seem that I had a choice. Left alone, Johnny was clearly doomed, and the longer he remained in that household, the more likely it was that he would infect the babies, assuming, of course, that they weren't already sick.

Jan and I had a long conversation, and jointly concluded that we had to bring the boy into our home. Our tiny apartment would become smaller still if we put another bed in it, but it was a small price if we could save the boy.

Taking my interpreter, I went to talk again to Johnny's foster parents, this time offering a bed and medical care for the boy. The old Eskimo, who until now probably had never heard of the germ theory, went into a rage. Eskimos don't often get angry, but when they do it can be serious. I hadn't expected that reaction, but my young guide explained, "It make him look bad."

I consulted with Henry Shade, who explained that the old man had been banished from his village years earlier, and consequently was something of a renegade. God alone knows what his transgression must have been, but it was serious. Banishment is the Eskimo equivalent of capital punishment.

From his point of view, the old man was living in a village populated mostly by aliens—by Filipinos and white men— Henry Shade, George the Greek, and me. He clung bitterly to the tatters of imagined respectability. Henry urged me in his indirect way to fly to Dillingham and discuss Johnny Miller's problem with the US commissioner. Then, almost as an afterthought, Henry casually added, "While you're about it, tell the commissioner that Carl Evon is in town."

I flew to Dillingham, and met with the commissioner, the deputy marshal, and Carlos Carson, the federal game warden. I'm still not sure why Carson was involved, except that he was also a sworn officer.

The Alaskan commissioner, in Territorial days, wore many hats, and occasionally made the law as he went along. After he heard my story, the commissioner advised me to simply take the boy away from the old Eskimo. He further suggested that I threaten him with the marshal if he gave me any trouble. Then, remembering Henry Shade's last remark, I repeated his message about Carl Evon.

The marshal looked startled, and Johnny Miller's difficulties abruptly receded into the background, while the commissioner began to recite Carl Evon's criminal history.

Carl Evon was an outcast. Only instead of settling down, Carl had become increasingly psychotic. He had first come to the attention of the authorities about ten years earlier when a pioneer bush pilot, "Red" Flensburg, flying along the Portage Creek trail, saw a bloody body lying in the snow. He landed nearby and went to investigate.

It was the corpse of a badly-beaten woman. Gaping wounds in her scalp suggested that handsful of hair and skin had been wrenched violently and with extraordinary force from her head. Her face and body bore the unmistakable wounds of countless blows by a small hard object.

The body was subsequently identified as Carl Evon's wife. Carl had forced her to help his dogs pull the sled. Apparently dissatisfied with her effort, he had beaten her to death with a dog chain. He was arrested and convicted of her murder. He was sentenced to six months in the Dillingham jail.

Two years after his release, again in mid-winter, a local missionary, driving a dog team from Levelock on the Kvichak

River to Dillingham, passed Carl Evon's cabin on Portage Creek. There was no smoke rising from the stovepipe, but the preacher heard a cry that sounded like a child. Curious, he stopped his team. He heard it again. He went to the door and listened. The cry, fainter this time, came from within the cabin. He forced the door open and found two young children inside. The stove had long been cold. The temperature inside the cabin was the same as outside—about –20°!

The baby was dead, frozen stiff. He opened his parka and lifting his shirt, tucked the surviving, but almost dead, little girl against the warmth of his body, and rushing back to his sled, forced his weary dogs to race madly through the dark, reaching Dillingham by midnight. The child lived, but lost an arm and a foot.

Carl was found by the marshal the next morning, wandering around town still drunk. He had left his children to freeze. This time, he was convicted of manslaughter. After serving a second six-month sentence, he was released. Two years later, he found a trapper desperate or foolish enough to take him on as a partner. Only one of them survived the winter. According to the commissioner, Carl shot his partner in the back.

This time, the case was tried in Federal District Court in Anchorage, and upon conviction, Carl was sent to the federal penitentiary in Washington State, where he served two years—long enough in close proximity to seriously hardened criminals so he became a postgraduate criminal—and was released. Now he was in Clarks Point. No wonder Henry was worried.

"What should we do if he gets out of hand?" I asked.

"Shoot him," the two officials said simultaneously. Not believing my senses, I looked incredulously at the men.

The commissioner looked somberly at me. "We're not kidding. He is dangerous as hell. Christmas is coming and there will be lots of booze around. If he gets drunk he's likely to shoot any white man he sees."

As soon as I arrived back in Clarks Point, I conferred with Henry Shade. Clearly, one of us had to take the initiative. We had to drive that fellow out of town before he hurt someone.

Although Henry had participated 20 years earlier in the hunt for another murderous Eskimo outlaw—a villain known as *Klootuk*—I was younger and considerably quicker than Henry. Also, my family obligations were not as great. Most importantly, however, I had a terrible advantage that neither of us recognized, but which I now think Carl Evon must have sensed, which tipped the scales in our favor.

Only three years before, I had spent 11 days on Iwo Jima in the bloodiest American engagement since Pickett's charge at Gettysburg. I know now that I was still a very sick boy.

Although I still wore a leg brace and found I needed a piece of string tied to the front of my right snowshoe to lift it when I walked in the snow, I was reasonably fit. At least in my case, emotional and mental wounds took much longer to heal than the physical ones. Apparently, I was still suffering from what was then called "battle fatigue," and is now termed "post-traumatic stress disorder." To put the matter bluntly, I was probably as crazy as Carl Evon, because I now realize I was fully prepared to execute him if it came to that.

Henry owned an Army 1911 Colt .45 pistol which I borrowed. Then I sent word down to the village that I wanted to see Carl Evon. I put the pistol in plain view on a small table and sat next to it after Carl arrived. Its heavy dark shape drew his black eyes like a magnet. After we were seated, I studied his face for a moment. He was an unusually dark complexioned, somewhat stocky Eskimo of indeterminate late middle age. His long black hair was combed straight back, revealing a deep crescent shaped scar near his hairline. I wondered if he had been hit on the head in prison.

I thanked him for responding to my invitation. Then I said as quietly as possible, "You have a hell of a reputation, you know." I paused, thinking he might have something to say, but he merely continued to stare at the pistol.

"The commissioner over at Dillingham warned me about you, and told me that you might try to hurt me if you got drunk." Still no response. His obsidian eyes flickered to my face and back to the pistol. He wasn't going to make this easy. I sighed. I really hated to do this. I knew it was wrong, but I thought it was necessary.

"You see the spot I'm in, don't you?" I continued, speaking very slowly and carefully. I didn't know how well he could understand English, although I was sure that two years in a Federal penitentiary would have improved his command of the language. "Now, just by talking to you this way, if you get drunk, you'll get mad. And if you get mad, you'll probably try to kill me like you did your partner."

"That's what this is for." I patted the .45. "You see my problem, don't you?" I asked again. Evidently he did. He never uttered a word, but rose silently, pulled his parka hood over his head and left. I never saw him again. He hooked up his team that evening and after stealing as much of Filipino Pete's dried fish as he could carry, he left the village.

The incident had its light side. When Carl Evon left town, he was not in a happy frame of mind. In addition to stealing the fish, he destroyed the animal traps he found along the trail. The next day, I was visited by a delegation of indignant Filipinos who seriously demanded that I go after him and bring him back to justice.

3

Settling In

Becoming an Alaskan required much more than facing down murderous Eskimos and rescuing sick children. Raised on a Montana ranch, Jan already knew about serious winter weather. But to me, a city boy from the Pacific Northwest, our new environment was alien and downright hostile. Puget Sound has an occasional sharp frost, and we expected snow three of four times a year, but I had never experienced sub-zero temperatures, and nothing had prepared me for a December northwesterly gale off the ice in the Bering Sea.

I received my first lesson shortly after we settled in. In the excitement and confusion of learning how to organize and teach school, I had neglected to care for the drums of fuel oil Emil Sorenson had dumped on the beach early in September. They had remained upended on the beach, I thought, well above the high water mark.

As needed, I had rolled them, one at a time, up a temporary ramp made of drift wood and discarded planks, over the gravel berm, and across the road to the schoolhouse. As it turned out, that wasn't good enough.

We had finished supper and settled down to a comfortable evening by the fire, reading and listening to the frigid gale whistling around the corner of the schoolhouse, when we were startled by a frantic hammering

47

on the door. I rushed to open it, and young Joe Clark, his face flushed with the cold, stepped in. His eyes rolling in excitement, he blurted, "Yer oil drums are floating away!"

Good God! This was awful! Slush ice starts running in the Nushagak in late October, when the winter gales begin, and Emil's scow had been hauled out of the water weeks earlier. There was no way lost fuel oil could be replaced before spring, and there were no reserves in the village. If we lost our oil, I knew we would be forced to resurrect the coal space heaters.

I quickly pulled on my rubber boots, heavy surplus Army parka, and gloves, grabbed a flashlight, and followed Joe out into the cold, dark, hostile night. The wind, a near gale straight out of the northwest, tore at my clothes and brought instant tears to my eyes.

When we rounded the corner of the school by the road, I was astonished to see a surf breaking against the berm and washing over the road. As green as I was, I knew instantly that the gale had caused an already high spring tide to rise several feet higher than predicted. Ice encrusted drums, gleaming wetly in my flashlight's beam, heavily bobbed and rolled in the crashing surf.

Handling a full 55 gallon oil drum, which weighs about 400 pounds, on dry land is a tough assignment. Wrestling many of them, coated with ice, rolling ponderously and dangerously at night in breaking surf, is nearly impossible.

Thrusting the light into my pocket, I pulled up my boots and waded out into the water, where I began rolling drums up out of the surf. Jan began to follow me into the water, but I ordered her away when I realized other men were also in that frigid water, working desperately to salvage the school's winter fuel supply.

I have no idea how long I splashed in the surf. I doubt if it was more than a few minutes, but I was quickly soaked and my legs became numb so I was unable to feel chunks of ice banging into them. After rescuing perhaps three or four drums—I really don't know how many—I was suddenly paralyzed from the waist down. I didn't fall, but however hard I tried, I had simply lost the ability to move my legs. I suddenly realized that if I fell, I might drown.

I called to a shadowy figure nearby. It was George the Greek. He hurried to my side and leaned forward, yelling over the crash of the surf, "Wassa matta? You no can walk?" His voice was heavy with concern.

"Help me, George," I replied. "I don't think I can make it to the beach."

He quickly and expertly sized up the situation, and called Joe Clark, also laboring nearby. "Hey Joe! Da schoolteach' is freezin'. Gimme a han'."

Supported by Joe Clark on one side and George the Greek on the other, I made it to the teacher's quarters. Jan and the two men pulled off my boots—it's always difficult to remove waterlogged boots because of the suction, but pulling them from feet and legs stiff and cramped with cold required a lot of wiggling and tugging. Chips of ice the size of ice cubes were poured from my boots when Jan dumped the water into the slop bucket.

She poured three fingers of 151 proof *Lemon and Hart's Admiralty* rum into tumblers and passed them around. George and I drank ours neat, but Joe cut his with water. Even in a warm room with my wet clothes off, full of rum and with Jan briskly toweling my legs to restore circulation, it was at least half an hour before I even started to shiver. God, I was cold!

However, thanks to the combined efforts of half the men in the village, when we took inventory the next morning, we found we had lost only one drum.

I mentioned the slop pail. Like other communities on the

Bering Sea coast, Clarks Point lacked even the most basic amenities. We couldn't install septic tanks because we were on the edge of the polar permafrost belt. We carried our household slops to the beach below the tide in a bucket, and used the outhouse for our more serious sanitary needs.

Another amenity most take for granted is a steady, if not always abundant, supply of fresh water. During the summer and autumn, we relied on a barrel that collected rain water from the roof for our fresh water. After freeze-up, however, water was hauled from a well under the hill half a mile across the muskeg swamp by dog sled.

My predecessor, Mrs. Ott, a lady of indeterminate years who had retired a year earlier, had arranged with one of the older school boys to haul her water during the winter, but her needs were far more modest than ours.

Remember, I was a young lad barely 21 years old, full of youthful energy and anxious to sample whatever life had to offer. I thought that having a team was desirable, because it would enable me to haul my own water, and enable me to go ptarmigan hunting when I wished. I thought it would also give me a certain stature in the village. It accomplished all those things, but not exactly in the way I intended.

On Henry Shade's advice, we bought a new knocked-down 100 gallon wooden barrel from Verner Wilson to use as a water reservoir. I assembled it in our windbreak (enclosed porch). I also bought a worn dog sled from him, and a 50 gallon barrel for carrying water from the well. The old Norwegian threw in several harnesses and a tow line. Now I needed dogs.

I had already identified myself as a fool by buying an old and perfectly useless biadarka (one-man kayak), and then paying an extra $10 for the paddle, before Henry Shade, no doubt worried that his recruiting efforts were about to vanish under a capsized kayak, could intervene. But he succeeded in persuading me that it would be suicidal to try to learn to use it in water that never warmed above 50°, even in July.

There were ten or twelve dog teams in the village. Like professional football teams, at the beginning of the season, each team had many more recruits than were needed, mainly from puppies that had matured during the summer.

School children watching fall ship leave

Since it was an unwritten but ironclad rule that all dogs six months old and older had to be chained, meaning they had to be fed, during the early fall sledding, the wheat was quickly separated from the chaff.

The rule about chaining sled dogs was universally observed in Eskimo villages. The reason was simple. Although every Eskimo child learned not to run in the presence of loose dogs, just as city kids learn not to cross the street without looking both ways, more than one youngster has been dragged down and killed by a pack of excited half-grown pups running loose.

Instead of being turned out to fend for themselves like football players, unwanted dogs were usually taken down to the beach and shot. But with a new, green, schoolteacher in town, dogs that otherwise would have been destroyed became valuable. Why not sell them to the schoolteacher? Suddenly I was inundated with dogs.

Eskimos have a wonderful sense of humor. They laugh often and well. From their point of view, there wasn't much wrong with a world that gave them the chance to get paid for getting rid of unwanted dogs while watching a cheechaco schoolteacher struggle with a team of renegade and outlaw animals! In the days before television, such entertainment provided a rich lode of humor that often became legend. It was not accidental that the Yupik phrase for a white man, *"ishtuk–a'sugaluk,"* literally translated, was "crazy white man."

I'm also sure they were not oblivious to the fact that whether they are worked or not, dog teams require fuel. Thus, the schoolteacher would be forced to enter the market for dried fish since he had none. Dried fish were salmon caught by the women during the days that commercial fishing was prohibited, then split and hung to dry on the racks that lined the beach side of the road. The going price was $40 a bundle (40 fish to the bundle).

Gingerly, I bought five dogs ranging in price from five to twenty-five dollars for my dogs. The higher price was for the leader. I knew it would cost roughly $2.50 per day to feed that many, but I felt I had to have a dog team, and I was told that five was a good number.

It's a good thing I acquired that many animals, because while all of them had faults, two dogs didn't last long. On the other hand, after learning to live with her most serious flaw, I wound up with a more than adequate leader.

I called her *Lady.* She was about three years old, and was very smart, but flighty. If dogs will cross with foxes, somewhere in her ancestry may have lurked a red fox. Her coloring, the shape of her muzzle and her alert pointed ears were those of a fox, but she was smooth haired, and much bigger than a fox. She was also sterile. I quickly discovered why this gem of a dog had been sold to me. As the local Eskimos explained it, "He eat harness."

Somewhere in this world may live a genius who knows how to break a dog from chewing its harness, but I never met anyone who did. I tried boiling the harness in a pepper soup laced with Tabasco sauce and kerosene. The dog loved it. I tried punishing her by sawing the cut harness back and forth in her mouth until her mouth bled. She wagged her tail and asked for more. I scolded, pleaded, and finally did the only sensible thing. Whenever I stopped the team and knew I'd be away from it for more than two minutes, I always unharnessed her and put her on a chain.

Bob was another recruit. He was a malamute, big, clumsy, and prone to breaking through crusted snow. You could forgive those things—but he was also an ancient, harness-wise wheel dog, and you couldn't forgive his skill at keeping his towline just tight enough to keep it off the ground.

On level ground, under good trail conditions, it's reasonable to expect a dog like Bob to pull 100 pounds all day. I suspected he was malingering. Once, when we were returning to the village with a barrel of water, I

Jan and Lady

proved it. As the team slowed, pulling the sled through a soft drift, I quietly sneaked up behind him, took his towline between my thumb and forefinger, and gently exerted a light pull. He instantly fell back to accommodate the extra drag.

That evening, I gave Bob back to his former owner. I told him I was sorry I didn't know how to drive a dog team well enough to handle a high class dog like Bob. That left me with four dogs.

George was a real piece of work. He looked like a big black Labrador. He seemed reasonably tractable, pulled hard, and appeared to exert a calming influence on a younger dog, Kodiak. How did I wind up with such a paragon?

Unfortunately, like the others, he was flawed. I discovered his fault one afternoon in late November, when I was out with the team hunting for ptarmigan.

We had flushed a small flock and I was leading the team on snowshoes holding one end of a chain that was snapped to *Lady's* collar. We were following a line of willows around a small hill, and I was intently watching where the birds had settled, shotgun at the ready.

It was a gray, shadowless day when the surface of the snow disappears in what bush pilots call a "white-out." Even to a person on snowshoes, the surface becomes invisible.

Suddenly, I pitched forward into a deep hole under a willow. As I was falling, I heard a snarl. Out of the corner of my eye, I saw George, eyes narrowed and lips peeled back, spring at me. Luckily, the other dogs were still moving, and their weight pulled George off balance, so he missed my throat. His teeth closed instead on my shoulder, and I dropped the gun.

He let go momentarily, probably to get a better grip, and although I was badly shaken and buried to my hips in the snow, I seized his collar with my left hand, and yanked his head toward me, while swinging my right fist with all my strength at the sensitive tip of his nose.

It was over in an instant. He yelped, and the other dogs dragged him away from me. Ptarmigan hunting forgotten, tremulously, I retrieved the shotgun and my broken snow-shoe, and directed the dogs back to the village.

By the time we arrived home, I had stopped shaking, but I knew what had to be done. After unharnessing the dogs, I led George by his chain down to the beach where I put the muzzle of my .22 rifle in his ear and pulled the trigger.

Later, when discussing the incident, I learned that poor George was, as a former owner expressed it, "goofy." It seems an earlier owner had carelessly struck poor George over the head with a board that had a protruding nail. The nail had pierced his skull, and although George had recovered from his impromptu brain surgery, ever after he was a little "funny."

In this case, "funny" translated into murderous. I think given the opportunity, the dog might have killed me. My thrifty nature came to the fore, however, as I stood gazing at George's lifeless carcass. Most Arctic furs reach their peak condition in late November, and George's fur was lustrous and thick. It seemed wasteful to discard it. So I skinned the animal and tacked his hide inside the cache to dry.

Later, I took a fair amount of kidding about skinning a dog, possibly because a schoolteacher willing to skin a dog was outside our new neighbor's experience.

When the hide was dry, I called on my next door neighbor, Mrs. Roberts, an Eskimo woman so ancient that her face bore status and beauty tattoos; lines that ran from the corners of her mouth down to the bottom edge of her jaw, and status marks tattooed in three vertical lines on the front of her chin. She spoke little English, but with the aid of my juvenile interpreter, she quickly grasped that I needed a pair of *mukluks,* known locally as *kamuksuks.*

She examined the stiff, untanned dog hide, and slowly nodded. Now on familiar ground, she grinned and said, "*EEEeeeEE,*" with the curious inflection that is the Yupik equivalent of "yes" or "OK." We quickly agreed on a price of $20, and I left the hide in her possession, not fully comprehending that she would use traditional methods, including soaking the hide in human urine, to tan it.

She did a splendid job, but unfortunately, whenever I wore

55

the boots into a warm room, they gave off a stench not unlike that of an ill kept barroom urinal. My new boots, in other words, were not suited to polite society. On the other hand, dog fur is exceptionally durable, and I wore them on the trail for years.

I kept two dogs in addition to Lady. One was a malamute named Kodiak, the other was named Jim. Kodiak's problem was exactly opposite from Bob's. Kodiak was a young dog, scarcely more than a pup, but he was a runaway artist and a fighter.

If I took my eye off him for a minute, he would bolt or snap at Jim. Jim, on the other hand, was a perfect gentleman. He looked like an Airedale, but had none of that breed's unpleasant disposition. Jim was tractable, hardworking, easy going. He was perfect in every respect save one. He only weighed about 35 pounds, and easily slipped out of a standard harness. But I had a dog team, even if it was part fox, part Airedale, and only 1/3 sled dog.

Although I truly believe that civilizations can be gauged by inverse proportion to the amount of armament in the hands of their citizens, I must confess that I've always been something of a gun nut. While at Clarks Point, for instance, I acquired a 20 gauge Mossberg double barrel shotgun, a 12 gauge model 12 Winchester shotgun, a S&W .38 Police Special, a .22 Winchester pump gun, a Spanish/American War .30-40 Krag, and an antique .31 caliber Schaarp cap and ball squirrel rifle.

Since Clarks Point was in the middle of the Pacific flyway, the muskeg swamp behind the village was host to thousands of migrating ducks and geese every autumn. Consequently, I got good use out of the 12 gauge shotgun. The Mossberg worked fine on winter ptarmigan. I never discovered what the Krag was good for, except it was cheap.

The muzzle loader was hard to justify, especially to a wife

who still lacked a washing machine. I had responded to an ad placed in *National Rifleman* by a dealer in Portsmouth, Ohio, who specialized in muzzle loading arms and supplies. After an extended exchange of correspondence, "Red" Farris set me up with the squirrel rifle for $75, which, as Jan pointed out, was almost exactly the same as the price of a gasoline powered washing machine in Ward's catalog. It helped some when I promised that we'd order a machine to arrive on the first available ship in the spring.

Jan was a wonderfully tolerant woman, putting up, as she did, with my various foibles. But that little squirrel rifle sorely tried her patience. In some ways, I suppose, it served as a domestic lightning rod. When storm clouds began to threaten our connubial bliss, the Schaarp could always be depended upon to attract, and deflect, most of the accumulated emotional overflow. Not being as wise—perhaps "seasoned" would be a more descriptive term—as I am today, from time to time I would feel called upon to defend my toy. Needless to say, whenever I tried that, it almost always ended badly.

For example, I remember once responding to the usual complaint about the muzzleloader's utility with an almost childlike, "Well, there's a lot of geese out there in the muskeg. I'll go shoot one for dinner."

If ever there were an award for foolish famous last words, my silly declaration certainly would be in the money.

However, to prove my point, I made a dozen "spills" of powder by measuring single charges of powder and wrapping them tightly in twisted pieces of wax paper. Then I soaked an equal number of cloth patches in gun oil, carefully selected my lead balls, shoved a box of caps in my pocket, and was off on the great justification hunt.

The ridge that meandered behind the village was nearly half a mile from the school. The muskeg swamp that lay between the village and the ridge was deceiving. There was just enough scrub brush and waist-high grass out there, so you couldn't see the little potholes and small meandering streams that seemed to connect most of them. Nor could you identify the floating mats of vegetation until you stepped on them.

Suddenly, as you stepped on seemingly firm ground cover, your feet would sink six to eight inches in spongy, watery muskeg. If you stood perfectly still and, flexing your knees, jumped up and down without actually jumping into the air, you could see how broad the patch of muskeg was by how far the ripples extended.

It seemed dangerous, but it was perfectly safe because underlying the water and vegetation was a solid stratum of ice and frozen earth called *permafrost*. While it was safe, it was very, very, cold and wet.

In responding to Jan's challenge, I had really painted myself into a corner. Since this was the fall, during the annual migration period, I knew there were several flocks of Canada geese in front of me. It was late in the afternoon, and the waterfowl were settling down for the night. My strategy was a simple one.

I would crawl silently through the wet grass, carefully (I thought) keeping the rifle out of the water, until I found a flock. My plan was then to get close enough to a sentinel goose so I couldn't miss a head shot.

A body shot was no good. Although it was a squirrel rifle, in modern terms, my muzzle loader was not a small caliber. A .31 caliber ball would so badly mangle the body of a bird that it would be inedible.

I must confess that I was then and am now strictly a pot hunter. Except for an occasional trout, I never got good at killing animals for fun. That's why it would never have occurred to me to gut shoot a goose just to prove it could be done. I did think of other strategies, however, before this hunt was over.

After seemingly hours of slowly, carefully, sliding through the muskeg, using the scant brush as a screen, making sure my head and rump never rose above a goose's limited horizon, I heard geese ahead of me muttering among themselves as they do when they are settling down for the night.

Suddenly, directly in front of me, not 15 feet away, I saw movement. I froze, scarcely daring to breathe. A sentinel goose was peering at me inquisitively, a low questioning murmur rumbling in its throat. Its head turned this way and that, while it strained for a better view. I slowly brought the squirrel rifle up, carefully cocked the hammer, put a percussion cap on the firing nipple, and sighted on my quarry. The goose's head was as big as a football over my iron sights, and my finger slowly, slowly, squeezed the double set (hair) trigger.

SNAP! The geese instantly fell silent.

Damn! Only the cap had exploded. The rifle had misfired. Despite my best efforts, evidently, the powder in the rifle had gotten wet!

The sentinel, my intended quarry, uttered an inquiring, almost collegial, squawk, as if reassuring the flock they had nothing to fear. Gradually, the geese began muttering again. I might as well try it again. I cocked the hammer a second time. Again I placed the cap on the firing nipple, took careful aim and squeezed the trigger.

SNAP! A second misfire. I knew the geese wouldn't stand for this much longer.

Again, the flock went on a silent alert. As if criticizing the quality of my woodsmanship, my intended victim uttered a reproving squawk. For a brief moment, since the sentinel and I seemed to have gotten on such good terms, I wondered if I could catch that bird with my bare hands. I quickly dismissed that idea as silly. Knowing I was whipped, but curious about the size of the flock I had found, I stood up.

59

Instantly, as far as I could see, the air was filled with desperately flailing wings and panicky cries of alarm. There must have been two or three flights of geese in that pond, in all, perhaps a thousand birds, possibly many more. As they milled in the air and quickly flew out of range, I couldn't help but speculate how many birds I might have killed with a single unaimed shotgun blast. More than a few, I'm sure.

Jan was good about it. She snickered quietly, as she watched me drag my wet, dirty, and weary self through the doorway, empty handed save for the disgraced muzzleloader.

I was more successful as a hunter the following autumn. The cannery was loading the summer's salmon pack on the Alaska Steamship Company's *M/S Rose Knot*, lying at anchor in front of the cannery. This was before the days of containers, and I had been sent out to the ship as a checker in the number one hold to represent the company by verifying the number of cases loaded there. The longshoremen working in the ship's hold were a crew of Eskimo fishermen.

The third mate, the steamship representative who counted cases as they descended into the hold, also supervised their stowage, making sure the hold was tightly packed.

The man was a serious racist. He was dissatisfied with the way the men handled the cases, and began making disparaging and insulting racial remarks. Perhaps he didn't realize it, but the Eskimos understood every word, and when we stopped work for lunch, they decided to quit.

I didn't have any authority over them, but they knew I was the local "school-teach'," and I was able to persuade them to ignore the boorish fellow and return to work.

That evening, after the day's work was completed, I was standing at the rail admiring the sunset when the mate joined me. Just then, a flight of Canada geese passed overhead.

"What wouldn't I give to take one of them home for Christmas," he said, more to himself than to me.

A diabolical scheme for revenge leaped into my mind. "Would you give, say, $25?" I asked.

"I sure would," he said.

His fate was sealed.

The following day, my gang was relieved by another gang from the cannery—the working conditions and food on those ships was so terrible, even by 1948 standards, that ship gangs were rotated every 48 hours.

As soon as I reached the shore, I rushed down to the schoolhouse for my .22 Winchester. Then I went back to the cannery. The tide was out, and the pilings at the face of the dock were dry. A mature sea gull perched on each piling.

I carefully scrutinized the birds, searching for the oldest, meanest, and scruffiest of the bunch. I finally settled on an ugly old bird, took careful aim at his right eye, and squeezed the trigger. Bang!

Killed instantly, the bird fell into the mud. I climbed down the ladder at the face of the dock and waded through the reeking mud to retrieve my prey. Then, instead of climbing back up the ladder, I worked my way out of the mud up to the gravel, and then walked back to the school along the beach. That way, I didn't have to explain to anyone why I was carrying a dead sea gull.

Once home, I quickly sharpened my knife and, holding my breath, skinned and gutted the bird. God, it stank! Then I wrapped it in paper, and took it back to the cannery, where one of the cooks obligingly tucked it into the freezer for me.

The next day, when we went back to the ship, I held a cold parcel in my arms. The third mate was waiting for me. He knew as well as I that it was highly illegal to sell game birds, so we quietly exchanged the parcel for two ten and one five dollar bills. A wink completed the bargain. I've often wondered how he and his family enjoyed their Christmas dinner.

True to my promise, the new washing machine arrived that spring when Alaska Steamship's *M/S Square Knot* dropped her anchor at the ship's anchorage in late May. It meant the world to Jan, of course, especially after Trina was born. But if the muzzleloader was a continuing source of irritation to Jan, I learned to hate that washing machine.

Don't get me wrong. I used to enjoy tinkering with the finely machined parts of weapons, and I've even had my share of manual jobs, but I never liked them. Even when I was a grimy 16-year-old working in the Puget Sound Navy Yard in the early war years, I was much happier when I was sent to hunt for lost parts than I was squirming my way into the guts of a cold, greasy, battleship.

That washing machine, to me, became a washing machine from hell. It seemed that every time Jan operated it—once a week before Trina was born, twice a week afterwards—I had to reassemble it. The little air-cooled gas engine that powered it vibrated so badly that nuts and bolts would come apart, and the dasher would begin scraping one side of the tub, or the wringer would fall off, or some other mechanical calamity would occur, often resulting in mangled or grease streaked diapers, shirts, pillow cases, or sheets. Not unreasonably, I soon became very prejudiced against household appliances powered with gasoline engines.

That washing machine led us down strange pathways. From about the middle of May until the latter part of October, during the five months of "bad sledding" as one old sourdough put it, we had to rely on our rain barrel for water.

Up to then, we hadn't had much experience with the rain barrel. Shortly after we had arrived the previous autumn, we had begun hauling water across the muskeg. However, during the brief fall interlude, after the rain turned to snow, but before the flats froze hard enough to support a dog sled, we had experienced a slight pinch in our water supply.

The problem was that while the water collected during the summer months, when the space heaters were cold, was sufficiently clean and abundant for our modest household needs, during the fall, when three stove pipes—one from each classroom and the kitchen—contributed to the accumulation of soot on the roof, the new snow quickly

Bill White

turned a dark gray as it melted and drained into the rain barrel. Clearly, we needed a well.

I ordered a well point, drive pipe, drive unions, a drive cap, and optimistically, a cast iron pitcher pump, from Ward's catalog. During the ensuing six weeks that it took our order to arrive, a bachelor friend, Bill White, and I scrounged through the cannery junk pile, searching for suitable scrap to fashion a heavy-duty drive hammer to pound the well point down to a water-bearing strata.

Bill was an accomplished, out-of-doors sort of guy. During the summer, he was a fisherman, but during the winter, he worked in the woods as a logger and rigger. He knew exactly how to drive a well.

Eventually, the well point—a heavy short length of galvanized iron water pipe with screened slots cut into its side and a heavy forged point welded to the lower end—arrived. We cut a hole in the floor where we wished to have the well and hung a pulley in the kitchen rafters above it. Then we rigged the hammer by tying it to a rope that ran over the pulley and fell to where we stood in the kitchen.

The point was joined to another short length of pipe by a heavy duty union. At the end was a heavy cast iron drive cap.

We stood the point on end and threaded it through the hole so it rested on the sand under the building. Jan steadied it while Bill and I seized the rope. Chanting to maintain a tempo, we began driving the well point by raising the hammer two feet above the pipe and letting it drop. The hammer struck the drive cap with an almost explosive, ear-tingling, crash that stood my hair on end. We weren't so sensitive in those days to harmful work conditions or we might have stuffed our ears with cotton.

It took longer to drive the well than I had expected. The work was hard and the conditions, unpleasant, but Bill stuck with us. As necessary, Jan fueled her human donkey engines with doses of rum and water. Late that afternoon, after driving the well 16 feet, we struck fresh water.

The well was only marginally successful. The meshes of the screen in the well point weren't small enough to filter out fine grains of sand, and the pump clogged almost every time we pumped enough water to do a wash.

After clearing the pump for the hundredth time, out of whimsy, I put the sand—about a cup full—in a shallow pan full of water, and began swirling it around and around, allowing the lighter materials to slop over the edge. Eventually, after adding more water from time to time, I reduced the solid material in the pan to little more than a thimble full.

Carefully, I examined that residue with a magnifying glass. There was no question about it. Tiny specks of yellow material were clearly present. I had gold in my well! I took my "strike" up to the cannery and showed it to Henry Shade.

He glanced at it. "Oh, yeah," he said, twinkling at me, "that's what we call flour. You find it all over. It's gold but it don't mean nothing. There's not enough to work."

I never thought I had made a serious discovery. It was fun to tell our correspondents Outside, whether they believed us or not, that gold clogged our kitchen water pump.

Frontier Nurse

O ur new neighbors soon learned about Jan's profession. Since her medical training was as good as that of the government nurses at Kanakanak, and since the nearest doctor (after the cannery closed in the fall) was in Bethel, 350 miles away, Jan was frequently called upon in medical emergencies.

She was never licensed to practice medicine, of course, but she never refused a request for help. She generously tended the sick, sutured wounds, delivered babies, and once even set broken bones.

Early during our first spring, after the dog team trail to Creek cannery had thawed but while ice was still running in the river, Harry Barnes, the 14-year-old who drove the Creek cannery sled, and another young man, came in a skiff with an urgent plea for help.

A childbirth at Creek cannery was going badly. Jan quickly assembled sterile sheets, packs, everything she could think of that might be needed, and left with the two young men.

I was worried, and I hurried to the cannery, binoculars in hand, to watch them as they made their perilous way through floe ice on the ebbing tide.

By the time I reached the dock where I had an unobstructed view, Jan and the two boys were half a mile out in the river standing on a large ice floe, dragging the boat across the ice to open water. Jan was then about five months pregnant.

A week later, she was called away to Ekuk on a similar errand, where another woman was having a difficult labor. She was always successful with those childbirth cases.

However, tuberculosis, in its many guises, always lurked in the background. While her common sense doctoring usually yielded good results, even she couldn't cure TB.

We kept Johnny Miller, the six-year-old waif, as quiet as possible on his cot in our quarters. If good nursing could have saved him, he might be alive today. We were willing to accept the increased risk of infection caused by Johnny's close proximity, but when Jan discovered she was pregnant, it seemed unfair to expose our unborn baby to that risk.

Consequently, we began pushing the buttons until, at last, a bed was found for him in the government hospital in Anchorage. We saw him about 18 months later in Anchorage, shortly before his death. He barely recognized us. His poor body was covered with tubercular skin lesions, and he was nearly blind. His was a sickeningly tragic and needless loss.

Our struggle against TB never ended. Toward the end of our first year at Clarks Point, some young Eskimo parents asked Jan to look in on their two year old daughter. Jan noted the symptoms of what she thought was a vitamin D deficiency, and since she had difficulty reaching the government doctor in Bethel on the radio, she began treating the child. In the meanwhile, however, the child's parents decided not to take chances, and one afternoon, when Jan called on the child, she found that old Mr. Roberts, our next door neighbor, was also treating the child. The old man was unperturbed, but the young parents were worried that Jan would take offense at this obvious sign of distrust on their part. Of course, they didn't know Jan.

We knew he was the village medicine man, but this was

Jan's first tangible evidence of it. She told me that the old man's treatment consisted of carefully placed holy pictures in the child's crib.

Frequently, her visits coincided with the old man's after that. Unfortunately, neither western medicine nor the best that Mr. Roberts could do prevailed.

Jan driving Lady on beach
Note floe ice in river

Jan knew the child was desperately sick. She finally succeeded in reaching the government doctor. She described the child's symptoms, and shyly offered her tentative diagnosis.

There was a long pause at the doctor's end. Finally, he said, "God, I wish you were right, Mrs. Moore. But that poor child has something you'd never see in the States. You've just described an unmistakable case of tubercular meningitis. There is nothing you could have done for her that would have made a difference. I'm sorry to tell you, but there is no hope. Tubercular meningitis is invariably fatal."

The doctor was right. The poor child lived another week. For reasons I never understood, the parents then asked me to read the burial service. I complied, of course, and did the best I could, but I never understood why I was selected, because almost without exception, the Eskimos in that part of Alaska were devout Russian Orthodox, and normally a lay Russian priest would have officiated.

Although the bacteria that caused the disease had been identified some 80 years earlier, there was an astonishing lack of knowledge about TB as late as the late 1940s, ignorance which nearly cost Steven Wassilly his life.

After the cannery shut down in the autumn of 1948, a small gang of local men remained on the payroll helping Henry Shade put things away, winterize the machinery, and haul the last of the floating equipment from the water. One of those men, a young Eskimo from a tiny village up the coast, came down with a bad cold that quickly deteriorated into pneumonia.

Henry asked Jan to take a look at him. We found the patient in a lower bunk, alone on the second floor of the fishermen's drafty, unheated, bunkhouse. His eyes were bright with fever. His temperature was 103° and rising. She took appropriate measures, but during the next few days, his temperature continued to rise alarmingly.

Jan was sick with worry. The irony was that while she had access to penicillin, an almost certain cure for pneumonia, it was then believed that antibiotics were seriously contraindicated for patients with preexisting tuberculosis because it was thought that penicillin suppressed "good" germs, thus indirectly encouraging the growth of tubercle bacillus. She was afraid to administer the medication, fearing it would cause his probable TB to flare up and kill him.

I remember walking with her on the beach while we tried to sort this problem out. "Tell me, Jan," I began, "if you withhold the penicillin, will the pneumonia kill him?"

Unhappily, she nodded. "I think so," she said.

"And if you give him the penicillin, the TB *may* kill him?"

Again she nodded.

"So either way, the chances are he's going to die?"

She sighed. "I'm afraid so," she said sadly.

"Well," I said, taking her hand, "You're not a doctor. Obviously the safe thing for *you* to do is to cover *your* ass by doing nothing. But that's not your style." I paused, then went on, "It's true, penicillin may cause his TB to flare up, *if he has*

TB. I realize there's probably a 90% chance he does, but you don't know that for sure. I also know there's a 100% chance he's dying of pneumonia. If it was me, I'd take a chance on the TB, and give him the shot."

Jan is a very courageous person. Personal considerations never entered her decisions about therapy. She always did what she thought was best for the patient. Even though she thought poor Steve's chance of survival was increased by less than 10% if she administered the shot—and she knew full well that if he died after she gave him the shot, whether it was deserved or not, she would have to accept some responsibility for his death—she administered a standard dose of penicillin.

Steve's temperature began to drop almost immediately, and in a week's time, he was out of bed, pestering Henry for work assignments. It was, quite literally, a miracle brought on by penicillin and Jan's courage.

Much later, we learned that medical orthodoxy, in this instance, was wrong. The drug is *not* contraindicated for people with preexisting tuberculosis.

Jan's medical training had not equipped her for a rough and tumble public health practice. But with her toughness of mind and spirit, and a few textbooks left over from her nurses's training, she accomplished wonders.

Frank's fingers were a good example. This happened in the late fall during our second freeze-up at Clarks Point. A few skiffs were still in the water. One of them, braving "pan" ice—thin, razor-sharp sheets of forming ice in the river—brought Frank Hiratsuka three long miles from Ekuk for desperately needed medical attention.

He came into our quarters, his left hand wrapped in a bundle of filthy rags, encrusted with dried blood.

While she soaked the bandages off, Frank matter-of-factly explained that he had fallen a week earlier against a piling stump on the beach while carrying a storage battery. His fingers were crushed between the battery and the stump. The battery had broken open and his damaged hand was bathed with electrolyte. I imagine that the agony caused by that sulfuric acid bath must have been almost unbearable, but I think it's fair to say that it probably saved his hand by preventing a crippling infection from setting in.

Nothing prepared us for the terrible picture his hand presented when the last of the bandages was peeled away. The bones nearest the knuckle on his first and middle fingers had broken, and jagged bone ends, glistening in the lamp light, extended through the bruised and bloody skin.

Frank desperately needed the care only a highly skilled orthopedic surgeon could provide. Unfortunately, because the accident happened during freeze-up, we were immobilized. Neither float planes nor planes equipped with skis could operate. It would have been suicidal to try to run a boat all the way to Kanakanak through the pan ice. Therefore, Jan felt she had no alternative but to try to reduce those fractures and repair the damage as best she could.

She had worked at the cannery hospital during the previous summer. Therefore, she knew where things were, and through Henry, had access to medical supplies and equipment, including sutures, Novocaine, and even morphine if required.

We knew the Novocaine had lost its potency. She had tried to numb a gaping wound in Charlie Nolay's scalp two weeks earlier, but the Novocaine had not taken effect and Jan had been forced to take seven unanesthetized stitches in his scalp while I struggled to hold the poor man still.

Therefore, rather than pointlessly jab needles into Frank's broken hand, she decided to administer a quarter grain of morphine. Although it's probably just as well, poor Frank turned out to be allergic to the stuff. He became instantly, violently, nauseated.

He was so busy retching and vomiting that he scarcely noticed as I took a firm grip with a pair of pliers on the ends of his broken fingers, one at a time, and pulled until the exposed bones slipped back into place. Stretching those cramped finger muscles was a surprisingly hard pull.

Jan, still worried about using penicillin on people with suspected tuberculosis, heavily dusted the bones and the wound with sulpha powder. Then, as the fingers were restored to their normal length and shape, she used tongue depressors as splints, and taped things tightly together. Frank recovered from his allergic reaction and astonishingly, eventually regained the full use of his hand!

Although I necessarily played second fiddle most of the time during these medical emergencies, on at least two occasions, mine was the lead role.

The first occurred one evening shortly after supper. We were relaxing after a frustrating day in the classroom. We heard someone loudly stamping the snow from their feet in the windbreak. Moments later, the door rattled under heavy and anxious knocking.

I knew before I opened the door that it was an emergency. But nothing could have prepared me for this. Henry Shade's ordinarily stolid brother-in-law, Emil Eglund, his eyes rolling frantically, was standing in the doorway making funny sounds and pointing desperately at the handle of a dental impression tray sticking out of his mouth. Emil had come to me because he knew I wore dentures.

Many Alaskans living in remote areas then patronized mail-order dentists who advertised in magazines like *Alaska Sportsman* and *Popular Mechanics*. There were a dozen such firms in the Chicago area. When a customer sent in an order, the dentist would mail back an appropriate impression tray, a small quantity of plaster of Paris, a color chart, and a price list. You decided whether you wanted all new teeth or would settle for second hand ones, and selected the color of teeth you desired. As I recall, new teeth cost around a dollar each, while used teeth were only a fraction of that. Usually, the finished denture cost between $15 and $25.

Also included in the package were explicit directions that concluded: *"Under no circumstances must this tray remain in your mouth longer than 30 seconds!"*

There was good reason for that warning. As any dentist can tell you, when God designed the roof of the human mouth, He undoubtedly had upper plates in mind. Emil, unfortunately, was not a literalist. He had reasoned that if 30 seconds were good, five minutes must be ten times better.

I sat Emil down. Together, Jan and I tugged and pulled. Nothing happened. Then I got out my tool box. While Jan stood behind Emil, firmly holding his head back to prevent whiplash, I rained sharp little blows on the handle of the tray with my claw hammer.

That broke the suction. The tray came out. I'll bet he got a tight denture, but that ever afterwards when the directions said "30 seconds" that's exactly what he allowed.

My role in the second episode was largely confined to stage management. Jan clearly was the star. This episode had to do with the birth of our oldest daughter, Katrina Anne.

Jan's pregnancy, as far as we knew, was more or less normal. Jan, always active, continued during the spring to care for our sick and injured neighbors. When the cannery opened, she worked regular hours in the tiny cannery hospital. After the commercial fishing season closed, she caught and split fish for our little dog team.

In late August, as her term drew near, we discovered that the doctor, who was normally stationed in Bethel, would be spending a week at Kanakanak. This seemed to be our best chance to have the baby close to home, yet with a maximum degree of safety for herself and the child. This alternative seemed especially attractive since she had "met" the doctor many times over the cannery radio discussing various medical problems confronting the local people.

How wrong can people be?

Never one to leave things to chance, Jan induced her labor by taking a quinine capsule washed down with a dose of mineral oil. Long before this medication could take effect, the pilot who had flown the school children to Kanakanak the previous winter, was summoned by radio. He arrived, and shortly before lunch, he flew us to Dillingham.

Jan wasn't even sure at first whether she was in labor. True, she had a low back ache, and had promptly vomited her lunch, but we waited in Dillingham until her first contraction. WOW! Then I found a taxi to take us the four miles of corrugated dirt road from Dillingham to the government hospital in Kanakanak.

After we arrived at the hospital, I paid the driver, but he refused to leave. "I've brought white people out here before," was all he would say.

Jan was ushered into the doctor's office while I sat in the waiting room. Jan later told me how the conversation went.

After examining her, the doctor told her to get dressed. "You're pregnant, and you're in labor," the doctor said, holding up two fingers. "Luckily," he went on, "you are a healthy young woman, and since this is your first baby, you still have time to get to a hospital in Anchorage."

Jan started to interrupt him, but he held up a restraining hand, "I know what you're going to say," he went on, "but you realize that as a white person you are a non-beneficiary, and I'm holding the only vacant bed I have for a Native woman in Dillingham who may be coming in this week. I'm sorry. I simply can't admit you." With that, he stood up to indicate that the interview was over.

Shaken and suddenly fearful, Jan came into the waiting

room to tell me what the doctor had said. I listened in stunned disbelief; how was this possible? That a doctor would turn away a woman in labor? Racial discrimination is a terrible thing, especially when you are on the receiving end!

We went out on the porch, and sat on the steps miserably reviewing our options. Our taxi driver sat patiently waiting for us to make up our minds.

However, we remembered that the cannery doctor at Clarks Point was still in residence. Therefore, we concluded we had a reasonable fall back position.

It was dreadful, knowing that each decision we made was irreversible. There wouldn't be any second chances. Despite the doctor at Clarks, we thought it might have been the safest thing just to wait the government doctor out. I felt certain even then that had she delivered her baby on the hospital steps, neither he nor the nurses could have remained indifferent to her plight. Beyond the shadow of a doubt, if I had it to do over again, there's not a force on this earth that could have induced me to put Jan back into that taxi.

But then, I was barely 22 years old, and I had been intensely conditioned in Naval hospitals to accept medical authority. Jan, with her nurses training, was similarly conditioned. Foolishly, the victims of our training, we got into the cab and bounced and jostled over that corduroy-like road back to Dillingham.

It was late in the afternoon when we returned to Dillingham, and the local happy hour was underway. However, I managed to find a sober pilot willing to fly us back to Clarks Point. His was a bi-wing Waco on floats. After an agonizingly long delay while he pumped water from his floats, we took off. Jan's contractions by now had settled down to 20-minute intervals, aided doubtlessly by the mineral oil, quinine, and eight miles of bad road.

We arrived back at Clarks Point at dusk. Jan went straight

to bed while I went to the cannery to summon the doctor. I found him playing pinochle with members of the beach gang in their quarters. Gasping for breath, I blurted the unwelcome news that the government doctor at Kanakanak had turned us down.

I was astonished by the doctor's hysterical reaction. "You're not going to put *me* behind the eight-ball," he screamed. "She's too old to have her first baby (Jan was 24)! There are no forceps in the hospital! I doubt I could save the baby, let alone the mother! I don't even have a sterile pack." He paused, looking pleadingly at the closed faces of his card playing pals.

Then he added, "I won't have any part of this. You got yourself into this fix; now you can get yourself out." With that he turned his back and resumed the game.

Stunned, I turned slowly away, hearing as I did so, his voice saying, "Whose deal is it?"

With a leaden heart, I hurried back down the road to the schoolhouse. Jan received my shocking news with astonishing equanimity. "Well," she said, "this won't be the first time a husband has delivered his baby. Hand me a sheet of paper."

I did as she asked and watched her prepare a list. Satisfied, she handed it to me. "Find Mr. Cooper. Tell him what's happened, and that you need these things from the hospital."

I rushed back to the cannery, this time going to the white house. It was my first visit there, and I was ill at ease for that reason as well as my larger problem.

Mr. Cooper listened sympathetically to my story. "I can't order the doc to look after your wife," he said slowly, "and frankly from what you say, that may be just as well."

He held out his hand for Jan's list. "Let's find the doc and get this stuff together."

The doctor had disappeared from the beach gang quarters

by the time we arrived. We went back to the hospital. The building was dark and silent. If he was in his quarters, he was remaining quiet. After hammering on the door without results, Mr. Cooper opened the door with his master key.

Together, we ransacked the storeroom and tiny pharmacy, quickly gathering things Jan had requested. Thanking Mr. Cooper, and receiving his concerned best wishes, I hurried back into the dark.

Jan had thoughtfully included bed linens and towels on her list, and she quickly folded them into a sterile pack, and told me to put them in the pressure cooker and cook them at ten pounds of pressure for 20 minutes. I already had water heating—isn't that part of the standard ritual when preparing for childbirth?—so the relief valve on the pressure cooker quickly began its cheerful little jiggling sound. While I was waiting, since we had no electricity, I decided I had better refill the Coleman gasoline lanterns.

Jan was becoming increasingly uncomfortable, and suggested perhaps I might improve my understanding of the process we were about to experience by thumbing through her obstetrics textbook. I tried, but that particular text was profusely illustrated with a variety of frighteningly abnormal birth pictures, and I found it impossible to concentrate.

Finally, I lost my nerve. With a hurried, "I'll be right back," I ran up to the Shade home. After pounding on the door, seemingly for hours, it swung open to a very annoyed Henry Shade. I blurted out that Jan was about to have her baby, and please could Mary come down and help out?

I hurried back to the schoolhouse and told Jan that I had gone for reinforcements. Mary showed up a few minutes later with a middle-aged, somewhat worldly Eskimo woman from Bethel, known as "Blue Annie," in tow. I have no idea why she was called that, but I felt better when I saw her because she had struck me as person who knew what she was doing.

Meanwhile, I had the sterile pack out of the pressure cooker, drying in the oven.

When she entered the room, Mary announced, "I've never done this before, and neither has Annie, but we've had plenty babies. . ." *God, now what have I done?!*

Jan ignored the two women who huddled in the corner watching me make up the bed with the sterile sheets. Jan told me how to set up the nursery with a pillow and towel, and how to tie the cord before cutting it. She also instructed me in examining the placenta and massaging her uterus after the baby was delivered, to express any clots.

By this time, it was nearly midnight. Jan was in serious pain, and kept asking me to watch her dilation. To her great annoyance, the two women alternatively urged her to assume a squatting posture in the corner and modestly kept pulling the sheet back over her.

Suddenly, Jan was seized with powerful contractions and sobbing and gasping, screamed, "I can't take any more. Give me a shot of scopolamine!"

This drug had been on Jan's shopping list and I had the cannery's entire supply. Dutifully, I plunged the hypodermic needle into the bottle, but just before I stuck the needle into her arm, I thought, *if you knock her out and get into trouble, who you going to ask for advice?*

Instead, I only pretended to give the shot. Things quickly became very confused. Mary and Annie were tugging on Jan's right arm, trying to get her to squat in the corner as they had done when they delivered their babies. In the meanwhile, Jan was exploring between her legs with her left hand. *"I'm having the baby!"* she screamed.

I ran to the other end of the bed. The first thing I saw was a pair of blue eyes. Even as I realized the baby's eyes were open, Jan had another massive contraction, and the baby literally squirted into this world. *Like toothpaste from a tube,* I thought, as I began tying the baby's umbilical cord.

Babies are normally born facing down with their chins tucked into their chest. Our baby was born upside down with her head back in what is called a "face up" presentation.

With the baby comfortably wrapped in a warm cotton flannel blanket and resting on the pillow, I was able to concentrate on Jan. Mary and Blue Annie left soon afterward, and I began to clean up.

Then Jan moved over, and I went to bed. It had been a long day. However, I didn't sleep very soundly. I heard every sound the baby made, and when I got up to check the baby, I shined the flashlight beneath the covers to make sure Jan wasn't hemorrhaging.

The next day, now that the emergency had passed, there was a great deal of huffing and puffing by our friends about the fix we had gotten ourselves into, and what people thought of the doctor, and so forth. I wrote a strong letter to our Delegate to Congress, Bob Bartlett, describing what had happened to us at the hospital.

I later learned that ours was the most recent and best documented of a long line of cases where Bureau of Indian Affairs doctors had failed, sometimes with tragic results, to provide needed emergency treatment to people classified as non-beneficiaries.

It materially contributed to the decision at the highest levels in Washington to shift the responsibility for Native medical services from the complacent and highly bureaucratic Bureau of Indian Affairs to the much more aggressive Public Health Service. That shift marked the beginning of the end of the tuberculosis epidemic that was then ravaging Alaska's aboriginal people.

5

The Sailboat Fishery

My chance in a fish boat came the third year. Under the terms of the union agreement, members of the beach gang had the right of first refusal for any fishing jobs that opened up during the season. If they turned a job down, by default, the "chance" was then open to a tallyman. That rarely happened, however. When it did, you knew something was seriously wrong. The shorthanded fisherman was being ostracized. If he had lost his partner by drowning, he might only be viewed as a Jonah, but if his partner had quit before or during the season, as my predecessor had, it was unlikely the survivor had many friends in the bunkhouse.

Mr. Cooper knew I wanted to become a fisherman. Shortly before the season opened in 1949, he asked Henry Shade to find me and have me report to the office as soon as possible.

Henry found me, paint brush in hand, working on the tally scow. "The Old Man wants to see you," he said solemnly. "He said to meet 'im in the office."

Puzzled and a little worried, I thanked Henry and after hurriedly scrubbing the paint off my hands, rushed to the office. The bookkeeper, John Cuthill, was standing in the room talking to a Native fisherman.

"Old Man wants to see me, John," I said nervously. Cuthill nodded toward the rear office. "He's in there," he said. "Don't forget to knock!"

Timidly, I knocked on the door. I hadn't spoken to Mr. Cooper since that terrible night the previous August when we had ransacked the hospital for the birthing supplies Jan had needed.

"Come!"

I pushed the door open.

"Come in, Denny," Mr. Cooper said, "and close the door."

I did as he asked, and sat in a straight chair facing his desk. I had no idea why I was there.

Mr. Cooper was in no hurry to enlighten me. Instead, although Jan took the baby with her every day to her job in the hospital, and he must have seen them dozens of times, he politely inquired after their health, and shook his head over the way the cannery doctor had behaved. Finally, he came to the point.

"Denny, do you still want to go in a boat?"

Of course I did. I nodded.

"Well," he began, "I'm not sure this is such a great idea with your bad leg and all. . ."

I interrupted him. "OK, I know my leg is still screwed up, but my knee hasn't gone out for a long time. Anyhow, we're going to need all the money we can earn because we're going Outside this fall so I can go back to school."

By mentioning school, I had played my ace card. Unlike his hard-bitten predecessors, Don Cooper was unremittingly enthusiastic about people improving themselves. I knew if anything could overcome his scruples regarding my physical limitations, that was it.

I wondered what he would have said if he could have seen me one stormy night the previous year, when I was on watch on Flounder Flats. Six to eight foot waves were smashing into the tally scow and the fish barge tied to its end. To prevent those heavy vessels from crashing into one another, we had slacked the lines holding them together as much as we could, and the two vessels were pitching and rolling about 20 feet apart in a near gale of wind.

It was near midnight. I was sitting on a bench reading a tattered magazine. The cook and the other tallymen were asleep, and I was sure the fishermen would be snugged down in a quiet anchorage riding out the storm. Thus, I was very surprised to hear a "monkey boat" horn, and see the beam of a searchlight play across the tally scow's window.

I jumped up, pulled on my oilskin jacket, and ran out into the stormy night. The *Murre,* a miniature (36 foot) tugboat, operated by young Henry Shade, Jr., was rearing and plunging in the lee of the tally scow.

When young Henry saw me, he stepped out of the wheel house and yelled over the shrieking wind, **"Turn on yer lights! I just brought a boat in. It's half full of water; those fellows need to tally their fish before their boat swamps!"**

I ducked back into the tally scow and threw the switch that connected the 12 volt flood lights to our storage batteries. The fish barge was suddenly bathed in light.

I went back outside, and considered my next move. In the daylight, with help, I might have attempted to haul the barge closer to the scow, using the hand-cranked windlass mounted on the bow of the tally scow for that purpose. But alone, I didn't have enough hands to crank the windlass and handle the rope on the capstan.

Seeing my hesitation, Henry shouted, "I'll put my bow up against the tally scow; that way, you can jump aboard. Then I'll drop you at the barge."

I waved my arm to signify I understood. He delicately nudged the wildly plunging *Murre* closer to the rolling tally scow. I stood on the side deck in the lee of the scow's box-like house, holding a hand grip while I watched the *Murre's*

81

erratic motion against the counterpoint of the scow's roll.

The *Murre's* bow reared five feet above my head, then was below my knees, as the scow rolled away. **"JUMP!"** young Henry screamed, as, not waiting to see whether I had made the leap, he shifted into reverse and opened his throttle, pulling away from the scow before it rolled toward him and crashed into the *Murre's* bow.

I had jumped an instant before he yelled, and still couching, clung to the anchor windlass on his bow. I suddenly felt as if I were on an express elevator as the bow shot into the air.

Wasting no time, Henry steered his little launch in a circle, coming into the wind and rain near the bow of the fish barge, which was rolling as heavily as the tally scow.

There was a big difference, here. The barge's bow was five feet higher than the side of the tally scow, which meant that I could leap from the *Murre* to the barge only when the launch's bow was on top of a crest. Henry turned on his spotlight, and yelled, "Don't jump until I tell you!"

I waved my arm in response. The *Murre's* bow sank in a trough, and I looked up to see the heavy planking on the underside of the barge's bow poised over my head. Henry delicately pulled us back out of harm's way as the doughty little launch began to gain momentum on her skyward leap.

Just as she reached the top of her rise, Henry shouted, **"JUMP!"** I was already in the air. I crashed heavily into the bin boards on the barge.

After resting a moment, tightly hanging on to the side of the fish bin, I walked around the side of the barge to the waiting fish boat. Two Native fishermen waited for me. They were taking turns using the awkward plunger-type bilge pump that those boats carried.

I yelled down, "OK. You can start delivering your fish!"

Somewhat to my surprise, one man remained on the pump

while his partner awkwardly pitched the 300 or so fish they had up to the barge. The man delivering the fish had a tough time of it. The incessant surge and roll of the heavy seas caused the boat to jerk continually against its restraining tie-up lines, and both men had great difficulty maintaining their footing. After the fish were delivered, to my surprise, the fisherman handed up a sleeping bag.

"What the hell?"

As he handed me the Swede stove, he said shyly, "Maybe him boat broken."

Of course. The boat had a broken plank. They were sinking. That was why one fisherman had continued pumping while the other man delivered their fish.

Their remaining personal gear and the all-important tally book were passed up while the other man abandoned his pump and began lashing the spars, sail, oars and nets.

Ten minutes later, we moved the boat's painter back to a bow stanchion, and we watched her slowly succumb to the sea. Wooden boats, of course, don't sink. They merely lie awash in the seaway, rolling over occasionally as especially powerful waves wash over them.

Then we made ourselves as comfortable as possible out of the wind in the fish bin, while we waited for daylight and the other tallymen to wake up and rescue us.

I smiled at the memory, and turned my attention back to Mr. Cooper. "I think I can handle it," I said.

"OK," he said slowly, "but you should know who your captain will be. Do you know Albert Larson?"

I did, but only by reputation. I knew he was a good fisherman, but highly eccentric. The old man had trouble keeping partners because of his strong, even irrational, views on labor-management relations.

There wasn't room in a two-man fish boat for gold braid

or formal protocol. The crew split their fish payday evenly and shared their living quarters. Usually, they slept on the bare floor of the tiny forepeak under the stars. But when the mosquitoes were bad or when it was raining, the men could lower the mast, and set up a tent that covered the exposed part of the fo'c's'le. The mosquitos were then held at bay by smoldering Buhach coils.

Bristol Bay sailboat.
Note the walking boards that
bracket the centerboard trunk

Albert believed the tiny cuddy under the foredeck was officer's country. Humble "boat pullers" should live in the rain and feed the mosquitos. He never mentioned it, but my predecessor may have suffered one mosquito bite too many.

It's a tossup whether I was dumber or tougher than my predecessor, but subsequently, I spent many restless nights sleeping on the walking boards over the main fish hold, rolled in a heavy canvas sail I had softened by dunking over the side. A wet sail doesn't have much to recommend it, but at least it protected me from the most voracious mosquitos in North America. I put up with it because I knew that without family connections in the fleet, I was damn lucky to have a chance in a boat, even with a Loony Tunes captain like Albert.

Our fishing gear consisted of two 75 fathom (450 feet) gillnets. A gillnet hangs vertically in the water like a curtain. It is supported at the top by buoyant "corks" or floats. The bottom of the net is held down by a lead line—a rope on which lead sinkers have been molded.

Most places, gillnets work best at night because then, the fish can't see them. The rivers in Bristol Bay, however, carry sufficient silt to render the water opaque. This was a boon to the fishermen because the gillnets were invisible to the fish that blundered into them.

That opacity was a two-edged sword. Several years later, on the Kvichak River, while I was watching arriving fishermen disembark from a small plane to a float tied to a cannery dock, I watched the last fisherman slip on a pontoon and fall into the river.

The unfortunate man disappeared in the muddy water and never surfaced. Whether the shock of cold water stunned him, or he was confused by his sudden loss of vision and light, or

Boats tied to the fish barge while their crews have dinner on the tally scow. Note the approaching boats.

the tidal currents boiling past the dock pilings overpowered him, we shall never know. His body was not recovered. His hat, like a felt wreath floating away on the current, was his only memorial.

A 20 foot tidal rise and *four knot* currents were the norm. You could expect a 25 foot rise at least once during the summer. When the tide was full, roughly twice every 24 hours, the fishing grounds on the Nushagak River comprised nearly 300 square miles, but at low water, the boats were crowded into less than 200 square miles.

The tides sometimes caused odd things to happen. For example, I remember the day a Creek cannery monkey boat attacked the United States Coast and Geodetic Survey ship *Pathfinder*. Jacinto, Floyd Eglund, and another boy and I had gone up into Combine Slough on a sea gull egg hunt. Spring sea gull eggs were a wonderful addition to the diet for people who had not seen an egg, fresh or otherwise, since the last of the "boat eggs" had been discarded around Thanksgiving. Our outfit included a case—30 dozen—eggs that had been fresh eggs sometime during the previous August. Even though we oiled the eggs to prevent air from penetrating the shells, by the end of October, they were pretty ripe, and Jan began breaking boat eggs into bowl. A really ripe egg landing in hot grease sometimes exploded. Wiping the residue of a rotten egg from the ceiling was not my favorite way of beginning a new day.

We had collected several dozen eggs from seriously protesting gulls, and were returning to Clarks Point in my new skiff (which Verner Wilson had built for me the previous winter) when we saw the Creek cannery monkey boat out in the river, running wide open, making probably ten knots, with the rudder hard over to starboard.

Something was wrong, and we set out in pursuit. When we came close to the boat, we realized that the boat was steering herself. No one was standing at the wheel. Our attempts to come alongside were frustrated by the considerable bow wave the boat was generating, but we followed close behind her as she raced through one circle after the other. The tide was strongly ebbing, and each circle brought her 100 yards closer to the *Pathfinder*, innocently laying to her anchor in front of Clarks Point. We failed one last attempt to get aboard, and fatalistically watched as the little craft inexorably plowed straight into *Pathfinder's* flank, hitting her square amidships!

The little boat appeared to jump in the water, and the engine quit. We were alongside the boat in an instant, and I leaped aboard, followed closely by Jacinto. While he went forward to take a line from *Pathfinder's* enraged leading chief, I ducked below to see if she was sinking. I had to step over the prone body of her skipper to reach the little forepeak.

I knew, at a glance, that Pete was alive; I could smell the booze as I entered the boat. But for all that, he had had a narrow escape. The boat's Northern radio had been dislodged in the collision, and rested on the wheel house deck scant inches from Pete's head. Those old fashioned, AM tube marine radios were heavy. If it landed on Pete's head, it might have killed him.

Of course, that would have saved the ship's leading chief the bother. His initial urge to kill Pete gradually changed to a more modest desire to lock him up. There was a long discussion on board about that, but finally, recognizing the many problems that arresting Pete would entail, the ship's officers decided to release Pete into our custody.

We found that the engine had stalled because the battery had become disconnected in the collision. After reconnecting it, I drove the monkey boat to the dock at Clarks Point, much to Mr. Cooper's disgust—"What did you bring him here, for?"—while Jacinto operated the skiff.

Pete had left his mark on the survey ship. The plating on her side where the monkey boat hit her was deeply dimpled.

That incident happened in unusually good weather. Most of the time, the weather was bad, and there were no weather forecasts. We relied wholly on our captain's skill at reading the sky and sniffing the breeze; hardly a reliable system. Consequently, we were often surprised by the Bering Sea's frequent mood changes, which were usually for the worst.

The fishery was conducted mostly upriver, in crowded company with hundreds of similar boats. Since the boats and their nets floated freely on the surface of the river, many fishing decisions were influenced by tidal factors, and were often implemented with a sense of urgency.

Fishermen hauling nets

Either we might be drifting into shallow water on a falling tide, or perhaps we were being carried too close to another boat.

Sometimes an anchored scow was in the line of our drift. Occasionally, it was simply time to move; to seek a more productive area. This sometimes resulted from a report by a passing monkey boat. Those boats, like the *Murre,* and the Creek cannery monkey boat we had rescued, carried radios. Their skippers were kept advised of the fish's movements. Their job was to tow the sailboats (at least those without the damning letter "A") to the new hot spots.

Since the boats were virtually identical, that identifying letter was required by the union agreement, so the monkey boat skippers, most of whom were nonresidents, could quickly identify their *paesanos;* knowing at a glance who to tow and who not to tow. (Note the boat on the cover.)

We retrieved our nets by hauling them over a dumb roller. One man heaved on the corkline, the other the leadline. Timing our movements to the rhythm of the sea, working in unison, we would pull two or three feet of net into the boat as the stern fell into a trough. Then, the man holding the corkline would swiftly lock a cork under the gunwale, holding it in place with his knee, while we renewed our grip on our respective lines, and waited for the stern's next plunge.

The net, heavy with water and flapping salmon, sometimes clustered together like grapes, would come over the roller, falling solidly into the boat. When fishing was good, the clearing room where we stood would quickly fill with twitching fish and net, all jumbled together.

Occasionally, when fishing was very good and the accumulating weight of fish and net caused our stern to settle into the water, so that wavelets began slopping over the gunwale, we would stop, tie the net off, and trim the boat by dragging the net and fish forward. After the loaded net was in the boat, we might set the other net, or sail (rarely, being towed) to a better location, then set the other net. While one net was in the water, we would pick the fish from the net in the boat.

We were usually bundled in wool watch caps and an outer layer of oilskin pants or an oilskin apron and jackets covering heavy woolen shirts and hip boots over wool pants. Because of our bulky garments and uncertain footing in those corky little boats, we moved carefully and with great deliberation.

That was especially true when we were handling the net. The safest way to set the net was when the boat puller stood on the walking boards facing forward, oars in hand, and pulled (actually pushed) the boat across the tide, in calm weather, while the captain fed the net into the water over a dumb roller in the stern.

But when the wind was fresh, the captain and boat puller stood on each side of the piled net, gingerly feeding it over the stern. That was very dangerous work.

Even a small piece of net in the water instantly became a massive sea anchor. For their size, those boats were heavy. Thus, in a fresh breeze, terrible forces were set in motion as the net slithered over the roller into the water. Although we used the net as a makeshift anchor rope to check the speed of our boat's downwind drift, lacking an engine, a drifting boat was basically out of control.

The meshes in a new net were incredibly strong, and while a hatchet and a sharp knife were always within easy reach, anything snagged by that net as it went over the stern roller either broke off or was pulled overboard.

In at least one respect, I was lucky. Under Albert's stern eye, I quickly cut the buttons off my jacket. During the years that followed, although I lost several gloves while laying out my net, other fishermen lost fingernails, and clothing. I knew a fisherman who lost his life when he was dragged overboard by his net.

Occasionally, a fisherman would be mentioned or pointed out in the mess hall or in the bunkhouse who had survived a swim across a channel separating adjacent sand bars, but those men were rare. Almost invariably, a man who went into the water was a goner, killed by drowning or more likely, hypothermia.

Boat pullers faced a special hazard. When a boat hit a sandbar on an ebbing tide, the boat puller would jump off the bow and, jamming his shoulder as low as possible against the boat's stem, lift with his legs and push with his back while his captain, still in the boat, hurriedly threw the net into the water behind the boat.

Those actions could be irreversible. More than one boat puller has heaved mightily at the same moment his captain snubbed a net upon which the tide had gained a firm grip. The snubbed net could literally yank the boat back into the water, stranding the unlucky boat puller on the bar.

If the captain was quick enough, he would cut his net free with a single blow of the hatchet and, scrambling forward, throw his anchor over the side while the boat was still within reach of the puller. Then, at low water slack, if the wind was calm, the captain would attempt to row back, or he might attempt to sail back after the tide turned, to rescue his stranded crew.

But in far too many cases, without an engine, those measures would fail. Then, unless the puller was an extraordinarily robust person and a strong swimmer, he was almost certainly doomed when the tide returned.

The Italian fishermen often nailed a small block of wood on the side of the boat's stem a foot or

CRPA boat sailing in the evening dusk

so above the water line, and permanently spliced a short lanyard to the cleat on the foredeck, or sometimes through a hole drilled in the top of the stem. This was the "save-a da'life," as they called it, a step and handhold to help the puller scramble back aboard after refloating the boat.

The night before the 1949 season opened, the sky held a sullen promise that frightful weather was in store. Sure enough, as I slipped into my clothes and oil skins in the two o'clock darkness the next morning, I heard a gale shrieking around the eaves. Jan was still asleep when I lightly kissed her goodby, and took a look at the baby, secure in her bassinet.

When the full force of the wind struck me, I began to regret Mr. Cooper's willingness to help me improve myself. I couldn't believe we'd be going anywhere in that terrible storm, but I knew I had to make an appearance at the bunkhouse. I struggled along the road leading to the cannery in the storm-darkened night.

Ordinarily, after our 3:30 breakfast, we would have been ferried to our anchored boats by the busy little monkey boats. By 4:30 at the latest, we would have set sail for wherever our respective captains wanted to be when the season opened at six am.

But not this morning.

The tide was full. As I staggered against the wind past the cannery dock, I saw great rollers from the Bering Sea coming in to strike the pilings and wash across the dock's deck to smash against the fish house. A handful of boats, anchored in front of the cannery, were exposed to the full fury of the storm. As those enormous waves rolled past them, they reared and plunged against their anchor rodes in the seaway, and yawed wildly in the gale force winds that buffeted them when they rose on the swell.

Breakfast forgotten, I went straight to the bunkhouse. Men stood at the window, somberly watching their boats. I couldn't see our boat but those that we could see, were not faring well. Some were rolling drunkenly, half full of water, in a losing effort to rise and meet each succeeding roller.

It was rare that an empty Bristol Bay boat would swamp at anchor, but from our window, we saw three boats showing first a gunwale, then their bottoms, as they rolled helplessly over and over, a jumble of nets, sail, spars, and gear trailing in the water behind them.

In an almost unprecedented gesture, Mr. Cooper came into the bunkhouse shortly after six. Seeing him enter, the older men faded into the background, sitting on the lower bunks that lined the wall, as if they were ashamed to be seen in the bunkhouse during an open fishing period. Lacking their inhibitions, younger fishermen like me, crowded forward.

Don Cooper was a big man, larger now in his storm gear. He removed his hat and said, "Fellows, we've got a hell of a storm out there." He was answered by an uneasy shuffling of feet, and averted eyes.

"I know the rules as well as you do," he went on, "but I don't want any of you to go out there before you think it's safe. A few more fish aren't worth a man's life."

The relief was almost palpable. The men now knew that when they applied for boats the following year, they would not be penalized for remaining in the bunkhouse this morning. They had reason to be concerned. Many superintendents would have insisted that they leave, regardless of the weather. That indifference to safety was matched only by the risks fishermen took in their own scramble for fish because a fisherman's career flourished or died by the "average."

At the end of each successive fishing period, the average catch for the fishing period, the running seasonal average, the average catch of the high ten boats, and the district averages, were posted in the fishermen's bunkhouses.

The men always crowded anxiously around the bulletin board to compare their individual catches with the company averages. More than simple vanity was at issue. The men who smiled and slapped each other on the back were usually at or above the company average and therefore were almost certainly assured of a fishing job in the next season.

Conversely, the men who quietly walked away from the bulletin board, avoiding eye contact, were those whose catch fell significantly below that magic number. They might have difficulty finding a fishing job the following year.

This sort of incentive system was at once fair and pernicious. It was fair because it treated everyone alike. But it was pernicious because it goaded fishermen into taking extraordinary risks in an already mortally dangerous fishery.

It was generally accepted that every summer each cannery would lose one or more boats by capsizing, swamping, and/or breaking up after stranding on a sand bar. In nearly all cases, the lack of an engine could have meant the difference between life and death.

I find it remarkable how much our attitudes concerning human life have changed during the past half century. Fishermen, like their boats, were then regarded as little more than interchangeable parts. The canneries practiced economies which would be wholly inexplicable today. The boats carried no navigation lights, and even after the Deadman Sands disaster, it didn't seem to have occurred to anyone that the boats should have been equipped with life vests. The really strange thing about it was that nobody seemed to care. Not the fishermen, not the Coast Guard, not even the fishermen's union!

The 1949 season was bad. There wasn't much fish, and from the first day to the last, the storms followed one another like beads on a string. Two boats at Clarks Point swamped and four men lost their lives. But nothing we experienced on the Nushagak River could compare with the July fourth calamity on our sister river, the Kvichak, when a sudden wind shift trapped a large part of that fleet on a great flat extending from the north shore of the Kvichak estuary, a flat known forever after as Dead Man Sands. Over 200 boats were crushed and 26 fishermen lost their lives.

During those years, I spent many summer evenings hanging around the fishermen's bunkhouse, listening to the yarns by the old timers. Jan and I knew by then that no matter what happened to my teaching job, our future was linked to Alaska.

The fishermen spent the evenings lounging on boxes and the stacked dock piling outside the fishermen's bunkhouse, filling the time after supper and before nine o'clock coffee, with stories. I listened to scores of tales told by men like "Pinky" Peterson sitting comfortably on a piling, idly brushing persistent mosquitoes away. Crusty Butch Smith, a lantern jawed, stubble-bearded, leathery old sourdough, whose thin gray hair was flying in the breeze, and who was always dressed in a heavy woolen shirt, 'Frisco jeans held up by heavy suspenders, and worn shoepacs, reminisced about trappers and prospectors long dead, and upriver exploits nearly forgotten. Butch had come to Alaska over the Chilcoot Pass in 1895.

My favorite story teller, however, was little "Glass-Eye" Billy Barton. He was a small, excitable London cockney who, until he had been rendered obsolete by construction of the Naknek Air Base, and the consequent introduction of scheduled airmail service from Anchorage only five years earlier, had driven the Bristol Bay mail sled, pulled by a 23-dog team, over a 600 mile route each month from November until breakup in early May. His route ran from Kanatak, a village on the Pacific Ocean side of the Alaska Peninsula, where he met the monthly mail boat, then through a pass in the Aleutian Mountains to Lake Becharof, down the lake, through Egegik, north to Naknek, and on to Branch River where he crossed the Kvichak River to Levelock, then north across the Nushagak Peninsula to Clarks Point, east up the Nushagak River to Portage Creek, and across the Nushagak and Wood Rivers to Dillingham.

After resting his dogs for a week, he would leave, following the same trail back to Kanatak. His trail crossed a mountain range, Alaska's third largest lake, and four major rivers.

By a very strange coincidence, I had met the long time captain of that mail boat, Captain "Squeeky" Anderson, in Seattle, while I was still in the service. He had served as the beach master on Iwo Jima and was a naval commodore when I knew him. We shared platforms for several weeks in and around Seattle during the Fifth War Bond drive. At his urging, I gradually grew accustomed to addressing him as "Squeeky," but it always seemed unnatural, almost obscene, for a buck private to address a commodore—the naval equivalent of a brigadier general—by his nickname.

Those who knew the land best were not the storytellers. They were people like Henry Ouye, a jovial middle-aged

Eskimo from Eek River, a settlement 75 miles away, up the coast. To him, and to a lesser degree to all the old timers, Alaska was a life; not a thing to be owned.

When nomadic spirits like Pinky, Butch, Glass-Eye Billy, and Henry Ouye described "the country," they meant a river course, a valley, a lake, or even a mountain range, where men and women could wander at will, unfettered by strange and artificial concepts of townships, counties, or fire district boundaries, and constrained only by the land's configuration and the personal spirit and determination of the traveler.

It was during those evening meetings that Glass-Eye Billy told us about the place Jan and I were looking for. Prospecting between mail runs, Billy had driven his dog team up into the Kulik Lake country, and lyrically described two long narrow lakes, Kulik and Nonvianuk, 15 and 19 miles long respectively, that met end to end, separated only by a short portage about a quarter mile long, through which a connecting stream ran. The valley in which the upper lake, Lake Kulik lay, penetrated deep into the heart of the Aleutian Range on the eastern edge of the famous Katmai National Monument, home of the Valley of 10,000 Smokes.

An old sourdough named Bill Hammersly lived at the lower end of Nonvianuk. Nobody lived on Kulik, although there was an abandoned cabin on the portage between the two lakes.

According to Billy, the portage and Lake Kulik were in a deep mountain valley, and thus were protected from the winter gales we experienced at sea level. The country was heavily timbered and teemed with game because the lakes acted as a natural funnel, directing migrating game in the fall to the portage which separated the two lakes. The lakes contained a virgin population of rainbow trout. Best of all, this wonderful *Shangri-la* was only about 100 miles away.

Jan and I had talked about the possibility of building a

hunting and fishing lodge. We were sure one in this part of Alaska would do well because of its close proximity to the Naknek Air Base, and a world class brown (Kodiak) bear population. I decided to visit the site.

I invited Jacinto Blancaflor to accompany me. I thought he could use a respite from the grind of caring for his sick sister and brothers, and, quite frankly, I wanted company on my first venture into the wilderness. Then I made arrangements with a local bush pilot to fly the two of us and our gear up to Nonvianuk Lake during the Christmas vacation.

Very soon after the pilot deposited us and our plunder on the beach at the upper end of Nonvianuk Lake, I knew I had failed to think very far ahead. I also realized that I had led a very sheltered life in the village at Clarks Point. Somewhat to my surprise, I discovered the same could be said of Jacinto.

Since the days were short, we wasted no time putting up our tent and gathering spruce boughs and dried grass for our beds. Henry had instructed me in some finer points of survival winter camping, and to that extent we were prepared with extra ground cloths and a tarp to throw over our tent. I had a good *Wood's* three star sleeping bag, but, stupidly, I hadn't thought to bring my new fur boots. Instead, I was wearing *L. L. Bean's* rubber shoepacs. Even dumber, I had brought only a light parka rather than the heavy alpaca lined one hanging in our windbreak.

Poor Jacinto was even more poorly outfitted, but he, at least, was more inured to the wasting hardship that accompanies unrelenting cold.

We spent three miserable nights in the tent before we gave up and moved into the empty cabin Billy had described. The cabin was furnished with crude bunks, a table, a chair, and a small sheet iron wood stove. There was no clue concerning the identity of the cabin's former occupant, but I'm sure he was a prospector and trapper.

97

The weather was worsening. The relatively balmy temperatures, ranging between 20° *above* zero and 0° that we had left in Clarks Point were now, according to a thermometer nailed to the outside of the cabin, ranging between ten and twenty-five degrees *below* zero! Those temperatures were far outside my previous experience.

Trapper's cabin at Nonvianuk Lake at 50° below zero!

The next morning, the temperature stood at **–32°**! I knew that bush pilots fly reluctantly at –30°, with great hesitation at –40°, and not at all at –50°. Therefore, if the temperature kept falling, I knew that we might be in for a long stay, and consequently, we had better rustle up some wood.

We had a tough time finding suitable wood. The cabin's former occupant had cleaned out the birch and dead spruce for a radius of a half mile in all directions. Even I knew that green spruce made poor stove wood, so Jacinto and I donned our snowshoes and set off in –30° weather to find fuel.

We worked all day and by late dusk, around three pm, we had accumulated a small pile of curly barked red and white birch and less desirable alder. After cutting it, we had stacked it on a ground cloth which we then dragged back to the cabin. It was miserable work.

The next day, we went fishing. We hadn't thought to bring fish hooks, but we found some in the cabin. I tied a hook on a string, using a nail as a sinker, and baited it with a strand of red wool from my cap.

I peered through our waterhole into the stream connecting the two lakes. Dozens of fat rainbow trout were aimlessly milling about in the shallow water. I lowered the baited hook into the water. The fish saw it instantly. One fish feinted toward it, possibly to see what it would do, and another darted past the first and triumphantly seized the bait.

I jerked the fish out of the water. It froze solid before it hit the ice, and my fishing line suddenly became a slender icicle that resembled a stiff wire. Careful not to break it, I unhooked the fish and put the bait back into the water. Almost instantly, I had a second fish laying next to the first. At least we now had a steady supply of food.

We spent ten days up on Nonvianuk Lake in terrible weather. The morning of our fifth day, the thermometer registered an incredible and frightening *–50 degrees!* A thin blue haze seemed to have settled over the land. Standing away from the cabin, we could see a plume of smoke and condensed moisture rising straight into the atmosphere. Nothing else moved in those temperatures. Even the wolves had ceased their nocturnal wailing.

While living creatures cowered in their burrows, more elemental forces were in motion, disturbing the cathedral-like silence of those frigid nights; the pressure of expanding ice crystals sometimes caused trees to crack open at night. We also heard the deeper, muffled, **BOOM** of thick lake ice cracking and sending up yet another pressure ridge somewhere out on the lake.

Each night, from about eight o'clock on, the northern

lights shimmered and gleamed, undulating in the northern sky. It was too cold to tarry outside, but we enjoyed brief glimpses of them.

Normally, this far south, the northern lights were white, shading into gray. Occasionally, at Clarks Point, we had seen hints of color, but only rarely. Now, however, looking north over Nonvianuk Lake, the lights became shimmering veils of delicately colored light that were like glimpses of Paradise.

Each evening, we stoked the stove so the top of it glowed a dull red—but the white frost never entirely left the stove's legs. Despite the cold, during the days, Jacinto and I hiked over a good bit of the terrain and found a likely spot for a small landing strip, suitable cabin timber (white spruce trees without too much taper), and even, taking into consideration such factors as protection from winds coming down the valley behind us, proximity to the water and the incipient airstrip, the view down the lake, and so forth, what we considered the best location for the lodge. It was fun picking the spot, even if I never had the chance to move in.

Jacinto was with me every step of the way, especially as we waited for our pilot. At the end of ten days, we were out of everything, and beginning to get very tired of fish.

Our pilot returned for us on January second. I imagine I'll remember that day for the rest of my life. The temperature had moderated a bit—it was then only −25° or so, and seemed almost balmy. We were standing on the lake shore.

Sound travels a long way in cold air. Jacinto heard the plane first. "Here he comes," he said, grinning jubilantly.

I didn't hear anything, and looked quizzically at him. "You're imagining things," I said.

"No, he really come. Don't you hear him?"

By God, I did. At first I heard a faint droning sound no louder than a mosquito, but the engine sound rapidly gained volume. Soon, Jacinto pointed out over the lake.

"There he is!" he yelled happily.

At first I saw nothing, but then a speck far out over the ice became a dot, and the dot magically sprouted wings, and suddenly to our huge, overwhelming joy, succor was at hand.

It was still so cold the pilot was unwilling to turn off his engine for fear he might not get it started again, so Jacinto and I quickly broke camp and crammed our gear into the plane. Within minutes, we were airborne. I looked back, briefly, at our camp site. It's well that I did because I never saw Nonvianuk again.

The last half of our second year at Clarks Point passed all too quickly. Although Jan had been appointed second teacher, leaving me the luxury of being able to concentrate on the upper five grades, there was so much I wanted to share with those children, and so little time, that I felt terribly frustrated as the year drew to a close.

Meanwhile, we had to consider our immediate future. The new school was a certainty. I knew my contract would not be renewed at the end of the school year, because I lacked the necessary credentials to continue teaching.

My brief experience with cold weather camping at Nonvianuk Lake caused me to rethink the implications of my disability. The shrapnel I had taken on Iwo had caused not only paralysis, but also had left me with limited circulation in my right leg and an unstable knee.

Moreover, as a city boy, I knew virtually nothing of farming or rural life. I knew it would be insane for us to move directly to Nonvianuk Lake from Clarks Point. First, I had to prepare myself and if possible, improve my physical condition before I dared commit my young family to such an exotic venture. But how?

The answer came during a counseling session with a VA officer. After I explained my dilemma, the officer thought for a moment, then said, "Well, there's the GI Bill, you know, only in your case, PL 16 would apply."

He explained that veterans with my degree of disability were entitled to rehabilitation training under Public Law 16. Unlike the GI Bill, which provided only a fixed amount of training commensurate with the length of the veteran's service, PL 16 training was goal oriented. Since my goal was to develop a hunting and fishing lodge, the counselor reasoned that the only academic program that would equip me for that career was a general purpose vocational agriculture curriculum. Every agriculture school in the United States offers one.

For me, it was an ideal solution. A curriculum covering mechanics, food preservation, welding, veterinary science, poultry science, livestock, feeds and feeding, and a potpourri of liberal arts and science courses was exactly what I needed. Since my counselor knew I enjoyed teaching, he reminded me that completion of this course would entitle me to a *permanent* teaching certificate.

The only thing left to decide was where I should apply for admission. Again, we were aided by an obvious choice. I felt I should study in a place where the climatic conditions were similar to Alaska's, where the cost of living was within our means, and where Jan would feel at home and could find a job if necessary. Montana State College at Bozeman was clearly the logical choice.

6

Stateside Interlude

We decided to take the long way around on our trip Outside. We reasoned this would give us a chance to see parts of Alaska that we'd never see again. Consequently, our trip involved a bush plane, a bus, two trains, and two steamships.

We flew into Anchorage aboard Dennis Fenno's Norseman, a high wing, heavy duty, bush plane on floats. Choosing a small aircraft for a four hour flight had advantages and disadvantages.

We had a wonderful opportunity to see the small upriver villages like Ekwok on the upper Nushagak River, and we flew *through*, not over, the famous and spectacular Lake Clark Pass in the Alaska Range.

On the minus side, it *was* a four hour flight, and there was no toilet on the plane. I was in serious discomfort by the time we arrived at Lake Hood, outside Anchorage. As soon as Dennis opened the cabin door, I sprinted for the nearest bush. Fortunately, it wasn't far away.

Anchorage had not changed much while we had been at Clarks Point, except they had paved 6th Avenue, and Cap Lathrop, a colorful Fairbanks entrepreneur who already owned radio station KENI in Anchorage, had started the *Anchorage Daily News* because, as he put it, he wanted to see a Republican paper in Alaska's largest city.

We spent several days at the Parson's Hotel, then boarded the train for the 400 mile journey to Fairbanks. A year earlier, the trip had taken two days. However, by starting early, running a little faster, and arriving later, the journey now took but a single day.

This burst of efficiency must have confounded Cap Lathrop, since the Truman Administration—Democrats—was still in control of the White House, and the railroad was operated by the US Department of the Interior.

The train ride offered spectacular views of the highest point in North America, 20,320 foot Mt. McKinley (which even then was sometimes known by its politically correct name of "Mount Denali"). Other than spectacular views of the mountain, the only thing I remember about the trip is that the roadbed badly needed reballasting.

Fairbanks, a smaller version of Anchorage, was suffering chronic growing pains. Hotel space was scarce. However, since we had reservations on the O'Hare Bus Line from Fairbanks to Whitehorse, in Canada's Yukon Territory, the bus company put us up overnight in a small apartment over the garage. I thought this was a friendly thing for them to do, especially since we were traveling with a baby. Trina was a happy, well behaved baby. A clean, dry, diaper and something to eat solved nearly all her problems.

The next morning, our cardboard box luggage was stowed in the luggage compartment of a big bus. Then, with some 30 other passengers, we boarded, and soon were on our way.

As soon we left the newly paved streets marking the downtown area, the pavement gave way to gravel, and in some places, the gravel gave way to dirt. However, when we reached the road connecting Alaska to the states, known around the world as the Alcan Highway, which had been open to the public only a year, we found it remarkably well

maintained. Of course, it had been built to military specifications. Also, I hasten to add that this was in the fall of the
year. I doubt whether people traveling the road during spring
breakup would have had such a congenial view of it.

We stopped at virtually every crossroad, discharging
passengers, freight, and mail sacks, until we reached Eielson
Air Base, some 30 miles southeast of Fairbanks. That marked
the end of civilization's reach. The driver then settled down
to the serious business of reaching Dry Creek, some 350
miles south of Fairbanks, across the border in Canada, as
soon as possible.

The road followed a valley tucked between two mountain
ranges. Much of the country was covered with arctic tundra
and birch. Although the view of snowcapped mountains on
both sides was spectacular, those of us who lived in the
country and listened during the winter to nightly weather
broadcasts, peered out the windows in awe. We knew that
this area, from Big Delta to Snag at the Canadian border, was
consistently the coldest, and in summer, occasionally the
warmest, part of Alaska. Winter temperatures in the –60°
range were commonplace. In January, 1952, the temperature
at Northway dropped to –72°. In June, 1969, however, the
temperature reached an official 91°. There aren't many
places in the world that can boast of an annual temperature
range of 167°!

We stopped briefly at a road house for lunch. Passengers
and driver were served family style at two long tables. There
was no charge for the meal; it was included in the bus fare.
Then on to Dry Creek. But first we passed through Canadian
customs at Snag.

Shortly after clearing customs, we arrived in Dry Creek
and pulled up to a somewhat bedraggled, single story, tarpaper covered, building that looked suspiciously like, and in
an earlier life probably was, a hastily constructed Army
barracks. Some of the passengers complained, but we were

used to tarpaper shacks, and quite happily accepted our assigned room. After a communal dinner, we relaxed for a time in the lobby with the other passengers, then turned in.

We arrived in Whitehorse the next afternoon. The bus stopped briefly while we unloaded our cardboard luggage and carried the half dozen roped cartons that contained our worldly possessions into the lobby. I was self-conscious about our cardboard luggage until I realized that the Inn was still on a war footing, and still rented beds instead of rooms. Not realizing that at first, I asked for a room with a bath. We were assigned beds in a large room that featured five beds on the second floor. There was no latch, and only a large hole where the lock had been. The "bath" consisted of a wash basin in the corner, and a toilet surrounded by a shower curtain, grandly mounted on a wooden pedestal in the middle of the room. When they talked about the "throne" in that hotel, they weren't kidding.

We spent two days in Whitehorse, always wondering who would rent the other three beds, poking around town, and trying to decide what to do next.

I knew that slightly over 50 years earlier, a major gold strike had been made in the gravel of Klondike Creek, a remote tributary of the Yukon River. By 1898, some 25,000 miners, including our friend Butch Smith, had swarmed into Skagway. Some carried their outfits over Chilcoot Pass, others hired human packers to carry their outfits. That wasn't cheap. Packers were charging a dollar per pound. Men soon began laying track for a narrow gauge line (the tracks were only 36 inches apart) at the salt water railhead in Skagway for the White Pass and Yukon Route Railway.

During the construction phase, two trains left Skagway each morning. The first was the freight train that carried miners and their gear as far up the hill as the tracks were laid. Then the engine reversed and returned to Skagway for the work train.

In less than two years, an astonishingly short time, considering the remoteness of the site, the climate, and the difficulties inherent in its construction caused by the dynamiting, trestle building, and switchback engineering that had to be done, the route was completed. Rails had been laid over a 3,000 foot pass, 126 miles from salt water to Whitehorse on the Yukon River. There were no government subsidies, yet the railroad was paid for before it was completed, because of the tariffs earned on the freight the train had carried almost from the first days of construction.

We decided to board that train, hoping to find steamship accommodations when we reached Skagway.

The tiny train left Whitehorse on schedule. We stopped at Carcross on Lake Bennett for lunch. Again, we were seated on benches at long trestle tables and served family style. The last 20 miles of the journey were almost unbelievable. Knowing the railroad's history, I hung out the window all the way down the hill to Skagway. This road has one of the steepest grades in North America. In about 20 miles, it climbs nearly 3,000 feet. I lost count of the trestles we crossed, but I'm sure this must be one of the most spectacular train rides anywhere.

The history of that region fascinated me, an absorption that would prove nearly fatal many years later. I'm getting ahead of my story, but 15 years after our first glimpse of Whitehorse, while we were driving south over the Alcan for the fourth or fifth time, we decided on an impulse to turn off the highway at the Tetlin Junction and detour over the "Top of the World" highway through the Yukon Territory to visit Dawson City and see the Klondike with our own eyes. That route still amounted to 150 miles of unimproved dirt road, and I remember the drive much more vividly than I do seeing Robert Service's cabin in Dawson City or the piles of placer tailings bordering the Klondike that marked the discovery of gold.

Shortly before the road entered Canada (the border was marked by an unattended shack on the Canadian side), we stopped at Chicken for gas. It was already dusk, and we toyed briefly with the idea of spending the night. However, we learned that the Taylor caribou herd was near the road, on its annual migration, and we were advised to keep moving; otherwise, the migrating herd might have blocked us for a day or more. Besides, it was only 75 miles further to Dawson.

We drove on into the night. Jan and the kids fell asleep, and I just kept plugging along. Most of the road followed the windswept, open ridges, but I noticed, as we began a long descent, that we seemed to getting into thicker brush.

Abruptly, without warning, I saw the familiar shape of an octagonal **STOP** sign in my headlights! I knew the Canadians didn't waste money installing meaningless signs, so I jammed on my brakes, only to find they had been glazed by that long descent from the ridges. I quickly pulled hard as on my emergency brake, and stopped just short of the sign. I still saw no reason for the sign, so I stepped out of the car, and walked ahead, out of the glare of my headlights.

Suddenly, to my horror, I realized I was standing on the ferry landing. Twenty-five feet ahead of me, below the reach of my headlights, the Yukon river flowed silently past the end of the road.

From my vantage point at the end of the landing, I saw the lights of Dawson City two miles upriver. I returned to the car and inched forward so my headlights would be visible to anyone watching from the city. Then I began blowing my horn and flicking my lights on and off.

Jan and the kids had awakened when I began blowing my horn. We were soon rewarded by the tinny, unmistakable rattling roar of a GMC 6-71 marine diesel engine starting, and soon the little two-car ferry was nosing up against the landing in front of our car.

Returning to the present, I found Skagway to be an interesting little town, very much a part of that early history. It was nestled on a wedge shaped alluvial plain facing Lynn Canal and backed against the St. Elias mountain range, over which the Chilcoot and White Passes led.

Main street was a single street of false fronted buildings, many of which were empty. People still talked about Soapy Smith, a nineteenth century rogue who had dominated the town, and swindled many unsuspecting prospectors with a ten dollar bill wrapped around a bar of soap.

Building lots were available for a few hundred dollars. I was tempted to buy one as an investment because I thought eventually organized tour groups would find the place. Unfortunately, I couldn't spare even the few dollars such an investment would have required.

The community was then focused on the possibility that a major aluminum company might build a smelter nearby, taking advantage of the local hydroelectric potential. The hotel was full of aluminum company engineers when we arrived. We were sent to prevail on Mrs. Palmer, an elderly widow who lived with another lady, in a hotel—the Golden North—that had been closed for several years.

In true Alaskan style, she graciously opened a room for us. The Golden North had its claim to an historical footnote. When she showed us to our room, she pointed to the door across the hall, and told us that in 1923, President Harding had contracted his fatal illness in that room.

The next morning, I walked down the town's main street to the dock where I found the Canadian Pacific Railway agent. I learned that the *Princess Louise* would be calling at the end of the week. It was the height of the cruise season, and accommodations were tight. The agent wasn't sure that there would be a vacant stateroom, but took my name and a deposit just in case.

Steamships then carried a good bit of regular passenger traffic between Canada and Alaska. Only three years earlier, in the spring of 1946, I had traveled to my first fishing job in Alaska in steerage aboard the *Prince Edward*, then the flag ship of the Canadian National Railway Line. (I last saw the *Prince Edward*, renamed the *St. Helena*, in 1986 in Cape Town, South Africa. She is still carrying mail and passengers to some of the more remote places on earth.)

Soon after the *Louise* docked, we learned there was an empty cabin aboard. We happily and gratefully thanked the old ladies in the Golden North hotel and took our cardboard luggage down to the dock.

Even then, the *Princess Louise* was showing her age (I last saw her tied in San Pedro, like the *Queen Mary*, reduced to service as a floating restaurant), but that was irrelevant as far as I was concerned. For me, that three day trip from Skagway to Vancouver set a lifetime standard for elegance and luxury that has never been surpassed. It was a wonderful experience.

By the time the fall semester began, I was enrolled as a full time student at Montana State College in Bozeman. We bought a tiny three room house on an acre of land for $5,000 on the outskirts of town. It was primitive by local standards, but almost luxurious compared to our previous accommodations. I applied myself to the mysteries of inorganic chemistry, sheep judging, agronomy, and veterinary medicine, while Jan went to work in the local hospital. The first winter passed quickly.

Our second daughter, Lynnie, was born in May with a minimum of fuss. However, she was an unusually active baby, and all too soon began to reduce her environment to rubble. I must have reassembled her crib a dozen times before she was able to stand without support.

Meanwhile, I decided to see if something could be done surgically to improve my physical situation. The VA doctors sent me from the hospital in Montana to an orthopedic center in Salt Lake for a consultation, then to Portland, Oregon, for surgery. The surgery stiffened my ankle. The doctors reasoned that this would reduce the stress on my knee, and obviate the need for a brace. They were right. But because my femoral vein had been severed, I healed very slowly, and it was an unexpected six months before the last cast came off and I began to bear weight.

School was not going well. I had postponed college math and had run out of interesting courses that I could handle with my limited secondary education. All was not well on the home front, either. Jan and I began behaving badly toward each other. I, at least, was feeling crowded; as if my back was to the wall. I finally concluded that there was no point in continuing my academic career. We decided to leave Montana in the spring, and return to Alaska.

We were still focused on the hunting and fishing lodge at Nonvianuk Lake. We thought we needed saddle and pack horses for the lodge. Therefore, much of our initial planning revolved around the logistical problems of moving animals from Montana to Nonvianuk Lake.

The only way we could get the horses to Nonvianuk Lake was to take them there by trucking them 2,500 miles over the Alcan Highway to Anchorage, and trusting to luck for the remaining 300 miles. It is a massive understatement to state that from where we stood that spring, the future was uncertain. Frankly, I simply assumed things would work themselves out as usual. Such rampant fatalism was at least partly a product, I'm sure, of my wartime experiences.

With the benefit of hindsight, and to be quite honest about it, I should have realized we were setting off on a fool's errand. We really had no idea how we would move the horses beyond Anchorage, but we had vague ideas about taking them overland if necessary. Consequently, our baggage contained not only saddles and ordinary camp gear, but also

111

included tools such as a saw and axe. The thing we lacked was sensible information. At first, we didn't even have a map.

We began this madness by buying a really beat-up 1936 International truck for $250. It had one outstanding feature, the significance of which at first escaped me. It came equipped with a five-speed transmission *and a two-speed axle*. But even with a two-speed axle, in 1951, any truck you could buy from a contractor for $250 was suspect, and on principle should never have been driven beyond easy walking distance to the nearest telephone.

We attended some ten to fifteen farm auctions in central Montana that spring; enough, so the auctioneers began to recognize us as people willing to bid on almost anything. We bought all sorts of stuff. Household equipment, like the old-fashioned wood stove with the reservoir and warming oven (for which we paid $35), copper clothes boiler, wash tubs, hand wringer, and so forth.

We had been impressed by the lush grasses that grew at Clarks Point, so fodder for the animals seemed assured. I bought old horse drawn hay-making equipment. We eventually accumulated nearly ten tons—a whopping truckload—of hundreds of items such as a used mowing machine, a dump rake, a post drill, a forge, a 100 pound anvil, hand tools of all sorts, including crosscut saws, axes, and a sledge hammer, the stove I've already mentioned, a bed, a sewing machine, kerosene lamps, dishes, a battery radio, ash lumber suitable for a dog sled, snow shoes, clothes—the list was practically endless. We packed everything in barrels and crates. I carried the load on our $250 truck (with 9x20 tires) to Seattle; nearly 1,000 miles, across two mountain ranges, mostly on secondary—some gravel—roads to avoid weighing stations, because I was so grossly overweight for my tire size.

The trip was not without incident. Four tires blew out. (They almost always pop in pairs when you're as heavily overloaded as I was) before I reached Seattle. I had to mount the "new" tires on split rims by the side of the road.

Then, shortly before I reached Seattle, I set my brakes on fire as I was descending US 10 from Snoqualamie Pass. Only the quick action of another trucker with a fire extinguisher behind me saved my truck and cargo.

However, when I unloaded the truck at Pier 42 in Seattle, I was pleasantly surprised. The rate clerk decided my shipment fit into the cheapest tariff available; that of "immigrant movables," which saved several hundred dollars.

The ride back to Montana was a much less stressful. My only cargo was a pair of pack saddles built on old US McClellen cavalry saddle frames, probably dating to the first World War, or even earlier.

Although I'm old enough to remember horse drawn milk wagons; my father was a trainer of polo ponies; and my youngest brother was a professional rodeo rider, neither history nor genes equipped me adequately to deal with our little herd of six horses.

The horses were a package deal. At one of the last auctions I attended, I had impulsively but successfully bid $100 for a decrepit 1925 John Deere tractor. I had no particular use for it, but with the instincts of a born trader, I thought if I could get it running, I might sell it at a considerable profit.

A college classmate helped me get the thing started, and he drove it home for me. Luckily, the lug wheels had been changed to water-filled rubber tires by a previous owner, so we didn't have to worry about chewing up the pavement.

Word that I had an unneeded tractor spread quickly, and the next day, a man named Frank Runlet came to the house to inquire about it. It turned out that he had six horses for sale. He was asking $400 for the lot, but offered to trade them straight across for the tractor.

This was almost too good to be true. It was exactly the deal I had hoped for. Since I knew practically nothing about

113

horses—even less than I did about old tractors—there was no point in my inspecting the animals, although another classmate who knew quite a bit about horses looked at them later. Frank claimed they were sound in wind and limb, whereupon we exchanged notarized bills of sale. I wanted to close the deal before he found out what I had paid for the tractor, and I suspect his motives were equally pure.

Maud

On our side of the bargain, we got four horses and two very young colts. Maud and Molly, mothers of the colts, were a team of big black mares, about 12 years old. Brownie, a bay saddle mare, was about nine. The fourth animal was an albino stallion, somewhat older than the others. His name was Smoky.

That Brownie was something else! The first time we saddled her, she stood perfectly still as the blanket went over her back, and didn't flinch, as many horses will, when the saddle arrived a moment later. Jan slipped the bit into her mouth and pulled the bridle over her ears. Lots of horses object to that, but not Brownie. Then Jan swung into the saddle. She clucked at Brownie, nudged her in the ribs and shook the reins slightly.

Unexpectedly, to my horror, Brownie reared—up, up—until I was afraid she was going to fall back on Jan. Just before she reached her point of balance, Jan reversed the quirt she was holding, and gripping the saddle horn in her left hand, swung the loaded handle as hard as she could, striking Brownie squarely on top of her head. Stunned, Brownie sagged forward. By that time, Jan had kicked her feet clear of the stirrups, and as Brownie fell, Jan rolled off the horse on the high side.

Meanwhile, Brownie was on her knees, slowly shaking her head. Jan yanked hard on the reins, and Brownie stood up.

Jan put her foot into the stirrup and again swung into the saddle. This time, when she nudged Brownie in the ribs and leaned forward, Brownie obediently began to walk around the yard. Jan nudged her again, and the horse began to trot.

Brownie was a good looking and well trained saddle horse, but she was stubborn and dangerous. She never reared again, but her rider always had to watch out for fence posts, door jams, and low hanging branches.

Smoky, on the other hand, was my kind of horse. He was moderately long in the tooth, probably 15 or 16 years old, but easy-going and very forgiving. Surprisingly, contrary to the conventional wisdom about stallions, he turned out to be the most tractable animal we had.

When Jan and I decided which saddle horse we should call our own, it was cowardice rather than machismo that led me to choose Smoky. Jan agreed. She was the horse expert of the family, and if anyone could handle Brownie, it was she.

The mares, Maud and Molly, were big draft horses, clumsy, stubborn, and phlegmatic. In that sense, they were well matched, but as we quickly discovered, they had quite different personalities. Maud had a bright, optimistic attitude while her teammate focused on the dark side of things.

Over time, they both learned to carry pack saddles, but Maud was much more willing than her partner. Molly was the clumsier of the two and also had a mean streak. Later, when we were harnessing them, she casually reached over and bit Jan on the shoulder (through a heavy coat) seriously enough to draw blood. She also had a split hoof that required a special shoe.

We were planning to truck the horses over 3,000 miles of mostly gravel and dirt roads. That would only get us to Anchorage. From there to Nonvianuk Lake is around 300 miles *by air.* On the ground, the distance would be twice as great because as far as we knew, there were no roads, but there were major rivers and a serious mountain range to cross.

I consulted an old cowboy, a life long bachelor, about caring for horses generally and especially about trucking them. Full of a lifetime of accumulated wisdom, he said, "You have to treat a horse like you would a woman. Be kind but firm."

He warned me specifically that if a horse fell down in the truck, it was imperative that I stop immediately and get it back on its feet; otherwise, it would almost certainly die.

Our $250 truck. Note the high ramp.

Because the horses would need to rest and graze every night, I built a sturdy twelve foot, cleated wooden ramp from three by ten inch planks. It was so heavy that the only way I could handle it was by hinging it like a grotesquely elongated tailgate at the rear of the truck bed.

The theory was that after the animals had climbed aboard, I would raise the ramp to a vertical position like a medieval draw bridge with a block and tackle. When it was time to unload the animals, I would simply lower the ramp to the ground and lead the animals down to feed and water. So much for theory. Reality was very different.

Unfortunately, the wagon bed was exceptionally high; therefore, on level ground, the angle of that ramp was acute; it required the horses to behave almost like mountain goats, scrambling up (or down) a 33° grade, but, like most things, it was the best I could do in the circumstances.

Jan and I left Bozeman on May fifth in separate vehicles. I was driving the truck; she and the kids were riding in the old station wagon. We were to meet at Jan's parent's home in Shelby, a small oil town near the Canadian border.

I drove the loaded truck, with breeching harness and saddles lashed to the top of the stock rack. My exotic appearance probably had much to do with what followed.

US 10 went straight through Helena. If you were turning off toward Great Falls, as I was, when you reached the intersection of the road leading north directly away from the Capitol, you made a hard right turn, which I did, and suddenly the bed of the truck shifted as 1,800 pounds of horse landed on its side.

Mindful of the old cowboy's dire warning, I sped up, looking for a place where I could safely park the truck and sort the horses out. There it was, just off to the right. A perfect place. An empty municipal ball park. I drove the truck up to home plate and put the bumper against the wire backstop. Then, erroneously assuming they would not stray far from their mothers, I unloaded the colts, and turned my attention to shuffling the horses around (without unloading any if I could help it) so I could rescue the fallen one.

I was sure the down horse would be one of the big clumsy mares. I was right. It was Molly. Just then, I heard a siren and looked up to see two police cars, red lights flashing, approaching, herding one of the colts back to the truck. *Oh, Lord, now what?*

It seems that the colts were even dumber than I had thought. That little fellow had not only left mama, but while I was trying to rescue his mother, he had gone out to play in the traffic. The motorists evidently thought it was a deer, because they were having fun flashing their lights and honking their horns to panic the poor little beast, when the police interfered. I was still wrestling with Molly in the stock rack, when a cop banged on the rack with his night stick.

"Hey, you!" he shouted. "What the hell do you think you're doin' settin' up a rodeo in our ball park?" Not waiting for an answer, he added, "Let me see your brand certificate!"

I wasn't intentionally rude. Fearful that Molly was going to die at any moment, I shouted back that I would show them my driver's license, brand certificates, marriage license, anything they wanted—*after* they helped me get that damned horse on her feet. I was disappointed with those guys. I would have thought Montana police would have known more about livestock. Unfortunately, they were focused on the idea that I was trespassing on city property, disturbing the peace, and creating a public nuisance.

I think Molly enjoyed the attention, but finally she got her feet under her, and with a desperate heave, stood up. Now I had to find and reload the colts.

It must have been a slow afternoon for crime because by the time I climbed down from the stock rack, the original pair of patrol cars had been joined by three more. All had their red lights going. This was beginning to look serious.

The first cop was still demanding to see the brand certificate, and I was insisting that we corral and load the colts before I produced any papers. Reluctantly—I suppose they were afraid of getting their hands dirty—the cops formed a human corral and slowly encircled the two skittish colts. The little animals were less than two months old, but they were already strong enough to put up quite a fight.

When they were safely back aboard, and the ramp stowed in an upright position, I displayed my brand documents, and explained what had happened.

There were hard feelings. The first cop kept insisting that I ought to be arrested for trespassing, if only to teach me a lesson. I'm afraid I wasn't very tactful, but one of the others

118

asked my tormentor if he wanted to look after the horses while I was in jail, and that cooled him off. Over the years, no doubt there has been more than one hanging in Helena, but I'll bet I'm the only horse wrangler in the history of the place who was run out of town with a five car police escort!

That wasn't a promising beginning, but I ignored what turned out to be a warning that worse was to come—if not today, then tomorrow, or next week, and much of the time in between. Then, however, the gods were content to smile and let me dig myself deeper. I had no more trouble during the remaining 200 miles to Shelby, except that I arrived long after dark and the folks at my destination were beginning to worry. Lee, my father-in-law, directed me out to brother-in-law Ralph's ranch five miles out of town, where I unloaded the horses in the dark. The next three days passed quickly as Jan and I attempted to complete our preparations for the long drive over the Alcan Highway to Anchorage.

Lee was born a Montana cowboy, and was raised, like his daughters, on a big ranch that was isolated much of the winter. He was too polite to say so, but I'm sure he thought our project reeked of madness. He had no confidence in the truck and not much more confidence in me. He let me know tactfully that if by some miracle, we actually got to Alaska, he doubted whether we could accomplish anything useful.

However, he and Blanche, my mother-in-law, were somewhat mollified that we were willing to leave our young children with them while we built a cabin and became established. Quite honestly, without their help, I doubt whether we could have accomplished, not the grandiose dreams that we had in the beginning, but the scaled down reality we ultimately achieved.

Lee was very worried about our truck, not without reason. For one thing, for some curious reason, the truck's former owner had *welded* its axles in place. That's why we carried the breeching harness. I couldn't repair an axle with horses, but

119

I thought if it came to that, I might use them to *prevent* an axle from breaking. Typically, axles are most likely to break when you are doing dramatic things with the clutch and accelerator, trying to extricate yourself from a mud hole. Thus, if we were bogged down in mud, for instance, I could harness the team and make life somewhat easier for the truck's drive system. At least, that was the theory.

Another way of protecting axles, of course, is to reduce the horsepower the engine is capable of delivering to them. We didn't have much to fear on that score. Our engine was barely capable of turning the wheels on a downhill pull, let alone breaking axles.

Although Lee was successfully involved in oilfield promotions when I knew him, he was still a cowboy at heart. He came from the old school where almost any malady that man or beast was heir to, could be remedied by a judiciously administered dose of salts. Salts were especially useful in treating colicky horses. That treatment required a cigar box full of Epsom salts and five gallons of warm water, and was called, appropriately, a "drench."

I had a colicky truck. Without consulting me (why bother?) Lee decided to give it a drench. Nobody in his right mind would pour salts into an engine. But there is an analogous product on the market called Casite that serves the same purpose for colicky engines. I don't know how much he bought, but I do remember sitting in the truck, desperately pumping the accelerator to keep the engine running, while Lee poured that vile stuff into the carburetor.

If he tried that stunt today, we'd both have been arrested. Great billows of thick black smoke rolled out of the exhaust. Lee was jubilant. The smoke was proof that he was "curing" my engine. Encouraged, he went to the gas station for more of the stuff, and kept pouring it in the engine as long as smoke came from the exhaust. People weren't so squeamish about air pollution in those days.

The next morning, Lee and I rose before daylight and met in the kitchen for one of his ranch breakfasts. Suitably fortified, we climbed into the truck and drove out to Ralph's place to load the horses. We hoped to get back to Shelby shortly after daylight so Jan and I could get a early start.

As the headlights illuminated the prairie pasture, I saw what looked like a slight depression in the contour of the land. I backed the truck into it to lower the height of the truck bed. Then, while I lowered the ramp and made the truck ready, Lee walked out into the dark, and began collecting the horses.

I watched closely, studying every move that master stockman made. An opportunity like this was unlikely to come again soon. Lee quickly captured the two black mares, and tied their halter ropes to the side of the stock rack. Their colts stood docilely at their sides. Then he caught Brownie, and tied her to the stock rack. Finally, he appeared from the dusk leading Smoky.

Since I had loaded the horses only once before, and then in Bozeman with the aid of our next door neighbor's stock chute, I had no better idea what to expect than Lee had. He suggested we load the team first. That seemed reasonable. We started with Maud because I already recognized that compared to her team mate, Molly, she was intelligent and cooperative. Molly was just the opposite. She was dumb as a post, sullen, and stubborn.

We thought Maud's good example might inspire the others. I led the horse up the gangplank while Lee pushed and clucked encouragingly. Not a bit of a problem. Maud scrambled up that ramp as if she had been doing it all her life. Then it was Molly's turn.

If Molly was inspired by Maud's example, she certainly concealed it. She balked and rolled her eyes, pretending to be terrified of the ramp, then as we insisted, she would step forward until her forelegs were well planted on the ramp, then as soon as a hind leg came forward, she would step off the ramp. It was very frustrating.

Lee finally lost patience; then I learned how to inspire a more cooperative attitude in a stubborn horse by fastening a "Irish twitch," a little rawhide noose on a stick, around the animal's upper lip. Lee stood high on the ramp above Molly, so by lifting and tugging, he kept her head high and her feet moving. I stood to one side, serving as a human fence.

Molly was on board. Then we turned to Brownie.

If Molly personified the klutz in horses, then Brownie was the clever embodiment of everything evil and iniquitous. Like Molly, she was no stranger to the twist, but where Molly would respond to one, Brownie merely shrugged it off. Eventually, I concluded that Brownie's lip was either so callused, or the nerves had been so bruised, that she was immune to its persuasion.

Hours went by. We tried every trick in Lee's considerable repertoire. Blanche and Jan drove out from town to see what was holding up the parade. I'm afraid we weren't very civil.

Eventually, we fooled Brownie into thinking she was in a stock chute by stringing ropes hung with pieces of sage brush, to give the illusion of something solid on the sides of the ramp. Lee also held in each hand an end of a rope that went around the pipes framing the stock rack gate, and the bight of which passed under Brownie's tail. Lee vigorously pulled the rope back and forth, causing it to saw against a very tender part of Brownie's anatomy.

Meanwhile, I was the anchorman. We had tied a long rope to Brownie's halter and led it over the top of the front of the stock rack. As Lee forced Brownie to move forward, I took up the slack in the line, which was wrapped around the truck's front bumper. My line suddenly went slack. Brownie was in the truck!

Lee joined me at the front of the truck, and as we were exchanging a congratulatory handshake, Lee saw movement out of the corner of his eye and screamed, *"LOOK OUT!"*

I had only a confused impression of a brown blur as I sprang away from the truck. By the time I regained my equilibrium, Brownie was standing by the front of the truck, calming browsing on a clump of bunch grass.

Lee's eyes were huge. "My God," he whispered, obviously shaken, "I've never seen a horse do that before!"

No wonder I got Brownie so cheap. She was a one-horse circus. She had reared and leaped like a goat over the front of the rack, landing on the cab, the hood and the ground. Nothing broken, but there was a hell of a dent in the cab.

We were seriously out of patience. Now that we knew how to load her, we didn't fool around, only this time, the rope I used to prevent her from backing out went *between* the slats in the stock rack. In 15 minutes, she was in the truck, securely tied to the stock rack.

We had saved Smoky until the last, since we were somewhat afraid of the fight he was likely to put up. He was as much a surprise as Brownie had been. He walked up that ramp with scarcely any coaxing at all.

We soon developed a routine. Because of Smoky's tractability, we loaded him first, and stood him crosswise against the front of the rack. Then we loaded the mares, first Maud, thinking her docile good manners would set a desirable example for her teammate, then Molly, ears back, eyes wildly rolling, and nostrils flaring, clumsily stumbling over her own feet, then Brownie. It was a struggle every morning to get her into that truck. You never knew what she would do.

The horses wore halters that I tied to the top rail over Smoky's back. Although most stallions would have considered such treatment a major affront to their dignity, and many would have let you know about it, he never complained.

123

The colts were lifted aboard, the ramp was raised, and I climbed into the truck, only some five hours late, and started the engine. Lee sat on the passenger's side. I put the truck in first gear and slowly let out the clutch. The wheels began to turn, but abruptly, the rear of the truck fell about a foot, and one set of dual tires began to spin. I turned off the engine.

"Shit!" Lee said.

I still wasn't sure what had happened, but Lee knew. We had broken through a gumbo crust.

The retreating glaciers that once covered the northern plains, including Montana, left behind shallow pockets of exceedingly fine clay particles to which water is bound. Mostly, those pockets are crusted, and are unnoticed. But in the days of dirt roads, hitting a patch of gumbo, as almost everyone did from time to time, was like driving on grease. Compared to gumbo, snow was like a dry gravel road.

We climbed down and took a look at our hopeless situation. The wheels were in gumbo. The differential and axle housing rested on the surface.

Lee looked grimly at me. "I'll tell you one thing, Denny," he said, his broad face betraying the emotional turmoil he was feeling, "I'm not going to unload those horses. First, I'll buy every God damned tractor in Shelby County!"

I heartily endorsed that idea. I knew that unloading the horses wouldn't get us out of that fix, although if I had been alone, and without a county full of farm tractors, I would have harnessed Maud and Molly, some 3,500 pounds of horsepower. I don't know, but I think there's a good chance they might have pulled the truck out of the hole.

Brother-in-law Ralph had been working in an adjoining field where he had watched our progress. Accurately diagnosing our last problem, he dropped his implement in the field and drove to the barn. In a few minutes, he returned. After letting himself through the gate into our field, he drove his big tractor toward us, directly across the field.

"I saw what happened," he said, "and I figgered you fellows could use a pull."

To that point, Ralph had not been my favorite brother-in-law, but he now stood at the head of the list.

He and I crawled under the truck looking for a strong place on the frame to attach the chain. Then Ralph took the other end and fastened it to the tractor.

Meanwhile, Lee said, "I want you to take it real easy, Ralph. I don't know how strong that frame is. It has at least one fish-plate—I think the frame must have cracked—and it's anyone's guess how strong those welds are."

Ralph nodded, and turned to me. "Denny," he said, "put your truck in its lowest gear. Then when you feel the truck lift out of the hole, *but not before*, slowly let your clutch out. I think I can get you up on the crust, but I can't guarantee you'll stay there."

"OK," I said, and I climbed back into the truck. After starting the engine, I pulled the Brownlite axle lever into low and shifted the transmission lever into first. Then I waited.

Ralph knew how to drive a tractor. He slowly took the slack out of the chain, and almost imperceptibly, the truck began to move. I waited until I felt the rear wheels begin to lift out of the hole, and I slowly let the clutch out. Suddenly, I began overtaking the tractor. We were out of the hole.

After thanking Ralph effusively, I climbed back into the truck. "We'd better hurry," Lee said, looking at his watch. "The women will be wondering what's keeping us."

They knew what was keeping us, all right! I parked the truck in front of Lee and Blanche's comfortable little bungalow. After washing up, we had a hurried lunch, and then began the painful farewells. While Jan and I hugged her parents, Trina stood silently to one side, solemn and big eyed. She was old enough to understand that Mama and Papa were going away for a long time. Lynnie then was almost a year old, much too young to comprehend anything other than her immediate needs.

Finally, it was time to go. Jan was in tears as we drove to the end of the block and turned the corner. We were on our way back to Alaska.

The Alcan Highway

I quickly discovered what large quantities of Casite will do to an aging engine before we even left the Shelby city limits. I found myself downshifting on overpasses and floorboarding the accelerator on level road to achieve a modest 30 miles an hour.

Lee followed us out of town in his new Studebaker, imploring me to turn around. He was right. Our poor abused truck was in no condition to tackle the Alcan Highway. Looking back, I can see how my foolish stubbornness led us, time and again, into unnecessary difficulties. This was one of them. But quite honestly, it never once occurred to me to turn back.

Shortly before dark, we arrived at the twin border towns of Sweetgrass and Coutts on the Montana and Alberta sides respectively. The Canadian customs officer eyed our rig very doubtfully. Then he demanded to know how much money we had. I told him, but he wasn't satisfied until he held the last $400 I had in this world in his hands, and counted it.

Then he inquired whether we had pistols. I confessed that I had a Smith and Wesson K-22; a .22 caliber revolver on a heavier .38 caliber revolver frame. He thought for a moment, then told me to walk to the store and buy a metal lunch bucket, which he would use as a portable safe. In the meanwhile, the truck was parked in the customs lot, and my pistol was in his safe.

I did as he suggested. He put the gun in the lunch box, and wrapped a metal seal around it. "You'll have to show this box to the customs officer at Snag when you leave Canada," he said. "Oh, and one more thing. Your transit permit and bond describes each horse and its brand. You'll have to produce these horses, dead or alive, before you can leave the country." Then he said, "Drive your truck down to the quarantine corral by the railroad. You'll have to unload so the vet can inspect the animals."

After my experience a few hours earlier, I had a strong inclination against voluntarily unloading the horses before we reached Anchorage, which, of course, was nonsense. I knew we would have to unload somewhere, if only because it was late in the day. The corral actually was a good deal because I was sure there would be a stock chute attached to it.

After we unloaded the horses, I found half a bale of hay. There was a water trough in the corral, so my animals were fed and watered. Jan and I walked into town and had a quick dinner. Then we rolled our sleeping bags out on the ground, and slept under the corral fence next to our animals.

The vet didn't show up until midmorning. He was mildly annoyed when he discovered I had helped myself to his hay, but I quickly paid him for it. He gave the horses a cursory examination, being mainly interested in their brands, signed the certificate with a flourish, and was gone.

I backed the truck against the stock chute, and in 15 minutes, we were loaded and ready for the road. I stopped at the customs office to exchange the vet's certificate for our transit bond, and we were officially on our way.

While we traveled through fenced country, we had to stop at farmhouses when the light began to fail and beg permission to unload our cargo and set up camp in a roadside pasture.

I hate having to beg under any circumstances, and it was

all the more difficult because of our poor appearance. Yet the people we contacted were invariably kind and generous. Without the spontaneous help and advice we received along the way, our trip would have been much more difficult. For instance, a young rancher we met near Calgary suggested that I build portable railings for the ramp, light enough to carry lashed to the sides of the rack, yet substantial enough to fool the horses. He even volunteered to take me to the local lumber yard, and to help with their construction. How can you say no to such generosity? His advice was sound. The light railings we built almost solved our loading problems.

I say almost because there were days when no matter what I did, Brownie simply refused to board the truck. As I've said, she was immune to coercion, even to an Irish twitch. Thus, when she stubbornly refused to climb into the truck, I tied her halter securely to the rear of the stock rack, and let her trot behind the truck for ten or fifteen miles. That tended to soften her up, and she was usually willing to ride after that.

That stubborn streak of hers nearly got us in trouble between Lethbridge and Calgary. Brownie was displaying her independence and refused to board the truck. I trotted her for ten miles, but she was still disinclined to ride.

I was searching for a solution, when I saw a sign announcing Lord somebody's racing stables. I was driving slowly enough, of course, so I was able to turn into the narrow dirt lane that branched off to the right, and which led directly to a maze of corrals complete with stock chute. There was the answer!

I backed the truck up to the chute while Jan held Brownie's halter. Then I dropped the pole gate into the corral, and led Brownie into the first chamber. I was so busy handling Brownie that I failed to notice the young stallion standing quietly in the inner corral until, in his view, I delivered Brownie to his amorous gaze.

I know she wasn't in heat, but it was a case of instant love on Brownie's part, as well, and she whinnied seductively. I waved my hat at her new friend who was prancing nervously and excitedly around us.

Luckily, the stallion was young and inexperienced, and I was able to divert him long enough to get Brownie into the loading chute unscathed, but I watched my rear view mirror for several miles half expecting an irate trainer to be following us demanding a stud fee.

The next day, I had a special fright as we drove through Edmonton, then Alberta's largest city. As you'll remember, the iron frame which supported the loading ramp extended 16 feet from the ground. As I drove along Edmondton's main thoroughfare, I noticed how the overhead trolley wires sagged between their supports, and it suddenly occurred to me that my ramp frame must be only scant inches below those wires! I have no idea whether the hazard I perceived was real, but taking no chances, I turned into a side street, at the next intersection.

We bought a 50 gallon drum of gas and four cases of lube oil in Edmonton. By now, we were nearly 400 miles into our journey, and I was shocked at how Lee's Casite treatment had increased the truck's appetite for gas and oil. We were getting only four miles to the gallon, and every hundred miles I was obliged to add another quart of oil. Moreover, although we were still navigating on relatively flat ground, the Canadian Rockies were often in view. I knew that sooner or later, we would cross that formidable range.

The pavement ended at Edmonton. So did most of the road signs. Until 1948, except for military convoys, all the traffic beyond Edmonton was local, and local folks, as a rule, don't need signs to tell them where they are.

It seemed strange that we had to travel nearly 500 miles of bad road, some of it merely an unimproved dirt track, to reach the Alcan Highway, which was graveled and built to military specifications.

Three days beyond Edmonton for instance, while we followed a pair of ruts across the prairie—this is no exaggeration—we had seriously begun to wonder if we might have turned off the main road. Much to our relief, a great 18-wheel highway transport truck came roaring down the grassy slope toward us. If we were lost, so was he.

As soon as we left fences behind, new problems about controlling our livestock emerged. In addition to her many other sins, we quickly learned that Brownie was a "bunch quitter," a mare that will stray from the herd.

The problem of a bunch quitter is compounded when you have a stallion, as we did. The stallion will attempt to keep his harem together by forcing the other mares to follow the bunch quitter. Thus, we faced losing not just the horse, but the entire herd. It was ironic that Brownie now had the power to destroy our project before it was well begun.

Lee had foreseen this problem, and on his advice, I had packed a cow bell in our baggage. He also had shown me how to tie a gunnysack hobble. Before that trip was over, I became something of an expert at applying one.

I remarked earlier about the helpfulness and generosity that characterized the Canadians we met. But to prove the rule, we had to find the exception. We found it in Grande Prairie. Four days after leaving Edmonton, we arrived in Grande Prairie, a little town, with a population then of considerably less than 5,000. The road went straight through the business district. The first thing that caught my eye was a garage with a big International Harvester logo on its sign.

I'm the impulsive sort and the truck practically steered itself into the service bay. The owner/mechanic walked over to see what I wanted. Briefly, I explained the problem, not neglecting to mention the Casite treatment.

"Well, let's see how much compression there is," the mechanic said. He removed the spark plugs one at a time, and inserted the test gauge in the spark plug port while I restarted the engine. Satisfied, he yelled for me to quit.

I climbed down from the cab to get the bad news. It was really bad. "Yer truck needs a major overhaul," he began, "but maybe if we just pull the head and grind the valves we can give you a little more pep."

Seeing the puzzled expression on my face, he explained, "I couldn't get any reading on number five cylinder. It's clear flat. Two of the others registered only around 15 pounds of pressure. One was about 30 pounds and two was 45, which is about half what you should have in this engine. Adding it all up," he concluded, "and I'd say you're putting out the horsepower of a small two-cylinder engine."

I asked the all-important question. "How much would it cost to grind the valves?" By now, our $400 bankroll had dwindled to just slightly over $200, and we still had the longest and most expensive part of the trip ahead of us.

I'm sure the mechanic took our obviously impoverished condition into account. He thought for a moment, then said, "$28," adding, "you'll probably save more than that in gas you otherwise will waste. It won't do anything for your oil consumption, however."

Jan and I had a hurried conference. Then, I turned back to the mechanic. "How long will it take? And is there some place near where I can unload the horses?"

The mechanic thought for a moment. "I can probably get the engine done by noon tomorrow," he said. "As for the horses, why don't you just take them out to the fairgrounds? There's plenty of spring grass out there. There's a fence there and nobody's around out there this time of year."

"OK," I said. "We'll settle the horses out there and I'll bring the truck right back."

Jan and I climbed back into the truck, and following the mechanic's directions, soon came to the fairground gate, which I opened. We drove into what seemed to be the midway area. There was broken glass on the ground, but we swept that to one side. After unloading the horses and hobbling Brownie, we unloaded our gear. Then I saddled Smoky and tied his lead to the back of the truck rack.

Jan stayed behind to set up our camp while I slowly drove the truck, Smoky trotting behind, back to the garage.

"I'll be back in the morning," I said. I swung into the saddle, and turned Smoky back toward our camp.

In the spring, twilight lasts a long time in that part of Canada. After we'd had our supper, and were settling down for the night, I went out for a last look around. It was almost dark. I saw a caravan of cars turn off the main road and come through the fairground gate. Oh, oh.

I leaned over the booth. "We've got company," I said.

Still in single file, the cars drove into the midway area, and came to a stop in a semicircle, all with their headlights focused on me. I was blinded by the lights and put up my hands to shield my eyes.

A man's loud voice yelled, **"What the hell you doin' in our amusement park?"** from the perimeter of cars facing me.

This didn't seem very friendly. I said, "Look, if you'd turn off some of those lights. . ."

"Don't you tell us what to do!" another voice shouted.

I almost expected to hear someone else ask, *who has the rope?* I thought this bunch probably had just come from a bar and was looking for trouble. I tried it again, gratefully aware that Jan was standing beside me. "Look fellows," I said, "the mechanic in the International garage told us it would be all right to camp here tonight. He's working on our truck, and we needed some place to pasture our horses for the night."

133

"Well, it isn't all right," the first man said. **"You've got 15 minutes to get yourselves and your horses out of here, or the constable will arrest you for trespass."**

I was genuinely glad to learn there was a policeman with them. This was a pretty tough crowd, and for some reason I didn't understand, they were in a bad mood.

"I'm sorry we made a mistake," I said, "but let's be reasonable. Two of our horses are black, and we'll never find them in the dark. We'll get our horses together at first light, and as soon as our truck is ready, we'll be on our way."

While the posse conferred, I reflected that this was a replay of the friendly experience I had in Helena, and I wondered sardonically if the constable had been warned about us by the Helena Police Department.

This was so silly. There was only one reasonable thing they could do, which was let us stay. If they didn't, I'd start limping around, and remind them that Canada had failed to see the necessity for selective service during the recent war, but as a combat wounded veteran, I didn't hold that against them. Some Canadians, especially men like these, were defensive about that at the time.

It didn't come to that. Reluctantly, grudgingly, their apparent leader said, "It's against our better judgment, but I guess it will be all right as long as you clear out at daylight. But you'd better be gone when the constable comes to check, or you'll be locked up!"

With much slamming of car doors and gunning of engines, Grande Prairie's motorized protectors backed their cars around and single file, as they had come, they left.

Just before the last car left, its driver fired the last salvo: **"Don't forget!"**

No problem. I didn't want to rub up against that gang of roughnecks again. Even though I thought it unlikely we'd see any of those fellows in daylight, we packed up and took the horses out to the road right after breakfast. I saddled Smoky again, and rode into town.

The mechanic was almost finished with the truck. "I heard what happened last night," he said, "and I hope it didn't give you the wrong impression of our little town." He went on to explain what I had already concluded; that this "posse" was only a collection of local barflies. I told him that they had mentioned the constable, and he laughed.

"We've got an RCMP constable, all right, but if Jim had been there, you can bet those drunks wouldn't have been talking for him."

That made sense. I felt a little warmer toward the town, especially after I paid the bill and found it was exactly what the mechanic had estimated, $28.

Notwithstanding the rude welcoming committee, I was glad we had stopped in Grande Prairie. The engine ran much better, and for the first time, I was confident we would be able to handle the mountain roads yet to come.

I unsaddled Smoky and loaded him in the truck, then drove back to the fair grounds where Jan and the horses were patiently waiting by the side of the road.

We knew we had reached the Alcan Highway when we saw the Mile 0 monument in the square of a small town called Dawson Creek (not to be confused with Dawson City in the Yukon) in central British Columbia. In 1951, the route we had followed through Alberta was the only way to get there.

The colts were not yet weaned. This presented a nice logistical problem. I had no intention of unloading the horses whenever the colts or their mothers began complaining. I found another solution involving an empty quart mason jar. When we stopped for lunch, we *all* stopped for lunch. I would reach through the slats in the stock rack, and milk first one mare then, on the opposite side, the other.

I served this warm milk to each colt by standing next to it, tipping its head up, and pouring the milk down its throat. Admittedly, this system was crude, but it worked.

Except for one thing. By lunch time, Molly was frequently in a reclining position. It's impossible to milk a horse that's laying down. Contrary to the conventional wisdom and strongly held opinion by experts on the subject, Molly preferred to ride in a prone position. Sometimes she would collapse the minute I engaged the truck's clutch. Other times, she would wait until I was steering around an obstruction in the road, but almost invariably by the end of the day, three horses would be standing on the fourth. I do not exaggerate when I say that she rode half the distance to Alaska on her side. Few horses can make that claim. She showed it, too. Her hide over her hip bones, was rubbed raw. I applied some salve to her wounds every evening. Fortunately, biting flies, of which the north country has many, are mostly daytime pests. In the daytime, because we were rocketing along at 30 miles an hour or so, the horses were out of their reach.

By now, we were settled into our routine. We were driving about eight hours a day, stopping only when we came to a recently abandoned construction camp. Those were great. They were conveniently spaced about 200 miles apart, and were usually composed of a large graveled clearing surrounded by abandoned barracks. Those areas were usually fenced, and knee high spring grass grew everywhere.

The clearings provided needed room well off the highway for unloading and loading the horses. When it rained, we sought shelter inside the building nearest the truck.

While 2,000 miles of gravel road has little to recommend it, the scenery along much of the highway varies between spectacular and breathtaking. Nowhere was the view more striking than at Muncho Lake. Muncho Lake was such an inviting expanse of water, surrounded by spectacular mountains, that we stopped earlier than usual. I thought perhaps I might be able to catch a trout for supper. But first, even though the camp was partly fenced, and there was an abundance of grass nearby, I knew I had better hobble Brownie, or we'd spend most of the next morning looking for the horses.

While Jan held her, I squatted at Brownie's forefeet. After twisting the gunny sack into a rope, I passed the bight of the sack around her off pastern, twisted it and was tying the ends of the sack around her near pastern when suddenly she reared!

Caught off guard, Jan lost her grip on Brownie's halter, and for a moment that seemed like an eternity, Brownie's hooves were raised above my head. Like ballet dancers in a frozen tableau, Brownie and I each moved slowly and deliberately, but with different purpose. While I concentrated on gently deflecting the threat of those raised hooves, she delicately shifted her weight to her off hind leg, and brought her near hind foot to rest on my newly operated ankle. Then, as her front hooves descended harmlessly to the ground, she maliciously shifted her weight to my ankle.

I screamed as a white-hot sheet of pain flashed up my leg. The searing pain in my ankle and knee was instantaneous. I lay writhing and sobbing on the ground for several minutes. Gradually the pain subsided to a dull localized, burning, ache in my ankle and knee.

Jan finished tying Brownie's hobble, then brought some pain pills and an Ace bandage to wrap my knee, which was already beginning to swell. We spent three days at Muncho Lake while I recovered sufficiently so I could help handle the horses and drive the truck.

That was not an accident. I think most horse people would agree that horses do not accidentally step on people, any more than they accidentally bite them. I'm sure the only reason she didn't bite us was because she didn't think of it.

We reached Lower Post, a former Hudson Bay trading

fort, located on the British Columbia/Yukon border at Mile 620, by noon the first day I was able to drive. My knee needed a rest, so we decided to stop for a cup of coffee.

We were sitting at the counter glumly reviewing the events of the past several days when a man came into the cafe and looked around before coming to us.

"Are those your horses out there?"

I was tempted to ask why first, but instead I said, "Yep, they sure are. Why?"

"They are making funny sounds like one of them is strangling," he replied.

That was something new. Sore knee forgotten, I ran out the door, followed by Jan and the other customers.

Climbing the side of the stock rack, I discovered to my horror that **both** Maud and Molly were down. Well, that's not quite true. Molly was in her usual reclining position, and Maud was off her feet, but she was gasping for air, since she was hanging from her halter, tied to a rope that ran across Smoky's back to the stock rack. I whipped out my pocket knife and slashed the rope. Maud collapsed.

This was serious. While Molly was sufficiently case hardened, having ridden hundreds of miles laying down, for Maud this was a new and potentially fatal experience. Horses are notorious for solving seemingly intractable problems by dying. I was sure that Maud would die if I didn't get her on her feet in the next few minutes.

I dropped the ramp. We quickly herded the colts out of the truck. I opened the inside gate, and after untying her halter, led Brownie over her fallen sisters down the ramp. Then I went back for Smoky, and led him down the ramp.

We foolishly neglected to tie Brownie, and while our attention was on Smoky, she bolted for the highway. I caught a glimpse of her just before she disappeared around the corner, and shouted, "Brownie's getting away!"

Holding his halter rope, Jan leaped on Smoky's back and kicked him in the ribs. It wasn't necessary to direct him. He knew Brownie was running away, and was only too glad to chase her. He and Jan thundered off in pursuit, leaving me to sort out the mess. It was a mess! Those two big draft horses were laying on their sides facing each other, their legs almost hopelessly entwined, crammed into the narrow space of the stock rack. This was no job for a guy who had spent the previous three days on his back waiting for his knee to heal so it would bear weight.

Remembering Doc Welch's advice—he was my veterinary professor—about his "oat sack" treatment, which required equal parts buggy whip and oat sack; the former to get the horse's attention, and inspire it to do something, and the latter to improve the animal's morale after the desired objective (standing up, climbing out of the hole, whatever) was achieved, but lacking a buggy whip, I used a quirt, the application of which lacked the elegance of a flicking buggy whip. I also used a twist, and God knows what else.

In the meanwhile, my impromptu rodeo had attracted quite a crowd that wasn't entirely sympathetic. I still remember some comments:

"Look at him stagger. He must be terribly drunk!"

"Can't someone stop him from beating those horses?"

"Isn't there a man here who will stop that?"

Just before I got Maud back up on her feet, Jan returned on Smoky, triumphantly leading an unrepentant Brownie. Our audience gave her a nice round of applause, and I distinctly overheard one woman pleading with her to "get that brute (I think she meant me) out of the truck."

Eventually, the horses were reloaded (Maud did not die) and we left Lower Post. It's probably a good thing we got out of there when we did; otherwise, I might have been arrested.

I did what I thought I needed to do to those horses to save them, but one sharp-eyed lady standing nearer than the others had been especially indignant when she saw me bite Maud's ear. Dentures can inflict a hell of a wound, and her ear bled profusely.

Smoky attracted a lot of attention, and I received several tempting offers for him. Our limited funds were nearly gone, and the the only thing that saved him was my memory of the customs officer's warning about our bond. I had to account for all of our livestock when we reached Alaska or face the consequences, whatever they were.

Yet when we pulled up to the same customs shed in Snag that we had visited on our trip south two years earlier, the officer merely wanted to see our papers. He had no interest in our cargo, and didn't even ask to see the sealed lunch box containing the .22 revolver.

Sixteen days after leaving Montana, we reached Anchorage. We had traveled nearly 3,000 miles from Bozeman, our point of beginning. The gas tank was nearly empty, and we had $20 between us.

Brownie's Revenge

Even though, as I grimly reminded myself, it was her own damn fault, it was no fun watching the horse die. Brownie was on her side, lying on the grass, her eyes rolling in fear, froth drooling from her open mouth, as she whimpered and kicked feebly at her side in the final spasms of a fatal colic, while the owner of the strawberry field she had ravished—which accounted for her terrible stomach ache—was screaming at me about lawyers and payment.

I hate to see animals suffer, and I felt terrible, even though Brownie had been a monumental pain in the ass right from the very beginning. She was a beautifully gaited horse, but she suffered from two major defects. She was a bunch quitter, a trait not uncommon among mares, and she was crazier than a March hare. Not Loony Toons, you understand, but crazy in a cunning, paranoid sort of way.

We had arrived in Anchorage the previous evening. I remembered congratulating myself on my good fortune when a gas station attendant casually asked if I was taking the horses to the riding stable. I hadn't known there was a riding stable in Anchorage. It seemed so unlikely, it wouldn't have occurred to me to ask.

Following his directions, I drove out of town and through a near suburb, Spenard. On the far side of Spenard, near what used to be called the "Y" where the road branched off to Lake Hood, we found horses grazing in a small pasture.

This had to be the place. We pulled into the yard, and I parked in the driveway next to a little barn. The door to the tiny house on the other side of the driveway opened, and a pretty young woman wearing worn Levis and a checked shirt came out to meet us. She was followed by a tall, thin man in his early 30s, who needed a shave and wore bib overalls.

We introduced ourselves, and shook hands. The woman's name was Betty. Her husband was called Doc. We explained why we had suddenly appeared in their driveway with a load of horses. We asked if we could pasture the horses for the night, and sleep in the barn.

Betty and Doc merely exchanged glances, then pleasantly agreed. I drove the truck into the pasture and unloaded the horses. Then we took our bedrolls to the barn.

Again and again, I was reminded of the characteristic generosity of people who, themselves, were obviously struggling to make economic ends meet, toward those they considered less fortunate.

Our hosts and new friends invited us to join them for supper. We gladly accepted. During the meal, we told them something of our experiences coming over the highway, and they in turn explained their business. Before the meal was finished, we were becoming fast friends. Doc's brother, Fred, joined us after dinner. We had a great time, relaxing and swapping yarns until nearly midnight, when Jan and I excused ourselves and retired to our beds in the barn. We were unaware that anything was wrong until morning.

However, we woke the next morning to the pitiful whinnying of a horse in serious distress. It was Brownie. She had evidently led the herd through a hole in the fence, and into the adjoining field which had recently been planted with young strawberry plants.

We didn't know whether she was sick from eating the strawberry plants, or had gotten into something else, but whatever it was, it was deadly. In desperation, I tried to find a veterinarian, but failing that, returned to the stable to find she was down. She didn't seem terribly bloated, but I thought briefly of jabbing a trocar, if I could improvise one, into her belly to relieve the pressure. That treatment almost invariably cures bloated cattle, but it is almost equally certain to kill a horse. But before I could do anything, Brownie gave a great shudder and died.

Unhappily, I knew I could have prevented this tragedy. This was the first night since we had left Montana that Brownie was allowed to graze without hobbles. And she took full advantage of it. What a grotesque irony! After fighting that damned horse for weeks, and hauling her 3,000 bitter, kicking, miles, she had the final laugh after all.

What do you do with a dead horse in Anchorage? In Montana, I would have called the nearest livestock disposal service. They would have picked up the carcass free of charge for tankage. However, there was no such business in Alaska. Here, on the last frontier, you buried your own dead horses. Imagine what it must be like to dig a grave for a *horse?* Especially in ground that was still partly frozen?

I shuddered at the thought, and forced myself to examine other, less morbid, aspects of our new and unexpected setback. Brownie had been Jan's saddle horse. The mares had already been assigned full pack loads, so even if she had been willing to try riding one of them, neither horse could provide Jan with transportation.

The only sensible solution was to find another horse. But in Anchorage? With only $20 in our pockets?

That last thought, of course, distracted me entirely. Apart from our immediate logistic problem caused by Brownie's untimely demise, somehow I had to augment our bankroll.

Sometimes, when the weight and bulk of my problems seems colossal and threatens to overwhelm me, I find the only way to deal with them is to pick them apart just as I would untangle a shapeless mass of snarled cordage. Find the end and begin a gentle tugging.

Brownie couldn't wait. We had to dispose of her in the most sanitary *(and, my instincts told me, inconspicuous)* way possible. Fred offered a possible solution.

Staring thoughtfully at the dead horse, he said more to Doc than to me, "You know where Mrs. Smith is subdividing her homestead?"

Turning to me, Doc explained, "Mrs. Smith is one of the real old timers around here. She and her husband home-steaded out by Jewel Lake 15 or 20 years ago. He's dead, and she has decided to subdivide her property." Then, back to Fred, he said, "Yeh, I know. What about it?"

"Just this," Fred said, conspiratorially lowering his voice, "I was out there yesterday looking for a job, and she's got a contractor with a D-6 Cat building an access road. Right now, they're filling across a little muskeg. Seems like that would make a pretty good place to leave Brownie."

Having envisioned myself laboring with a pick and shovel for a week to dig a grave big enough for a horse, I quickly and enthusiastically agreed. "That sounds like a great idea, Fred," I said, ignoring a nagging little voice in the back of my head that monotonously warned over and over, *"But suppose something goes wrong?"*

Ever helpful, that afternoon Doc and Fred drove their pickup over to the Widow Smith's place to reconnoiter. They returned to report that while the road project had shut down for the weekend, it then being Saturday afternoon, the fill across the muskeg was only partially completed. We ought have no trouble at all disposing of our dead horse by dragging it out to the edge of the fill, then pushing it over the edge where it would tumble to the bottom. We could complete the ceremony with a few shovelsful of dirt.

Thinking that three o'clock on Sunday morning was the most inconspicuous time possible for our little trespass, we dragged Brownie's carcass behind Fred's pickup about a mile down the road to the Smith subdivision turnoff without seeing a soul, even though it was already broad daylight.

Having reached the turnoff, we dragged the carcass another quarter mile until we reached the end of the road building project. Then, after dragging the carcass as close to the edge of the soft fill as we dared, Fred stopped the truck while we untied Brownie's towline. Then, with enormous effort, we rolled the carcass over and over until it reached the edge of the fill. A final shove pushed it over the edge, and it tumbled down a 15 foot slope to the bottom. Taking shovels from the truck, we hastily spread loose earth over the carcass, tossed our shovels back in the truck, and left the scene as quickly as possible. On reflection, I'd say we left the scene a little too quickly.

Four days dragged by. We were just beginning to relax, thinking that Brownie was gone forever, when a Highway Patrol car rolled into the yard.

The conversation began amicably. The officer rolled down his window and asked, "Are you missing a horse?"

"No, Officer," I assured him, "we know where all our horses are."

The policeman abruptly changed tactics. "Let's quit fooling around," he said. "You guys tried to plant a dead horse on the Smith subdivision. Mrs. Smith's madder'n hell. Her cat-skinner came to work Monday, took one look at that dead horse, went into town, and has been drunk ever since.

"It's hard to find a good cat skinner, these days," he added philosophically. Then, looking me straight in the eye, he delivered his ultimatum.

"I'm giving you two days to get that horse out of there! If you don't, I'm going to arrest the lot of you for trespass, malicious destruction of property, and anything else I can think of. *Don't make me come back.*" With that, he rolled up his window and backed his car out of the driveway.

We silently and unhappily looked at each other. All I could think of was *God! Won't that damned horse **ever** leave us alone?*

Without going into nasty detail, let me tell you from the heart that it's easier and a whole lot more fun to roll a dead horse downhill than it is to carry one up a 15 foot slope of loose dirt in small, smelly pieces. Especially a horse that's been dead for five days. To give our new friends credit, Doc and Fred never flinched. They were right there with me, helping me retrieve Brownie's carcass. That was a chore that may have been one of the worse jobs I ever had to perform.

Soon the pickup bed was filled with Brownie parts. Glad the wind was blowing Brownie's foul odor away from us, we drove across town to the dump where, surreptitiously, we reburied her carcass under a mound of garbage.

Soon after, the king salmon season began and Betty persuaded Jan to join her in applying for a job at Emard's salmon cannery on Ship Creek.

Both women were hired instantly to work on the packing table, a piece work operation where women hand-filled half pound cans with fresh king salmon meat. I went to work in the cannery as a general laborer. One day I might be assigned to caulk an old work boat; another day, I would find myself hanging spare gillnets or stirring a huge stinking kettle of simmering cat food made from equal parts of salmon offal and oatmeal.

Our only expense was food, and although our wages were low for that time and place, we found we were saving money at a prodigious rate. After a month or so at the cannery, our bankroll had grown to about $150.

The Fourth of July, always an important holiday in Alaska, had come and gone. Our hosts had borrowed Smoky and saddled him with an elaborately decorated and very expensive saddle and bridle for the parade. I'm sure he enjoyed his brief moment of glory as the Parade Marshal's mount.

We never forgot that we were 300 miles away from Nonvianuk Lake. The unpleasant fact was that we really weren't much closer to our goal now than we had been in Montana.

I kept my ears open at the cannery, and learned that a large barge was sent almost every month to Kodiak

Smoky in his 4th of July finery

for a load of pumice for the local cinder block industry.

After examining a chart of lower Cook Inlet, Jan and I realized that the barge's route took it close to Nonvianuk Lake. Therefore, we paid a visit to Captain Jack Anderson on the tug *Tiger*. Anderson's father owned the *Anderson Transportation Company,* a local water freight company.

Captain Jack, as we came to know him, was a tall, slender man, not much older than us. He received us graciously aboard his tug, and listened to our story. Then he stood and took a Cook Inlet chart from a drawer. His first remark made me wish there was another water freight company in town.

"My old man hauled horses for the railroad contractors," he said, "and he swore he'd never have another one on board any boat he owned."

Seeing the expressions on our faces, he relented. "But I'm not my father." He winked at us, then went on, "We could

147

drop you in Iliamna Bay, here. A road connects Iliamna Bay with Pile Bay up on the upper end of Lake Iliamna. You'd still be a long way from Nonvianuk Lake, but at least you'd be in the same watershed." His finger pointed to an indentation on the sea coast about half way from Anchorage to Nonvianuk Lake.

"The thing is," he went on, "if we land you here at Diamond Point," he pointed to a spit extending from the shore furthest from the bay's entrance, "we'd have to anchor 500 yards off and you'd have to swim the horses ashore."

He paused to let that information sink in. Hearing no response, he continued, "Horses are terribly unpredictable. You must realize that we might drown half of them just getting them ashore. That's what happened when Dad was landing horses."

This was getting worse and worse!

"You've also got to realize that I can't fool around in there all day. This will be a quick detour, mainly to save you from killing yourselves. How much money have you got?" Captain Jack was direct.

"$150," I said, too startled to lie.

He was silent for a moment. Then he shrugged. "OK," he said. "I'll drop you in there for $150, but don't tell my Old Man. He would skin me."

He was leaving the following week for Kodiak. Suddenly, we had much to do and little time in which to do it. For openers, I had to sell the truck and find a replacement mount for Jan.

I knew that selling the truck would not be easy. I had planned to ask $250, but as Doc pointed out, since $250 was enough for a down payment on a new truck, why would anyone chose mine?

I placed an ad in the *Anchorage Daily Times* without result, and I was seriously beginning to wonder what I could do when someone told me about a fellow named Johnny Vanover who had a hog farm on the edge of town, and who dealt in horses and trucks.

My kind of guy. I paid a visit to Mr. Vanover, and found him feeding his hogs. After we shook hands, and I explained my mission, he said, "You see that horse over there?" waving his hand to indicate an odd looking creature in the corral. "Take a look at him and tell me what you think."

Profoundly wishing that Jan was doing this instead of me, partly because she was the family horse expert, but mainly because I was selecting a horse for her, I walked over to the corral and peered over the corral poles at the most peculiar animal I had ever seen. I wasn't even sure, at first, that I was looking at a horse.

The animal was a gray gelding of indeterminate but obviously advanced years. He was still shedding his winter coat, and great gobs of dirty matted hair hung from his back and sides.

His posture seemed strange, possibly because he appeared to be leaning against a high feed bin. I may be wrong about this, but I came away with the distinct impression that his front legs were crossed.

However, the most peculiar thing about this horse was his diet. When I first looked at him, he was contentedly munching on a cantaloupe rind he had evidently picked out of the garbage Johnny fed his hogs.

I walked back to the truck where Johnny was standing. He eyed me, waiting for my reaction. "Well?" he prompted.

"I don't know," I said. Then I had a flash of inspiration. I was sure a horse trader would want to see whether the animal was lame. "Would you mind leading him around the corral so I can see him walk?"

Johnny quickly entered the corral, and seizing the animal's

halter, led him around in a circle.

The ground in the corral was soft sticky mud, and I couldn't see how the horse was placing his feet.

"How about walking him on hard ground?" I suggested. I was beginning to worry because he was so obviously anxious to sell the horse. I was glad he hadn't looked in the bed of the truck and seen that I had come equipped with a saddle and bridle. I didn't want him to know how eager I was.

Johnny led the horse out of the corral. The animal was unshod and had an odd way of placing its feet. Still, an old packhorse was better than no horse.

"What kind of a deal do you have in mind?"

Johnny looked at me for a moment. Then he said, "You've had a chance to look the horse over. Tell me about the truck. Does it use much oil?"

"That's like me asking you if the horse is lame," I cleverly countered.

He ignored my parry. "Does it?" he insisted.

I certainly wasn't going to tell him I had to add a quart every 100 miles. On the other hand, I knew he would suspect the truck burned oil—the only question was how much. I equivocated.

I said, "Yes, like all old engines, this one uses oil. You have to watch the oil level. Otherwise, you could get into trouble."

He accepted that. "Tell you what," he began, "suppose I give you the horse and $100 for the truck?"

I was expecting an even trade. "That's fine," I said, offering my hand. "I came prepared," I added, as I drew the truck title from my pocket. Johnny filled out a bill of sale, and we exchanged documents and shook hands again before I climbed into the truck to get the saddle, bridle, and blanket.

Johnny gave me a wry smile. "I see you did come prepared," he said, watching me saddle my new horse.

We shook hands again. I swung into the saddle, and was both relieved and a bit surprised to find that Dusty was trained to neck rein.

Although I had no claim to expertise, I guessed, when I saw the horse's gait on firm ground, that his problem might be the result of walking on soft footing for nearly a year. First the winter snow; then, since the spring breakup, the mud. His toenails were much too long, forcing him to walk on his heels.

Horses loaded aboard the barge

It was a long ride back to Spenard. After we arrived, Doc and Fred, the experts, quickly trimmed his hooves. His posture and gait immediately improved.

Three days later, we saddled our little pack string and made the long trek in from Spenard, through town, and down to the docks where the barge was waiting.

Folks in Anchorage weren't accustomed to pack strings. Consequently, the downtown traffic became somewhat snarled until (again!) we acquired a police escort, as we moved at our usual sedate pace through the city.

Since Jack had instructed us to be aboard no later than 10:30 that morning, I had assumed we would cast off directly after our arrival, and that we would soon reach Iliamna Bay. Consequently, I had made no provision for feeding or watering the horses en route. That was a serious mistake.

We cast off as expected, but instead of heading down the Inlet, we went across Turnagain Arm and anchored in the lee of Fire Island. I still have no idea why. We had spread our bedrolls on the barge with the horses, partly to reassure them, and I think partly because we felt obliged to share their discomfort.

It's a long way to the water!

The crew had maneuvered the tug so it and the barge rested side by side in the water. We were able to step across to the tug, and join the crew for meals. I begged several buckets of water from the cook for the horses. Unfortunately, she had nothing to feed them.

We spent nearly 30 hours at Fire Island, and finally got under way for the journey to Iliamna Bay, arriving shortly after daylight, the following day. Jack brought the barge alongside the tug again, and dropped his anchor.

We looked around with considerable apprehension. There was no beach in the usual sense. Instead, we found ourselves in a deep bay surrounded on three sides by sheer rocky cliffs towering 100 feet or more above our heads, and dropping straight into the water. Dead ahead, however, the rocky precipice ended on a narrow strip of gravel that rose two or three feet above the water. Sea gulls, disturbed by our appearance, wheeled overhead, protesting our presence. It didn't help matters that it was a gray, cloudy day.

"That's Diamond Point," Captain Jack said, pointing toward the gravel beach a quarter mile away. "Now, it's up to you. I'll have the boys put the lifeboat in the water."

I hope nobody's life ever depends on that boat. About ten feet long, it was a flimsy, low sided, flat bottomed, plywood skiff that barely carried two people. Still, it was all we had.

Jan and I had worked out what we thought was a sensible strategy for unloading the horses. We didn't know whether the colts could swim to the beach, so we decided to carry them ashore in the boat. We assumed that maternal devotion would cause the mares to leap into the water and swim to their babies, and that the stallion would follow the mares, and that poor Dusty, fearful of being alone, would gamely leap into the water and rejoin the herd on the beach.

That kind of thinking is the way politicians balance budgets. Like us, starting with a false major premise, they inevitably wind up with a logical fallacy. In other words, we were not only wrong in our assumptions and conclusions; we were grossly, 100% wrong!

Somewhat inexpertly, we hogtied the first colt and laid him in the bottom of the skiff. Jan sat in the stern while I pulled on the oars. About halfway to shore, the struggling colt came untied. Anyone can tell you that a ten foot skiff is too small for two people and an anxious horse, no matter how tiny that horse may be. With great presence of mind, Jan promptly sat on his head, which gave him something to think about besides trying to kick the sides out of the boat.

As we approached the beach, I paused to examine the place. I didn't like the looks of it. The cliff went straight up almost like the side of a building. Judging by the rings of fresh algal growth on the cliff face, at high tide this narrow strip of shingle beach would be covered by about four feet of water. Clearly, we had no time to waste.

153

Just before we touched the gravel, we gently rolled the colt over the side of the skiff and watched him splash his way to the dry gravel. I started rowing back for the second baby. We hadn't gone very far, however, before I noticed an object in the water which appeared to be pursuing us.

It was the colt struggling to return to the dubious security of mama and the other horses still on the barge. We now knew that given adequate motivation, colts swim very well. What we didn't know, and wouldn't discover until the next morning, was how powerfully motivated the horses were to *avoid* landing on that particular shore.

I turned the boat around, and rowed back to intercept the colt. Jan slipped a noose around his neck, and I towed him back to shore. This time, Jan remained behind restraining the frightened little animal by wrapping her arms around its neck while I rowed back to the barge.

One of Jack's deck hands volunteered to help me in the boat. The men remaining behind lowered the second colt into the water, and tossed its lead to my helper. I quickly towed it to the beach. Now Jan had two colts to look after.

As we had anticipated, the mares were becoming seriously agitated, but we had underestimated their instincts for self-preservation. Or perhaps it was unreasonable to expect *Montana* horses to voluntarily hurl themselves off the bow of a barge 12 feet above the water.

Climbing back on the barge, I led Maud to the very lip of the bow, where she stood, nostrils flaring, anxiously eyeing her colt on the beach. Satisfied that her attention was firmly on her baby, I gave her a mighty shove.

She struggled briefly to regain her balance, but it was too late, and she fell into the water with the same odd *Kerrr-PLUNK* you hear when large stones are dropped into deep pools. Almost instantly she bobbed to the surface, and her gaze never wavering from her baby, she set out for the shore with such powerful strokes that, even though I had hurried into the boat as soon as she was in the water, I barely caught up before she reached the beach.

Back to the barge for Molly. Molly quite obviously lacked Maud's maternal commitment. Or perhaps having just seen what had happened to Maud, she was too canny to be taken for a walk to the forward edge of the barge.

The two deck hands and I pulled, and tugged, and prodded that poor horse, and finally she fell overboard in the narrow space between the barge and the tugboat. Jack later told me he felt her strike the keel of the tug twice as she struggled back to the surface. Mislead by Maud's purposeful performance a few moments earlier, when Molly surfaced, I watched her swim around the barge and tugboat, seeking a way back on board. Finding none and obviously confused, she forgot about her baby or the beach, and struck out for sea, directly away from the beach.

My deckhand assistant rejoined me in the skiff. Frantically, I rowed to overtake her, and none too soon. She sank from view as I approached her, surfaced, sank again. She reminded me of a surfacing whale, but I knew I was looking at a drowning horse.

We reached her as she started to sink, I'm sure, for the last time. The deckhand grabbed her halter, and pulled her head over the transom so her nostrils and eyes were out of the water.

The weight of her head threatened to pull the transom of our tiny boat under water, so I slid my weight as far forward as possible, and in that awkward position, began pulling for the beach. The instant Molly's head came out of the water, she gave up, and switched on her dying mode. Realizing this, I redoubled my efforts, and pulled like hell on the oars.

The tide was still dropping, so dragging her bulk through the water, I barely made headway against it. Meanwhile, remembering my veterinary professor's "oat sack treatment," for heading off the tendency of distressed horses to die, I made reassuring sounds, hoping to keep her interested in living.

After an incredibly long and hard ordeal on the oars, I dragged that useless animal to the beach. When she felt the gravel, she awkwardly stood and casually strolled up the beach as though nothing had happened.

Back to the barge. Dusty was the next to go. It's quite possible he had done something like this before. The deckhand led him to the bow and gave him a shove. He fell into the water, surfaced, and swam straight to the beach. I hardly needed to escort him.

If Smoky had been upset by losing his harem, he was now frantic to see Dusty with them. But his imperious whistles and whinnies as he ordered the mares to return to the barge went unheeded.

I thought his high anxiety level would make it easy to put him over the side, so I remained in the skiff and watched the deckhand lead him to the edge of the bow. I was even wrong about that.

Stallions, deservedly, are reputed to be nimble and short tempered. Although Smoky was unusually tractable for a stallion, there was nothing wrong with his reflexes, and even his placid temperament had its limits, as the unfortunate deckhand soon discovered.

Seeing that Smoky's attention was riveted on the beach tableau, the deckhand gave him a hard push on the shoulder. I thought Smoky was going over, but he regained his balance, and shot the offending deckhand a reproving glance before resuming his dialogue with the gang on the beach.

This time, the deckhand pushed on his hind quarters. Again, Smoky teetered on the lip of the bow. Seeking to follow up while the horse was struggling to regain his balance, the deckhand gave him another hard push. That was one push too many!

Smoky's ears went flat. Instead of worrying about his harem, he now focused on his tormentor, the deckhand.

I can't tell you how Smoky did it, but instead of falling overboard, he whirled, and sprang for the suddenly terrified man who turned and wisely sprinted for the tugboat. Smoky was just behind him, snapping at his haircut.

The deckhand almost made it, but he waited a fraction of a second too long before deciding to dive over *Tiger's* railing and into the safety of the ship's galley.

The barge was some 80 feet long by perhaps 40 feet wide. Its cargo space was defined by a five foot plank bulkhead that was set in about five feet from the sides of the barge and about 15 feet from the ends. This walkway suddenly became a track where the unfortunate deck hand found himself in a desperate race for his life.

Ordinarily, there would have been no contest. Smoky was much faster than even the most terrified human alive, but he was shod on his forefeet, and iron shoes in contact with the steel deck created an uncertain and slippery surface. Thus, he was forced to slow down to get around the corners. This gave the deckhand a slight advantage, since he could grab the corner stanchion and swing himself around the corner without losing precious momentum.

From my vantage point in the boat, I heard the deckhand's frantic screams for help but all I could see was the brief moment the deckhand, still hotly pursued by Smoky, flashed across the barge's bow and down its side.

I also saw his captain, Captain Jack, standing comfortably on the *Tiger's* bridge, shouting encouragement to his deckhand, and thoughtfully taking pictures of the race with his Polaroid.

The race ended as abruptly as it began. Near the end of

the second lap around the barge, Smoky unwisely waited a fraction of a second too long before applying his brakes. Unable to stop in time, he flew off the bow of the barge, landing in the water with a horrific splash. After he surfaced, he looked around, got his bearings, and quickly swam ashore.

The unfortunate deckhand, meanwhile, lay on the steel deck trying to catch his breath. When he was able, he stood and wobbled down below to his bunk.

Several years later, we learned the rest of the story. We were talking to Captain Jack on the radio, and after we identified ourselves as the horse people, he told us the deckhand was so offended by his captain's perceived insensitivity that he refused to participate further in the ship's activities, but stayed in his bunk until they returned to Anchorage, where he demanded his pay.

"If I'd known you were going to cost me a deckhand," Jack concluded, "I'd have charged you a lot more than $150!"

It took two additional trips to ferry our baggage ashore. Then we watched as the *Tiger's* crew hauled the skiff aboard and raised the tug's anchor. Soon she was underway. Just as she reached the bay's entrance, Jack blew a last lingering blast on her whistle. I hope I never again feel as lonely or hear such a lonesome sound as that final salute. The echoes reverberated from cliff to cliff, sending the gulls into another frenzy of protest.

We had no time to waste. Jack had confirmed my suspicion about the tide. Even as we saddled and packed the horses, the water was visibly beginning to rise. I prayed that the narrow beach we were following around the bend wouldn't already have disappeared. If the rising tide trapped us, we would almost certainly lose our animals and equipment, and might even lose our lives. The rock face was a virtual wall. There was no way we could have scaled it.

By the time we worked our way around the corner, past

the little gravel beach and into a patch of slippery, moss-covered rocks, the tide was within 20 feet of the cliff wall, and coming fast.

We didn't dare hurry the horses because they were seriously weakened. They had been a day without water and without food for nearly three days. Moreover, we knew their reserves had been further depleted by their enforced swim.

Worried about the narrowing trail ahead of us, I left Jan coaxing the horses along while I hurried ahead around the bend, to reconnoiter. As I feared, less than a quarter of a mile ahead, the beach was covered by rising water.

As I came closer, however, half hidden to the left, almost out of sight behind an outcrop on the cliff's face, I found a steep but not quite impassable rocky cleft which opened on a tiny, hillside meadow carpeted with lush grass. A brook bubbled through it. We were saved!

I hurried back to tell Jan the good news. The horses smelled the water and grass, and broke into a clumsy trot toward the tiny mountain meadow I had found.

Jan held them on the beach while I led each, one at a time, over the sharp boulders and into the miniature meadow above the beach. After we and the animals were twenty feet above the beach, we unsaddled the animals and let them graze. We found a small space that was nearly level, and unrolled our bed rolls. We were too tired to eat. We crawled into our sleeping bags and fell into deep slumber.

It was full daylight when we woke about four o'clock the next morning. The horses had eaten all the grass in a radius of about 25 feet from our bed rolls, even nibbling the grass from *under* us as we had rolled back and forth in our sleeping bags during the night. I built a little fire, and while Jan started to fix breakfast, I walked down to the beach to see if the tide had dropped far enough so the beach was passable. It was. I also saw something else.

A bear track, *I'll swear as long as my forearm,* was pressed deep into the wet sand at the water's edge. Looking closer, I saw additional bear tracks, all freshly made. No wonder the horses stuck so close to us!

I hurried back to report what I had found. We decided we had best get moving and perhaps have breakfast a bit later. Realizing we would still be leading the animals rather than riding them, we put the pack saddles on Maud and Dusty, and our riding saddles on Molly and Smoky.

After breaking camp, we continued that terrible journey around the cliff, leading the horses over jagged shale and jumbled boulders slippery with moss. Several times, the horses slipped and nearly fell.

I was leading our little procession, rifle in one hand and Smoky's reins in the other, when Jan, 50 feet behind me, called out, "Look at that!"

I turned to see Dusty upside down, all four feet in the air, rolling back and forth on his pack. No wonder Johnny Vanover wanted so badly to sell him!

Unfortunately, one of the *panniers* hooked to his saddle contained our food; for weeks afterward, we picked grains of coffee from our pancakes. That was his way of telling me I had pulled his saddle cinch too tight. I loosened the cinch, and he never rolled on his pack again.

Gradually, the boulders disappeared, and Jan mounted Molly. It was obvious that she had been ridden before, but probably not often. I climbed aboard Smoky, glad to give my bum leg a rest.

An hour later, we came around the last bend on the beach and to our astonishment, saw a small dock, a huge pile of empty oil drums, a couple of trucks, and several buildings including a very substantial looking home!

What in the world was this?

While we sat there trying to sort this out, an equally befuddled man came out on the porch to greet us.

"Hello there," he called. "Come in and have some coffee."

Still feeling disoriented and wondering if we were dreaming or had suddenly gone mad, we dismounted, and climbed the steps to the porch.

"My name's Carl Williams," the man said, extending his hand, and turning to the pleasant middle-aged woman who joined us on the porch, he added, "and this is my wife, Wilma."

We introduced ourselves and I examined our new friend while we shook hands. Carl was a big man, well over six feet, and he must have weighed 250 pounds. It was hard to tell in the overalls he customarily wore. I was still trying to adjust my thinking to accommodate this new reality.

Later, Carl told us he had seen us coming around the last bend, and was so confused by what he thought was an hallucination that he had gone back to see if he was still in bed dreaming that people on horseback were approaching.

Carl was employed by the Territorial Department of Highways to maintain the 23 mile road known as the Iliamna Portage, which connected the saltwater terminus at Iliamna Bay with the tiny community of Pile Bay at the head of Alaska's largest lake, 80 mile long Lake Iliamna.

Carl operated a small freight business over the portage, mainly hauling diesel fuel in 50 gallon drums over the road. He operated a small, home-made, self-propelled, barge from Pile Bay to ports around the lake; places like Pedro Bay, Newhalen, and Igiguig.

No attempt was made to keep the road open during the winter, but during the spring and summer months, Carl had more work than he could possibly handle. Within a few hours of our arrival, Carl made us a proposition:

If we would remain with them for a month, Carl offered to provide room and board and carry us and our horses to Igiugig at the far end of the lake. He wanted me to drive his truck over the portage, hauling drums of diesel fuel to Pile Bay. He also expected me to help him in his chores as needed. Having glimpsed the harsh realities of travel on foot through the wilderness during our brief excursion along the beach, we readily agreed. After all, Igiugig was within walking distance of Nonvianuk Lake. We spent a happy and productive month in the Williams' household.

Carl was quite different from the colorful old-time miners, trappers, and dog team drivers we had met at Clarks Point. Unlike them, he was a well settled small business man with a growing family. Like them, however, he was tough and enormously resourceful.

He taught me much about self-sufficiency. For the first time, I began to understand why Jan's father's had been so concerned. I was beginning to realize that I had viewed our project through glasses that if not rose tinted, were at least tinged with romantic optimism. Realism was beginning to replace my romantic daydreams.

With Carl's help, I soon began to distinguish between the casual subsistence-level existence that Jacinto and I had experienced at Nonvianuk Lake, the sheltered life Jan and I had led at Clarks Point, and the self-reliant, disciplined way that Carl lived, as he built a home and a business from the ground up. Something we planned to do.

While I learned rudimentary mechanics at Carl's side, and drove loaded fuel trucks over the portage to Lake Iliamna, Jan was absorbing practical information about the peculiarities of wilderness housekeeping from Wilma. But Jan's interests and responsibilities were much broader. In addition to learning the finer nuances of sourdough cookery, Jan also had to keep one eye always peeled on the horses.

By late July, the small alluvial plain around the Williams' homesite was covered with high, thick, grass that reached above our heads. Every day, our horses ventured out of sight into the grass in search of younger, more succulent stems.

One day, however, glancing out the window toward where she had last seen the horses, Jan saw a big brown bear 200 yards away, sliding and crawling down the slope that formed the southern boundary of the grassy plain.

In a moment, the bear was lost to view in the grass. Jan realized instantly that it was after the horses. She knew that if the bear stayed downwind from them, they would have no warning of a pending attack because they wouldn't be able to see him approach.

I'm sure most people would have considered it foolish and even reckless, since brown bears can be very dangerous to man, but without hesitation, Jan pulled on her shoes and plunged into the grass to find and recover the horses before the bear could kill one.

It *was* a reckless thing to do, but it was also an act of consummate bravery for her to plunge unarmed, without visibility, into a thicket of grass to deprive a hungry bear of its dinner. I don't know many people with that sort of courage.

Bear scares were by no means unusual. Iliamna Bay and the adjacent countryside literally crawled with brown bear. This species, better known as Kodiak bear, ranges from the western side of lower Cook Inlet along the Pacific Ocean rim covering all of the Alaska Peninsula, and inland as far as Lake Iliamna and the Kvichak River.

Carl was an inveterate bear hunter, and he worried that my arsenal, composed of a shotgun and a Spanish American War rifle, (the .30/40 Krag), was unequal to the demands of serious bear hunting, so he *gave* me his old bear gun, a Model 95 .405 Winchester.

Less than a week later, I had an opportunity to try it out.

I was sitting on a log behind the house, repairing a pair of shoes I had damaged in the rocks during our desperate march from Diamond Point two weeks earlier, when Carl's youngest boy came running from the house.

"Denny, Denny," he called, "there's a bear out in front after the horses!"

Carl was up on the portage working on the road. So, barefoot, I rushed into the house and scooped up the Winchester and a fistful of cartridges. I couldn't push the front door open because the horses had come up on the porch and held it closed.

I dashed back through the house, out the back door and around the side of the house, loading the rifle on the run. On my right, I saw the horses bunched around the front door. In their hour of distress, Smoky had allowed Dusty into the group. But I didn't see a bear.

The Williams' front yard contained several hundred empty 50 gallon fuel drums, stacked four or five high. To get a better view, I climbed on an empty drum that stood on end next to the pile.

As I straightened up, a bear on the other side of the pile stood on its hind legs. We were eye to eye less than 50 feet apart. It paid no attention to me. Its eyes were fixed on the horses, and it shuffled forward on its hind legs, forelegs out-stretched for balance.

I took careful aim at the spot on its chest where I thought the heart should be, and pulled the trigger.

WHAM!!

I was prepared for a recoil, but I never imagined that the rifle would kick so violently that it would capsize the drum on which I was standing. But there I was, flat on the ground, scrambling to my feet and running away and around the stack of drums. If the bear was still alive, I was sure it would be looking for me.

I needn't have worried. The bear lay on its back, paws still twitching, but it was as dead as a bear can get. That rifle was powerful medicine, and Carl was proud of both of us.

The Model 95 was a lever action rifle, popular around the turn of the century. Teddy Roosevelt took a battery of Model 95s in various calibers with him to Africa on his famous safari. Like the .30/40 Krag, it had a box magazine.

The magazine was a particularly desirable feature. You could load this rifle while you were sprinting for the nearest tree or running around the corner of a building as I had done. To load, you merely snapped open a small door on top of the magazine, poured in a handful of cartridges, let the door snap shut, and operated the lever. Just that fast, you were open for business.

The caliber also deserves special mention. The .405 designation referred to the diameter of the rifle's bore. The cartridges were the same size and shape as small cigars. The rifle would comfortably chamber .410 shotgun shells.

But it was the weight of the slug that stopped bears cold. The bullet weighed nearly 500 grains—about three times as heavy as a standard military load, or twice the heaviest *modern* sporting load. Its range wasn't great, but in the brush, or at close quarters around a pile of oil drums, it was deadly.

In early August, as promised, Carl had the barge ready. Jan and I saddled the horses and rode over the portage road to Pile Bay village on Lake Iliamna, where we boarded it.

The next morning, we left Pile Bay. Although the run to Igiugig took 24 hours, water was not a problem. We were surrounded by potable water, which needed only to be dipped up in a bucket.

As we motored the length of the lake, I was struck by the constantly changing landscape. Pile Bay is a sequestered little inlet at the head of a long bay surrounded by Alpine-like mountains that even in August were snow capped. As we ran

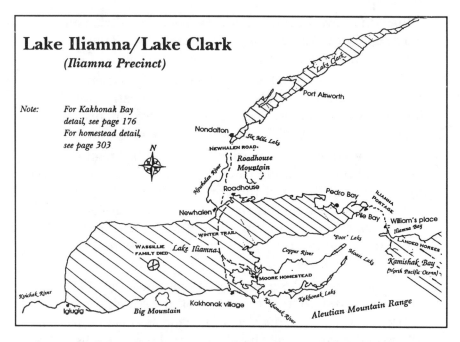

Lake Iliamna/Lake Clark
(Iliamna Precinct)

Note: *For Kakhonak Bay*
            detail, see page 176
            For homestead detail,
            see page 303

down the lake, the mountains fell behind us and the uplands seemed more open, less timbered. Two-thirds of the way to Igiugig, we pasted a very prominent, solitary hill, possibly a thousand feet high. Carl said it was Big Mountain. Beyond Big Mountain, we could see a distant mountain range. The timber near the shore gave way entirely to monotonous brown tundra. We arrived in Igiugig. I looked around while Carl nosed the bow of his barge against the river bank.

The most prominent landmark was a Civil Aviation Authority (now FAA) control tower painted a startling white looming above a small Russian Orthodox church, and a dozen Native huts with their attendant pungent fish racks on the river bank. A small nondescript trading post on an island in the mouth of the river completed the picture.

The horses stepped ashore, and immediately began to graze. Eskimo children, never afraid and always curious, came running. The sight of the horses stopped them.

166

They had never seen horses. At first, they thought we had somehow brought funny looking moose. A couple of the older youngsters spoke some English, and we carefully explained that our horses were like dog teams; that children should not try to pet them or get too close.

While we were talking to the children, a young white couple dressed in light parkas came down to the beach to greet Carl. These were the Stiles, Jack and Barb, who looked after the small emergency landing field for the CAA. We shook hands and chatted in a perfunctory way, but we were too worried now, to feel very sociable.

We belatedly realized that we were in a race with the calendar. It was now mid-August. Freeze-up would begin in less than two months, and we were *still* 50 long miles from Nonvianuk Lake. Moreover, presumably, we had at least ten tons of freight waiting for us in Naknek. Some of that, such as our heavy tools and the stove, would have to be transported to Nonvianuk Lake before we could even begin making preparations for winter. Then there was the problem of hay. We had to have hay to get the horses through the winter. Suddenly, the project we had started so blithely a few months earlier was becoming impossible to accomplish.

Jan, Carl, and I had one more conference. It seemed as if our best bet would be to move the freight upriver as close as possible to Nonvianuk Lake. If I could catch a ride down river, and get that operation started, and then return and, with Jan, take the horses overland, perhaps we could still meet nature's freeze-up deadline.

Carl's next port was the Newhalen roadhouse, about halfway up the lake on the north side. He agreed to take me as far as the roadhouse, but he made it clear that from that point on, I was on my own. Jan would stay with the horses.

Although the CAA people had only recently come into the country, Jack understood the complexity of our problem, and he and Barb invited Jan to stay with them until I returned.

Late the next afternoon, we reached the roadhouse. Art Lee, the owner and operator of the roadhouse, immediately sent word down to the village in Newhalen that I needed a ride down river, and the following morning, I boarded another small barge, and a day later I stepped off the barge in Naknek.

Naknek was not a very big place—in the 1960 census it had a population of 271—but because it was the center of the largest of several Bristol Bay salmon fisheries, it boasted several bars and two coffee shops.

I found Stan Chmiel in a coffee shop. I talked first to the waitress, seeking information about my freight. She had pointed to a man seated nearby eating his lunch. "That's my brother, Stan," she said. "I'm sure he can help you."

I introduced myself to Stan and as we shook hands, we sized each other up. Stan was a clean shaven, stocky, prematurely balding, man in early middle age. He was dressed in typical rural Alaska style in a Pendleton woolen shirt, heavy twill pants held up by broad suspenders, and shoepacs.

I explained we had a small herd of horses at Igiugig being looked after by my wife while I was in Naknek locating our freight, that had arrived sometime during the summer. I told him I hoped to arrange transportation for that freight to a site as close as possible to Nonvianuk Lake.

Misinterpreting the quizzical expression on his face, I explained that I had visited the site during the 1949 Christmas vacation, and knew exactly where we wanted to settle.

"But you don't understand," he said. "Northern Consolidated Airlines got the jump on you. They staked that area over a year ago, and they're building what they call *Kulik Lodge* there, right now!"

Starved Out

S uddenly, we were in a terrible bind. Worse, the planning, effort, money, and that long, difficult, trip with the horses was wasted. We would have been better off had we remained in Montana.

Stan accurately read my stunned expression. "Look," he said, "that's not the only place around. Off the top of my head, I can think of two or three other places that would serve your purpose just as well."

I knew he was trying to cheer me up, but how terribly disappointing it was to think we had lost that beautiful site. Still, that was the way things were, and there was nothing I could do about it.

"What other places?" I asked.

"Well," he said. "Let's make a list of your requirements." He took a pencil from his pocket. "Mary, do you have a piece of paper?"

His sister handed him a sheet of note paper, and he began writing a list.

"If you're going to start a lodge," he began, "you'll need a place where there's lots of game." He began his list by writing **1. Game** "OK, what's next?"

Together, we compiled a reasonably detailed list of perhaps 15 or 20 criteria. We separated those items into two columns headed MUST HAVE and NICE TO HAVE.

We had to have access to a good fish and game population. We had to be close to building timber and firewood. We had to have an abundance of grass so we could make hay for the horses, and we had to be adjacent to a good sized body of water to facilitate air travel.

Everything else fell into the second category. It would be nice to be able to reach the place any time of year, to have water access, to be reasonably isolated but not completely cut off, to have hydroelectric potential, and so forth.

Stan looked at his watch. "It'll take three hours to reach the place I have in mind," he said. "We'd better get going."

I hadn't the least idea where we were headed, but on the way to the pond where Stan kept his plane, he told me we were going to fly up to Lake Iliamna. He said we could stop at Igiugig and pick Jan up so she could help decide if the place he had in mind was suitable for our purpose.

We quickly took off and in minutes were flying in a northeasterly direction up the Kvichak River. This river was not much larger than the Nushagak, but it was home to many more canneries than the Nushagak.

Forty five minutes later, we circled Igiugig. The horses were near the river. I hoped Jan was with them, and would come to the plane.

We landed, and she hurried down to meet us. I told her the bad news, and explained that Stan was going to show us a couple of alternative sites that he considered just as promising. I wanted her to come with us so she could help decide what to do.

Jan climbed into the plane, and we quickly took off. We followed the southern lake shore for about 30 miles. Stan leaned over to shout above the engine's roar, "Looks like it's closed in ahead." He pointed to lowering dark clouds ahead.

"I don't think we're going to be able to make it."

As we flew nearer to the squall, visibility rapidly fell to zero. Stan banked the plane away. He shook his head. "You know what they say about old bold pilots," he shouted. "Looks like we're going to have to give it a miss."

Minutes later, we landed a second time at Igiugig. This time, he dug into his map case and pulled out an aeronautical chart. "I couldn't show you the place on the ground," he said, "but this is what it looks like on the chart."

He pointed to a large bay on the south side of Lake Iliamna that was labeled "Kakhonak Bay." A large peninsula shaped something like a partly eaten pear extended about eight miles from the eastern side of the bay. The narrow part of the peninsula next to the mainland was further reduced in size, because a small, narrow bay or lake—it was hard to tell which from the chart—extended like a finger from the sheltered inside waters of Kakhonak Bay almost, but not quite, severing the peninsula's connection with the mainland. That was the spot Stan had in mind.

There was grass there, plenty of game, wonderful fishing, a good quantity of timber. And the post office and store were directly across the lake.

Jan nodded. "Let's go for it," she said. Thus, the really important decisions in life are made.

I flew back to Naknek with Stan. During the next couple of days, I was introduced to a bewildering number of people in Naknek, among them, a very special, middle-aged, Aleut widow named Emma Nicolet.

By an extraordinary coincidence, I had read about her and her remarkable family in a tattered copy of *Reader's Digest,* when I was aboard a troopship bound from California to Hawaii in late 1944.

The article focused primarily on her daughter as "A Most Unforgettable Character," but Emma's powerful presence as a self-sufficient widow, single-handedly raising three children by trapping and fishing in desolate Port Heiden on the Alaska Peninsula, dominated the story.

I wonder, now, what effect that article may have had on my subconscious interest in Alaska. I mean, how many magazine articles do most of us remember after seven years and a major war? Not many. It was a rare privilege to meet Emma Nicolet.

After we chatted for a short while, and Emma learned something of our plans, she abruptly asked, "You like to buy my dog team?"

I was momentarily speechless. She didn't wait for my reply, but explained that she had retired from trapping, and since she was then living in Naknek, she had no need for dogs. "I t'ink you be good to my boys; I sell 'um cheap," she concluded.

I definitely needed a dog team, but I had so many more urgent needs that I had not given dogs much thought. In the back of my mind, I suppose, based on my experience at Clarks Point, I had expected to acquire village castoffs. The flaw in that reasoning, of course, is that there was no village.

Controlling my excitement, I asked, "How many dogs do you have, and how much are you asking?"

"I have t'ree. Feefty dolla fo' each dog."

A well trained dog team for $150? Fantastic! My few dollars were vanishing like a snow drift in July, but I couldn't pass this up. "Let's look at them," I said.

Those dogs were special. They were malamutes, weighing perhaps 80 or 90 pounds. The leader, Buck, was considerably older than his team mates. I asked about his age.

She said, "Buck, him maybe eight years." Nodding toward the other two, she added, "them boys young dog, maybe t'ree." She then told me the two wheel dogs were named Bill and Pan. She gave me a thumbnail character sketch of each.

"Bill like young puppy. Him like to play. No make trouble. Pan like old man. No play. But him no make trouble, either."

Emma had taken good care of them. Even though it was mid-August, when the cumulative neglect in local dog yards always became obvious, these animals were clean, in good flesh, and very happy to see Emma. I understood her desire to find them a good home.

Emma's "boys"

I handed her the money and promised to take good care of them. I had a dog team again.

Then I contacted Sonny Groat, owner and captain of a small surplus LCVP or "Higgins boat," a landing craft like the one that carried me ashore at Iwo. He agreed to transport my freight, which had arrived on the summer boat, and my new dog team, upriver to Igiugig where we would stop for Jan and load the horses, then on to Kakhonak.

As usual, my ointment contained a large, rather nasty fly. We had placed a big order with Sears, Roebuck shortly before leaving Montana for roofing paper, window sashes, nails, hinges, barbed wire, and so forth, with instructions to ship it to Naknek via Alaska Steamship. I had also ordered a minimal amount of lumber. I expected those orders would have arrived on the same ship as our "immigrant's movables."

However, when I collected our mail, I found two letters from Sears. They both contained the same message. "We regret to inform you. . .temporarily out of stock. . .shipment in 30 days. . ."

For us, there was no practical difference between 30 days and nine months. If you missed the last boat of the season, which Sears had done, you'd have to somehow get through the winter without it. Other than that, things went very well.

We stopped in Igiugig, loaded the horses, then traveled up the lake. It wasn't until we were approaching the site we had selected that Sonny confessed that he had never been there before. However, his deckhand, Jackie Drew, was from Iliamna. Guided by Jackie's recollection, we carefully felt our way among dozens of small islands, cautiously watching for submerged reefs, until we reached a steep gravel beach. "I think this is it," Jackie said.

"The knoll rose about 15 feet"

Sonny shut his engine down. Rifles in hand, we stepped ashore. There was disappointingly little grass, but we found a well defined trail, and followed it through stunted spruce, over a low rise, across a short stretch of muskeg, and came to a little knoll overlooking the finger-like bay on the opposite side of the peninsula. Although it seemed longer, the trail, or "portage" as the Eskimos called it, was only about 400 yards.

The knoll rose about 15 feet above the lake. It formed part of a ridge that continued to rise to our left up a heavily wooded hill over 200 feet high. There was an abundance of cabin timber on the land surrounding the bay in front of us.

We quickly retraced our steps to the boat.

Jan and I walked away from the barge. We needed a few moments to sort things out. We were confronted by what amounted to an irreversible life-or-death decision.

We were very worried that there wasn't more grass, but I don't think either of us fully comprehended that the horses simply could not survive the winter without hay. On the other hand, we were sufficiently concerned about it that we pressed Jackie to suggest an alternative site.

He suggested a site in Copper River, two miles east of the portage, but our efforts to reach it were blocked by a barrier reef in the mouth of Copper River. Sonny wasn't inclined to fool around in unknown waters. He laid down the law. It was either the portage or back to Naknek.

In the long run, it was unfortunate that neither of us thought of wintering in Naknek. Instead, we unloaded the horses and dogs. The four of us set to work, lifting, pushing, and carrying things. By dark, the beach was littered with barrels, crates, boxes, bed springs, agricultural tools, a stove, and sled lumber.

We pitched our tent, and set the bed springs and mattress on the ground inside, next to a box on which the Coleman stove resided. Our camp was made.

The next morning, I shook hands with Sonny and Jackie. The little barge backed away from the beach, turned, and we watched it out of sight. Just before it went behind an island, Jackie stepped out of the wheel house with their foghorn and blew a long farewell salute.

It was some time before I got used to the idea that we had reached the end of that particular trail, and that we were now entirely on our own. We had no boat or radio, and other than Stan, Sonny and Jackie, nobody even knew where we were. Here, there was no Carl Williams living around the corner. Our nearest neighbors, as it turned out, were 12 miles away at an isolated Eskimo village. Then, however, both they and we were ignorant of each other's presence.

When I think about the box we were in, I marvel at Jan's courage and loyalty. Alaska had been almost entirely my idea.

175

She had followed my lead without regard to the hardships we faced, and even without overt concern that in a harsh and extremely physical environment that did not forgive the weak or disabled, she was relying on a person with a severe physical handicap to do the heavy lifting.

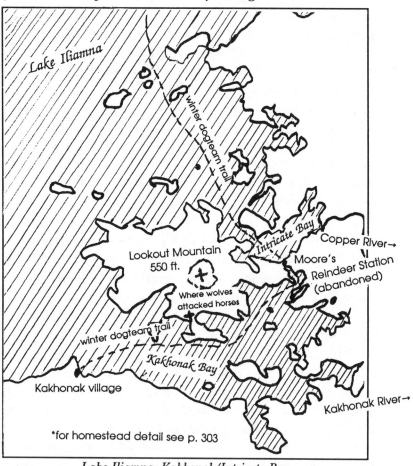

Lake Iliamna, Kakhonak/Intricate Bay

Unfortunately, it rained almost every day. We were careful to avoid trampling what little grass we found, hoping it would dry so we could make some hay. Meanwhile, we saddled

Smoky and Dusty, and rode for miles, looking for grass. Other than the small amount at our campsite and an equal amount across the portage, there just wasn't any.

Instead, the rocky soil was covered with Arctic tundra. Here and there were tiny islands of brush—alder, swan and goose berries, high bush cranberries, and a few birches.

As we explored our new home, I began to understand why we had seen so much grass at Clarks, and why there was so little here. The game trails, especially those made by larger animals, offered a mute explanation.

Arctic tundra is composed of a dozen species of dwarfed plants and lichens. It can be resilient and spongy in some places and in others it might be nothing more than a thin surface layer of lichens and reindeer moss on rock. But everywhere, it grew on a very irregular surface. In short, tundra is hard going for man or beast.

That simple fact probably accounts for the game trails. Humans aren't the only animals that seek the least difficult path. After countless generations of hooves and paws have smoothed the trail, why walk elsewhere?

Invariably, those trails were overgrown with grass. Apparently, grass replaces disturbed tundra. That's why there was so much grass around the buildings at Clarks Point.

Unfortunately, the tundra here was little disturbed except for an acre or so of grass where we had landed. Sad to say, we did not find any meadows. Instead, we found rolling uplands carpeted with tundra that was dotted with islands of deciduous growth.

White and black spruce were the only conifers. Both species were short, stunted trees. White spruce grew on well drained slopes, in gullies, and places somewhat sheltered from the wind. The largest of those trees were two feet or more in diameter at the base, but in less than 40 feet, the trunk often tapered to six inches. These were majestic trees, however, when compared with black spruce, which were found in the cold, wet, acid soils of the muskeg, and seldom grew larger than Christmas trees.

Although our search for grass was unsuccessful, we also had to provide for the three dogs I had bought from Emma Nicolet. And we had to find a reliable source of food for ourselves.

Knowing that Lake Iliamna is the world's largest red salmon nursery, we had brought a scrap of old salmon gill-netting with us. We saw dozens of schools of spawning salmon swimming along the lake shore. But we needed a way to set and retrieve the net.

Lacking a boat, our best bet was to rig a running line. But that meant I had to find a way of setting an anchored buoy and pulley 100 feet or so off the beach. The running line was a light rope 200 feet long that would run from the beach out to the pulley fastened to the buoy, and back to the beach.

I made a temporary boat from one of the larger crates—a wooden box three feet wide by perhaps four feet long and 18 inches deep—by wrapping a tarpaulin around its bottom and sides, bringing the ends into the box. It was crude and wobbly.

Judging by the beach's slope, I guessed the water might be 25 or 30 feet deep 100 feet out from the shore. I carefully tied a heavy chunk of cast iron to a 40 foot piece of anchor rope, and spliced the other end of the rope to a five gallon jerry can to which I tied the pulley. A light 200 foot rope running through that pulley completed the rig.

I loaded this apparatus in my box-boat, the buoy and rope on the bottom of the pile and the anchor on top. Then I pulled my strange little craft into deeper water and gingerly stepped aboard, taking care that I wasn't standing or kneeling on any of the rigging.

With exquisite care, I gently pushed myself away from the

shore, using a board for a paddle. Jan stood on the beach, anxiously watching while she slowly paid out the doubled running line piled at her feet.

She seized the end of the line as it slipped through her fingers, and yelled, "That's it. You have all the line!"

I put the paddle to one side and gently lifted the anchor over the side. I should have eased it down to the bottom, but my craft was leaking badly, and I had to hurry. I dropped the anchor. I wasn't quick enough. My boat was immediately unbalanced, and rolled heavily in the opposite direction. In a moment, it rolled over.

Lake Iliamna is glacier-fed. The water temperature in the deeper bays never rose above 50°. I sputtered and gasped at the shock of the sudden cold, and instinctively bent over in the water, struggling to pull off my boots.

My left boot fell away. I had to come up for air. Then, taking a deep breath, I bent over again and tugged on my right boot. That was tough. Because of the ankle surgery the previous year, my foot and ankle had lost flexibility, and the ankle tended to swell to roughly twice its normal size.

Luckily, I had the flotation of the wood in my box-boat to support me while I worked to get that damned boot off and regain my breath. The boot finally fell away, following its mate to the bottom of the lake, and now, nearly paralyzed by hypothermia, I feebly swam ashore.

We had our running line. That evening, Jan ran the net out, and the next morning, we had a dozen big salmon piled on the beach.

Although we hung those first salmon in the bushes to dry, this wasn't at all satisfactory, and I soon cut posts and poles, and built a fish rack, where we hung the fish to dry after they were headed, gutted and split.

The gravel beach marked the edge of a small shallow bay. An enclosed pond occupied the western portion of the bay.

Our first camp. The dead sea gull on the fish rack was a scarecrow.

We quickly discovered that a trickling water course fed into the pond. Curious, we followed the stream inland. Not more than 300 yards upstream, we came upon a second, secluded pond, 100 yards long by half that wide, which was hidden between two steep ridges.

We explored further and discovered another stream entering the pond at its opposite end. The brush was too thick here for the horses, so we tied them, hiked up the gully, and topping a short rise, came upon a large beaver dam holding back a small round lake, perhaps half mile in diameter.

It was getting dark and it was very still. Ducks were feeding in the shallows near us. We clearly heard their splashing and nervous chatter as they dove for succulent roots. Suddenly, somewhere out of sight, we heard the warning splash of a beaver's tail. It must have seen a fox or some other predator. There wasn't enough wind to carry our scent to them. On the far side of the lake, we heard the lonely whistle of a loon. It was a magic moment. Suddenly, I felt as if I belonged.

We had two calendars. One hung in the tent. The other was Roadhouse Mountain, rising 3,200 feet 30 miles away, behind the Iliamna roadhouse (postoffice, store and airstrip) across the lake. Although the calendar said it was only September fifth, the snow was already nearly halfway down the mountain's sides. That snow line was a constant reminder that the brief autumn season was fast drawing to a close.

Unless we wanted to spend the winter in a tent, which certainly wouldn't have much to recommend it, we could no longer wait for the grass to dry. We had to build a cabin.

Where should we build? Obviously, we had to build near our present location because winter was closing in, and because we couldn't move our heavy equipment far.

We had to be close to a year-round water supply. That ruled out the little feeder streams we had seen. We had to build near brush to provide firewood, and timber suitable for cabin construction. Another requirement was that we be sheltered from the northerly winter winds.

The only site we knew that seemed to meet these requirements was on top of the little knoll across the portage. We were excited to be making permanent plans, and although it was beginning to get dark, we walked across the portage to take another look at our proposed cabin site.

The knoll was as near perfect for our purposes as anything could be. We were facing in a southerly direction as we looked over the bay (or lake; we still weren't sure which). The north winds would be behind us on the other side of the portage. The lake was perhaps 100 feet away down a 15 foot slope. That was not an inconsequential consideration when you reflect that every drop of water we used would have to be carried up that slope. The hillside to our left fairly bristled with cabin timber, and there was an abundance of birch and alder within easy reach.

We knew that while our cabin would be a permanent structure, within a reasonable period of time, I hoped to build the lodge we had come to establish, and I had to make sure I saved the best site for that. However, I also realized that the requirements for the lodge site might be considerably different than those for our cabin.

The next morning, after considerable trial and error (neither of us having harnessed horses before), we harnessed Maud. Then we shackled the slip scraper to the harness, and led Maud across the portage to the building site.

The slip scraper was a digging tool about the size and shape of a large, shallow wheelbarrow bowl. It had handles like a wheelbarrow, but instead of a wheel and legs, it was fitted with a stout steel yoke which looked like a giant steel wishbone. The ends of the yoke pivoted on steel pins welded to the sides of the bowl. The front of the yoke was fastened to the horse's harness.

The operator held the slip's handles as he walked behind the horse. When he wished to load the slip, the operator simply raised the handles and allowed the lip of the tool to bite into the soil, as the horse walked forward. When the slip was loaded, the operator simply dropped the handles and let the tool skid to where the operator wished to dump it, which he did by simply flipping the handles up while the bowl was still moving.

That's the theory. I know this seems like harmless fun, but Maud had only one forward speed, and it was hard for me to keep up. I imagine there are easier ways to learn how to handle a draft horse and/or slip scraper than stumbling behind a determined horse with lines looped around your neck while you dig a foundation in rocky soil. The first time I tried it, the damn thing bit too deeply into the ground, and the scraper flipped over, carrying me with it. After that, I quickly became more cautious, and tried to avoid using my weight to hold the handles down, but there wasn't really any way to prevent the damn thing from accidentally flipping when, as frequently happened, the cutting lip hit a buried rock. As primitive as this seems, in less than a week, Maud and I excavated about 200 cubic yards of dirt; and dug a hole approximately two feet deep. The foundation was ready.

Then Jan and I took our crosscut saw, axes, and wedges, into the woods and began cutting logs. I had had some experience as a boy with logging operations and crosscut saws, but this was all new to Jan. However, she quickly picked up the fluid, reciprocal rhythm two people develop as they pull their saw back and forth, making it sing as it cuts ever deeper through a tree trunk.

We took turns driving the team when they were skidding the logs out of the woods. The drover walked beside the load, reins in hand. Again, the horse's fast pace caused the logs to bounce around a good bit.

Late one afternoon—this was our last load for the day—the team and I were moving through the last heavy brush before emerging in the clearing, when suddenly an unseen bull moose standing silently in the brush less *than 30 feet away* bellowed a passionate mating call! *My God!* His roaring bellow sounded as if he was standing at my shoulder. I must have jumped a foot. The horses didn't like it much, either!

This was clearly a case of mistaken identity, but I wasn't sure how I could explain that to him without someone getting hurt. A bull moose in rut is a dangerous animal, and I had an awful vision of the moose attempting to mount one of the mares and getting tangled in the harness. There was no possibility of a happy ending if that happened.

Jan was standing near the pile of logs. I yelled to her to run across the portage and get the Krag. I thought I should stay with the horses and try to defend them if that was possible.

Jan ran across the muskeg and disappeared on the trail leading to our camp. She returned in less than five minutes. Then it was her turn to stay with the horses, while I went looking for the moose.

I searched through the brush where he had been, and circled around as I imagined he might have done when he was trying to get the wind. Nothing. After about 15 minutes of quietly combing the woods, I returned to the knoll where Jan was standing. Then I realized she was looking at something. It was the moose standing in our portage trail on the edge of the brush, about 200 yards away. The failing light reflected off his magnificent rack—I never saw a bigger one—causing it almost to glow.

I didn't want to kill him. There was no way we could have preserved the meat, and it would have been wasted. On the other hand, I didn't want him beating up on the horses that night, either. I hoped to drive him away. I'm a good shot—I qualified as a high expert in the Marine Corps—and I took careful aim, holding for the top curve of his rack. I squeezed off a round. I'm pretty sure I nicked his horn. He jumped a bit, then turned and walked into the brush.

He swam across that little bay in front of the building site the next morning. I watched closely as he climbed out of the water. He didn't seem to be any the worse for the experience, although he may have had one hell of a headache.

I don't want to sound too noble about this, or deny that I was tempted. We certainly could have used a change in our diet. We had been eating fish twice a day for a month, but even that abundance was coming to an end.

Since all Pacific salmon die shortly after they spawn, and the spawning season had ended a month earlier, the quality of the fish we were catching had been steadily deteriorating. The fish's flesh color had long since changed from bright reddish-orange to a pasty white. Now, even the brilliant spawning skin colors were fading; from a bright green head and scarlet body, to a dull, lackluster gray. Many females had worn away parts of their tail digging nests for their eggs, but now, some fish were exhibiting a more general decay.

Once, we caught a loon in the net. Jan boiled it a long time in a vain effort to tenderize it, but no matter how long she cooked it, eating it was like trying to eat a rubber ball. You might have driven a nail into it, but you could barely break the skin with a fork! It was simply inedible. Perhaps it was retribution for the sea gull I had sold to the nasty third mate at Clarks Point.

I was too driven by that steadily descending snow line on Roadhouse Mountain to take time out from building our cabin, to go hunting. Then, one morning, a small miracle occurred. I had just stepped out of the tent and was standing near the fish rack, waiting for Jan, when *thump!* Something hit the ground immediately behind me. I wheeled around and discovered a dead spruce hen—a species of wood grouse—on the ground. It was freshly dead, but it bore no talon marks or wounds. I have no idea where it came from, other than to suppose an owl might have dropped it, or that it had suffered a fatal heart attack.

It didn't matter. We gratefully accepted the gift, and enjoyed our first bite of meat in a month, even though the little bird, scarcely larger than a robin, yielded just a single morsel for each of us.

The cabin was originally planned to consist of two rooms of equal size, in a building approximately 18 by 30 feet. However, we ran out of logs and time before winter overtook us. The room on the left, facing the water, became our living quarters. The room on the right, which was only partially finished, became a cold weather cache, windbreak, and barn.

The largest trees we could find yielded 36 foot logs. Those were adequate for the back wall, common to both rooms. The three perpendicular walls required 25 foot logs. These had less taper, and were correspondingly easier to work. The front wall of the enclosed room required only 24 foot logs. The front wall of the windbreak was constructed of vertical poles, designed to keep most of the wind and snow outside.

We built the cabin in layers. The first logs were peeled, then dragged into position in the excavation, notched with an axe, and fitted together. The second tier followed the first. There was so much taper in the logs—some of the longer logs were 30 inches at the butt and eight inches at the top—that I had to reverse them on each layer. The resulting joints where the sides met the back wall were almost grotesque.

185

"Cut the doors and windows..."

Those green logs were slick, and the larger ones were very heavy. Raising them was especially tricky. After each was peeled, we positioned it on the ground parallel to the wall it would join. Maud, in harness, would pull from the opposite side of the building on a rope that was tied to the log. If all went well, the log would obediently slide up stout poles leaning against the building. When things did not go well, which was most of the time, all I can say is that we were awfully lucky neither of us was seriously hurt.

When the walls were about seven feet high, we cut the windows and door with the crosscut saw. I felt a warm little glow of satisfaction after cutting the doorway, as, for the first time, I walked into the building. That was a major milestone. Up to then, when I needed to recover a tool or adjust a log or do something else inside the building, I had to climb over the wall to get inside, then climb back out.

The logs were in place by mid-October. The snow on Roadhouse Mountain had nearly reached its base, and there was frost in the tent every morning. Luckily, it had not yet begun to snow, but the salmon were nearly gone. The net continued to supply trout, an occasional pike, and once, a whitefish.

We were discovered by our neighbors around the first of October, shortly before freeze-up. We were in our tent eating lunch when we heard the unaccustomed sound of human voices from the direction of the portage trail. What on earth?

Two stocky Eskimos emerged from the brush. One was wearing a summer parka, the other a worn plaid jacket. Both were wearing hip boots rolled below the knee. One man carried a rifle, the other a shotgun. Since they came from the direction of the partly built cabin, they knew someone was here, but they took us completely by surprise.

The younger of the two men, whose name, I later learned, was Feeny Andrew, was less shy and spoke better English than his companion.

Who were we? Where had we come from? Why were we here? It was only later, when I understood how out of character such direct questions were for normally polite and reserved Eskimos, that I realized how startled they must have been to find us there.

After that initial visit, we saw villagers quite frequently. They began bringing gifts of food, mostly meat, for which we were very grateful.

Our race against the first snow was compounded because the days were becoming noticeably shorter. By the middle of October, full daylight was delayed until 8:30 in the morning, and dusk began to fall by 5:00 in the afternoon.

It was time to build the roof. When I was in Naknek arranging for the dogs and freight, I had bought several old cannery windows and ten pounds of spikes to replace some of the materials Sears had failed to deliver. Unfortunately, I was unable to find roofing paper.

Therefore, I split some fifty poles, which I laid side by side from the ridge pole to the cabin eves. These, I covered with

Feeny Andrew

dry grass. Then Jan and I dug squares of tundra and placed that on top of the grass. We weren't any too soon. The ground was freezing. It was five degrees above zero the morning we decided to move.

It was the fifth of November, and I had yet to chink the walls or install the windows and build a door.

But we were desperate, because our tent was no longer habitable. Whenever Jan cooked a meal, the water vapor condensed on everything, coating the inside of the tent, our clothes, tools, books, everything, with a fine glaze of ice. In addition, every morning when we woke, the inside of the tent was white with frost from our breath.

By contrast, even though the warm air the big wood range in the cabin generated immediately dissipated, the moisture it created did not condense on our immediate surroundings, and at least we could maintain a zone of warmth in the stove's immediate vicinity.

While I used the lumber I salvaged from the crates for the window frames and door, Jan collected dry moss. After the windows and door were framed and closed in, I began to close the spaces between the logs with the moss Jan had collected.

Meanwhile, the poor horses were ranging further and further afield in search of food. We comforted ourselves with the rationalization that after all, they were Montana horses, accustomed to foraging in severe winter temperatures. We even talked ourselves into believing that Sear's failure to deliver the wire fencing was a disguised blessing. Since we couldn't control their movements, they were free to find the best opportunity they could for survival. But I hadn't reckoned on the wolves.

Dusty, on the other hand, knew all about wolves. Early in the fall, he had followed the other horses, staying the discreet distance behind

At last a roof over our heads!

them that Smoky required. However, when the wolves began howling in the late autumn evenings, Dusty left the herd, and sought the company of humans.

It was the first of December; we were down to about six hours of daylight, and the nightly temperatures were regularly dipping well below zero, before I drove the last caulking in place to seal the walls.

The Eskimos had made several visits following their original one. During one of his earlier visits, Feeny had told us he had seen the horses on the shore from his boat. Later, shortly before freeze-up, we were terribly shocked and saddened when, Feeny shyly reported that one of the black horses had been killed by wolves. He hadn't seen the kill, but another hunter from the village had found bits of hide and a hoof near the outer end of the peninsula, across the bay from the village. If one was gone, they were all gone. The only survivor was Dusty.

During freeze-up, after the ice was strong enough to bear the weight of a wolf pack, we were subjected to almost nightly visits by the wolves. I think they were primarily interested in Dusty, although the dogs, chained in the dog yard next to the house, always stopped making a fuss when the wolves approached the cabin, and instead hid in their houses. They knew that hungry wolves would eat dogs.

Jan and Dusty

At first, I failed to appreciate the meaning of certain night sounds; the frenzied barking of the dogs, followed by silence and an occasional muffled whimper, and the sound of Dusty in the windbreak nervously stamping his feet. But the wolf tracks in the snow outside the cabin the following morning told me what I needed to know. The next time I heard that sequence of sounds, I joined Dusty in the windbreak, rifle in hand, hoping for a shot at one of the wolves. The federal government was then paying a $50 bounty on wolves, and the hide, in prime condition, was worth an additional $35.

The animals returned, night after night, and I caught occasional glimpses by star light of dark shadows moving rapidly in the snow past the cabin, but I never succeeded in shooting one. Eventually, they moved on.

Dusty was a survivor because he ate almost anything. Although nature hadn't equipped him for it, somewhere, Dusty had even learned to browse like a moose. I remember how surprised I was when I first saw him strip a willow of its leaves and bark. He would also eat table scraps. Jan always fried three or four extra sourdough pancakes for Dusty.

Some days, he got a whole pan full of hotcakes, because Jan and I were then still too squeamish to eat pancakes after she had fished one or two dead shrews out of the batter. We had discovered that any lump in the sourdough batter was suspicious, because more often than not it turned out to be a little ball of fur.

The shrews were everywhere. Attracted by the relatively more congenial temperatures and (for them) abundant food supplies the cabin offered, we were inundated by literally hundreds, perhaps thousands, of the lively, squealing, bickering, inquisitive little animals. They raced back and forth across our bed all night, and we quickly learned to turn our shoes over and give them a good shake while getting dressed in the morning. Shrews are capable of delivering a painful and mildly poisonous bite. While Jan was preparing our meals at the counter next to the stove, I grew accustomed to the periodic **thump** of a large wooden spoon she kept handy, landing on an overly bold shrew.

By this time, the ice on our side of the lake was thick enough to permit safe dog sled travel, and the men from the village began stopping by on a regular basis. Eskimos must be the most pragmatic people in the world. When Feeny realized that we were infested with shrews, he told me how to build a shrew trap.

Kerosene, Blazo (white gas), and aviation gas came in five gallon tin containers that were neatly packaged, two containers to each stout wooden box. As you can imagine, those boxes and cans—"gas boxes" and "gas cans"—when emptied, had many uses. Feeny introduced me to a new one.

Following his instructions, I cut the top out of an empty can. Then I dug a hole in the cabin floor—this was easy since the floor was dirt—and sunk the can in the hole until its top was just level with the floor. After I firmed the earth around the top of the can, we had a 14 inch tin-lined hole in the floor measuring ten inches across at the top. That was the trap. The trigger was a slender stick 11 inches long that was laid across the top of the can. The bait was a piece of meat (anything edible would do) tied to the middle of the stick with a piece of thread.

The trap was a wonderful invention. It was both self-baiting and self-emptying. At night, Jan and I would lie in bed listening to our trap conduct business. Attracted by the bait, the greedy little animals would run out on the stick, which would roll under their weight, dropping them into the can.

Then, we'd hear a muffled thump followed by a startled squeal as the trap claimed a new victim. We'd hear additional squeals and the sound of serious little claws scratching fruitlessly against the tin walls. Then silence, followed by another thump. This may bother some animal-rights people who worry about scientific experiments involving rats, but the more thumps we heard, the wider our smiles became. The trap was even self-emptying. Shrews have an extraordinary metabolism and are highly cannibalistic. In the morning, we'd see one fat shrew in the trap and a dozen tails.

The village people soon learned about Jan's profession. When they had a serious medical problem, she was often consulted. In exchange, as Feeny had, they tutored me in woodcraft and fur trapping techniques, and gave us meat from time to time. In that way, we gradually met Pete Mike, Little Joe, Nick G, Pete Andrew, Simeon Zachar, and Simeon Wassilly, most of the adult male population.

In the meanwhile, I built our sled, using the lumber I had brought from Montana and scraps of rawhide I begged from Feeny. Then I established a small trap line. It wasn't very productive, partly because I was a poor trapper, but also because the local fur bearing predators had such easy pickings, they could afford to disdain my baits.

Animal populations usually maintain a stable existence within a subtle framework of checks and balances. However, because some rodents, especially mice, rabbits, and lemmings, are so well endowed with reproductive capacity, the slightest environmental wrinkle—a flareup of distemper among the foxes, for example—and it's "Katie bar the door!"

Like the shrews, the local population of snowshoe rabbits—scientifically known as varying hares—was nearing the top of an extraordinarily powerful population explosion.

I hadn't realized we were overrun with rabbits until Mother Nature played an awful trick on them. They changed color before the snows began. During that brief interval, it seemed that every bush sheltered at least one, sometimes several, rabbits. The poor animals were blissfully unaware that their bright white coats contrasted as sharply against their drab surroundings as a neon sign on a dark rainy night.

My old muzzle-loader was a perfect rabbit gun. Until I learned to snare rabbits, I needed one. I had exhausted our meager supply of .22 cartridges. Luckily, I had a good supply of black powder and several hundred caps. I melted lead from the net's lead line, and molded .31 caliber balls.

We gradually settled into our new, very restricted, life. The days were short. We had little kerosene for our lamp, and usually blew the lamp out right after supper. We also rationed the hours—no more than one hour a night—we spent sitting in the dark listening to the old fashioned tube radio, which required 15-pound batteries. I spent most of the daylight hours out of doors running the trap line, cutting wood, or fishing and hunting, desperately trying to augment our minuscule food supply. Jan freely pitched in with the outside chores. And because she had two sound legs, she was the better water carrier.

Log cabins are tinderboxes, and I had a horror of fire. We always allowed the fire in the stove to go out at night. I was afraid that if we burned out during the coldest nights, when I was most tempted to keep the fire going, and lost our outdoor clothing in the process, we wouldn't have survived to reach Kakhonak village.

Because we had no heat during the night, by morning the inside of the cabin was downright chilly. By tacit agreement, possibly because I spent nearly all the daylight hours out of doors, Jan pampered me. She almost always rose first and started the kitchen fire. She even gave me a cup of coffee while I was still in bed. I remember one morning when I dozed off before drinking my coffee, and waking an hour later, I found that a sheet of ice had formed in the cup.

During the winter, the sod roof provided excellent protection. On the rare occasions when the cabin became overly warm, the frozen sod would begin to thaw, and we would have a taste of what we could expect in the spring. But mostly, we were reasonably comfortable.

Christmas came. Our celebration was meager, and we missed our children very, very much. Two weeks later, on January seventh, the Kakhonak people treated us to our first real *Slavik*, or Russian Christmas celebration.

We had celebrated Russian Christmas with our students at Clarks Point, but the *Slavik* practiced in that heavily Catholic community was little more than a village open house.

Here, ten or twelve dog teams came racing around the corner of our little bay and up to the cabin. A brief flurry of gunfire—we later learned this was to drive the devils away from the roof—and the celebrants, every man in the village, filed into the cabin.

Two of them reverently laid an alter cloth on our table, and placed several holy pictures on it. Then, three men holding "stars," stepped forward. These were light wooden frames built in the form of classic five-pointed stars mounted on a freely spinning axle and elaborately decorated with tinsel and pieces of colored Christmas tree garlands. Each bore a holy picture pasted on its hub.

The congregation then began to sing Christmas songs. The men holding the stars twirled them in time with the music.

At intervals, the star bearers would change direction and twirl their stars in an opposite direction.

It was a serious ceremony, and we felt honored that they had chosen to share their Christmas with us. Knowing how straitened our circumstances were, they declined our offer of coffee, and instead, after wishing us a Merry Christmas, they filed outside and left.

The cupboard was really bare! Although we had learned to order large quantities of food in the fall when we were living at Clarks Point, any shortages were easily made up simply by asking Henry to open the store. Plus, we had the benefit of easy credit from Mrs. Bradford.

Unfortunately, we had neither at Kakhonak. I had only been able to buy a small quantity of basic supplies in Naknek, because we were unknown in the community, and people seemed skeptical about our ability to survive. Therefore, we had begun running out of things—including coffee and tobacco—weeks earlier.

Cigarette smokers are a disgusting and shameless crowd. I rolled cigarettes, using Velvet pipe tobacco, when I could get it, or any other brand when I couldn't. When I realized it would be a while before I could buy more tobacco, I had begun saving my cigarette butts and had rerolled the unburned tobacco at least twice, rationing myself to one cigarette a day. That's the mark of a true addict.

Accordingly, as the men filed outside, I spoke quietly to Feeny, and asked when he would be traveling to the roadhouse. I explained that we needed supplies, but that I didn't feel ready to tackle a 30-mile crossing on my own.

He said, "Maybe I go roadhouse nex' week. We see 'bout the weather. Maybe ice in the middle still soft; better we go by Ten Mile Island."

I said, "OK. First good weather next week I'll come to the village. Maybe we can go then."

He nodded his assent.

The following Tuesday was a perfect day. The temperature was about −10°, and the air was barely moving. After a hearty breakfast, I harnessed the dogs. Then I gathered the letters we had written during the previous three months to relatives, friends, and the government complaining about wolves killing our horses. As daylight was beginning to color the eastern sky, I left for the village. This was serious business. It would be my first overnight trip away from the cabin, and Jan's first night alone.

The dogs quickly settled into a fast trot. Buck needed no guidance. He was following a well established trail which was identical to the path a boat would take in summer. It followed the peninsula's shore for about six miles, then turned slightly toward the southwest and headed for the village, a further six miles away.

I stood on the runners, enjoying the feeling of movement, and clapped my hands to encourage the dogs. They always enjoyed the chirping and clapping and other sounds I made. Clapping was especially effective in speeding their cadence.

I tired of standing, and swung a leg over the side of the sled and climbed in. I sat until I began to feel chilled. Then, I climbed out and standing on one runner, I scooted until I warmed up. This was good going, and the dogs made an easy five or six miles an hour. Soon I saw the village, straight ahead. White plumes of mingled smoke and steam rose straight into the air from a dozen stovepipes. This was the perfect day to cross the lake.

I drove the team through the village. The chained dogs, seeing my team, set up a terrific din, leaping against their chains, giving every indication of incipient violence, but it was all show.

I stopped in front of Feeny's cabin, and chained Buck to a pole sticking out of the frozen ground. Feeny was ready and waiting for me. "You want coffee?" he asked, his round face creased by a wide grin.

I shook my head. "We have a long way to go," I said.

Feeny nodded, and began shrugging his way into his bulky trail parka. "I hook up de dogs," he said, adding, "you wait here, stay warm."

I sat on a gas box by the kitchen table and glanced around the tiny cabin. There wasn't much to see. The kitchen table, two chairs, the gas box on which I was sitting, an Aladdin lamp in the middle of the table, and a small wood cook stove completed the furnishings. A calendar, pictures cut from magazines, and a holy picture over the bed decorated the walls. I absently watched Feeny's shy wife, Madronna, bustle around the cabin, first soothing the fussy baby, then putting another piece of wood into the stove's firebox. The young baby was playing on a sagging double bed in the corner of the cabin.

Feeny's dogs were barking excitedly as he unchained and dragged them, one at a time, to their assigned positions. My dogs, stimulated by the strange sights and smells around them, added their voices to the general uproar that always accompanied the harnessing of a dog team.

Feeny opened the door. "I t'ink we go now," he said.

Thanking Madronna for her hospitality, I pulled my parka over my head and stepped out the door into the windbreak. The sudden blast of cold air contrasted sharply with the moist overheated cabin. Feeny was already out on the lake ice.

I unchained Buck and, standing on the brake, pulled on my mittens. Then I slipped my foot off the brake, deliberately allowing it to bang against the sled's frame.

"All right, boys!" I called loudly. My dogs, hearing the brake release and my command, began running furiously to catch Feeny's team.

"All right, boys!"

Although I had gained a good bit of experience with dog teams at Clarks Point, nothing had prepared me for the trail Feeny made as he found our way across the lake. Much of the distance was smooth; almost too smooth. Wisps of fine powdery snow lay on glare ice, looking like mare's tails of high cirrus clouds on a clear day. The bare ice was black, and Buck tended to shy away from it at first, but it easily bore our weight. Then we entered a zone of pressure ridges. Water expands as it freezes. When the water body is covered with ice, and further natural expansion is blocked, forces within the ice will build until, with a shattering roar, the ice buckles, releasing the pressure.

These ridges were only three or four feet high, but extended for a hundred yards like miniature mountain ranges. Since freeze-up was still occurring, the ice was new, and these ridges were still sharp and jagged. They seriously slowed our progress as we picked our way through them.

In a few more miles, we came upon a different sort of ice jumble that required slow, careful driving. While freeze-up is a continuous process, it is never constant. Freezing weather will be interrupted by periodic storms that shatter newly formed ice. The ice floes thus created batter and break heavier ice. The process goes on as long as the storm continues. Then, when the storm passes, the broken ice chunks, like a bowl of partially melted ice cubes placed back in the freezer, will freeze in place. The results can be grotesque and humbling. For example, I remember a piece of ice ten feet long and perhaps eight feet wide—but only about eight *inches* thick—resting on edge, firmly welded to the ice on which it perched. It looked like a sail. What possible chance for survival would a person have who witnessed such an event taking place?

It was late in the afternoon, already getting dark, when we arrived at the beach near the Iliamna roadhouse. Feeny stopped in the adjacent village to spend the night with relatives, while I went on to the roadhouse.

I had met Art and Helen Lee a few months earlier when Carl Williams had deposited me in Art's care after leaving Jan and the horses at Iguigig. Now we shook hands.

"I heard you were over in Kakhonak," he said, "and I wondered how you were getting along."

I said we had had a tough time of it, and briefed him on our experiences. He led me to the store/postoffice and handed me a bundle of mail. Then we went back to the house. I sat at the table, sorting through the mail, looking for my disability compensation checks. All the money I had in this world was in those little tan envelopes. There were three of them. Two were for the standard amount, nearly $300, but the last one was for only $120. What the hell was this?

Searching for an explanation, I sorted through the mail again and found a letter from the Veterans Administration in Juneau which explained that since I was now presumed to have recovered from the ankle surgery, my disability evaluation had been reduced from 100% to 60%.

Oops. Although the cost of living in Kakhonak was somewhat commensurate with our standard of living, which was about as low as you could get and still survive, in a country where a case of ordinary evaporated milk cost $20, $120 a month was not going to cut it.

Moreover, Jan's mother planned to bring the children to Kakhonak in the spring. Somehow, I had to earn a few hundred extra dollars to cover the expenses we faced.

The next day, I cashed my checks with Art and bought a sled load of supplies. The local airline, Pacific Northern, made a scheduled stop at Iliamna three times a week, and I asked Art to make a reservation for me the following week, and to send a local bush plane to Kakhonak to pick me up so I could meet it.

Feeny was waiting for me at Newhalen, and together we crossed the lake a second time. For me, that trip was a doleful one. For the first time since we had left Montana, I was seriously questioning my ability to provide for my little family. For all practical purposes, we were broke. The supplies I carried on the sled would not last more than a month or two. To put it bluntly, we had simply starved out.

While the wisdom of leaving Jan alone while I went into Anchorage seeking work may seem open to debate, for us, there was no alternative. It is sad but true that poor people lack the options others take for granted.

While we were still teetering on the edge of physical survival, we had an enormous advantage. We were young enough to believe we were invincible.

10

The Hungry Years

Shortly before we left Clarks Point, we had sold nearly all our household equipment, including that washing machine from hell, to a cannery carpenter and his wife. They had decided to remain in Clarks Point for the winter so he could build the new school.

The carpenter, Clarence, had been short on cash. Still, since he was our only buyer, we gladly gave him all the credit he needed. Not surprisingly, during the following two years while we were in Bozeman, we never saw a dime of that money. I knew he and his family had subsequently moved into Anchorage. Consequently, when I arrived there in mid-January, the first thing I did was look for him.

He and his family were living in a three-room shack on the edge of town. The place had been a farm, but the animals were gone. A goat shed remained on a corner of his lot.

We struck a bargain. I offered to forgive the debt in exchange for the opportunity to live in the goat shed and take one meal every day with the family for about four months. Clarence agreed, so I installed an army cot and my sleeping bag in the shed. I "heated" the shed with a portable kerosene space heater; the kind that uses a wick.

In my experience, finding work is never difficult if you need it badly enough. I quickly found work with the US Weather Bureau at Merrill Field as a

GS/3 clerk. My job was to prepare synoptic charts for the forecasters by hand plotting the coded weather sequences as they came over the teletype.

It was night work, and the pay was barely above the minimum wage. Nevertheless, it was regular. My only expenses were for gas in my old jeep and breakfast at the *Sportsmen's Club* on K street after work, so even those small paychecks quickly added up.

Blanche, Jan's mother, came through town in late February when she brought the children to Alaska. I missed seeing them as they passed through on their way to Kakhonak. But I was probably damned lucky that she didn't see me when she returned on her way back to Montana. I can't imagine she was too thrilled to find her eldest daughter living in a sod-roofed log hut with a dirt floor!

Jan and I had planned that she and the kids would move temporarily into Anchorage in the spring when her mother returned to Montana. We weren't giving up on the homestead; we simply had to regroup.

It was OK for me to live in a goat shed, but I could hardly ask my family to do that. Consequently, shortly before their arrival, I began searching for a small, cheap, apartment.

Meanwhile, Jan closed up the cabin, and boarded the dogs with Feeny Andrew. She then rode Dusty across Lake Iliamna on the ice behind a dog team, and left him in the care of Eskimos in Newhalen.

I was put in touch with Fred Thomas, a local radio personality. He and his wife had a lovely home in a convenient downtown location. They had carved their basement into three one-room apartments (with shared bath). Before Jan arrived with the children, I rented one of them. Our new neighbors were pairs of stewardesses. It was a wonderful arrangement, except things got a bit tight in the bathroom when the girls weren't flying.

When Mrs. Thomas heard our story and realized I was a disabled veteran, she urged me to come to her office—she worked at the local office of the US Bureau of Land Management (BLM)—and file a homestead claim on the Kakhonak property.

My claim was filed under the Civil War Soldiers and Sailor's Homestead Act of 1862. Ordinarily, three years were required to "prove" a homestead. The first year, the claimant was obliged to build an habitable dwelling and live in it for seven consecutive months. The second year, the claimant was required to cultivate 1/16th of the land area claimed. On a 160-acre claim, this amounted to ten acres. The third year, the claimant was obliged to bring an additional 1/16th of the claim under cultivation.

However, the statute exempted *disabled* veterans from the cultivation requirements. All we were required to do was build the cabin and live in it for seven months before applying for our free survey.

Although the BLM office looked like any other drab federal office, it was, in fact, a veritable cornucopia. Mrs. Thomas explained that two years earlier, several hundred acres of public land near Anchorage had been divided into five acre lots and sold to veterans. Some buyers had failed to make the necessary payment. Those tracts were now available to new buyers. The price was $15 an acre!

I couldn't open my wallet fast enough.

Three weeks later, I learned that I had won the drawing and I now owned five acres of unimproved land on Spruce Road near the Campbell air strip.

We carried some old plywood cement forms out to the site and built a cabin. Then I dug a shallow well; a process which nearly killed me. I had dug down about ten feet, when I ran into a layer of small boulders about the size of grapefruit.

Any experienced well digger will tell you that you must be

very careful not to allow a cone of earth to accumulate around the edge of the well. Such cones build as the digger throws successive shovelsful of earth up over his shoulder.

Author in 1952

I wasn't an experienced well digger, and I had foolishly allowed a large cone to accumulate. The trouble arose when I picked up a ten pound boulder and flung it back over my head with both hands. Then I bent over to pick up another.

I never reached it. The first stone landed on the slope above the well, and rolled down the slope. It landed on my back just above my right kidney. God, that hurt!

I sagged to my knees, and rested my forehead against the cool wall of earth as waves of excruciating, nauseating, pain washed over me. It seemed like an hour before I could even yell for the ladder. Then, I crawled out of the well, and spent the rest of the day trying to find a way to lie comfortably. It was a week before I went back into the well to finish the job, and then I was moving only very slowly and carefully.

The 1952 fishing season was about to begin. Since Jan had worked as a hand packer at Emard's cannery the previous summer, we drove to the cannery to look for work after pursuading a neighbor lady to look after the kids.

Jan was hired on the spot. I was promised a job on the beach gang as soon as I could report for work, after I gave notice and resigned from the Weather Bureau. Soon, Jan and I were going to work together. About three weeks into the season, Henry Emard came to see me as I was caulking a tender.

He stood quietly for a few minutes watching me work. "You still want to go in a boat, Denny?" he asked.

"I sure do, Henry," I replied.

"Well, this ain't a boat," he said. "This is a setnet deal down at Kenai near the East Foreland."

Jan and I talked it over. We decided I ought to take the fishing job. It was early in the season, and yet there was no indication what the season would bring.

I packed my duffle bag, and the next day, boarded the cannery tender on its outward journey from the cannery to lower Cook Inlet. After running for hours, the tender delivered me into a big skiff run by a wizened and crabby old man named John (Salt-House) Utterstrom. He and an elderly Indian woman named Mary eked out a stingy existence so parsimonious that I nearly starved.

Before I was 11 years old, I had learned one of life's great lessons: The basic distinction between those who sit and those who stand; those who ride and those who paddle.

In 1936, Mother had sent me to a boy's summer camp where there were two kinds of campers. The little rich kids in one category, and the rest of us, called "hustlers," in the other. When the cry for "Tennis!" went up, the rich kids ran for their tennis rackets. We ran for the lawn roller. When we went camping, the little rich kids sat while we paddled.

Nothing, however, had prepared me for the miserable living conditions John and Mary imposed on their hired help.

My accommodation was a log hut four feet high, and approximately eight feet square. It was roofed with rusty and badly used, corrugated iron. There was no door or window, just a hole in front of the hut to crawl through.

The place could have been a fat farm; the meals at chez Utterstrom were simple and far apart. Mary bestirred herself every morning, and mixed thin sourdough hotcakes. A stack of them, a strip of bacon, and a cup of the thickest coffee I ever drank, constituted breakfast.

The second meal of the day, served in mid-afternoon, was usually fish head chowder, heavy on fish heads (which were free) and potatoes. When she lacked fish heads, we had plain potato soup. Eventually, driven by starvation, I walked to a store in Kenai where I bought canned spaghetti, baked beans, and sardines, which I wolfed in the privacy of my "cabin."

Salthouse John, or "Salty," as he was known, operated a setnet on the beach. His nets reflected his general lifestyle and attitude. Nylon nets were then just coming into wide use. Salty's nets were a patched-up lot of old-fashioned linen nets that the local canneries had discarded. I got a lot of net-mending practice that summer from those rotten old nets.

Utterstrom's property was on top of a high bluff overlooking lower Cook Inlet. It was about six miles north of the Kenai River, and was immediately adjacent to Ted Mining's low-lying homestead on which he had made an important discovery; a large deposit of diatomaceous earth, useful as a jeweler's fine polish. Before he could get rich on the earth, however, Standard Oil bought his homestead and dredged it, converting it into an oil terminal named Port Nikiski.

Jan was paid off at the cannery in late August. She drove down to Kenai with the kids in our old jeep. By this time, the season was all but over, and I was ready to call it quits.

1952 was not a good year in Cook Inlet, and my share of the catch was only slightly more than I would have made working for wages in the cannery.

We closed the shack out on Spruce Road, sold the jeep, and flew back to Iliamna. Jan had been gone for six months. Our dogs had been well cared for by Feeny and his family, but Dusty, our only surviving horse, was dead.

Art Lee was reluctant to tell me what had happened, because he feared I might seek revenge on the young men who had so badly abused that gentle, resourceful, animal.

Eventually, I got the story. It seems that for fun, several young Eskimos in Newhalen had set their dogs on the poor animal, running it as hard as it could go. When Dusty collapsed, they then beat the poor horse to death trying to force it to rise and run again. As Art sadly put it, "it was a prime example of savage cruelty."

I asked Art not to tell me who was responsible. The famous Hatfield-McCoy feud began over a smaller provocation than this. I was afraid if I knew who the miscreants were, it might affect my relationship with them and their families.

We bought a big pile of supplies from Art. We also bought an old river boat from a local Native. "Little" Joe's gas boat was tied to the roadhouse dock. He planned to return the next day to Kakhonak, so I persuaded him to tow our boat and deliver us and our cargo across the lake.

Late the next afternoon, we arrived on the gravel beach where Sonny had unloaded our freight and horses almost exactly a year earlier.

The cabin was just as Jan had left it. Before Jan, her mother, and the two children had come in to Anchorage the previous spring, the sod on the roof had thawed. Since there was nothing to prevent melting snow from penetrating the sod, the floor had quickly turned to mud. In a nearly vain effort to keep the two toddlers out of the mud, Jan and her mother had paved the floor with tree limbs.

Jan had described the frightful scene, but nothing prepared me for the awful sight of those limbs, now bare of needles, embedded in the muddy lake that was our floor. Everything inside the cabin; stove, walls, table, beds, was covered with thick mold from the nearly incessant drip, drip, drip of rain water trickling through the sod roof. The smell of decay was almost overpowering.

There was no point standing around feeling sorry for ourselves. We soon had a fire going in the stove. Then we had supper, and put the babies to bed. The next morning, I dug a ditch from the rear of the cabin to drain the water that created a small lake inside the cabin.

We had brought sheets of plastic from Anchorage. We tacked them against the ceiling. It wasn't stylish; it was almost like pitching a tent inside the cabin. But at least our beds were no longer wet, and we hoped the floor would soon dry.

Simeon Zachar

We were interrupted by a delegation from the village that arrived in a skiff around noon.

Nothing at Clarks Point had prepared me for dealing with these upriver Eskimos. There, visitors usually had business to conduct. While the protocol required a ceremonial offer and acceptance of coffee, the visitors generally got right down to business.

Not here. Possibly because of their isolation, these Eskimos retained much of their aboriginal mores. Their courtesy required a decent social interval before business could be conducted. Although their English was much better than my Yupik—limited, as it was, to a few phrases—neither of us had much small talk.

Therefore, it was not uncommon for three or four Eskimos to sit silently at the kitchen table sipping coffee for an hour or more, before addressing the issue that brought them in the first place.

This visit was an exception. My guests wanted immediate action. It seems that my complaint to the government about the wolves had caused the US Fish and Wildlife Service office in Anchorage to send a predator control agent to deal with this particular wolf pack.

According to my guests, the agent had set poison traps in

the brush surrounding my cabin. "Him very bad, very danger," Simeon Zachar said, his drawn face reflecting the gravity of the problem. "If dog or baby pull bait, him die!"

Although I never saw one, they were described as a stick supporting a baited capsule. When the bait was disturbed, the capsule, which I later learned contained cyanide or strychnine, would break in the animal's mouth or at least within lethal proximity to its head. Not the sort of thing you want scattered around your back yard. Especially not if you had young children.

Little Joe's English was not as good as Simeon's, but he interrupted Simeon to make sure I understood they wanted me to write a letter to the game warden asking him to retrieve those traps before they killed a dog or hurt some-

The babies were put to bed. Note sheets of plastic on ceiling.

one. I was only too glad to oblige.

Someone was planning to cross the lake the following day, so I wrote the letter while they waited. The letter would be mailed at the post office in Iliamna. I had no idea where to address it, but I had gotten good results in the past by communicating directly with our Delegate to Congress, Bob Bartlett, so I addressed the letter to him.

It worked. About six weeks later, shortly before freeze-up,

a small two-place Piper Cub on floats bearing US Fish and Wildlife markings, landed in the bay in front of the cabin.

The pilot was the federal predator control agent who had set the poison traps. His name was Jay Hammond. His passenger was his boss, the area supervisor.

While Jay quietly retired to retrieve the traps, his boss, who had a keen appreciation for political nuances, sat with us in the cabin, urging me to write a follow-up letter to Mr. Bartlett, which I did, extolling the service provided by the US Fish and Wildlife Service.

In later years, Jay and I would come to know each other well. He credited me—accurately, as you shall see, but with heavy irony—with starting his political career, which ended after he successfully completed two terms as Alaska's Governor. However, I have often wondered whether, or to what degree, the unfortunate circumstances of that initial meeting were to have on our future relationship. We never discussed it. I suspect, however, that it may have been profound.

Of nearly equal significance, a US Geological Survey team had come to Kakhonak while we were in Anchorage, and had established a base camp at the old deserted reindeer station, about three miles away.

We were unaware of their presence, as they were of ours, until one day, much to our astonishment, a small Bell helicopter appeared overhead, and slowly landed in the swamp behind the cabin. This turned out to be the clearest manifestation of manna from heaven one could imagine.

The pilot and passenger climbed out of the odd-looking machine. We introduced ourselves and invited our visitors to the cabin for coffee. They explained that they had spent the summer conducting a geodetic survey redrawing the base atlas sheets, using the helicopter to carry the surveyors and a modern theodolite to the tops of all the major local hills.

Since the project was nearly completed, they expected to

leave in about three weeks, and would not be returning. Therefore, as they studiously avoided looking at our dirt floor, they wondered if we would like to have their leftover lumber and supplies.

Does a bear live in the woods?

Christmas came early that year. I thought it strange that the Eskimos hadn't mentioned the survey team. However, common sense told me that they probably had their eyes on the leftover supplies, and hoped I wouldn't discover the camp until it was too late.

I was wrong. I didn't know the upriver Eskimos very well. They knew about the camp, but they had no interest in salvaging any left-over supplies.

I went to the abandoned reindeer station in my "new" boat, and helped the last of the survey party load their expensive equipment aboard the helicopter. After they left, I quickly built a raft by lashing empty oil drums in a frame constructed of 2x4s, shiplap, and plywood, and piled my scavenged plunder high on it. It took three hours to tow that awkward and ungainly raft five miles to our cabin. I immediately used most of it to build a floor in the cabin to get the kids out of the mud.

The first full winter we spent on the homestead was long, hard and cold. Despite the lucky windfall we had received, we were still living very close to the edge. For example, we had started the winter with only a single case of kerosene (ten gallons) to provide our light and to aid Jan when she laid a morning fire in the stove. Luckily, we inherited a case of candles from our surveyor benefactors, and we rationed ourselves to one candle per night. When the candle went out, we went to bed. Considering that we lived at 55°N, you'll realize that we were forced to light that candle about four pm, and as a result, we went to bed very early.

I established a short trapline, but most of my waking hours

were spent in the endless chore of hunting and cutting firewood. Luckily, the rabbits were even more abundant now than they had been the previous year. It became something of a family joke that Jan learned how to prepare a dozen varieties of turkey tetrazzini using rabbit meat. We were barely subsisting on a very marginal level. We knew we had to take a dramatic first step to break the poverty cycle we were in. Otherwise, we would never achieve our dream of a hunting and fishing lodge, or even a reasonable amount of financial independence.

Bath night

Although the horses originally had seemed essential, and we would have been hard pressed to build the cabin without them, it now appeared that we could have accomplished just as much with a small crawler tractor.

However, in defense of our decision to use horses, I should explain that in 1951, only a few manufacturers were building farm crawler tractors, which were then extraordinarily expensive. I knew from the beginning that wheel equipped farm tractors would not be practical in the rugged terrain where we planned to build the lodge. Also, a tractor would have required a far greater capital investment—money we didn't have—then the horses.

Frankly, even if money hadn't been a consideration, I doubt whether I would have considered that alternative. My imagination had leaped over the mundane problems we now faced, and I had a head full of romantic pictures featuring myself leading a pack string of horses across the tundra.

Our greatest need, now, was lumber. I had to replace our

sod roof. Also, my family was growing, and I needed to add a room to our tiny cabin. Where many people in our circumstances might have written to a stateside lumber yard, I immediately began thinking about a sawmill. Luckily, there was plenty of raw material. We were surrounded by a good growth of white spruce.

Lynnie

I knew the Small Business Administration existed, but I didn't realize that agency had never made a direct loan in Alaska. Largely out of ignorance, I submitted a loan application. Months later, after an unbelievable amount of paper work, my request to borrow $4,000 to finance a sawmill and power plant was approved.

I wasted no time. I found an address in a copy of *Popular Science* I borrowed from Art Lee—the same periodical where my friends ordered their new teeth—and ordered a new 16-foot Belsaw sawmill. Then I ordered a 28-HP stationary gasoline power plant from Sears for an additional $400.

Our third daughter, Debbie, was born the following summer, but not before we had a terrible fright.

Paradoxically, spring was the most dangerous season of the year. In the first place, there was the ice to consider. Unlike major rivers where the transition from solid, safe, ice to open water was only a matter of a week or two, lake ice didn't break up or even melt.

First, as the ice began to "honeycomb," its surface would lose its smooth texture and instead became jagged and sharp, requiring dog team drivers to tie leather booties on their dog's feet to prevent them from being cut. Then the ice slowly turned black, and gradually rotted. Although visible holes opened in the ice here and there early in the spring, most of the ice remained in a solid sheet, floating on the water. It would become very dangerous. While it was still a foot thick, the thoroughly honeycombed ice would crumble under the slightest touch.

Travel by plane, boat, or dog sled was impossible while this condition, which usually persisted for a month or six weeks, lasted. There were also other, less visible, but potentially more dangerous hazards.

Drinking water was always suspect, but in the spring, it was lethal. For the previous six months, the now mushy ice had served as a thoroughfare for dog teams, wolverines, moose, rabbits, weasels, shrews, and other animals. During that period, it accumulated, buried in layers of snow and ice, a rich variety of animal excreta.

During cold weather, the public health menace it presented was small because that filth was frozen in the ice, but when breakup came, and the ice melted, our drinking water always became seriously contaminated.

We knew enough to boil our drinking water, but somehow, and I'm sure the contaminated water was responsible, a few germs got to Jan, and she became horribly ill.

Travel across the ice was then impossible. There were no alternate methods by which we could seek help, so we were forced to rely on luck and our own resources to deal with what may have been a deadly disease. Jan's illness was never diagnosed, but it resembled typhoid fever. Of course, it helped not at all that she was then five months pregnant.

The onset of the disease was similar to flu. Jan had a headache, a fever, and was nauseous. However, instead of running its course in four or five days, the fever steadily climbed to 104° by the end of the seventh day.

She subsisted merely on sips of water. She was not able to retain any solid food. After the first or second bite, any food she had swallowed was instantly and violently vomited.

Jan was blessed with robust good health, but she became so weak, so spent, after the first seven or eight days of fasting that I was almost afraid to try to feed her because the violent re;ching that invariably followed took a visible toll on her fading strength.

Lynnie, the youngest child, at three, was still too young to comprehend what was happening to her mother. Trina, however, knew about death. I still remember after Jan had experienced a particularly severe spasm of retching, her fearful whisper in the evening dusk, expressing the forbidden thought: "Is Mommy going to die?"

Although I did my best to reassure both frightened little girls by hugging them close, I was hardly as confident as I hoped I sounded.

Quite honestly, I had nearly given up. I had no medicine to give her, and Jan was steadily growing weaker. There was no way I could get help. I did something then that I had done only once before, when Jan was in labor at Clarks Point. Although I consider myself an atheist, I prayed that night for her life. The next morning, to clear my head, I walked the 400 yards across the portage, and stood, lost in my doleful thoughts, staring at the rotted, blackened lake ice beyond our gravel beach.

Suddenly, I heard the muted squawking and murmur of feeding ducks! There were three mallards in an open patch of water next to the beach near the lagoon.

As quietly as possible, I rushed back to the cabin and grabbed the shotgun and a handful of shells. I loaded the gun on the way back across the portage, and when I drew near the fringing brush, I dropped on my belly, and began the most cautious and careful stalk of my life.

Slowly, gently, I worked my way through the budding willows and alders, grateful that the leaves I was crawling over were soaked with melting snow. The duck sounds grew steadily louder as I drew closer to the beach. Finally, I parted a tuft of grass and peered through it at my prey. The three mallards, a drake and two hens, were swimming lazily along the edge of the ice about 75 or 80 feet away. I took careful aim and squeezed the trigger.

BOOM!

Two ducks died instantly, the third flopped reflexively for a moment or two before it too became a bundle of feathers floating quietly on the water's surface.

The birds were almost 50 feet from the beach. I was on the point of stripping down and taking my chances swimming in that frigid water to retrieve them, when a light breeze came across the ice, nudging them toward the shore.

I took a long pole from the fish rack. By wading out, nearly to my waist, floating that pole in front of me, I was just barely able to reach the birds, and coax them toward me.

I ran home with the three birds. After changing out of my wet clothes, I quickly skinned and cleaned them. I put them in a pot of water to simmer. Later, I added two cans of vegetables to what became a thick duck soup.

It was a miracle. Jan kept the first few bites down, and asked for more. Careful not to overdo it, I gave her a few spoonfuls at a time, letting her rest between bites.

Her fever broke that evening, and I knew she would live. I'm convinced those ducks saved her life, but I'm willing to concede that other folks might have a different explanation.

I hitched a ride with Feeny Andrew to Nakeen cannery (otherwise known as "Squaw Creek") in Bristol Bay, 150 miles away. Meanwhile, Jan and the children flew to Anchorage where she delivered our third child.

Jan was her father's daughter. Truly an amazing person. After the hospital bill was paid, she used what loan money was left to do something I would never dared even contemplate. She used it to make a down payment on a brand new John Deere crawler tractor.

Entirely on her own, she negotiated a deal with the Northern Commercial Company. As she later pointed out, the mill wasn't much good without logs. The tractor and the sawmill were to be delivered on the fall ship.

We were awash in debt. It's a good thing we hadn't known while we were getting in so deep that the 1953 season would be a complete bust. The fishing companies on the Kvichak, and their fishermen, took serious economic losses that year.

The previous year, 1952, had been a year of little fishing effort because the canneries were converting their sailboats to power. This involved major surgery on as many as 200 boats in each cannery. A deep notch was cut low in each boat's stern, through the horn timber, seven frames, and associated planking. Then, prefabricated stern bearings and rudder posts mounted in a metal shell were slapped over the gaping hole and bolted in place. Prefabricated engine beds and 4-cylinder gas engines replaced the centerboards. Hydraulically powered net rollers were fitted in the stern where the dumb rollers had been, and finally, prefabricated dog houses were bolted to the fore part of the vessels, replacing the tents of an earlier era. Crude as they were, those conversions were light years ahead of the infinitely more primitive sailboats.

1952 was a year marred, as 1949 had been, by almost continuously stormy weather. Several million fish that otherwise might have been caught, even with the reduced amount of effort available that year, had escaped unnoticed to the upriver spawning grounds. When the spawning surveys were conducted that fall, the industry was surprised to learn how strong the 1952 run had been.

Wishfully believing that the strength of the 1952 run foretold an even stronger run in 1953, the companies on the Kvichak River opened closed canneries and launched every boat they owned in preparation for what they thought would be a banner year.

I signed on to fish with Nick Nowatak, also from Kakhonak, as a company fisherman at Nakeen, a cannery owned by the great A&P Tea Corporation, the same company that owned Waterfall cannery where I had worked as a trap watchman in 1946. We were assigned to sailboat 110.

Besides the technological revolution—the watershed shift from sail to power—that was changing the Bristol Bay fishery forever, powerful social issues were also bubbling.

Until 1951, the Alaska Fisherman's Union (AFU) was the exclusive bargaining agent for all the fishermen in Bristol Bay. However, because nonresident fishermen easily outnumbered residents by a ratio of at least ten to one, where it mattered, the AFU agreements tended to favor nonresidents at the expense of residents. There was some—but not much—historic justification for that discrimination.

Traditionally, the fishermen were paid "run money" for pre- and post-season work such as sailing the ships north from San Francisco, unloading cannery supplies, hanging their nets, preparing their boats; then after the season was over, putting their boats away, loading the salmon pack, and sailing the ships south.

The local resident fishermen were an independent lot, and inspired resentment by the outside fishermen, especially after a good fishing season, because they sometimes avoided the unpleasant and time-consuming job of helping load the salmon pack at the end of the season.

The logical argument that "run money" shouldn't be paid to men who didn't do the work was extended illogically to paying the residents as much as three cents less than the outside fishermen were paid for their fish. There were additional forms of discrimination. The residents almost always were assigned the older, more dangerous, boats. They were obliged to identify themselves as residents by painting a telltale letter "A" on the bow of their boats. (See cover.) In most canneries they were even housed in segregated bunkhouses. In short, the relations between the two groups were anything but cordial.

The Alaska Fishermen's Union was one of the 11 unions expelled from the CIO in 1948 for Communist leadership under the Taft/Hartley Act. The International Longshoremen and Warehouseman's Union (ILWU), based in San Francisco, was another. An attempt to merge the two unions was defeated by resident AFU members in 1950.

Sensing an opportunity to enter a new jurisdiction, the powerful Seafarer's International Union (SIU, AFL-CIO) decided to organize the disaffected Bristol Bay resident fishermen. In 1951, while I was in the Veteran's hospital having my ankle fused, the resident fishermen, led by Jim Downey and Truman Emberg at Dillingham, had formed the Bering Sea Fishermen's Union, as an affiliate of the SIU. The canning companies, naturally, had refused to recognize the new union, so the resident fishermen had mounted a jurisdictional strike.

The organizers knew that a regular jurisdictional strike would have been cause for industrial rejoicing, since the nonresident (AFU) fishermen were more than capable of catching and delivering all the fish available. However, the strike strategy devised by the SIU was worthy of a Clausewitz.

Before World War II, the canneries had used their own ships to carry their crews and supplies north in the spring and the crews and salmon pack south in the fall, in their own ships. However, the new Naknek Army Air Base now offered a much cheaper way to transport crews to and from Alaska.

The shift away from water transportation for cannery crews undercut the economic rationale for company flag shipping fleets. Alaska Steamship Company, which had operated the wooden hulled *S.S. Tongass* between Seattle and Ketchikan before the war, now proceeded, with a fleet of leased Liberty and "Knot" ships, to fill the vacuum left by the vanished company fleets. The Liberty ship *S.S. Denali*, operated by the Alaska Steamship Company, sailed north in the spring of 1951 laden with can stock, food, and other essential cannery supplies.

When a supply ship arrived at the ship's anchorage in the Kvichak River, five miles offshore, the cannery superintendents would send several barges and gangs of fishermen out to offload the ship. While fishermen and sailors shared jurisdiction over loading and unloading cargo, the steamship company preferred to hire fishermen, because the fishermen were paid only 55¢ an hour, while for the sailors, the work was paid at the overtime rate. This practice caused considerable resentment among the sailors.

Although the fishermen and the sailors shared that grudging jurisdiction over the longshore work in the ship's holds, the sailors, (who conveniently for the strikers were members of an SIU affiliate) had <u>exclusive</u> jurisdiction over the work of opening the ship's hatches.

Knowing that, and armed with a formal refusal of recognition by the canning industry, key members of the new Bering Sea Fishermen's Union took a member's boat to the ship's anchorage to meet the *Denali* as she anchored. Before the cannery barges arrived, the boat was circling the ship, displaying a large picket sign.

Since this strategy was devised by the SIU, the sailor's shop steward undoubtedly had been well coached, and knew what to do if something unusual occurred when the ship reached Alaska. The first pickets were greatly relieved when the sailors waved as they approached the ship. They knew then that the sailors were expecting them, and would respect their picket line by refusing to open the ship's hatches.

The cannery barges with AFU work crews arrived, but they had nothing to do. They could not unload cargo that was sealed beneath closed hatches. As long as the resident fishermen maintained their picket line, the cargo hatches remained closed.

There was an immediate and enormous outcry by the canneries and the steamship company, but the fishermen and sailors stood their ground. After two weeks of shouting and foolish fist shaking, the canneries gave in and the Bering Sea Fishermen's Union was formally recognized by the industry as the exclusive bargaining agent for resident fishermen. But it was the Fourth of July, when the annual salmon run was half over, before the canneries got into full production.

Now, in 1953, the National Labor Relations Board held a formal representation election by the fishermen to ratify (or reject) the new union as the exclusive bargaining agent for resident fishermen.

The politicking by various factions among the fishermen paled in importance, however, to reports some of us were beginning to receive from friends and family upriver.

Ordinarily, by the Fourth of July, large numbers of fish would have arrived at fish camps in Igiugig and further down the lake. This year, however, something was very wrong. Few fish had yet reached the fish camps.

On July tenth, a delegation of resident fishermen from Nakeen lead by a local school teacher named Bob Kallenberg, who served as an advisor to the American Section of the International North Pacific Fisheries Commission, called on the US Fish and Wildlife Service agent at his King Salmon airport headquarters. They reported to him what they had learned from the upriver communities, and strongly urged him to consider an early closure of the commercial fishery.

221

The official, a man named Bert Johnson, listened to them, then shook his head, saying, "Look. You fellows don't have the whole picture. Be patient. I know the fish are coming."

He was wrong. A week later it was obvious to everyone that the season was a bust. We thought there was no use going back to the Fish and Wildlife Service. Bob Kallenberg called a fisherman's meeting Sunday morning in the bunkhouse.

He had prepared an argument for everyone, based on the undeniable fact that there were no fish to be caught, and therefore, no money to be made. To the resident fishermen, however, he added the need for a sufficient salmon escapement to provide winter food for themselves and their dog teams. To the nonresident fishermen from California, he stressed that many were missing lucrative alternate fishing opportunities in the tuna fishery. To the fishermen from Seattle, he pointed out that they were missing valuable fishing time in the halibut fishery. A long, sometimes heated, debate followed. The fishermen were worried about breaching their contract and being compelled to pay their own airplane fares back to the states. However, one astute fisherman pointed out that the contract merely required them to put their nets in the water once every 24 hours, so by noon, they voted to begin a modified "sit-down" strike.

With the tacit permission of the cannery superintendent, Kallenberg made the announcement over the cannery radio to a startled audience of Bristol Bay cannery radio operators that Nakeen cannery was on strike!

Like annoyed wasps, small airplanes soon began buzzing in and out of Nakeen's dirt airstrip as fishermen delegates from other canneries arrived to find out what was going on.

After they returned to their canneries and meetings were held, one by one, announcements began coming over the air:

"This is Diamond J cannery announcing that the fishermen are supporting Nakeen . . . "

"This is Libbyville cannery announcing that our fishermen will not cross Nakeen's picket line . . . "

"This is PAF cannery . . . "

"This is New England cannery . . . "

All afternoon, and into the evening, the announcements came in from nearly every cannery in the Naknek-Kvichak District, and by midnight, some 2,500 fishermen had pledged to support our effort to cause an early closure of the 1953 salmon season.

As usual for a Monday, long before daylight the next morning, the fleet departed their respective canneries. But instead of scattering over the fishing grounds to wait for the six o'clock opening, most of the boats went to Coffee Point—a generic term for a sheltered anchorage near the fishing grounds—where they anchored and began the strike.

Unrest in the fleet always meant good business for local bush pilots as cannery superintendents sought to discover what their fishermen were doing, and all day, as the fishermen visited back and forth, drank coffee, and yarned, bush planes buzzed overhead. The US Fish and Wildlife plane also appeared, as Mr. Johnson came to see for himself that the fishermen had taken matters into their own hands.

The strike continued all night, but by ten o'clock the next morning, the canneries capitulated and called their boats in. The season had ended! I was at the Telephone Point tally scow when the word came. Nick had been injured by this time, and I was in command of A&P 110. Kallenberg was fishing a converted sailboat. He offered to tow me upriver to the creek where Nakeen cannery was sheltered behind a wall of steel sheet piling.

Being something of a romantic, and savoring the historical significance that the sailboat era had ended, and that I commanded the last company sailboat to return to a Bristol Bay cannery, I declined Bob's offer. I explained that I wanted personally to close that dark chapter in Bristol Bay history by making the last sailing return to a cannery unassisted.

Bob understood and appreciated my quixotic impulse. But as a man who had sailed his share of Bristol Bay boats, and realizing the wind was calm and that the tide was strongly flooding, he never let me out of his sight as I bravely stepped into the boat.

We cast off from the tally scow and began "sailing" backwards up the river! There wasn't enough wind to turn the boat around, much less give us steerageway. The cannery was less than a mile up river, and the flood was making at about four knots. Kallenberg loafed along, behind us, watching as I drifted helplessly past the quoin leading into the creek.

"Now will you take a tow?" he yelled from the bow of his boat.

There was no point in going further. I motioned my acceptance, and an important era ended, ignominiously, at the end of a towline.

The battle was won, but, as the resident fishermen were soon to discover, the war was only beginning. I don't know if we could have dodged what was coming, but the next few years were painful.

11

The Disaster Years

The *Fajen*, Hermy Herrmann's 110-foot, steel war-surplus scow arrived at our gravel beach on schedule. It was mid-September. I had been home from the fishing grounds for a month, getting acquainted with my new daughter, cutting firewood for the winter, and taking care of the thousand and one things that needed attending to before freeze-up. As usual, I was driven by the descending snow line on Roadhouse Mountain, because I knew that after the scow arrived, I'd be totally engrossed with setting up the sawmill.

Before leaving the Bay, I had gone to Hermy's house and alerted him to the cargo—the sawmill and tractor—we expected on the fall ship. I had also bought several heavy timbers at the cannery to use as a base for the mill, and I asked him to pick them up. Finally, I had asked him to bring five drums of gas.

Hermy announced his arrival by a loud blast on his horn. We'd been watching for him, and even if we hadn't seen him coming, we surely would have heard the tinny roar of the three GM 6-71 diesels that powered the *Fajen*.

Jan and I stood on the beach straining to see if our precious cargo had made the ship. All we could see was the rust-streaked black up-ended bow ramp creating a froth of white foam. The bow soon brushed the beach. After considerable hammering, and with loud screeching, the winches supporting the bow gate reluctantly gave way and like a medieval drawbridge, the bow descended to the beach.

Hermy stood on the deck grinning down at us, his round, almost cherubic, face topped by wispy, thinning hair, lifting in the breeze. He wore Frisco jeans held by heavy suspenders, and a heavy plaid shirt.

I took the grin to mean that everything we expected had arrived. "Is the tractor here, Hermy?" I asked, moments before I spied that jaunty John Deere green color buried in the cargo.

He confirmed it. "You've got enough plunder here to keep you busy all winter," he said. "Of course, we've been playing with that tractor all the way up the Kvichak." He, his two deckhands, and I quickly unloaded the drums of fuel and case of lube oil I had ordered, the timbers from the cannery, the four crates of sawmill parts, several rolls of roofing paper, and other hardware. Hermy personally drove the little green tractor ashore. It was still mid-afternoon when we finished unloading. I invited him to stay for supper, but he declined. He wanted to go on to the roadhouse before dark.

I'm convinced that Hermy made those fall trips up to the lake more out of a sense of duty than anything else. It was a marginal proposition for him no matter which way you looked at it. The *Fajen* was so big that she could navigate through the Kaskanak Flats in the upper Kvichak River only during the late fall when the river was at its greatest height for the year. He always carried a good load of freight, but it was strictly a one-way deal.

I thought his rates were extremely reasonable. For instance, he charged only $250 for lightering my stuff off the ship, loading the gasoline and the timbers, and hauling the lot 150 miles up the river and down the lake to our place. I knew he couldn't get rich that way.

After he left, Jan and I looked wonderingly at our shiny new tractor. I carefully read the instructions, then climbed into the driver's seat and turned the key. The little two-cylinder engine, for which Deere tractors were justly famous, started flawlessly. I'm glad to report that during the following years, although I drove it in all kinds of weather and under the most difficult conditions, that little engine never gave me a moment of trouble.

Jan and I retrieved the cryptic sawmill instruction sheet from one of the sawmill crates, and almost wore it out from studying it. At first, I was afraid to open anything for fear I'd get things mixed up. However, by the time we sank ten pilings for the foundation, and tied the whole business together with the 6x10 stringers Hermy had brought from Nakeen, I was ready to set up the machine.

Reading about things often will carry you only so far. I was reminded that when Jan and I were married, the preacher had ended the ceremony by handing us a manual mysteriously titled, *The Fellowship Side of Marriage*. It was interesting reading, but it was almost too vague to be useful. It contained hints, promises, innuendoes, even a couple of testimonials, but you were never entirely clear what the subject matter was.

The sawmill instruction manual was like that. Vague, but full of promise. One thing was certain. Those directions weren't written for a city boy. Only half understanding what I was reading, at first, I set the damn thing up backwards.

After I put the thing together properly, I had to level it the way nature and the saw's designer intended. This was crucial; a running saw is like a gyro—when it's out of plumb, it'll wobble, struggling to regain its balance. Also, I had to learn how to "lead" the saw. Unfortunately, like some of the finer points of fellowship, leading a saw is something no manual can teach.

227

The saw was driven by an endless 50 foot flat belt, six inches wide, that connected the small pulley on the engine's power take-off to the saw's mandrel pulley. That belt was a continual headache. If it was too slack, it would quickly run to the high side of the mandrel pulley and fall off. If it was too tight, it could pull the saw out of alignment.

If ever I wanted to improve on the most awful, fiendish punishment hell has to offer, I might furnish the penitent with a flat belt driving an unstable mandrel under widely variable loads. On a good day, after I had gained some skill and had learned how to load the saw properly, the belt might fly off the mandrel pulley only once or twice in an afternoon.

The tensions within a circular saw blade are incredible. Even a small, 40-inch saw's rim travels 10,000 feet per minute. That speed creates enough centrifugal force to stretch the saw's rim, possibly causing it to crack under a load. Blade manufacturers solve that problem by "pretensioning" the blades at the factory. Each blade is hammered in its center. When the blade is at rest, the hammering treatment gives it a slightly dished appearance. However, when the saw is running at its "hammered" speed, the dish in its center disappears, and the surface of the saw is flat. Magically, the saw is now infinitesimally larger than it was at rest.

This carefully balanced tension must be maintained as a log is fed into the running saw. Great care must be taken to prevent the saw from slowing in the cut, which would cause the center of the saw to rub against the log. Such friction will cause the center of the saw to heat and expand. That's why the saw blade must be tilted slightly toward the log carriage.

That was a delicate adjustment. Not enough lead, and the saw would heat, slow down, and eventually stop, unless you backed the log out and let the saw cool. In the extreme case, you could even "burn" your saw and ruin it. On the other hand, if your saw had too much lead, it would wobble, run crooked, pull the log off the carriage, and in the extreme case, run into the carriage. I did that once.

The log on the carriage was a big one, and I was feeding it slowly because the saw was buried in the log's end. From my position in front of the saw, holding the carriage control lever, I couldn't see what was going on.

I don't know whether the log rolled slightly, or the belt was too tight, or what. But suddenly, the log jumped, and I heard a hideously loud metallic screech, accompanied by a shower of sparks. The belt flew off the mandrel pulley, even as I was reflexively yanking on the control lever to pull the log back.

As dramatic as this incident was, there wasn't much damage to the saw. Of course, it cost a day; it took that long to refile and swage the saw teeth.

All sawmills are inherently dangerous. But little "peckerwood" mills like ours were far more dangerous then big commercial ones. Our mill had none of the built-in safeguards that surround most moving machinery, especially where workmen's compensation is involved. Second, and most importantly, the human/machine contact was infinitely more intimate and direct on the smaller machines. When something failed to operate properly on a commercial mill, it would be stopped and the problem would be remedied. We, on the other hand, were somewhat inclined to force it, usually to our sorrow. Both Jan and I bear scars as a result. As a matter of fact, it's something of a miracle that we remained physically intact.

My turn at accumulating scars came when I attempted to remove pitch from the blade by washing it with kerosene. The idea was sound; it was the method I chose that led to trouble. The engine was running at a low idle, slowly turning the saw while I held a kerosene soaked rag tightly against its surface. I wiped the rag back and forth across the blade as it turned, but carelessly allowed a corner of the rag to come into contact with a tooth. In an instant, my right glove was pulled into contact with the teeth. Before I knew it, my right glove was blood soaked. I began running, holding my wrist tightly in my left hand, for home and Jan.

She carefully peeled the tattered remanent of glove from my bleeding hand and inspected the damage. The several little wounds suggested that successive teeth had seized and turned my hand. The major injury, a lengthwise incision deep into the back of my third finger between the two finger joints, was harder to explain.

It was obvious that the tooth had damaged the bone. Jan poured copious quantities of sulfa powder into the hole, then took six stitches to close the wound. It reminded us of Frank Hiratsuka's injured fingers at Clarks Point. The only difference was that we had nothing to deaden the pain or distract the patient. Jan wasn't sure whether the bone was intact, so to play it safe, she splinted my finger like she had splinted Frank's.

Jan's turn came later, and also involved a finger. The mill's reversing drive—the gearing that caused the log carriage to return for another cut—was temperamental, especially when I was sawing unusually heavy logs. When I was working alone, I'd baby the damn thing, sometimes throwing sawdust on the belting to improve its traction.

But Jan tended to be impatient. When the carriage return balked, and she was standing at the end of the mill, she would sometimes reach over the end of the sawmill bed and grab the drive cable with both hands. Then she'd yank on it, always being careful to let go before the moving cable reached the iron pulley bolted to the end of the bed. Her strength always provided the necessary extra steam needed to get the carriage moving.

But even we knew that practice was fundamentally unsound. One day, a fishhook in the wire—a broken strand—snagged her glove, and pulled her hand over the pulley under the cable. The iron rim partially peeled the skin off the side of her little finger. Then it was my turn to install sutures without anesthetic.

The first halting production from the mill—it was nearing freeze-up by this time—was used to put a new roof on the cabin. The eternal drip, drip, drip of a sod roof ended.

I drove the tractor across the ice to neighboring islands where I cut three thousand board feet of timber, hauling some logs to the mill, making log rafts with the others.

The sawmill

My activities somehow came to the early attention of the district forester at Homer. Looking back on those early years at Kakhonak, it seems we had continual involvement with various government agencies.

I suppose some would find it flattering, but had I been given the choice, I would have preferred his attention had been directed elsewhere. The forester, a man named Scott, evinced his interest by flying a Forest Service plane from Homer across Cook Inlet, and then across the Aleutian Mountains, to land in the bay by the sawmill.

I guess he didn't have anything better to do. He inspected the site of a nearby logging operation, and complained that I had left the slashings piled wrong and that my stumps were too high. Also—and this was his chief complaint—I hadn't paid for my stumpage. I suppose he somehow had to justify the expense of his trip. I gave him a check for $10 and promised to mend my ways.

Months before we met Mr. Scott, however, while I was still

nailing the new roof together, President Eisenhower had declared Bristol Bay a federal disaster area, because of the terrible 1953 fishing season. That declaration made us eligible for surplus food.

A new roof

Stocks of surplus agricultural commodities were flown to Iliamna (and other Bristol Bay airfields) by the Air National Guard. When the ice was safe, and I was able to travel by dog sled across the lake, early in 1954, I received our share of the free food. It was an odd assortment. It consisted of cans of meat and gravy, tins of butter, cheese, dried milk, and sacks of dried beans.

Bristol Bay was temporarily in the public eye. Following the near calamity our dangerous isolation had caused the previous spring, I had applied to another agency—the Territorial Department of Communications—for a territorial coastal marine radio station. Our application was granted.

During the following summer, we received a 50 watt transmitter, antenna wire, a generator, and a coastal marine radio license. We now had the ability to participate in the nightly round-robin radio schedules led by Carl Williams, and could send and receive telegrams, through a nightly radio schedule with the US Army Signal Corps' Alaska Communications System (ACS) station in King Salmon (formerly the Naknek Air Base).

Two more governmental agencies—the US Justice Department and the US Fish and Wildlife Service—entered our lives that winter. First, Art Lee nominated me to succeed the local US commissioner.

Just as Art Lee reminded me of my earlier mentor, Henry Shade, the nomination process reminded me of my appointment years earlier as schoolteacher at Clarks Point. I didn't think I was qualified for the position. I was still a relative newcomer to the area, I didn't know many of the local people, and I knew even less about local customs.

On the other hand, I had three qualifications. I could read, I was a registered Republican, and I was not a missionary. It was the last virtue that had engaged Art's attention.

Although I was not aware of it at the time, the communities at the upper end of Lake Iliamna, Pile Bay in particular, were suffering a plague of missionaries. These earnest men and women were fundamentalist Christians, several of whom had come into the community as schoolteachers. Using the school as a base of operations, they had aggressively proselytized the school children, and through them, the villagers.

Aware that a new commissioner for the Iliamna Precinct was soon to be appointed, they made every effort to see that one of their own was selected for the post. Frankly, at first I thought that Art's objection to the appointment of a missionary was based merely on unreasoning prejudice, but shortly after my appointment, which dragged on for months, I quickly learned differently.

I had just returned from the disastrous 1954 fishing season in Bristol Bay when I was visited by one of the Pile Bay missionaries with an unusual request. It seemed that an elderly citizen, Tom O'Hare, a pioneer who had almost singlehandedly built the community, was now exhibiting possible signs of senility. Or perhaps he simply had prostate problems. He had recently begun relieving himself when he felt the need, wherever and whenever he happened to be as long as it was out-of-doors. According to the missionary, this behavior was unbearably embarrassing to Tom's young, recent converted, Athabascan wife, Annie. The preacher wanted me to send Tom to the Pioneer's Home in Sitka, or hold a sanity hearing.

I couldn't find anything in my Commissioner's Handbook about sanity hearings, but I was sure that the Pioneer's Home wouldn't tolerate such behavior. Sending Tom to Sitka was really condemning him to spend the rest of his life in Morningside Sanitarium in Oregon where Alaska's mentally ill were warehoused. It didn't sound to me as if Tom posed a threat to himself or others, and I wasn't inclined—even if I had the authority—to give him a one-way ticket to Sitka.

I was frank. I told the missionary, "Sending Tom Outside would kill him. He's looked after his wife for 15 years. Now it's her turn. She can take care of him for a change."

To my great surprise, the preacher became very angry when he realized I wouldn't cooperate with what I considered a transparent scheme to get rid of the old man. Evidently, he was used to having his own way, and didn't appreciate being frustrated. That attitude, I later learned, is not uncommon among the holy.

Only later did I discover what may have been the real motive for wanting to send Tom away. Apparently, Annie had been ready to give their house to the missionaries, but Tom, stubborn old man that he was, had refused.

That incident will give you some idea how broad an Alaskan commissioner's powers were. Each commissioner served a geographic area or "precinct." Commissioners served as county clerks, issuing marriage licenses, and recording mining claims, deeds, wills, and other documents. They also served as justices of the peace, trying criminal misdemeanors and small claims civil cases, and performing marriages. They also served as coroner, and when necessary, had the power to convene a coroner's jury. Less commonly, they also served as juvenile judge and as probate judge.

These paragons were appointed by and served at the pleasure of the respective federal district court judges in the several judicial divisions.

At roughly 9,000 square miles, the Iliamna Precinct was about the size of Vermont, but had a population of only slightly over 500 people, nearly half of whom lived in Nondalton, the Indian (Athabascan) village on Six-Mile Lake at the head of the world-famous Newhalen River, between Lake Clark and Lake Iliamna. There was a small settlement on Lake Clark, but the rest, mostly Eskimos, lived in scattered villages around Lake Iliamna. A handful of people like ourselves lived apart from everyone else.

The prospect of my appointment did not meet with universal approval. The religious folks didn't know me, but as far as they were concerned, I already had two unforgivable strikes against me. First, I was not one of them. Second, I was an unknown quality. Fundamentalists of every stripe hate to deal with the unknown.

My first inkling of opposition from another quarter came early in the spring when the game warden's plane with its clear US Fish and Wildlife Service markings, landed on skis on the ice in front of our cabin. The district game warden, Bob Mahaffey, climbed down from the pilot's seat. The passenger's door opened, and another game warden, Sid Morgan, climbed down on that side. Then a third, stocky figure emerged from the plane. It was Nick, an Eskimo from Newhalen.

I walked down to meet the men. After we shook hands, Bob Mahaffey motioned toward the Eskimo and said, "Nick, here, tells me he saw a dead moose here last week. Can you tell us anything about it?"

I was stunned. The basic charge was a lie. I hadn't seen Nick for two months. On the other hand, my conscience wasn't entirely clear. One of the men from the village had brought a moose haunch about three weeks earlier. A good bit of it was still hanging in the windbreak when the plane first appeared. As soon as I realized who our visitors were, I had swiftly cut the leg down and concealed it in a box at the bottom of a stack of empty cardboard boxes.

I am not a successful liar, but by focusing on Mahaffey's blatant falsehood, I was able to muster what I hoped was convincing indignation. "I haven't seen Nick, here, for two months. He's crazy if he told you that!"

"Well, maybe so," Mahaffey replied, smiling his infuriating *gotcha!* grin. "Do you mind if we look around?"

I didn't know then that Mahaffey had gone to the trouble of swearing out a search warrant. I was (sort of) innocent, and innocent people have nothing to hide, so I shrugged. "Sure, why not if it will make you feel better."

Mahaffey merely grinned again. Then the two wardens went to work. They searched the cabin first. I watched Morgan sort through the top four empty cardboard boxes on top of the box containing the contraband. But he didn't go deep enough. Then they examined every conceivable hiding place outside. I followed them for a while, but finally went back to the cabin and was sitting at the table drinking coffee when Mahaffey and Morgan returned from a long walk in the woods. They had followed each of the trails I had made cutting logs. They had even searched the sawmill.

Then, sitting at the table sipping coffee, the cross examination began. "We heard that you had moose snares set up in the woods," Mahaffey said.

Ah, ha! I said to myself. *That explains it.* The previous summer, I had amused the other fishermen in our bunkhouse by telling about my efforts to salvage a small wrecked amphibian—a Republic Sea-Bee—that had crashed the previous spring in shallow water near Kakhonak River. Kallenberg had asked what I wanted it for, and I had replied, "I could use the wheels, the control cables, perhaps even some of the hydraulic equipment."

Bob had heard only "control cables," and began teasing me about making moose snares with them. That was where *that* story had come from. I explained the origin of that rumor to my inquisitors. Then, looking straight at Mahaffey, I asked, "This search party couldn't have something to do with my nomination to be the next commissioner, could it?"

Morgan looked uncomfortably at the ceiling. Mahaffey looked me straight in the eye, and beginning that *gotcha!* grin again, said, "Well, it wouldn't do to have a poacher as a commissioner, now, would it?" I suppose he had a point. A few minutes later, they left.

Shortly before dark, we saw a lone dog team approaching from the direction of the village. It was Feeny Andrew. I went down to the ice to greet him, while he tied his dogs. Then we went to the cabin and sat at the table while Jan poured coffee. Feeny came right to the point.

He unwrapped a flat package, revealing an old, battered, cigar box. "I bring church money," he said, "to pay fine."

I realized immediately that he—and the village—knew about our visitors. Feeny was thinking about the meat I had hidden in the windbreak. He knew I didn't have a moose hidden on the property. I couldn't see why they felt obligated to make up for the misdeeds of an Eskimo from a different village, and I said as much.

It was Feeny's turn to be surprised. He hadn't known that Nick had accompanied the game wardens. "Day catch Nick Nowatak on Tommy Point with moose," Feeny said, "and make 'em say you catch moose."

Ah, Now I understood. I could well imagine Mahaffey

scaring poor Nick half to death. Nick could neither read nor write and his English was scarcely better than my Yupik. I was surprised he was able to understand what Mahaffey wanted.

"He boy wid 'im," Feeny explained. "He talk fer 'im." I knew the boy. He was about 11 or 12, somewhat of a smart aleck, whose English was quite good.

The cigar box was still on the table. "Feeny," I said, "they didn't find anything. There isn't any fine."

A relieved Feeny soon left for the village, church money intact. I'm not sure exactly how they operated the church money box, but it served as a community bank. The funds were loaned to needy parishioners. They were also used for community projects, and on rare occasions, were even used to pay game violation fines when a member of that community helped frame an unsuspecting commissioner candidate.

I had another unwanted visit from Mr. Mahaffey again that spring, shortly after we received our "Dear John" letters.

The fishermen's union agreement assumed that all members in good standing would be rehired by their cannery year after year. However, in case a superintendent decided not to rehire a man, the agreement required him to notify the fisherman of that fact by registered mail no later than April first so the man would have a chance to seek another job for that season.

By April Fool's day, 1954, *all* the fishermen in the precinct, including me, had received such letters from our respective canneries. Although the canners later denied it, I am convinced this was a pay-back for the jurisdictional strike of 1951 and the sitdown strike in 1953.

Jan and I were sitting at the kitchen table reading and re-reading that terrible letter and discussing the best way to meet this latest problem, when a small plane buzzed the cabin. We rushed outside to see the Fish and Wildlife Super Cub banking in a tight turn, preparatory to landing. In minutes, our game warden, Bob Mahaffey, was entering the cabin. This time, he was alone.

Coming straight to the point, as he stirred his coffee, Mahaffey said: "As you know, Denny, the canneries took a big financial hit last year."

I nodded.

"We have a new director in Fish and Wildlife, a man named Colonel Farley," he continued, "who has rewritten the regulations this year. The old fishing regulations allowed any amount of gear in the fisheries the canneries wanted to use. But since the sailboats are gone, the new director is convinced we must now limit the number of boats in the fishery.

"He can't do that directly. But he can control the amount of fishing time available. So, he has developed a formula that makes fishing time proportional to the number of boats in the fishery. The more boats, the less fishing time per week."

I thought I saw where this was taking us. He continued, "We think the optimum number of boats in the Kvichak this year will be 450. Under the formula, that number of boats would have 96 hours of fishing time per week."

"What happens if there's 451 boats?" I asked.

"According to the formula, fishing time would be cut 12 hours, so you'd only have 84 hours per week."

"Where does that leave us?" I asked.

"I understand the canneries have notified all the Native fishermen that they don't have jobs this year," he said.

"That's not my question," I said. "Suppose the upriver fishermen all went independent. What then?"

He shook his head. "There isn't room for your fishermen this year," he insisted. "I think it's your duty to see to it that the local men all stay home this summer."

At first, I thought he must be joking. I couldn't imagine any responsible person asking people not to work at the only occupation they know so others could make more money. But that's exactly what Mahaffey was doing.

I did some fast calculations in my head. Then I turned to Mahaffey, and asked, "Suppose 50 Native boats outside the quota show up. Then what happens?"

"We'd probably have to close the fishery," he said.

"That's fine," I said grimly. "Because if we can't fish, nobody fishes!"

Later, after assuring Mahaffey that I would do everything in my power to flood the river with local boats and gear, I escorted him back to his plane and stood outside, watching him take off. I wondered what must happen to a man's self-respect when he knowingly served as a lacky to the billion dollar corporations which thought they owned the Bristol Bay fisheries. As much as I disliked Mahaffey, I didn't envy him.

Breakup was eminent. The next morning, I harnessed the team, and drove to the village. The men quickly gathered in Feeny's tiny cabin. Pulling no punches, I told my audience about Mahaffey's visit. Then I outlined a possible strategy to counter it. My idea was to flood the Naknek–Kvichak fishery with as much non-quota gear as possible. I felt that unless we struck back with all the force we could muster, we might be squeezed permanently out of the fishery.

Although the upriver Eskimos were understandably shy about things they didn't understand, and tended not to be aggressive in any case, the men agreed with me. The next day, dog sleds from our village fanned out. Some went to Igiugig at the mouth of the lake where their drivers conferred with the half dozen Eskimo fishermen who lived there.

Another delegation went in the opposite direction, to Pile Bay and Pedro Bay at the head of the lake. The residents there were Athabascan Indians. I wasn't sure how the Eskimo delegation would be received, but I needn't have worried. The Eskimos and Indians didn't always get along, but on an issue of common interest like this, there was no problem.

Two days later, I made my last dog team trip of the year across the lake. I explained the situation to Art Lee. Then, after spending the night at the roadhouse, a local bush pilot, Oren Hudson, flew me to Nondalton so I could meet with those fishermen.

Nearly 100 people crowded into the schoolhouse to hear what I had to say. I explained the situation, and told them how we at Kakhonak planned to respond. Then I asked for a show of hands of those with boats and nets willing to join us, even though it meant facing the certain wrath of the canners. At least 25 hands shot into the air.

Three days later, back in the village, the couriers and I compared notes and discovered, somewhat to my surprise, that we could muster 73 boats. Most of them were long, narrow, river boats from Nondalton, which would have to be trucked over the portage from the lower end of Six-Mile Lake to the roadhouse. I admired the spirit and courage of their owners, but seriously doubted their wisdom. Those boats were entirely unsuited to Bristol Bay conditions.

Nearly every household on the lake boasted a skiff. Feeny and Little Joe, in Kakhonak, had gas boats. Feeny invited me to join him. There were another half dozen gas boats up the lake. One lucky fellow in Igiugig had a sailboat complete with mast, boom, sprit and sail.

Almost every man who wanted to go fishing had a chance. Where we fell short was nets. The Bristol Bay canneries had made a partial switch by that time to nylon nets, but they were still using wooden corks and cotton lines. The old linen nets had found their way upriver where they were used during the salmon runs by the women and children, to catch salmon to dry for winter food, and for dog food.

Those nets never received any anti-bacterial treatment, and consequently most of them were seriously decayed. However,

I was quickly learning never to underestimate an Eskimo. The nets that could be salvaged were stretched over net racks, and men and women with net needles began repairing them.

To make a maximum impression on the authorities, we hoped to arrive in Naknek in a body. Therefore, everyone agreed to rendezvous at Igiugig on June 15. We were there a day early and camped on the beach next to the village.

The boats from Nondalton were the last to arrive. They had to watch the weather very closely. It was 45 unsheltered miles in a straight line from the roadhouse to Igiugig. If a strong wind suddenly began to blow, the lake could become violently dangerous in a very few minutes, even for a gas boat like Feeny's. The river boats were infinitely more dangerous, and were entirely unsuited to travel on the open lake.

The "mosquito fleet," as this nondescript flotilla became known, arrived in Naknek on June 18. I had distributed license application forms to the fishermen and collected them back with the appropriate fees before we left Igiugig. While the fishermen set up camp on the beach at Naknek Point, I took a cab out to Fish and Wildlife headquarters at King Salmon to purchase their licenses. The place was a madhouse. The authorities knew we were coming, and the Governor had sent the lieutenant governor to try to resolve the problem. He was seated at a table in the corner, meeting with the cannery operators when I walked through the door.

The room fell silent as I entered. Ignoring the meeting in the corner, I went directly to a young man at a desk piled high with license application forms. "I have a few more applications to add to the pile," I said pleasantly.

He looked despairingly at his supervisor across the room. A man detached himself from the crowd in the corner and took a step in my direction. I had never seen him before, but from Bob Kallenberg's description, I knew I was looking at Bert Johnson, the Fish and Wildlife fishery supervisor. "Can't you see there's a meeting going on here?" he demanded.

I shrugged. I'd been thrown out of better places than this. "OK," I said, and I turned toward the door.

"Wait a minute, fellow," someone else called as I reached the door. I paused, my hand on the knob.

"Are you connected with those Natives down on the beach?" the same voice inquired.

I turned to face the crowd. "Yes," I said. "My name is Denny Moore. I'm from Kakhonak Bay up on the lake."

I had a good look at the man. He was balding, in late middle age. When he stood up, I saw he was well over six feet tall. He stepped forward, holding out his hand. "I'm Hugh Wade," he said, adding, "I'm the lieutenant governor. I think you'd better join us."

The other men around the table quickly identified themselves. The two whose names I remembered were Aubin Barthold of Alaska Packers Association, a heavy-set, dark haired man, and Win Brindle of Red Salmon. Mr. Brindle was a small, slender, man with gaunt features, a very prominent nose, and the sharpest eyes I ever encountered.

Inside or out, Mr. Brindle almost invariably wore a cloth cap. If Barthold resembled an English squire, Brindle looked like his cockney game-keeper. As I studied his features, Brindle picked up the thread of his argument.

". . .those AFU fellows have me over a barrel. If I buy even one fish from Moore's mosquito fleet—this was the first time I had heard that expression—and it causes a 12 hour loss in fishing time, I'll have to pay every fisherman on the Kvichak an indemnity of 1,000 fish for every day of lost fishing time. It would cost me $60,000 a day!"

"Well," Governor Wade said, "suppose Bert Johnson, here, let the Native fishermen fish outside the formula? Then there's no loss of time."

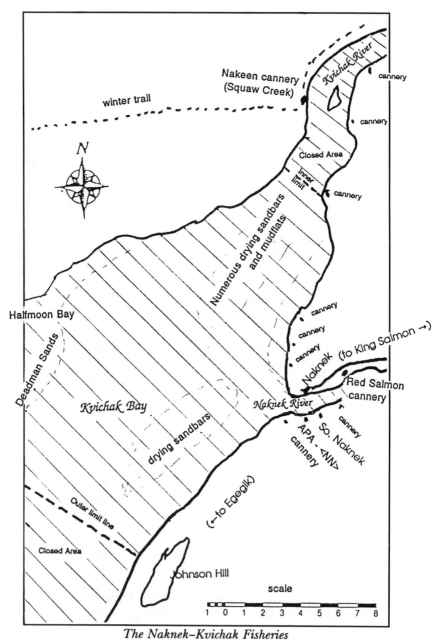

The Naknek–Kvichak Fisheries
—Drawn by Capt. Jim Hogan

244

"It makes no difference. I don't dare take the chance."

I was right. It was obvious that Brindle was using a "sweetheart" clause in his AFU Agreement to break our resident union. Wade argued and pleaded, but Brindle was unyielding. He would not accept our fish, and that was all there was to it.

The meeting broke up on that inconclusive note. I thumbed a ride back to Naknek where I met the fishermen I now thought of as my own. I told them what had happened. It looked like we had gone to a lot of trouble for nothing. While we stood on the beach trying to think what to do next, Gunnar Bergen and Father Endahl, the Catholic priest I had known at Clarks Point, drove up in Gunnar's truck.

After we exchanged greetings and shook hands, Gunnar said, "I hear dot Homer Kyros on de *Arctic Maid* down off Egegik might buy your fish."

I quickly learned that Homer Kyros and Gunnar were old friends, and that Kyros had spent several winters in the country. I also knew that Gunnar, not an easy man to fool, thought a great deal of him.

"How do I get down to Egegik?" I asked.

"Vell, Taddy Moonson says ve can borrow Charlie Herrmann's conwersion," Gunnar replied, "as long as Taddy runs it, that is."

We were a strange crew aboard an even stranger craft the next morning when we left Naknek on top of the morning tide. There were three of us aboard beside myself. Gunnar Bergan, a thin, intense man in late middle age with brilliant blue eyes and a thick Norwegian accent, Father Endahl, a big, jovial Jesuit priest, smart as hell and genuinely concerned for the fishermen, and Taddy Monsen, a member of a large local family. He was our skipper.

The tide carried us along nicely, which was lucky, because when Charlie had converted the boat to power, he had been obliged to mate a right hand engine with a left hand propeller. We had forward motion only while we were in reverse gear.

The engineers who design reverse gears never imagine they will be used hour after hour for primary propulsion. They are not designed to withstand the stress of 50 mile runs. Ours failed about five miles north of the *Arctic Maid*.

Luckily, a fish patrol boat was in the vicinity. The officer, seeing we were in difficulty, took us in tow and delivered us to the *Arctic Maid*.

The *Arctic Maid* was a small war-surplus Army supply ship that had been converted into a 400 ton tuna seiner. Like all tuna seiners, she preserved her catch by freezing the fish in super chilled brine. That was also the way she preserved the salmon brought aboard by her catcher boats. The *Arctic Maid's* most serious limitation was her size. With a 400 ton capacity, she could carry only about 150,000 salmon.

Homer was a stocky man with graying black hair, heavy eyebrows, and unmistakably Homeric features. He greeted Gunnar with easy familiarity and shook hands with Father Endahl and me. We sat in the galley while he listened sympathetically to our story, shaking his head when I explained Brindle's attitude toward us.

He thought for a few moments, then he said almost more to himself than us, "Maybe I can help. We could put Bob Young's scow *Columbia* in the Naknek River to receive fish. I will pay 73¢ for red salmon, but no writing, no contract."

Father Endahl smiled his sweet smile, and said, "But a contract merely avoids misunderstandings."

Homer shook his head. "I can't give you a contract," he said firmly, "because I already have 11 boats. I'm going to get heat from those guys just by trying to help you out, because they will fear that this extra effort will fill the boat too soon." He spread his hands and shrugged his shoulders. "I'm sorry," he said, "that's the best I can do. You'll just have to trust me." He paused, then added, "One other thing. If the fish hit and I have to put my guys on limit, I'll have to cut you loose. You'll be on your own. I won't be able to take your fish, too."

Gunnar, Father Endahl, and I retired to a corner and discussed Homer's offer. Nobody likes a take it or leave it proposition, but we really had no choice. Making the best of it, we shook hands, and began working out the details, such as nets. Luckily, Homer had plenty of spare gear, and was willing to give it to us on credit.

1954 turned out to be a poorer season, even, than 1953. Ironically, the low point for us was on the Fourth of July when, poor as it was, the only semblance of a run to appear that year occurred. Unbelievably, in 24 hours, our despised mosquito fleet in its weird, almost bizarre, collection of river boats and cast-off sailboats, caught and delivered to the *Columbia* over 63,000 salmon. Roughly 1,500 of those fish belonged to Feeny and me.

My first inkling of trouble came the next day when we came alongside the *Columbia*, prepared to deliver our usual 50 fish and saw that the previous day's catch was still on board. *Columbia's* skipper, a tall slender man with blonde hair named Bob Young, who seemed much too young to be operating his own scow, was standing on the deck, watching our approach. He shook his head as I offered our line.

"I can't take your fish," he said quietly.

It took a moment for those words to penetrate. My ears suddenly began to ring, and I felt as if I had received a massive blow in the midriff. I had trouble breathing, and I even wondered briefly if I could be dreaming.

When I felt I could trust my voice, I asked, "Why not?"

He sighed. "Come aboard," he said. "I need to tell you, so you can pass the word."

Feeny and I secured the boat and followed Bob into his

247

galley. He poured three cups of coffee, and sliding two across the galley table to us, he sat on the bench opposite.

"It's Brindle," he said. Then he explained that the same tide which had brought the fish run into the Kvichak had also brought fish to Egegik, and that Homer's 11 boats had loaded up.

"Homer was trying to save room for your fish," he said, "but one of his generators broke down. That cut his freezing capacity in half." Bob stopped, and stared at his coffee cup for a full minute before he resumed.

"When he realized that he couldn't even process all the fish his own boats had delivered, he called the other floating processors, but only Augie on the *North Star* had room for more fish. That's how he took care of his own boats."

Bob then explained that the old US Fish and Wildlife ship *Dennis Winn* had gone alongside the *Arctic Maid* and had passed a heavy electric cable over to provide emergency power until the fish on board were frozen.

"In the meanwhile," Bob continued, "Homer flew up here to see Win Brindle about saving these fish."

Bob didn't need to explain why Homer had called upon Mr. Brindle. Numerous consolidations had occurred as the industry retrenched after the economic debacle the canners had experienced in 1953, and only two canneries were open in the Naknek–Kvichak district in 1954, Mr. Brindle's Red Salmon cannery and the big Alaska Packer's plant across the river in South Naknek. Bob didn't mention Alaska Packer's, and I don't know why Homer passed them up, but evidently he had gone directly to Red Salmon.

"The first person Homer saw in the cannery," Bob continued, "was Floyd Olson, Brindle's cannery foreman. Olson already had the crew washing up, but when Homer explained the problem, he said, 'Sure, we're all cleaned up. Bring your scow up on the next tide.' Then, as an afterthought, he added, 'But you'd better check with the Old Man, first.' So, Homer went looking for Brindle. He found him in the warehouse. He explained the problem, and told Win what Floyd had told him. Brindle stared at him for a moment, then said, 'Hell, no! I won't touch your fish!'"

Bob went on to say that Homer had pleaded with Brindle, offering in the alternative to sell the fish to him outright, or hire the services of the cannery to custom pack the fish for his account or Washington Fish and Oyster's account; anything to save them.

"Nothing doing. Brindle was unyielding. He would not allow the fish on his property."

Bob stood up. "I've got to get busy," he said. "I wanted you to see those fish before they went overboard so you'd know there wasn't something funny going on."

Bob followed me out the galley door. I went back to my boat and watched while Bob rigged his fire hose and washed 63,000 fish overboard.

It was incredible that in what turned out to be the poorest season since 1910, one man's stubbornness was responsible for the wanton waste of over 5,000 cases of salmon. Brindle didn't even have the grace to plead the sweetheart clause in the union agreement to justify his action.

For us, as I'm sure he intended, his refusal was an economic catastrophe. A full two-thirds of that year's payday went overboard with those fish. At the end of that season, with my truncated paycheck, I was able to buy just over $300 worth of groceries to see us through the winter. And I was one of the luckier ones. Some of those river boats carried three men, and they undoubtedly earned much less than I.

Years later, when we were discussing this terrible situation, Mr. Brindle hinted that others—my guess is, Alaska Packers— were the real villains behind his refusal. "There are things about that incident that you don't know, Moore," he said darkly, adding, "I wasn't entirely a free agent."

Jan used to say, during those years, that she could estimate how many fish I had caught when, after a two month absence, she saw how heavily laden my boat was as it came into view around the bend.

The President again declared Bristol Bay a disaster area, which meant that we would again count our wealth by the number of sacks of beans that were piled in the windbreak.

As a surrealistic end to an utterly bizarre season, the Bering Sea Fisherman's Union found itself in trouble with the Federal Trade Commission for "conspiring to fix the price of raw fish" by attempting to bargain on behalf of independent fishermen such as my ragged cohorts and me.

The FTC also took a dim view of the restraint of trade practiced by Mr. Brindle and his associates. Before the winter was over, the industry had signed a consent decree admitting nothing, but promising not to do it again.

I thought the only appropriate remedy was to sue Mr. Brindle for what seemed to me to be a clear anti-trust violation, but cooler heads prevailed. The folks in Dillingham, Truman Emberg and Jim Downey, who, three years earlier, had formed the Bering Sea Fishermen's Union, now focused on meeting the FTC's objections by forming an agricultural marketing cooperative which they called the Bristol Bay Fish Producer's Association.

In the meanwhile, President Eisenhower declared Bristol Bay a federal disaster area for the second year.

12

The Tough Years

J an was appointed postmistress of a newly created fourth class post office at Kokhanok Bay the summer of 1954. We hadn't moved; we simply changed the way the name of the place was spelled to conform with the way local people pronounced it, **Kok-ha-nok**.

Although President Truman had been out of office nearly two years when Jan received her appointment, her commission bore his signature. Of course, postmasters of fourth class post offices didn't rank high in the pantheon of presidential appointees. They were paid $600 per year, more if their stamp sales warranted it.

Jan the postmistress

Unknowingly, with the establishment of this post office, we were indirectly responsible for retiring the last dog sled mail route in the United States. Nels Hedlund had distributed the mail from Iliamna to smaller post offices at the eastern end of the lake by dog sled. However, when the Kokhanok Bay post office was created, the Post Office Department decided to switch from dog teams to airplanes, and an ex-bomber pilot named Oren Hudson successfully bid the air mail contract.

The Kokhanok Bay post office was established at almost the same time as my appointment as US commissioner for the Iliamna Precinct became effective. Commissioners were equipped with a safe, a typewriter, a table, two straight chairs, a volume of Alaska Statutes, and a Commissioner's Handbook. Everything except the safe was new, and was delivered by Hermy Herrmann on his annual fall delivery run.

"Little" Joe

The safe was a different story. My predecessor was the wife of a federal employee at the Iliamna airfield. She had never bothered to shelter the safe after Carl Williams had brought it to Iliamna from Pile Bay on his scow, and it had remained on the beach, looking like a small, forlorn, steel outhouse.

The Administrative Office allowed $50 to pay for moving it across the lake. I dangled the money in front of Little Joe, and urged him to ferry it to Kokhanok on his gas boat.

The damn thing weighed nearly a ton, and it took a dozen husky men to push it, on wooden rollers, up an impromptu gangplank, until it rested on planks laid across the boat's gunwales.

It was dangerously high in the boat, and caused the boat to roll slowly and deeply. We needed more ballast, and scoured the beach looking for small boulders to pile in the boat's bottom. At last, Little Joe was satisfied, and we left Iliamna for Kokhanok Bay.

I had great confidence in Joe. They called him "Little Joe" because his body was deformed. He was a hunchback dwarf. That was a serious handicap in an environment as physically demanding as ours. Nevertheless, the other Eskimos accorded him a great deal of respect, not because he had overcome his limitations, but because he was smarter than most. He was a natural leader, and others willingly followed him.

Little Joe was sufficiently dubious about this venture, so Feeny Andrew accompanied us in his gas boat, just in case our boat rolled over halfway across the lake.

We had no trouble. When we arrived at our gravel beach, I used the winch on the tractor to pull the safe off the boat and onto a wagon. It was a simple matter, then, to move it across the portage. I stood it upright on a newly constructed floor (that sawmill was a blessing!) and built a third room, appropriately defined as the office, around it.

The US commissioner worked on a set fee basis, depending on the job. Simple filing and recording chores paid two dollars, while conducting a criminal trial, performing a wedding, or serving as coroner, paid the maximum, $25. Some commissioners did better than that. Art Lee liked to tell about a former commissioner who granted informal divorces as well as performing marriages.

It seems that the old chief in Newhalen had tired of his wife. She had grown old and wrinkled. Her teeth were worn down by chewing leather and her eyesight was failing because she had taken too many stitches by the light of a kerosene lantern. A younger woman was available.

The chief hitched up his dog team and drove to interview the commissioner. He came straight to the point. "Sam," he said, "I want a divorce."

The commissioner looked grave. "Divorces are very expensive," he said.

"How much?"

"$600," the commissioner said.

"OK, I pay $600," the old man said, pulling his wallet from under his parka. He handed the money to Sam.

Sam said, "OK. It will take two, maybe three weeks. Come back then, and I'll have your divorce for you."

Feeling as if he had recovered his youth, the old chief happily returned to his village. His joy was short lived, however, because a week later, the bishop arrived on his annual visit to his far-flung parish.

The Russian Orthodox Church of North America played an important role in the social lives of those coastal Eskimos, and a visit by the bishop was almost like a visit from God.

Eskimos love to gossip. The bishop hadn't been in town 15 minutes before he had heard about the chief's pending divorce. He and the old man had a heart to heart talk about Hell and Eternity, and various other unpleasant things. The old man was instructed to walk around the village all night, seeking God's counsel.

Art would smile at this point, describing how the children ran behind the chief, mocking and making fun of him while he was performing his penance. The next morning, having seen the light, the chief harnessed his team and returned to Pile Bay. Again, he came straight to the point. "Sam, I want to call off the divorce."

Sam sadly shook his head and sighed. "Chief," he said, "what you're asking is very expensive."

The chief was resigned. "How much he cost?"

"$600," Sam said.

Silently, the old chief paid his money.

Art swore the story was true, and having known some of the characters involved, I don't doubt it. There is no question that the early white people in the Territory were not always of unblemished character, and if the Eskimos knew anything about white man's law, they knew it was expensive. They always came prepared for the worse. That was why Feeny had appeared the previous spring with the church money to bail me out after Mahaffey's visit.

The earlier settlers weren't the only rogues. Shortly after I obtained the commissioner's files, I discovered that when Mahaffey had searched the homestead the previous winter, he was armed with a search warrant he had obtained by using a false affidavit.

I probably should have referred the case to the US attorney in Anchorage. Had I done so, he might be alive today. However, since I merely hoped to see him transferred to some unpleasant place where he would spend the remainder of his career counting ducks, I only advised the Interior Department of the facts in this case.

Frankly, I never liked the man. He had a mean streak in him. Stan Chmiel used to complain that he had maliciously ruined the commercial value of a wolf pelt Stan had offered for bounty by "accidentally" mutilating the hide while he was hole punching the ear to prevent the hide from being offered for bounty again.

I watched him prosecute several commercial fishing violations in Naknek when Albert Davy was the commissioner. Albert wasn't very strong on procedure, and Mahaffey took full advantage of it. The hapless defendant would stand in front of the commissioner while the complaint was read to him. Then he would be placed under oath, and be required to explain himself. Only after the defendant had exhausted his defenses would Mahaffey, smiling his usual wolfish grin, state the government's case against him. The poor defendant never had a chance.

Apparently, there was another side to Bob Mahaffey that presumably none of us in Bristol Bay knew. Shortly after his transfer to Kodiak, Bob and his wife, Betty, went to a New

Year's Eve party. When they returned home, according to the widow, they had indulged in a foolish three am, in-depth analysis of their relationship; a discussion which inevitably included the Other Woman.

Anyone with a lick of sense will tell you that three o'clock of a New Year's morning is not the time for this kind of discussion. Judgment is likely to be fuzzy, and perspective may be lost. This would be especially true for a guy like Mahaffey, who already was strongly inclined toward pulling the wings off flies. It was to be his undoing.

At his widow's trial, it developed that he had been involved with the wife of a Seattle dentist. According to his widow's testimony, she had asked the old, and sometimes fatal, question. "What do you see in her that you don't see in me?"

Mahaffey was lying on the bed at the time, his arms folded behind his head. I can well imagine how that wolf's grin might have crossed his face as he yielded to the temptation of pulling yet another wing from that tormented fly.

"Because she's better in bed than you are, my dear," he said, not realizing he had just uttered his death sentence.

Betty responded by grabbing his service revolver and shooting him full of holes.

Few tears were shed in Bristol Bay. But Betty wept copious tears at her trial. Her primary defense was simply that she did not want to be separated from her four children. Judge J. L. McCarrey, the same federal judge who had appointed me commissioner, sentenced her to serve two years for manslaughter. Since she had been in jail for nearly a year and a half awaiting trial, he merely suspended the last six months. She walked out of the court, a free woman.

Unlike their brethren in the "lower 48" who held life appointments, Territorial federal district court judges in Alaska were appointed for four year terms. According to the gossip in local legal circles, President Eisenhower had a very difficult time finding a Republican lawyer in Anchorage willing to give up a lucrative law practice to serve a short term on the federal bench. Then he found Mr. McCarrey.

McCarrey was the quintessential Alaskan success story. He had come to Alaska as a salesman for the Utah Woolen Mills. He soon began to study law and eventually obtained a mail order law degree. According to his detractors, he had studied while he was traveling up and down the Yukon River, selling woolen long johns to the Indians.

The judge was a very compassionate man, as his handling of the Mahaffey case illustrates. He was so compassionate, in fact, that, partly in reference to his earlier profession, his fellow lawyers had nicknamed him "The Great Suspender."

A much more profound tragedy occurred a week later, during the Russian Christmas celebration. The first inkling I had of trouble was when I received a telegram informing me that " . . .all five bodies have been found and there is no evidence of foul play. Therefore, the marshal's office has no responsibility for recovering the bodies. (Signed) Fred Williamson, US Marshal."

I had no idea whose bodies had been found, or where. However, on the evening radio schedule, I quickly learned that the victims were Simeon Wassillie, his wife Annie, a 14-year-old daughter named Octrina, an 11-year-old son, Steven, and a baby. Oren promised to pick me up in the morning so we could recover the bodies.

I didn't sleep well that night. My imagination kept repeating one dreadful scenario after another. I couldn't imagine what had happened to that unfortunate family.

Oren was then flying a four-place Piper Pacer on skis. He arrived shortly after nine o'clock. As I climbed into his plane, he told me that 12 sleds had left Newhalen bound for Igiugig for the annual *Slavik,* or Christmas visit. Simeon and his family had been part of that group.

The weather had been bad. The temperatures had remained between minus 20° at night to minus 10° during the
day for the past week. Compounding the weather problem,
a chill northwesterly wind had been blowing much of the
time. What I didn't know was that out on the lake, low-lying
ice fog had obscured visibility. Apparently, Simeon somehow
became separated from the others in the fog. The others
arrived at their destination, but poor Simeon and his family
didn't. The CAA caretaker at the little dirt airstrip at Igiugig
alerted the Civil Air Patrol, and an aerial search had been
launched from King Salmon. After searching for three days,
Dick Jenson had found the sled and its tragic cargo.

Oren and I quickly took off and soon reached Kakhonak
village. Simeon's brother, Gabriel, was waiting for us. He
climbed in the back seat and we began the search again.

Oren explained, shouting over the engine's roar, "Dick
found the bodies just before dark two days ago," he said. "He
landed just long enough to see that everyone was dead. It's
too bad he didn't take five more minutes and put up a
marker!" Then, after thinking a moment, he added, "We
were grounded yesterday because of the ice fog."

We were flying at about 500 feet. There was no fog today.
The ice stretched away in all directions. Seen with half closed
eyes, the alternating, smoothly contoured, windrows of snow
contrasting with the narrow streaks of glistening black ice,
looked like an utterly desolate seascape with frozen white-
caps. I couldn't understand how Oren could hope to find
anything as small as a sled in that immense expanse.

But Oren knew his business. He flew transects, back and
forth, back and forth, for over an hour, before Gabriel said
quietly directly in my left ear, "I see 'um."

Oren spotted the sled at the same moment, and as we
swung low over it, I saw a lonely sled, half buried in a snow
drift, with what looked like two bundles of rags, one in the

sled, the other draped over the sled's bow. The outline of a dog team showed through the snow.

"I wish I knew how high those drifts are," Oren muttered to himself as we braced for the landing. Then to us, as he closed his throttle, he said, "Hang on; this could be rough!"

We touched the top of a snow drift, and plowed through the next, as the plane lost momentum. Oren had timed his landing to minimize the taxiing he would have to do, and we came to a stop abreast of that tragic scene.

Gabriel was openly weeping as we slowly, reverently, approached the sled. Annie was in the sled, inexplicably sitting on the canvas sled cover and sleeping robes. They had made no attempt to save themselves by making a camp. She cradled the frozen baby in her arms. I have seen many more than my share of violent battlefield deaths, but nothing in my previous experience had prepared me for the sight of one tiny, pathetically bare, foot escaping her dead mother's grasp.

We can only guess, but quite possibly, knowing his family was gone, Simeon had simply died of despair while sitting on the bow of the sled. We found him sprawled across his sled, face up, lying backwards in the snow. His head and shoulders were buried in the snowdrift. The marshal's telegram notwithstanding, there were no additional bodies.

We struggled to fit those rigid bodies into the plane. When the door was finally closed, Gabriel and I watched the plane fly toward Igiugig. Not for the first time, I marvelled at the selflessness of ordinary Alaskans I knew. Oren knew he was performing this macabre task as a community service; that he would never be compensated for it.

Then Gabriel and I resumed our search, thinking perhaps another body might be concealed under a nearby snow drift. While we examined the drifts, Gabriel turned to me and answered the question—*how could this happen?*—that had been uppermost in my mind since I learned of this tragedy.

He had two explanations. First, he gestured toward the team. "Dogs, he quit," Gabriel said. "No fish, dogs can't pull good; they all the time hungry." Then, he added, "Simeon like to talk to the wind! Maybe wind get mad."

His remark triggered a memory of a stormy day by the sawmill when, after discussing the weather, Simeon had faced into the wind and shaken his fist, shouting, "I don't care if you blow; you can't scare me!" I specifically remembered my surprise at the reaction of the other Eskimos, who were obviously a little shocked by his defiant attitude.

Although the southern Eskimo's conversion to Christianity dates back to the first Russian fur traders over 200 years ago, their animistic faith—the belief that all physical phenomena, moose, trees, rain, even rocks, had souls—still heavily influenced their day-to-day lives.

By a miracle, two of Simeon's dogs were still barely alive. Cannibalism among dogs is almost unheard of, but they had survived by eating a dead comrade. Gabriel quietly put them out of their misery.

Then he pointed to the towline. For the first time, I realized a dog was missing from the team. Both its towline and collar line had been cleanly cut, as if by a knife.

I had known Simeon well. As one of the more independent thinkers, he was a leader among the Eskimos. We had worked closely together in Bristol Bay the previous summer, and I had come to have enormous respect for him.

It was painful to try reconstructing what must have happened. Unavoidably, I shared a faint echo of the agony Simeon must have experienced. I was certain that it was not coincidental that the girl and the dog were both absent.

I could imagine how he might have behaved after discovering that his wife and baby were dead. He might have cut the strongest dog from his failed team, handing the animal's towline to Octrina. Then he would have pointed downwind toward Big Mountain, visible above the fog, ten miles away.

He would have known, as I did, that if a resourceful Eskimo girl as old as Octrina could reach the brush with a dog, there was an good chance that she might survive.

When Oren returned to pick us up, he told us that Steven was alive. The boy had ridden on another sled. But nobody knew what had happened to Octrina.

As soon as I returned to Kokhanok, I sent a wire to the marshal describing what we had found and what we suspected had happened to Octrina. I also sent a telegram to the Commanding Officer, 10th Rescue Squadron, USAF, asking that the search for the missing girl be resumed. At daybreak the next morning, an old, slow flying, C-54 with Air Force markings, and an observer in every window seat, began combing the lake's shoreline. Dog teams from Kakhonak drove to Igiugig, meeting other teams from Newhalen that had similarly examined the northern shoreline. Unfortunately, no trace of the girl was ever found.

A young man named Gene Pope came from Ohio to live with us. This was an outgrowth of my continuing friendship with my black powder correspondent, Red Farris, in Portsmouth, Ohio. Red, you'll recall, was the man who had sold the antique squirrel rifle to me when we lived at Clarks Point.

I had mentioned in one of my letters the frustration I felt at not being able to accomplish everything I wanted to do because I was partly crippled, short handed, etc, etc. Red took me seriously, and asked if I could provide room and board for a young man, 17-years-old, who wanted to relive Daniel Boone's life.

By then, we had the room for another person. I had not only added two rooms to the cabin but had moved a decrepit old cabin built by an early day trapper up to the knoll next to our cabin. This was to become part cache, part bunkhouse. We had installed a space heater and a cot in it.

Lynnie and Trina playing in front of bunkhouse. Garage in background.

I said yes, as long as it was clearly understood that all we could pay was board and room. Wages were out of the question. It seemed like a godsend to me, and we enthusiastically welcomed our new recruit.

Oren Hudson brought Gene to Kokhanok on a cold day in February. As advertised, he was a husky, well-mannered young man. He was an eager and willing worker with a good outlook. The only problem was that he was 17 years old. That wasn't his fault; I knew he'd outgrow it if we survived.

My survival was problematical almost from the beginning. As soon as Gene was settled in his new quarters, I decided to show the kid around so he could get the lay of the land. Foolishly, I grabbed the .30/40 Krag and handed it to him.

"You might as well get used to carrying this; you can never tell what we might run into." We set off across the portage.

After crossing the portage, we went through some heavy brush near the mill. I noticed that the rifle's muzzle had somehow filled with snow.

"Hold on a minute, Gene. You've got some snow in the muzzle. If you fire the rifle now, you will likely blow up the receiver. Wait until I clear it."

I broke off a twig and began digging at the snow. A part of my mind noted that he was doing something with the rifle while I probed at the snow.

BANG!!

My hand was instantly numb. I stared at it in disbelief. My

thumb was bent back at an unnatural angle. It was also naked and black with powder burns. I had been wearing two pairs of cotton gloves. The cloth surrounding it had disappeared.

My forefinger was similarly denuded and blackened. I knew this was going to hurt like hell very soon, so I quickly peeled the gloves off my now bleeding hand, and pulling my shirt loose, put the injured hand against my bare stomach.

We hurried back to the cabin. Jan quickly snapped my thumb back into its proper orientation, and dressed the wound. It looked much worse than it was.

The part of my thumb and forefinger that was exposed after the cloth was blown away was indelibly tattooed with powder burns. There was a huge burn blister on my right index finger and my thumb print was gone. The skin and a tiny bit of meat at the end of my thumb was missing.

I was some kind of lucky! Fortunately, the most elemental rule of gun safety—to <u>always</u> keep the muzzle pointed away—had become an automatic reflex.

I didn't blame Gene. I knew he hadn't tried to murder me. But I'll tell you, that hand hurt for a long, long time.

A month or so later, he got me again. We had just finished supper, but were still sitting at the dinner table. My lower plate had been bothering me. Although it doesn't sound very elegant, I had removed it after dinner. Lots of men with ill-fitting dentures did that, but they usually slipped their teeth into a shirt pocket. I foolishly laid mine on the table.

Gene was telling a story. As he reached the climax, he made a dramatic sweeping gesture with his left hand and. . . It wasn't so much a crash as it was a quiet thud when my denture hit the floor, but it was broken in half.

Home remedies abound these days for fixing broken false teeth. There's Marine-Tex, Crazy Glue, all sorts of stuff. But then, the only remedy was a visit to the dentist. We were so poor, however, that a trip to the dentist in Anchorage was out of the question. I couldn't even think about a trip across the lake unless I traveled by dog sled. So I wrapped the broken denture in tissue, and put it out of reach of the children.

I planned to order a new mail-order plate from Chicago. But the mail service, such as it was, was interrupted by spring breakup. I became so accustomed to "gumming" my food (it's a gross exaggeration that toothless people necessarily subsist on a diet of mashed potatoes and Pablum) that I scarcely noticed when mail service was resumed until one day when "Babe" Alsworth landed in our bay.

Babe lived in a small settlement he had named for himself—Port Alsworth—on Lake Clark. It was about 50 miles from our homestead, on the other side of Roadhouse Mountain. He, his wife, Mary, and a grizzled old A&E (aircraft) mechanic named Mike Vandergrift, had single handedly built a settlement that subsequently attracted several retirees including a retired dentist.

Knowing that, I tucked the teeth into Babe's shirt pocket, and asked him to see if the doc could repair it. I didn't have much hope, but I thought it was worth the chance.

Two weeks later, when Oren made his next mail delivery, there was a small $10 C.O.D. package addressed to me from Port Alsworth. It was my repaired lower plate. It fit so well that I wore it comfortably for the next ten years.

The only major case I had during my tenure as commissioner involved a suspected murder at Nondalton.

Shortly before freeze-up, two men from Nondalton had whiled away a lazy afternoon lounging around the roadhouse drinking vanilla extract. When Art Lee cut them off, they summoned the local taxi, a 4-wheel drive Power Wagon, and were driven over the portage road to the landing on Six-Mile Lake where their skiff was tied. That was the last time anyone saw them both alive.

Sometime later, the survivor, Mike, still three sheets to the wind, arrived alone at the village. He explained that he and the other man had attempted to change places in the boat. Riverboats are notoriously cranky. His partner lost his balance and fell overboard, leaving only his wallet behind.

Possibly buoyed by the alcohol in his system, the deceased unexpectedly floated—this was unusual in such cold water—and as coroner, I was obliged to inspect the remains and decide whether to convene a coroner's jury.

When I arrived in the village, the deceased had been laid out in his house, and was lying on the kitchen table. His widow had dressed the corpse in fresh clean clothes, and had even prepared it for cold weather by wrapping a heavy muffler around its throat. I was curious about that muffler, and began unwinding it. The widow violently objected. That only whetted my curiosity, and I insisted on removing it.

I scarcely qualify as a forensic pathologist, but to my untrained eye, the bruises on the deceased man's throat looked suspicious. I decided to convene a jury.

Finding six adults in a village of 200 who are willing to swear they are unrelated to either party may seem a trifling task, but it was difficult. I nearly exhausted the voter list before I had my six jurors.

The jury and I inspected the dead man's throat. There were no other signs of foul play. Then the jury retired to consider whether the evidence was inconsistent with a finding of death by natural causes.

We left the deceased and returned to the village chief's house. The jury retired to the kitchen and deliberated for more than an hour. When it returned, the foreman said, "We t'ink Willy was killed."

Invisibly, I took off my coroner's hat and donned the hat of a magistrate conducting an arraignment. Then I sat in the kitchen and summoned the survivor.

I explained the procedure to him. Then I told him of the jury's finding. "What this boils down to, Mike," I said, "is that the jury thinks Willy was killed. I agree with them. That means that someone or something did the killing. Since you are the only possible suspect, I have no choice under the law but to bind you over to the grand jury for possible indictment." I then explained that the US marshal would come down from Anchorage in the next day or two, and take him into custody.

I returned to Kokhanok Bay, and sent a wire to the marshal in Anchorage. In due course, a deputy marshal arrived and took Mike to Anchorage where he spent the winter in jail, waiting for the grand jury. In the spring, when the grand jury convened, it refused to indict him. He was released and returned to Nondalton. That fall I performed the wedding ceremony that made him the wealthiest man in the village. He married Willy's widow and became an indirect beneficiary of the social security survivor's benefits paid to Willy's eight little orphans.

Weddings were an important adjunct to the commissioner's office. I suppose this was hardly surprising; when you think about it, even in Alaska, people are much more likely to get married than they are to be murdered or file mining claims. Especially after the bishop's annual visit. He would really get after the young folks who were living in sin. After a particularly good sermon, I'd sometimes get two or three weddings. On the other hand, although the bishop never realized it, I considered him to be substantially in my debt as the spring of 1955 rolled around.

I happened to be at the roadhouse. As usual, Art Lee and I sat up late gossiping and telling each other stories. Art was worried. He had a problem that only an innkeeper in a very rural setting would appreciate. It seems the bishop was scheduled to arrive two days hence. Art had enjoyed an unusually busy and prosperous year, what with all the federal and Territorial relief folks hanging around making sure the disaster relief was properly distributed. There had not been a January thaw that year; the temperature had remained unrelentingly at zero or below for four solid months.

As a result of the heavy traffic and continuous freezing weather, Art's outhouse had taken on a disgusting appearance as a frozen

*Nondalton wedding party
Oren's plane is in background*

brown cone interleaved with bits of white paper emerged from the toilet seat and jutted proudly in the air several inches above it. It didn't trouble Art that relief officials and humbler folk like me would have to crouch over that threatening cone as we responded to nature's call. But to ask a *bishop* to do that seemed somehow sacrilegious.

The guest bedroom was upstairs in an unheated, semi-finished room beneath the rafters. When I woke, it was full daylight. As I stretched and the sleep fell away from my mind, I became aware of a muffled rhythmic **thump! thump! thump!** Curious, I went to the window and rubbed a hole in the frosted pane.

Art was standing outside dressed in a jacket, mittens, fur hat, and boots, white breath rising from his effort, as he slammed a sledge hammer into the dirt near the outhouse.

Something I didn't quite understand was going on. I hurried into my clothes and rushed outside to get a better look. Art saw me coming.

"Ah, you're just in time," he said. "Give me a hand with this thing."

I realized then that he had been beating on the mudsills on which the outhouse rested, jarring them loose from the frozen ground.

"First thing we're going to do," Art said, "is lay this outhouse on its back."

We both pushed until it began to teeter on the rear sill. Then I went around in back to catch it, and as I took more weight, Art joined me, and we gently laid the little structure on the ground.

"Don't go away; I'll be right back," Art said, as he went to the garage, leaving me to contemplate those obscene twin brown cones, looking like negatives of nearly symmetrical miniature mountains.

Soon Art returned, bearing a crosscut saw over his shoulder. I almost went back into the house. I could only conclude that Art must have been raised a Catholic. I wasn't. I've done some bizarre things in my life, but when I accepted the other handle, and helped him fell those towering peaks of frozen shit, I wasn't doing it for Jesus. I was doing it for Art.

After Jan replaced me as commissioner, she had a criminal case involving an illegal wedding.

Alaska has a three-day waiting period between the time a marriage license is applied for, and when the wedding may be conducted. Obviously, this presented logistical problems because of our isolation. However, as far as I was concerned, notice was notice, whether it was expressed on a legal document or given over the radio. Therefore, rather than requiring the betrothed to make two trips across the lake, I accepted verbal license applications over the radio. The licenses were dated and filled out when I was notified. I think that procedure satisfied the law. No one complained.

Yet a year later, after Jan had replaced me as commissioner, she had to send me to arrest a preacher who had violated even that lenient notice requirement.

An oldtimer named Charlie Dennison up on Lake Clark had sent away for a mail order bride. The bride, a pleasant, middle-aged lady, originally from Switzerland, arrived at Iliamna. She was met by Oren and flown up to Lake Clark. When the missionary up at Port Alsworth discovered that Charlie intended to take his bride home and get married later, he raised so much hell that the parties reluctantly agreed to tie the knot on the spot without bothering with silly formalities, such as a marriage license. Missionaries tend to think that way when there's a question of divine as opposed to secular law.

When Jan heard what had happened, on the advice of Fred Williamson, the US marshal in Anchorage, she appointed me an acting deputy US marshal, and sent me to Nondalton to arrest the offending preacher and bring him in for a trial.

Nobody can get as mad as the truly righteous! Handling that fellow was like sorting wildcats. He was livid with anger when I placed him under arrest. In his eyes, everything he did was God's work; therefore, my objection was literally the work of the devil. I was a blasphemous heretic.

Jan heard the case and assessed a modest fine. She patiently explained what the consequences for Heidi, the bride, might have been had Charlie dropped dead of a heart attack on their wedding night. No Social Security, no inheritance, nothing.

None of this made much impression, of course. The missionary raved on and on about suing us—those people always have to have the last word—but we heard no more about it. Three days later, Jan flew up to Lake Clark with a properly seasoned marriage license, and did the job right.

In the spring, I made a swing by dog sled around the lake, visiting the villages, hearing small claims cases, registering the unrecorded births and deaths, helping seniors file for Social Security benefits, and poor people file for public assistance.

My last stop on this two-week trek was Newhalen.

There I met a man who would become one of the world's oldest persons. His name was Evon Olympic. A slight Eskimo with thinning gray hair and a wispy beard, he was neatly dressed in a clean checkered shirt and pants. The cornea of both eyes was thickly clouded. He was blind. He sat quietly at the kitchen table in the chief's house.

He spoke very little English, but finding good interpreters in a place like Newhalen was no problem. I quickly discovered that the old man was penniless. He wasn't receiving Social Security benefits because he lacked a birth certificate and thought he was unable to prove he was eligible.

However, the law provides for people like Evon. Church records are almost as acceptable as birth certificates, but he had none. However, the next best evidence, also acceptable, is the testimony of contemporary witnesses. Two men and a woman in that village were receiving old age retirement and survivor's benefits. According to the Social Security records the men were 69 and 76 while the old lady was 81.

I asked them how long they had known Evon. The oldest man said that he had known Evon all his life. Then I asked if he remembered when Evon had gotten married.

The old man grinned a toothless smile. He spoke briefly to the interpreter who then turned to me. "He say, Evon always got wife. Even when I little boy, Evon got wife."

The other man's memory wasn't as strong, but he tended to corroborate what the first man had said. It was the old woman's testimony that settled matters. She hailed from Togiak, and had come to Iliamna as a bride of 17. She said that Evon already had two children by then. If her age had been accurately estimated, she was born in 1874, and had come to Iliamna around 1891. The Russian-American Fur Company maintained a trading post and fort at Nushagak Point as late as 1890. I asked if she had visited the fort.

She replied, "Eee-e," adding, through the interpreter, details of the fort that a little girl might have noticed.

Evon described the Russian fur traders he had met. They had ventured as far inland as Newhalen in their endless search for fur.

I asked Evon how old his children were when the terrible flu epidemic obliterated whole Eskimo villages in 1920.

He replied that two *grandchildren* had died at Kaskanak, one of the villages obliterated by the epidemic.

I thought Evon might have been born as early as 1850, which would have made him 105 years old *at that time*. But, rather than risk straining the credulity of the person who would review the evidence we were offering, I backed off, and set an estimated birth date of 1857. The evidence was persuasive, and Evon began receiving his old age benefits.

Subsequently, he underwent successful cataract surgery in both eyes and in 1976, celebrated his official 119th birthday. He died the following year. He could have been 127 years old at the time of his death!

April was the perfect month for extended dog team trips. The trails were packed and well defined. The ice was as safe as it ever would be, the weather was good and the days were warm and long.

Almost as soon as I returned to the homestead, Jan tucked Debbie in a bedroll, and drove the team back across the lake to spend a few days with Helen Lee. It had been almost two years since she had spent any amount of time with another white woman. She never complained about it, and I don't know whether she missed the company of other women.

Of course, we were raising our own little women. Trina would turn six in August and would be starting school in September. The Territory provided correspondence courses through the Calvert School in Baltimore for students like Trina who lived in isolated circumstances.

Jan driving the dog team. The girls are standing in the sled.

The Territorial library system also provided a mail order service. Every month, we received a new package of books selected for us by the librarian, and returned the ones we had read. This was a wonderful convenience for people like us, who lived in such deep isolation.

The summer of 1955 promised to be a busy one. Jan was heavily pregnant again, and planned to fly into Anchorage about the first of July to deliver her baby. We decided the risks we had taken two years earlier when Debby was born were no longer necessary; that Gene would stay on the homestead with her while I went to Bristol Bay to go fishing.

Feeny had made other arrangements for this season, so I had to find another way to go fishing. I had acquired an old sailboat hull that I had used in a very limited way as a barge, towing it behind my skiff and outboard. I decided to convert it to a powered fish boat.

I bought a reversible propeller of Canadian design, and installed that in the boat. Then Gene and I took the four cylinder industrial engine from the sawmill and mounted that on a makeshift engine bed in the boat. Finally, we built a small cuddy forward, enclosing the tiny fo'c's'le.

Early in June, Little Joe's gas boat came around the corner. Half dozen young men jumped off after it was tied up, and climbed the hill to our cabin. Nothing unusual about that except it wasn't a mail day. Then I noticed another man painfully step from the boat to the dock. He was seriously hurt. I rushed down to offer assistance. It was Pete Mike, a young man for whom I had performed a marriage ceremony several months earlier. His left foot was wrapped in what looked like a bloody bath towel.

I hurried up to him, and offered my arm. "Let me help you, Pete," I said.

He shook his head. "Is OK. I make it."

I saw it was a point of pride with him, so I shrugged, and helplessly stood by, watching his slow, painful progress up the hill to the cabin. Obviously, Little Joe had brought him to Jan for medical assistance. Then I hurried back to the cabin to alert her that her services were needed.

Jan soaked the towel loose, and exposed a wound about four inches long in the top of his foot. Pete had slashed it with an axe while chopping firewood. Luckily, the wound was shallow. The bones, tendons, and ligaments appeared to be intact. The blow apparently was glancing, probably deflected by his shoepacs.

Pete had a difficult choice to make. We could summon the 10th Rescue Squadron at Elmendorf Air Force Base in Anchorage. They existed to provide emergency service to the military as needed, but unstintingly extended that service to the rural civilian population as well. They would send a small plane for him, and deliver him to the Alaska Native Service hospital in Anchorage. If he chose to go to Anchorage, he would receive excellent care, but he would miss the fishing season. On the other hand, Jan could sew the wound shut, and a cannery doctor could remove the stitches two weeks later. The only problem was, she didn't have any Novocaine.

Nevertheless, rather than miss the season, he asked her to repair his foot.

Jan chased his escort out of the cabin. She sent the children outside, as well. Then she poured Pete a stiff drink while I sharpened her curved suture needle.

As I braced Pete's foot to prevent involuntary flinching, I was reminded of the similar operation she had performed under nearly identical circumstances to Charlie Nolay at Clarks Point. Pete was more stoic than Charlie had been—or perhaps the scalp is more tender than the foot. In either case, Jan did her usual excellent job. When I later escorted Pete to the cannery doctor and explained what had happened, he was surprised and very complimentary.

I was ready to go fishing, but I needed a partner. Gene indirectly solved that problem. Shortly after breakup, a boyhood pal of Gene's, a young man named Frank Filoso, came to visit from Ohio to visit him. After spending two weeks with us, he agreed to go fishing with me.

It may seem unfair that I didn't ask Gene, but there was a good reason. Gene knew his way around the homestead by this time, while Frank was still a very green young man. When Jan left to go to Anchorage, Gene would be left alone. I didn't think Frank was ready for that.

Frank was a giant of a boy. He was built like a wrestler. His life's ambition was to become a military policeman, an ambition, I'm happy to report, that he subsequently achieved.

Things were very different in 1955 compared to 1954. The bitter controversies that had marred the 1954 season were ancient history when 1955 arrived. The canneries, in an outwardly astonishing turnaround, willingly, and even eagerly, sold converted sailboats to resident fishermen on easy terms.

Obeying the Federal Trade Commission order, the fishermen abandoned the Bering Sea Fisherman's Union and signed up with a new fish marketing co-op called the Bristol

Bay Fish Producer's Association (BBFPA). I served on the first board of directors, representing the Iliamna fishermen, and participated that spring in our first successful negotiations with the cannery operators.

Pete Mike

I imagine the debates in industry board rooms that winter must have been fierce. However, management evidently realized that a basic sea change had occurred in the fishery when the sailboat restriction was lifted. That change was underscored by the bitter events of 1954. Undoubtedly, they also realized that a captive fleet of "independent" fishermen could be a valuable adjunct in years of poor salmon runs when it would be far cheaper to buy independent fish than pay the costs—transportation, room and board, insurance, nets, boats, and other equipment—associated with "company" fish.

The superintendent at Nakeen cannery, a well respected and liked gentlemen named Tom Ryan, did everything he could to help us. But somehow, this new prosperity passed me by. I seemed to be stuck in a time warp, still wrestling with last year's problems. I could have bought a "new" boat, too, but I was struggling to make payments on my SBA loan and to NC Company for the tractor. Also, I faced a huge bill for the winter groceries we had ordered from the cannery that spring. Frank and I were forced to make do with what we had and fish as diligently as we could. Nevertheless, in retrospect, I now realize I was foolish not to contract for a new boat, because I had grossly overestimated the seaworthiness of the boat I owned.

275

Frank and I traveled with the Eskimo boats from Kakhonak to Naknek. I knew I had struck pay dirt with Frank, the very first set we made. When the time came to haul the net, Frank gestured me to stand aside, and he pulled the net into the boat hand over hand as lightly and easily as I might have plucked a string from the water. He was enormously strong.

The 1955 season was only marginally better than 1954 had been. Shortly after the fourth of July, we got into trouble. We were on a long drift out in the middle of the river. The weather was rough, and we were in a fairly stiff southwesterly breeze. I knew that the waves would calm when the tide turned. Lacking a power roller, I thought it best to wait until slack water to pick up our gear. I was lying in the cabin, reading a magazine. Frank was on watch. Suddenly, he yelled, **"Denny! We're sinking!"**

I jumped up and looked into the boat. Inexplicably, Frank was standing in a foot of water, frantically hurling water over the side with a large bucket. I was instantly reminded of that ancient saw about the most efficient bilge pump being a frightened man with a big pail. I took the bucket and continued bailing while Frank hauled the net into the boat.

I couldn't tell where the water was coming from, but it was coming in fast. I was able to hold it, but not until the net was in the boat and Frank replaced me on the bucket did the water continue to recede. In the meanwhile, I started the engine and began running slowly through the breaking waves for the nearest scow. Since the canneries had all consolidated, any scow would do.

A Libby scow was about three miles away, and I headed for it. I carefully instructed Frank to ask the scow captain to send the engineer to talk with me. I explained that we would have to use the scow's pumps to get the water out of the boat so I could locate and plug the leak. He seemed to understand.

We slowly approached the scow, and at the proper

moment, painter in hand, Frank stepped across to the scow's deck and made our boat fast to a stanchion. Then he disappeared into the galley.

Meanwhile, the water had risen ominously in the boat, so as soon as I shut the engine off, I rushed back into the stern and began bailing again. I wondered when the engineer would put in an appearance.

Minutes that seemed like hours passed. No engineer. I was getting frantic. Losing the boat would be a great inconvenience, but losing the sawmill engine would be a disaster! Where in the hell was that engineer!

"Hey! If you're not going to deliver fish, you can't stay here!"

I looked up to see an angry young man standing on the stern of the scow staring at me. It was Alvin Asplund, a local man I knew only slightly.

"Hey, Cap," I replied, "I'm in serious trouble here. I've got a leak I can't find. If your engineer could pass a suction hose over to me, we could get the water down so I could at least slow the leak."

Just then, Frank came strolling out of the galley with his mouth full, holding the remains of a sandwich in his hand.

Alvin at first refused to help. However, by alternatively threatening and pleading, including a poignant argument blending the potential loss of my sawmill engine with the loss of his Coast Guard license, he finally, reluctantly, agreed to send his engineer to help.

The engineer, a laconic older man, glanced briefly at my rapidly sinking vessel, and disappeared below. He reappeared moments later, dragging a two inch hose. "Here. Put the suction end in the deepest part of the boat," he said. Then he disappeared into the engine room again.

The sudden roar of his main engine was accompanied by

a loud sucking sound from the boat as the water magically disappeared. The leaks were suddenly visible.

A four foot row of tiny spurting fountains between the keel and the garboard, the bottom plank next to the keel, appeared. Luckily, I carried caulking cotton. Using a table knife as a caulking tool, I pushed tiny bits of cotton into each fountain until the arterial spurts were quelled. Then I handed the hose back to the engineer with my heartfelt thanks.

It took some doing, but I persuaded Frank to come back on board, and we headed for Naknek Point, some ten miles away, where we beached her. After the tide went out, we found that about four feet of cotton and putty caulking had washed out of the garboard seam. No wonder we were sinking!

We rolled the boat over on her side, and I crawled under her, cotton, caulking iron, and putty in hand. After I repaired the seam, just for luck, I nailed a long narrow strip of lead over the seam.

When the boat floated on the in-coming tide, Frank and I ran up to the Standard Oil fuel dock where we filled our gas tanks, preparing to return to the fishing grounds.

Hermy Herrmann's *Fajen* was slowly approaching the fuel dock as we were leaving it. Frank ran forward. I thought he was going to push us away from the big scow, so I was surprised to see him grab one of the truck tire/fenders hanging on the side of the scow. Our vessels were slowly moving in opposite directions. Frank had a firm grip on his tire, and allowed himself to be dragged out of the boat.

The last I saw him, he was climbing up the *Fajen's* side. I never saw him again. I later learned, however, that he had gone to the cannery and collected his pay on his way to the airport, and presumably went straight back to Ohio.

I continued fishing alone. Without a hydraulic roller, however, it was tough going. Besides, there really wasn't enough fish to make it worth while. 1955 was poorer, even, than 1954 had been, although local fishermen did much better, since they were now fishing in decent boats, and none of their fish was thrown away. But much was happening at King Salmon that I thought required my attention.

Following the industry's attempted lockout of resident fishermen, which marred the clumsy introduction of the new management strategy, and the failure of the lieutenant governor to mediate the issue, Alaska's Delegate, E. L. "Bob" Bartlett had raised the problem in Congress. Partly in response to the criticism the Fish and Wildlife Service had received for its role in the 1954 debacle, Bert Johnson was sent to the Pribilof Islands. He was replaced by Donald L. McKernan, a big and very physical man, who tended to dominate his surroundings with an impressive presence.

I was driven by a bitter and very angry memory of Simeon Wassillie's lonely sled and its tragic cargo. That terrible scene had a profound impact on me. I realized for the first time how the lake's ecosystem inextricably linked fish with people. Therefore, following Kallenberg's example, I was beginning to express my concern about what appeared to be yet another failure of escapement (salmon which escape the commercial fishery and reach their natal spawning grounds).

The Fish and Wildlife folks were friendlier than they had been. I took advantage of it by learning to read the daily catch and escapement figures, researching old records, and asking questions. The junior scientists were sympathetic and showed me where things were and explained the significance of the data they had. There was a reason. They were as concerned as I, but since they were employees, their views counted for very little. I was a free agent.

The FRI (Fisheries Research Institute from the University of Washington), had been working on the Nushagak River under contract to the salmon industry when we lived at Clarks Point. The industry had hired that private group in an effort to improve salmon forecasts. Now, under contract to the US Fish and Wildlife Service, the FRI was investigating the biology of the Kvichak–Iliamna system. As an initial step, in 1955, they were actually counting "escaping" salmon into Lake Iliamna for the first time since 1932.

From reading the daily FRI escapement reports, I knew that by the Fourth of July, virtually no fish had reached Lake Iliamna. The daily escapement figures coming in from Igiugig and key Kvichak tributaries combined with the pack figures from the canneries indicated that as of that date, when the salmon season was about half over, the total salmon run in the Naknek–Kvichak rivers had been slightly over three million fish. Of that number, about 262,000 fish had been counted into the Kvichak tributaries but only 187,000 fish had gone past the towers at Igiugig into Lake Iliamna, the world's largest red salmon nursery. Mr. Brindle, on the other hand, had canned 2.6 *million* fish. Remembering how futile Kallenberg's arguments had been with McKernan's predecessor only two years before, I tried to open a dialogue with McKernan early about what seemed to be another failing season. However, McKernan wasn't accustomed to taking advice from a roughneck fisherman. He paid my suggestions little heed, although he was always courteous to me.

I continued to urge McKernan to act. As each day passed, it was increasingly obvious to me that we were facing another tough winter, and possibly no future fishery at all. Of course, I had no scientific credentials, but you didn't have to be a scientist to realize that three failures in a row did not auger well for the fishery. Overriding all else was a fear that we might be reenacting the Karluk River tragedy on Kodiak Island, where a red salmon fishery was exterminated in the early 1920s by greedy and shortsighted salmon canners.

In 1925, to correct such abusive practices, Congress had passed the White Act prohibiting the practice of blocking salmon streams. It also established a remarkably farsighted conservation standard. That law, still in effect in 1955, required that in any salmon stream of Alaska where the fish were actually counted, at least half of those fish had to be permitted to escape to the spawning grounds. Admittedly, that wasn't a particularly scientific solution.

For years, Fish and Wildlife biologists contemptuously ignored the plain language of the statute, preferring a theoretical management system based on an abstract concept called "population dynamics," which involved hypothetical escapement goals. I failed to understand how a management system based on questionable assumptions, false information, and a keen desire to appease the power brokers in the salmon industry could possibly succeed. Frankly, I thought the existing management system smacked of Russian roulette, since the results were always after the fact and irreversible.

I was also driven by a bitter memory of Simeon Wassillie's forlorn dog sled and its tragic cargo. I felt it was especially important to challenge a system that ignored the needs of local people.

Dennis Winn, a legendary fisheries biologist who, before the days of airplanes, came to Bristol Bay by dog sled, knew what his successors had forgotten; that the people who lived on the lake would set nets in the mouths of key spawning streams. Instead of providing seed for future generations, the first 500,000 fish in the escapement would end on fish racks.

Ironically, without an adequate fish payday, the Eskimos and Indians of the Lake region would be forced to depend even more heavily than usual on subsistence trapping and hunting, which meant relying on dog teams already weakened by two previous winters of short rations.

I wish now that I had acted more decisively that summer of 1955, but I was still influenced by early conditioning which caused me to defer to knowledge and to respect authority. Still, by the tenth of July, I knew I could wait no longer. I made one last entreaty to Mr. McKernan, pointing out that instead of the required statutory ratio of 50–50, the catch to escapement ratio then was more like 80–20, and there was no hope the deficit could be made up so late in the season.

After being told by Mr. McKernan that he was on top of things and all was well, I went next door to the Alaska Communications System office. The new Distant Early Warning line (the DEW line) had opened scant months before, and made possible long distance telephone calls from Bristol Bay. I placed such a call to the Governor in Juneau.

When Governor Heintzleman came on the line, I recited the catch and escapement numbers and explained that the White Act was now applicable to the Naknek–Kvichak system since salmon were being counted into Lake Iliamna for the first time in many years. I mentioned the escapement requirements in that Act, and explained that a gross violation of that act was occurring in Bristol Bay. I asked him, as the senior Interior Department official in Alaska, to order an immediate closure of the commercial fishery.

Within 24 hours, the 1955 season was closed.

13

Blue Tongue Treatment

President Eisenhower declared Bristol Bay a federal disaster area for the third consecutive year in 1955. Again, we reckoned our wealth by counting the sacks of relief beans stacked in the windbreak.

I knew that wild European cranberries, lingonberries, a rare and costly fruit imported from Scandinavia, were virtually identical to our wild low-bush cranberries. Tons of those berries grew wild in the tundra. They fed a few people like ourselves, birds, and some bears. The rest rotted. Almost as if Mother Nature were trying to compensate for the disastrously small salmon runs we had been experiencing, the tundra was practically awash in berries that fall.

I wrote to the Agricultural Extension Service in Palmer, inquiring about more efficient methods of harvesting berries than picking them individually by hand. They responded by sending a working model of a cranberry scoop. The device they sent was a wide scoop with a stout metal comb fastened to its leading edge. The comb's stainless steel teeth were about four inches long and 3/16ths of an inch apart.

The picker simply combed through lowbush cranberry plants with the scoop. The ripe fruit and some twigs and leaves were retained in the scoop. After picking, the wheat and chaff were separated in a time-honored fashion by pouring the berry-twig-leaf mixture from the scoop to a blanket in a strong breeze. The heavier berries would fall to the blanket while the twigs and leaves fluttered away on the breeze.

In a rich patch, the picker could make three or four passes with the scoop and empty a quart or more of mixed berries, twigs, leaves, and so forth, into a bucket. I'm sure this basic technology seems crude by comparison with modern harvesting methods, but it was far superior to hand picking.

One of the principle virtues of low-bush cranberries was their indestructibility. You could mash one with a hammer if you wanted to, but, like the ball bearings they resembled, they were impervious to anything short of total destruction. More to the point, they were eminently mailable.

I wrote to the buyer at Frederick & Nelson's department store in Seattle, explaining the project and inquiring whether they would be interested in buying our berries. We received an enthusiastic and encouraging reply; a firm offer to buy berries at $1/pound FOB Seattle.

Although $1/pound doesn't seem like much today, it handily covered the actual shipping costs and resulted in good hourly wages for the pickers. After the shipping costs were deducted, the balance was paid to the pickers.

We derived a considerable financial benefit from this transaction. Jan started with the Postal Service at $50 a month. That salary was based on a level of activity commensurate with the sale of up to $150 worth of postage per year. During August, September, and part of October, however, the postage on those boxes of cranberries totalled three times that minimum. Her salary was adjusted accordingly. Because she sold $600 in postage that year, her salary shot up to $1,500. This was clearly a win-win proposition.

After the first shipment had been paid for, we knew what the berries were worth. Freeze-up was approaching. We knew the pickers needed as much cash as possible for their last boat trips to the roadhouse. Consequently, we began paying for the berries when we received them.

Freeze-up was early that year. We got stuck with a 50-gallon barrel half full of berries we couldn't ship because the early formation of ice suspended mail deliveries for six weeks. The barrel was in the windbreak; we didn't think we had room for it in the cabin.

Cranberry pickers at work
(Copper River in background)

Moreover, we had eaten lots of cranberries in the spring that had been frozen all winter, and I didn't think it would hurt them much. But I was wrong. When the barrel full of berries thawed, they had lost their flinty hardness, and were somewhat mushy. We ate a lot of cranberries that fall. I suppose it was good for us. I even tried to make wine out of them, but they were too acidic to ferment.

The previous spring, Oren Hudson had brought a young fisheries biologist named Dean Paddock, from the Department of Fisheries, to see me. He had an ambitious investigation in mind, and needed a partner.

He wanted to inventory the fishery resources in the Iliamna watershed, especially in the higher and normally inaccessible lakes above Lake Iliamna. He also wanted to study the water courses immediately above Lake Iliamna to determine whether it would be feasible to open additional spawning grounds for the salmon which use the Iliamna drainage as their spawning grounds.

Such a trip was feasible only in the fall when the streams and lakes would be at their highest level of the year. This was important. The lakes usually rose about six feet during the summer. Therefore, he proposed to make this trip in early September. He offered to pay $20 a day and found, meaning he would provide the necessary food and equipment.

I was delighted to join him. For a man who had earned less than $500 for the entire salmon season, $20 a day was good pay. In addition, this project fit nicely with my long range plans for a lodge. Finally, I was as curious as the next fellow about what lay over the next hill.

Dean returned on September second. After Oren landed, I hastily gathered my sleeping bag, the .405 Winchester, my light parka, and a dry change of clothes. After kissing Jan and the kids goodby, I squirmed into the back seat of the plane which was already crammed full of groceries, a bundled rubber boat, paddles, a tent, a small outboard motor, tins of gasoline, nets, and God alone knew what else.

We flew up the Kakhonak River. Dean carefully noted landmarks above the falls, so we would have ample warning as we approached the falls coming down the river in our rubber raft. Oren patiently circled and banked so Dean could get a better view.

Flying at 500 feet, we continued up the river until we came to a long, sinuous, irregularly shaped lake. As we flew its length, we entered a narrow timbered valley between a craggy snow capped ridge that rose some 1,500 feet above our wing tips on the right and a large, isolated mountain on the left. Gradually, the mountains gave way to a tundra clad plateau. It was a spectacular ride.

We reached the end of the lake, and followed a meandering stream five miles further until we reached a second, much smaller, lake. The chart identified it as Moose Lake.

Oren saw what looked like a sandy beach at the far end of it, and pointed it out to Dean. Dean nodded. Oren skillfully read the wind direction in the riffles on the water, and in moments, we were skimming the surface of the water, our pontoons barely touching. When we were near the beach, he pushed the throttle in, and the plane settled into the water. Almost immediately, I felt a gentle lift as the pontoons touched the sandy shore.

Dean sprang down from his seat next to Oren, while I slowly untangled myself in the back seat. Then, taking the rifle, I walked into the brush beyond the beach and quickly checked for bear sign. There wasn't any.

Meanwhile, Dean and Oren unloaded the plane. I had only seen part of the load. Oren kept pulling bales and packages

Moose Lake camp

out of the plane like a magician pulling rabbits out of a hat, until I was beginning to wonder how we would fit it all into the surplus two-man life raft that was to carry us back to civilization.

Two cans of gas for the outboard topped off the load. Oren asked if there was anything more he could do for us. Dean shook his head. Oren offered his hand to each of us, pushed his plane back into the water, and soon disappeared flying back the way he had come.

Dean and I were about the same age and size. Like me, he wore typical Alaskan bush clothing, a plaid jacket and gabardine pants from Sears, warm but not too expensive. Unlike me, however, he had a pair of light sportsmen's hip boots. I envied him those boots. All I had were heavy commercial fishermen's boots and the ubiquitous waterproof shoepacs—boots with rubber bottoms and leather tops.

Dean was anxious to go fishing. He was the boss. We inflated the rubber boat, and carried it to the water. After paddling a 100 yards off the beach, he began casting. The evening air was so still I heard the *plop* of his lure hitting the water. Also, far down the lake, I heard loons calling.

I watched him fish for a few minutes, silhouetted against the mountain backdrop. I consciously wondered if this were the first fishing lure to enter the pristine waters of that little lake, before I began setting up the camp.

We hadn't discovered Moose Lake, of course, but it was an insignificant body of water, and so far out of the way, that I couldn't imagine why sportsmen would have bothered with it when the bounty of the world famous rainbow and steelhead waters in Copper River and Newhalen were so close at hand.

Dean, or his wife more likely, had provided an assortment of canned goods, including several tins of something called "gluten steaks," and a variety of dried vegetables. I remember, in particular, a sack containing a pound of dried carrot chips. We had a frying pan, two pots, plates, cups, utensils, and dish soap. The only thing I couldn't find was coffee or the coffee pot.

I had the camp sorted out, the tent up, and a fire started when Dean let out a whoop, "I've got a big one," he shouted. Dean was standing in the boat, his rod nearly doubled. I watched as he lifted the rod and quickly reeled in the slack.

The fish stayed deep. Judging by the way the line zigzagged back and forth where it entered the water, the fish was making short runs beneath the boat, acting, I thought, like a char; a Dolly Varden or a lake trout.

"He's too big to bring into the boat," Dean shouted. "I'm going to try to beach him."

The fish had tired by this time, and Dean held the rod between his knees as he paddled slowly toward the beach. I walked down to meet him. I was as curious as he about the monster on his hook.

When I reached the water's edge, Dean was already

wading, his doubled over rod in one hand, the boat painter in the other. He pushed the boat toward me. "Here," he said, "you grab the boat while I beach this guy."

I grabbed the boat. Then I watched him gingerly work his quarry into shallow water. Suddenly, he bent forward and bear like, batted the fish out of the water.

I was astonished. The "monster" fish looked like a 10 inch rainbow trout. "What the hell, Dean. . ." I began, but he interrupted me. "I think we've got something special here," he said. "I'm going to take a careful look at him after dinner. First, though, let's set the net."

Hell. I thought that fish *was* dinner. We piled the little variable mesh net into the boat and paddled a short distance from shore. Dean had tied a rock to each end of the net's leadline to anchor it. While I paddled—once a boat puller, always a boat puller—he paid the net over the side into the water. In ten minutes, the net was in place.

Then it was dinner time. We celebrated our first night on "safari" by dining on canned gluten steaks. They were awful. The kindest thing I can say about them is that they tasted like and had the texture of fried library paste. I knew I would be very hungry before I ate another.

After supper, I learned why I had been unable to find the coffee pot. There wasn't one. Dean explained, "You see, Denny," he said, "I'm a Seventh Day Adventist. We don't believe in any stimulants—including caffeine."

This was going to be a long two weeks. Lacking coffee, I did the next best thing, and made Russian "tea," as the Eskimos did when they were on short rations, from a plant that grows in the tundra. I doubt if was a stimulant, but it boiled up into a colored liquid with a slightly bitter flavor.

The next morning, while he dissected the trout, I paddled out to retrieve the net. We had gotten skunked. The net was empty. I hurried back to the beach.

I wanted to get back before he threw the rest of that fish away. I didn't want more gluten steaks (his wife had thoughtfully included a half dozen cans in our outfit).

Dean was a highly competent biologist. In the field, he was meticulous almost to a fault. When he expressed surprise about a biological phenomena, I was sure something extraordinary had caught his eye.

He counted the gill rakers on the specimen I hoped to have for supper. "I think we have either a mutation here," he said, "or a hybrid. You might find almost anything in these land-locked lakes. This fish, for instance, has some of the physiological characteristics of a rainbow, but others of a red salmon. Moreover, it's sterile. Its gonads are so underdeveloped I can't determine its sex."

My hope for a fish dinner was rapidly eroding.

"Just look at that flesh color," Dean went on. "It's redder than that of a red salmon! And it acted like a red salmon when I hooked it."

I admitted that we had stumbled onto something unusual.

"The gill rakers and fin rays are those of a rainbow, however," he concluded.

Just as I was trying to think of something good about gluten steak, he handed me the fish carcass minus entrails and head. "We might as well have this for supper," he said.

This became our standard procedure. He measured, weighed, and gutted the fish we caught. After saving the guts, the fish were handed over to me for a final treatment in the frying pan.

The next day, we struck camp, packed our gear into the rubber life raft, and made our way to the opposite end of the lake. This put us three or four miles closer to the solitary mountain to the south, which somehow was comforting. I guess I've never completely gotten over my battlefield conditioning. I'm always uneasy in an open field or when I'm in an exposed position.

That night, we set the net near the stream that flowed from Moose Lake to Kakhonak Lake. In the morning, we had more fish than we could eat. Most were small rainbows, but Dean identified two more hybrids, if that's what they were. There was also a small lake trout in the catch. None were as big as the trout Dean had caught the night before.

"Lining" through the rapids.

While I sorely missed my coffee, the next several days passed quickly. Every day we moved our camp a few miles closer to "civilization." We discovered that Kakhonak Lake was actually *two* lakes. The first one, about five miles long, was two feet higher than the second Kakhonak Lake.

The two were connected by a short, somewhat turbulent stream. We lined the boat down through the short rapids. Finding a reasonably level place in the sand, we decided to camp there, within ear shot of the rapids.

Had there been salmon in the lake, camping near the rapids wouldn't have been a good idea. Very likely we'd have had bears around our camp all night. But there were no salmon here.

The resident fish knew the advantages of moving water. We set the net, and in the morning had as good a profile of the lake's inhabitants as we were likely to get.

The fish population mirrored Lake Iliamna's. We caught two suckers, a ten pound lake trout, several Dolly Vardens, two more hybrids, several small rainbows, and a dozen ciscos, or lake herring. The wide diversity of fish life suggested to us that the blocking falls in the Kakhonak River might be a fairly recent phenomena; perhaps the result of an earthquake some time in the last 10,000 years or so.

By comparison, a year later, we explored the Copper River drainage (the Iliamna Copper River; not the one in Prince William Sound). The upper Copper River was also blocked, but there, the falls were much higher.

The most remote lake on that chain is officially named *Meadow Lake*. However, after we found it contained miniature Dolly Varden trout—we caught a ripe female three inches long—and zillions of fresh water clams half the size of my little fingernail, Dean and I informally renamed the lake *Poor Lake*, "poor" being both a contraction of Paddock and Moore and an accurate description of the lake's ecology.

Poor Lake was typical of many small Arctic mountain lakes. The surrounding ecosystem of such lakes is lean and mean. There is practically no bacterial activity in the ecosystem because of the cold temperatures and the lack of human activity. Thus, apart from a scattering of moose and rabbit pellets, the uplands surrounding such lakes are nearly sterile. The water feeding such lakes comes from melting snow and glaciers, and is almost as pure as distilled water.

Moreover, because the lake was almost continually shaded by the steep mountains around it, the water received few of the sun's rays necessary to trigger photosynthesis in the carbon cycle.

But for the annual infusions of salmon carcasses, especially red salmon, much of the Iliamna watershed and possibly Lake Iliamna itself, might be no more fertile than Poor Lake.

I was beginning to worry because we were finding shell ice in the shallows each morning when we got up. Razor-sharp pan ice was dangerous for wooden boats, but it was deadly for rubber ones. But Dean was in no hurry. In his meticulous way, Dean sampled each stream feeding into the lake.

Copper River falls

Shortly before we entered the Kakhonak River on our final leg, we saw an odd looking rock. Investigating, we discovered that the "rock" was the fresh carcass of a bull moose sticking out of shallow water, a gaping hole in the top of its skull where its antlers had been.

Evidently, the poor animal had been spotted from a plane while it was swimming across the lake. We couldn't tell whether it had been shot from the air, but my guess was that the plane had landed, and the "sportsman" had killed his trophy while the animal was helplessly wading ashore. Then the guide, most likely, had chopped off the animal's rack, illegally leaving the rest of the animal to rot.

A few hours later, a local guide, Bud Branham, saw us from the air as he flew down the lake in his small amphibian airplane. He landed at our camp to ask whether we had seen anything "unusual."

I don't know why, but we assured him that we had seen nothing. After our return, however, Dean reported our discovery to the game warden in Dillingham. I understand Bud was fined and lost his license for a time as a result.

As we began to descend the river, the species mix changed. Now all we caught—and we caught hundreds of them—were six to eight inch rainbows. Virtually every one of those little fish was digesting a tiny ball of fur. On closer examination, those bits of fur proved to be young shrews.

Devout Seventh Day Adventists do not fool around with their Sabbath. Dean celebrated two of them while we were exploring the Kakhonak River drainage. When the first one came, we were still camped on the shore of Kakhonak Lake. Dean stayed in bed all day reading his Bible, while I, .405 Winchester in hand, went for a long, exploratory walk.

The second time, however, we were on the Kakhonak River, working our way through an extended marshy area when Friday afternoon came. Shortly before dusk, we found a dry hummock where we made camp. Promptly at sundown, Dean put down the axe he was using, and turned to me with a wry grin. "Well, Denny," he said, "I guess it's up to you, now. My Sabbath has begun."

It was a repeat of the previous Saturday except I wasn't able to go for a long walk. Rustling up firewood was as far away from Dean as I could get. Still in ear shot, I spent several hours patching holes in the boat caused by the rocks in the rapids and abrasion from the cargo we carried.

Whether Dean was trying to do me a favor or felt it was his duty, even though I pointedly ignored him, he began to preach around noon. He went on all afternoon, and quite frankly, it annoyed me. I have always resented the smug arrogance of people trying to do things for "my own good."

I'm sensitive about this. Purely by accident, I was "saved" once. I should explain that my early religious training was casual. I attended various Protestant Sunday schools, all within walking distance of my grandparent's home on Seattle's Capitol Hill, guided more by a desire to be with my best friend of the moment than theological convictions. The only reason I went at all was because I had an informal arrangement with Jesus. Mother gave me a dime for the collection plate, not an inconsequential sum for a young boy during the Depression. I'd faithfully put the dime in the collection plate and take back a nickel. That seemed fair. After Sunday school, that nickel became an ice cream cone as quickly as possible.

I mentioned having been "redeemed." That happened in the most unlikely way. I was on a brief liberty from Camp Pendelton in Oceanside, California. Barely 18, just out of boot camp, I was standing on the sidewalk in front of the USO watching the cars go by, when a flashy civilian drove up in a flashier station wagon, and asked me if I'd like to "have a good time." I was his man.

Like most of my generation, at 18, I was as virginal as the day I was born. I suppose it's indicative of my innocence that I honestly thought I was being offered an opportunity to rectify that sad situation. I hopped quickly into the car before my new friend could change his mind, foolishly believing he was going to deliver me to a whorehouse. Instead, in company with several other teen-age sailors and marines, all wanna be rakehells, I was delivered to the Kingdom of God. My captor was a Jehovah's Witness. Before the party was over, we were all on our knees repenting our sins.

The experience proved to be a spiritual vaccination. I haven't felt the need for much religion since. During the question and answer period following Dean's sermon, I asked who did the cooking and dish washing on the sabbath in a place like Aleknagik (a Seventh Day Adventist colony and Dean's home) where there were no heathen servants?

The next morning I extracted a moderate revenge. Rejuvenated by his spiritual experience the previous day, Dean bounced out of his sleeping bag at first light. "Come on, come on," he sang, "it's a beautiful morning, let's get going!"

I stretched slowly and deliberately. I was going to enjoy this. "Don't you know what day it is?" I asked.

He looked at me, puzzled at first, but gradually he comprehended my meaning. "Aw, come on, Denny. I know you're kidding. Aren't you kidding?" he asked.

"Fix my breakfast," I said, "Then we'll see."

Dean was a good sport about it. I treated him pretty much

as he had treated me when he had felt his religious tides rising. I'll say this; although we continued to make our upriver explorations every fall for as long as I remained at Kokhanok, and although he religiously observed his Sabbath, he never preached to me again.

Kakhonak River falls
(over Dean's shoulder)

It took two days to descend the Kakhonak River. The rapids we had seen from the air proved more formidable from the water, and several times, Dean decided to line the boat, when I would have been inclined to ride. But I'm sure, in each case, his judgment was better than mine.

We portaged around the blocking falls Dean had seen from the air. We knew they were there, of course, but we weren't sure exactly where. The wind was mostly behind us, carrying the sound of the falls away. Luckily, we became entangled in a sweeper just above the falls, and when we began fighting our way clear, the unmistakable rumble of the falls came to us.

It was getting dark when we completed the last portage. We had "channel fever" rather badly, so rather than camp and wait for daylight, which sensible people would have done, we decided to press on; after all, we were back in Lake Iliamna, less than five miles from home.

When the sun went down, so did the temperature. The boat began losing its shape and became flaccid while we were struggling through what seemed to me to be mountainous waves. But we kept going, and soon we were rewarded by the welcome sight of a lighted window at the head of our bay.

Dean gave us the remaining food. Since I was the camp cook, that included the dried vegetables, including those flinty little orange chunks of dried carrots.

After Dean left, Jan sorted through the remains of our outfit and found the carrots. "What are these for?" she asked.

Attempting to be sarcastic, I looked at her with a straight face and said, "If you eat them slowly, one chip at a time, they taste just like peanuts."

Jan never understood sarcasm. I returned from the mill for lunch the next day. She and the children were solemnly crunching those dried carrots, remarking to one another how much they tasted like peanuts! Unfortunately, I could not control my reaction. Any imaginary resemblance those carrots may have had to peanuts vanished the instant I started laughing.

A person's body will usually, but not always, let you know what it needs. For example, cold weather always meant heavy inroads on our brown sugar supply. When I came in from logging or working at the mill on a cold day, or from attending the trapline or whatever, as soon as I peeled off my mittens, shook off my mukluks, and hung up my parka, I would dip up a cup full of brown sugar which I ate with a spoon like normal people might eat a pudding. Obviously, since I needed those extra calories, I must have been burning a lot of them.

Late that fall, I thought of another natural resource that might support a cottage industry. I knew there were whitefish in the lake; we caught one now and then in the net. I wrote to the Director of the Territorial Department of Fisheries, Mr. C. L. "Andy" Anderson, outlining my idea of developing a commercial fishery in the lake, and asking for technical assistance.

He responded by sending Jim Brooks, a young wildlife biologist, to Kokhanok to work with me exploring the fishery potential. Jim spent several weeks with us. He was slightly older than I, and had served as a bomber pilot during the war. Jim's early history was like mine. We were both high school dropouts. I remember once asking how he had managed to get to flight school when his educational background was no better than mine.

He looked at me and grinned. "Never tell the truth when a good lie will serve," he said.

He had spent several winters trapping in the Noatak River country north of the Arctic Circle, and was that rare individual who was capable of pulling his own teeth when necessary. I learned a good bit of woodcraft working that fall with Jim.

Jim and I traveled over much of Kakhonak Bay by dog sled. He showed me how to set nets under the ice. We caught a variety of fish, during these trials, but not enough whitefish to justify a commercial effort. Also, the whitefish we did catch carried skin parasites which rendered them unsuitable for the market.

Money was awfully tight. We were really scratching to make our payments to the SBA and Northern Commercial Company. My fishing payday, such as it was, had gone for food. I had earned about $250 as Dean's assistant, and now we were being paid $10/day for Jim's board and room. I was easy to talk to, when Jim took a fancy to the two treasures we owned. My antique squirrel rifle was one.

The other was a primitive oil painting we had commissioned at Clarks Point. The artist was a member of the beach gang; an old sailor named Walter Schultz. This was his form of scrimshaw. Every year, the old man would stretch and prepare half dozen canvases. Sailor-like, he used whatever material was at hand. His canvases came from the sail locker. He made his brushes from rope ends. The paint came from the cannery paint locker. Logically enough, he painted only maritime scenes. Our's was a painting of a full rigged ship in a rising sea. It was a wonderful example of sailor art.

I had commissioned it in 1948 for $25. A carpenter at the cannery had framed it, and we had it hanging in the cabin. Jim offered $100 for it, and we let it go. However, as a sequel, I repurchased the painting in 1975 for $200. Art gets more valuable as it grows older.

The radio schedules with our friends around the lake and with the ACS station in King Salmon became an important daily social event. Late that fall, the radio became even more important when we were inducted into the Ground Observer Corps, and wired into the "Sadie Hawkins" radio network.

Worried about the slow construction of the electronic fence that the DEW (White Alice) project was supposed to provide, someone in the Pentagon had thought of enlisting people like us to serve as interim observers. A network of Air Force stations was established along the Bering Sea coast, and people with coastal marine licenses like us were recruited to join the net.

The first we knew of it was when an Air Force Norseman on floats landed in front of the cabin late in the autumn. We went down to the beach to meet a pair of uniformed airmen—these were real Air Force people. One of the Air Force men, the captain flying the plane, swore us in; the other man, a tech sergeant, installed a Sadie Hawkins crystal and tweaked our transmitter for maximum efficiency.

Every evening after that, after our regular round-robin lake schedule and ACS schedule, we checked in with *Sadie Hawkins 68* (their call sign). We learned the operator's names, but they would never tell us where they were located.

Sadie Hawkins 68 became the equivalent of today's 911 emergency number. Only once did we call to report an unidentified flying object. It was a bright, slowly moving light that seemed high, but not an astronomical body. I even took pictures of it.

The night following our sighting, the Sadie Hawkins operator told us someone else had also reported it, so they had scrambled a jet to take a look. It turned out to be a comet; one I had never heard of: *Arends/Roland.*

Rabbits still dominated our ecosystem. I no longer shot them. Instead, I snared them. Every morning, I would visit my rabbit trapline—less than a hundred yards from the cabin—and retrieve five or six freshly caught rabbits. They were so plentiful that I even chopped up two or three every evening to add to the pot when I cooked the dog's dinner.

We had been acutely aware of the terrible consequences of short rations for the dogs since the Simeon Wassillie tragedy. Every evening, I would build a fire near the dog yard, and put a two gallon pan half full of water on the fire. When the water began to boil, I'd add two chopped up fish, rabbit if I had it, three cups of oatmeal, and three big spoonsful of cannery lard. The cannery fry cooks saved the fat drippings and scrapings from the top of the stove in five-gallon coffee tins. A tin full of accumulated cooking fat cost $5. You had to get in line early for one of those tins because almost everyone recognized the nutritional value of fat for dogs who spent their lives out of doors.

While Jan was splitting fish to dry for dog feed, she usually saved a five gallon tin of salmon eggs for fish bait for me to use during the winter. Each skein of eggs was carefully preserved by coating it with *Twenty Mule Team* Borax soap. It took a box of soap to properly cure five gallons of eggs.

Shortly before freeze-up, we were raided by a huge bear. I never saw him, for which I am profoundly grateful, considering the circumstances. Luckily, nearly all the fish had been bundled and put away before the bear came, so our loss was not serious.

However, the bear knocked all the poles to the ground, and ate the few fish still hanging on the rack. Then, for dessert, Mr. Bear attempted to eat five gallons of salmon eggs, tin can and all, in a single bite. The animal crushed the can in his mouth, his incisors making neat holes in the tin about 12 inches apart. That was a big bear.

He spit the tin shell out, but licked up all the eggs. No matter how big he was, I wouldn't want to meet *any* bear that had just eaten a box of Borax!

The population of rabbits was soon to crash in a classic example of a wildlife enzootic, due to starvation and disease (in the spring, we would see girdled spruce trees, where winter-starved rabbits had gnawed the bark from the trees, and begin to find ticks infesting the rabbits we snared). Yet the presence of those hundreds of thousands of rabbits over such a long period of time had proven an irresistible magnet to every predator for hundreds of miles around. Like their other predators, their abundance certainly made life easier and, paradoxically, (although we were slow to realize it) much more tenuous for us.

When the wolves moved in, the moose moved out. For years, no matter how strenuously I hunted, especially during the winter season when the snow aided my tracking (and the cold weather provided natural refrigeration), I failed to get my moose. However, we leavened the unlimited supply of rabbit meat with fish from the net I kept under the ice, an occasional porcupine, and from time to time, spruce hen. I thought we were doing just fine.

But that spring—it was early in April—Jan and I simply ran out of gas. It was an astonishing experience. Normally active and robust, I was overwhelmed by a feeling of lassitude. During daylight hours, I sat hour after hour in a rocking chair listening to the radio, watching the children play, overcome by a great listlessness.

Jan was feeling the same way. I remember wondering vaguely if something could be wrong, but I'm sure, like most victims, I was slow to recognize the symptoms. We learned later that rabbit meat lacks one of the essential amino acids. Obviously, there was good reason for our listlessness. Our bellies were full, but we were starving.

I was sitting in the rocking chair, when five-year old Lynnie suddenly shouted, **"There's a moose out on the ice!"**

I didn't even bother to look. I grabbed the Krag, and ran outside. Lynn was right. A gaunt, scarred, old moose was slowly picking its way on the ice across the bay. It was about 400 yards away.

Lacking a criminal mind, it didn't occur to me that shooting a moose out of season a stone's throw from the cabin was about the dumbest thing I could do; but shooting one out in the open on the snow where airplanes (including the game warden's) usually landed, was even dumber.

All I knew was that the our diet was about to change. I sat in the snow, wrapped the rifle sling around my left arm, aimed slightly above the animal's left ear, and squeezed the trigger.

BANG!

The unfortunate animal crumpled and was dead before it hit the snow. Jan and I rushed out with knives and a big washtub; the one the kids used as a bathtub.

After I bled the animal, I realized that shooting a moose in the snow in front of the cabin was not the smartest thing I had ever done. It is an exaggeration, of course, but to my guilty eyes, the animal's blood stained at least an acre of clean white snow. Its liver must have weighed 100 pounds. We rolled the three lobes into the wash tub and struggled up the hill with it.

Ordinarily, hunters will wait until the meat of a fresh kill cools before eating it for fear of (sometimes) becoming violently ill. The liver is an exception. I'm no great fan of liver, but later, I watched approvingly as Jan cut inch-thick liver steaks for supper. I can tell you, that was good eating!

We quickly skinned the animal, and carried it, in pieces, to our cache. The job was much more pleasant, but it reminded me, as I toiled up the hill, staggering under the weight of a hind quarter, of the last rites we had performed for Brownie.

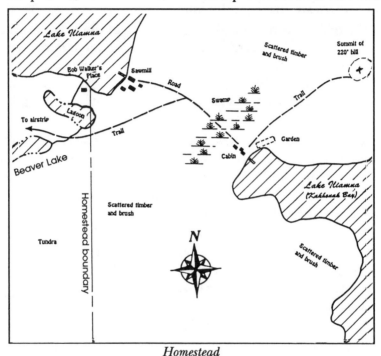

Homestead

—Map drawn by Capt. Jim Hogan

It took hours to complete the job. Then I chopped a hole in the ice in the center of the bloodstained snow, and began sloshing buckets of water over the bloody snow. It took a lot of buckets, but I erased most of the evidence before dark.

Within two days, Jan and I experienced an almost miraculous recovery. Our lassitude vanished. Full of pep, I returned to my work at the sawmill. Jan, also enjoying restored good health, had an unaccustomed variety of meat to serve her family.

303

By this time, we were maintaining climatological records for the Weather Bureau. The winter of 1955-56 was unusually severe. On Christmas Eve, 1955, the temperature dropped to an astounding (and to me, frightening) *minus 48°!* That, as far as I know, was the record low temperature during the nine years we lived on the lake.

We had been reasonably comfortable in the original cabin, but by 1955, the original one-room, 270 square foot cabin had grown to four rooms with over 700 square feet. The kitchen stove could not heat the enlarged space. Eventually, we added a Franklin heater, thereby almost doubling cold weather wood consumption.

The first addition was a room measuring 16x12 feet. I divided it into a relatively larger room for us and a smaller room for the children. I built two bunks against the back wall for the older children and two shorter bunks against the inside partition for the younger ones.

In the years to come, when my children are telling their grandchildren about their childhood hardships, I hope Lynnie won't forget to tell how her blankets occasionally froze to the log wall against which she slept.

I was reminded, during that cold weather, of the brief visit Jacinto and I had paid to Nonvianuk Lake in 1949. We heard the same frequent rumbling **BOOMs,** sounding like distant artillery, caused when thick ice, sometimes two and three feet thick, cracked and buckled, forming pressure ridges out on the lake. The occasional sharp report that sounded like a rifle shot, caused by expanding internal ice crystals splitting a frozen tree, was also familiar, as was the color provided by the northern lights. We often saw those phantom like, shimmering, undulating curtains of light in the northern sky, but only on the coldest nights did we see them in technicolor. Sometimes, they were so bright they seemed to reflect from the snow.

Even though our cabin was four years old, the cabin logs were still drying and trying to reconcile the dry, frigid air on the outside with the warm, moist air on the inside. As a result, on especially cold nights, we occasionally were wakened by the sharp report of a suddenly splitting log.

Lizzy in her crib (This photo shows cabin's interior. Our bedroom is in the background behind the bookcase)

Usually, when a Siberian high pressure system was in charge, and the temperatures were as low as they were going to get, the air would be absolutely still. Outside the cabin, you would see tiny vents of steam betraying the leaks in the cabin's caulking. Unless the leak was serious, I would defer repairing it until the weather moderated.

I found those extended periods of bitter cold weather depressing and, to be honest about it, frightening. Perhaps it was my imagination, but the same faint blue haze I had noticed years before at Nonvianuk Lake seemed to settle over the land. My outdoor options were so sharply restricted by the combined low temperatures and short days that I would began to experience pangs of something closely akin to claustrophobia colored by a mild paranoia. I would begin to personalize my environment, and feel as if I were the victim of ill-defined, malevolent forces set loose upon the land. It wasn't hard to see how a more primitive people living under those conditions might embrace animism.

The tractor wouldn't start when the temperature reached
-20°. It was unsafe to work the dogs in temperatures colder
than -40°, because too much exertion could cause them to
die a particularly painful death from frosted lungs.

There wasn't much you could do outside when the
temperature dropped into the minus 30° range. But there
were some things you had to do. You had to feed the dogs
no matter how cold it got, and you had to cut firewood.

Every fall, I cut and stacked several cords of birch—the best
firewood available. But I never accumulated enough to last
the winter. Other chores always took precedence.

As a result, when the temperature dropped into the low
minus 30s, I would begin anxiously watching the thermometer with one eye and the wood box with the other. Almost
always, the thermometer won. While my better organized,
better disciplined, peers were sitting around their warm
cabins in their slippers, I was struggling into my parka, mukluks, and wolf hide mittens. There were even times when I
had to walk into the brush in search of a birch not yet cut.

Although I was desperate to get back into the friendly
warmth of the cabin, I forced myself to move slowly. My life
depended on it. A single hasty inhalation could result in a
paroxysm of painful coughing that could last an hour.

There was more. Frozen wood splits almost too easily,
since it's inclined to shatter like glass. But cutting it with a
saw is a different story. The Swede saw is a highly efficient
tool, but not on frozen birch. It will do the job, but slowly.
So there I was, crouching in the snow, chilled to the deepest
marrow in my body, afraid of any exertion which might force
me to breathe through my mouth, with a saw that could only
scratch its way through a birch log.

After the log was cut, I could drag it behind me on a tarp
or reduce it to a size I could easily carry. Sometimes, it took
all morning to cut those few extra sticks of firewood.

There was one thing about it. The body does make some internal adjustments. Thus, a person in my situation became inured to the cold or they found a different line of work. However, even the most Spartan regimen could not have prepared me for the first dog sled lake crossing of the year.

If ever my dogs were inclined to quit, I'm sure it would have happened then. It was after Christmas, and that terrible cold spell of 1956. Although the mail had been moving for several weeks, we were plagued with shortages of one sort or another, and it was time to go to the store.

Everything—even air temperature—is relative. After experiencing temperatures near fifty degrees below zero, a mere twenty degrees below seemed like a balmy spring day.

It was tacitly agreed that two teams should always make the first crossing of the season, in case of trouble. Consequently, I had arranged to meet Pete Mike in the village. Pete, you'll remember, was the man with the new scar on his foot. He also wanted to make an early trip across the lake.

There was not the slightest breath of moving air. The snow crunched underfoot like corn flakes as I walked around the dog yard in the dark, that morning, harnessing the dogs.

In the bright dawn, even though the temperature was still minus 20°, the dogs enthusiastically galloped across the ice, the sled runners squeaking through the fresh snow. The trip to the village was fast and easy. Plumes of smoke and steam rose in the air from village stovepipes as we approached. Chained dogs, seeing us, began their usual frenzied clamor, barking, howling, leaping against their chains.

Pete was just getting up. Somewhat impatiently, knowing we had only about five hours of daylight left, I sat at the table in his cabin's only room and sipped a cup of coffee.

After a long delay, Pete finally went outside to harness his team. When he was ready, he poked his head inside the door. "I t'ink we go, now," he said.

I unchained Buck and standing at the back of my sled, waited for Pete to start his team. Then I yelled, "All right, boys! All right!"

The dogs were watching Pete's team and when they recognized the command, and felt the sled move as I pushed it to get it going, they leaped into their harnesses. The sled's steel runners worked fine on ice, but tended to stick in very cold snow, especially after a run. My dogs had to work a bit harder to overcome that initial stickiness.

Three hours later, as we approached Halfway Island, we ran into a little patch of green ice; ice that, considering the weather, inexplicably had just frozen, and was probably less than half an inch thick. Pete, 200 yards ahead, crossed it without difficulty, but it was flexible and it scared the hell out of me when I felt it sag under our weight. It was also very slick. Buck didn't like it. He tried to shy away and had trouble maintaining his footing. This was no place to stop. I didn't dare try to walk on that thin ice to lead them.

Trying to keep the panic out of my voice, I shouted, "Come haw, Buck, come haw!" Then, as he swung to the left, I yelled encouragingly, "All right, boys! Keep going! Good boys!" Encouraged, but against his better judgment, Buck swung back to follow Pete's team across the thin ice.

A short while later, the wind began to blow. We had worked our tortuous way through the jumbled ice of several pressure ridges, some of them like miniature, ten foot high, mountain ranges. That sharp, jagged, ice was tough on the sleds, dogs, and people. It slowed our progress. I suddenly realized it was beginning to get dark.

We were moving straight into the wind. My face was nearly numb and my eyeballs ached from the cold. Remembering Simeon and his family, who had died the previous year, I was suddenly frightened and felt a momentary twinge of panic.

Both teams were showing signs of exhaustion. Scared as I

was, I noted that even though my three dogs had traveled 12 miles further than Pete's five, and my sled was heavier than his, his dogs appeared to be in worse shape than mine. Pete stopped and waited for me to catch up. "Maybe it get dark soon. It's better we chain sleds together," he said.

He dug in his sled bag and pulled out a 12 foot dog chain which he handed to me. I snapped an end to Buck's collar. Pete fastened the other end to his sled.

"I drive. You ride and get warm. Then you drive and I ride and get warm. That way better," he said.

I didn't need a second invitation. I huddled in my sled, back to the wind, parka hood over my head, eyes tightly closed, desperately wishing I were somewhere else.

All too soon, Pete stopped our odd little procession. "Maybe you drive, now," he said. We changed places. Then he snapped his end of the chain to his leader's collar, and I tied the end to my sled. I whistled at the dogs, and yelled, "All right, boys! Let's keep going!" I stood on the runners and slapped my hands together.

The dogs hated to face the wind, but Buck, seasoned leader that he was, kept his nose to the ice, and led his team through the night. When I could stand the cold wind no longer, I stopped the teams. Pete and I changed places again and again. I was beginning to wonder if I could be imagining this terrible experience when Pete stopped.

"We're here," he said.

I turned around. In the starlight, I saw dark, shadowy structures lining the shore. It was so cold and windy that the chained dogs next to the building neither smelled nor heard our dogs.

Pete tied his leader to a fish rack. "Let's go get warm," he said. I was beginning to think I'd never hear that word again. Numbly, I nodded, and followed him through the snow to a small hut.

He pushed the door open and we entered. An elderly Eskimo couple sat next to the stove by the light of a kerosene lantern, blinking their surprise as we walked into the tiny, smelly room. Pete said something in Yupik, and the old lady cackled. Pete turned to me. "Is OK. We're t'ree, maybe four miles from Newhalen. But we get warm first."

When I was removing my parka, the front of my right thigh began to tingle. The tingling quickly changed to a sunburn-like pain, which rapidly began feeling as if it was on fire. Pete saw my discomfort, and said, "Maybe you got frostbite. Maybe old woman can fix."

I never learned whether these people could speak English, but it didn't matter. Paying no attention to me, the old Eskimo woman set two mugs on the table and began pouring steaming tea into them. I stood up.

As young as I was, modesty was still very important, and I didn't want to take my pants off, but by that time my thigh felt as if it was being cooked by an acetylene torch. I pulled down the two layers of pants I was wearing, and modestly rolled my underwear leg up, exposing a white spot slightly larger than a silver dollar on my thigh just above my knee. "Eeee-e," the old lady said, when she saw the frostbite.

She poured a small amount of the boiling tea on a rag, and handed the hot wet cloth to me, motioning me to hold it against the frostbite.

By God, I'll tell you, that <u>hurt</u>! But I knew she was right; the foolish idea of rubbing snow on frostbite probably resulted from a desire to minimize the agony of thawing nerve ends and blood vessels. But everything I knew about Arctic survival told me to grin and bear it.

Sure enough, in less than 15 minutes, the pain began to ebb, and soon the white spot was an angry red color. I carefully dried my leg and pulled my clothes on. We thanked the old couple for their hospitality, and went back out into the night. The cold air hit me like a club!

Hurrying, we unchained the dogs, and headed them up the trail along the lake shore. The dogs were on an established trail, and they ran much more easily than they had across the lake. Soon we came to Newhalen. Pete waved good night, and turned his sled in among the buildings. I knew where I was, now, and pressed on until I reached the roadhouse.

Again, I was almost paralyzed by the cold. I chained Buck to a bit of drift wood, and ran to the roadhouse windbreak to let the Lees know I had arrived. Then, before I had a chance to get used to the warmth of the house, I rushed back to the sled, and quickly unharnessed the dogs, chaining each out of the wind to different pieces of drift wood. Then I fed them their trail rations—each dog got a whole fish.

I don't know what the wind chill factor was, but the wind was blowing 25 miles an hour with gusts to 35, and the thermometer stood at −27°! I don't think I have ever been colder in my life than I was that night.

Fortunately, there were no lasting ill effects from the frostbite. The skin sloughed off and a sore developed, but Jan treated it with sulfa powder and sterile dressings, and eventually the sore healed.

If I had been alone on that trip, I hope I would have had sense enough to turn back when the wind began to blow. Otherwise, I have to wonder whether I would have survived.

In a way, the hardship of that trip marked a turning point. Nothing like that occurred again. In fact, without realizing it, we had turned an important corner. With Gene's help, we had done a lot of expansion work the previous spring. In addition to planting a garden, and brooding 25 chicks we had ordered from Sears, we built a garage to house the tractor, and a chicken house for the pullets. Of course, then, I didn't know how badly the season was going to turn out, or that we would be scratching pretty hard just to feed the birds.

Chickens made good sense. After our experience with semi-starvation the previous winter, having a steady supply of fresh eggs meant insuring an adequate diet no matter how poor moose hunting proved to be. Besides, we *liked* eggs. The brief sea gull egg season, when we picked eggs on nearby islands, provided fresh eggs for only about three weeks in the spring. After that they were gone.

Fortunately, chickens will eat just about anything. We had a small amount of mash shipped from Anchorage (the freight bill doubling the already excessive Anchorage price), but for the most part we relied on cornmeal, oatmeal, ground up dried fish and even rabbit from time to time.

The chickens flourished until shortly after New Year's. The accident was commonplace; somehow, the kerosene heated water fountain in the chicken house capsized and set the litter on fire. I heard the distressed squawking and saw smoke trickling from the chicken coop ventilation ports. I rushed in with a fire extinguisher, and quickly put out the fire.

Within four months, the chickens were all dead. There were differences in degree and location, but they shared a common fate. They all died of cancer. Some developed tumors as large as small grapefruit in their abdomen. Others had cancerous growths in their crop and gullet. One or two had skin cancer. I'm absolutely certain the carcinogenic factor was the carbon tetrachloride fire extinguisher.

This was a shocking event. The cause and effect relationship seemed so dramatic that I wrote a letter to the cancer research facility at Johns Hopkins Medical Center in Baltimore and reported what had happened to my chickens. Six weeks later, I received a very nice letter from a doctor at Johns Hopkins thanking me for bringing this incident to their attention, especially since, as the doctor said, it was ordinarily very difficult to induce cancer in chickens.

My learning never stopped. For instance, Babe Alsworth,

who originally hailed from the farming country in southern Minnesota, had noticed the clumsy way I had attempted to plant a garden. He knew better, and he showed me the proper way to hill potatoes.

After the fishing season, Ole Wassenkari, an elderly sourdough fisherman I had met at the cannery, who lived on Ole Creek, a tributary of the Kvichak River, some 80 miles away, showed me how to convert a portion of our potato harvest into potato whiskey.

Ole had come to Kokhanok, largely out of curiosity, I suppose, to visit for a few days. He brought with him a jug of white lightning, or "Ole's Moonshine" as he called it. Luckily, his booze was about gone by the time he reached Kokhanok.

Don't get me wrong. Ole was a great guy; knowledgeable, friendly, and extremely generous. But like so many of us, booze didn't improve him at all. He wasn't a mean drunk. He was a crying drunk. At the cannery, when he had a bottle in the bunkhouse, other fishermen would leave the room because they knew that with two or three shots, poor Ole would begin feeling sorry for himself. The more he drank, the sorrier he became, and without exception, before the bottle was empty, Ole would blubber all over anyone foolish enough to stick around and listen to him.

When Ole saw our potato patch, he began to extol the virtues of potato "whiskey." I was amused but not particularly interested. Ours was basically a dry camp. Jan rarely took a drink when it was available, and while not as abstentious as she, I drank only moderately. When I made one of my infrequent trips to Anchorage, I would sometimes bring home a bottle of 190 proof grain alcohol called *Everclear.*

However, inspired more by curiosity than anything else, I set up a kitchen still. Before I go further, there are two points that require clarification. The first is a matter of nomenclature. Is it possible, you may ask, that a beverage based on water, sugar, and potatoes can even be called whiskey? I think an argument could be made either way. Reserve judgment until you see how the stuff was made.

The second point is a sticky one. The government takes a particularly dim view of distilled alcohol that has somehow escaped the tax collector's attention. Therefore, what follows is merely a description of a picturesque process, not an invitation to do likewise.

The recipe required a 50 gallon barrel tucked away in a warm corner. Since I had placed our stove at an angle to the corner of the room to keep heat away from the log walls, there was room behind it for the barrel. The raw materials were 36 pounds of diced potatoes, 36 pounds of sugar, a pinch of yeast, and 40 gallons of (warm) water. It was a good idea to cover the barrel with a tarp so that while the gases generated could escape, mice and shrews were kept out.

As the barrel "worked," the cabin would fill with an aroma similar to that which might be caused by a massive rising of sourdough bread. After about ten days, the foam in the barrel would subside. Then, the "wash," as it is called, would be ready to distill. Ten quarts of wash would yield approximately one quart of high proof alcohol. I had no way of measuring the specific gravity of the alcohol; I could only judge by a test of my own invention, striking a match over a sample in a teaspoon to see how readily it burned.

The "still" was a big, old-fashioned, pressure cooker on a Coleman stove. A wash boiler served as a condenser. The "worm," ten feet of copper tubing that connected the two, was connected to the pressure cooker's lid where it received the vapor coming off the heated wash.

I'd fill the condenser with five gallons of water, and the cooker with about ten quarts of liquor from the barrel. Then, I would light the Coleman stove. The ability to regulate the heat, as every successful moonshiner knows, is the critical step in the manufacture of OLD STUMP PULLER. The alcohols in the wash must be *gently* separated from the water.

I'm not a chemist. I don't know how many alcohol fractions there may be. But I do know that higher gaseous fractions of alcohol will start flowing invisibly from the worm—they don't condense—but you can get a nice buz by just standing next to the pipe taking deep breathes.

Soon afterward, you could expect to see a tiny, diamond-like, glistening drop of almost pure ethyl alcohol trembling on the lip of your worm. Soon, alcohol would be running in a thin but steady trickle into a measuring bowl.

That was where the sure hand of the experienced moon-shiner paid off. If the wash was heated too rapidly, or its temperature was too high, everything would begin to vaporize at once, and the product would be heavily contaminated with condensed steam and toxic (and explosive) fusel oils, leading to yet another risk. You might unwittingly build a head of steam inside the cooker with certain and always dramatic results. That once happened to me.

I had set the rig up as usual, and was waiting for the still to begin running. The cooker was making plenty of noise, and I knew something would soon happen. It did. The cooker's lid blew off. An instantaneous flash of blue flame enveloped the end of the cabin above the counter. The force of the explosion caused one of the wire legs on the stove to collapse, and boiling wash sloshed on the floor, nearly scalding the cat, while the thatch in the roof caught fire.

After we put the fire out, Jan and I had a long and serious conversation about my hobby. On pain of my project being banished to the bunkhouse I promised to be much more careful and alert after that.

A year and a half later, on my first trip to Seattle, I discovered five-gallon charred oak sherry barrels at the Sweeney Cooperage. I brought three of them back to the homestead. I put them in the root cellar under the office floor, and "aged" my potato whiskey in them, sometimes as long as six months. I must say, it gives a man a world of comfort, knowing he has 15 gallons of whiskey in the cellar.

Purists will argue about it, (just as they argue whether bourbon can properly be called "whiskey") but my claim to the use of the term is based on that final step of the process.

Surprisingly, the distinctive flavor of my whiskey was strikingly similar to Irish whiskey, and the whiskey that remained in the barrels the longest time actually turned a light amber color.

It never occurred to me to find out what wash tasted like, but it couldn't have been much different from a local Native tipple called *bevok*.

As far as I know, the Eskimos and Indians who lived in the Iliamna precinct abstained from making bevok, but the Aleuts and Eskimos in South Naknek made it regularly. They used essentially the same recipe, but usually substituted raisins, canned fruit, or rice for the potatoes. This was basically the same beverage that goes by the generic name of "sneaky Pete" many places where legal alcohol is unavailable.

I never attended a bevok party, but from all accounts they could get rough. When I was in Naknek during the 1955 season, for instance, the commissioner and a marshal from Anchorage were trying to solve a bizarre death arising out of such a party in South Naknek.

It seems that when the guests regained consciousness the next morning, they discovered Martha, their hostess, jammed head first into her own bevok barrel. She was dead.

At first glance, it appeared to be a case of monumental ingratitude, or at the very least, terribly bad manners, but it was never fully established whether her death was involuntary manslaughter, or murder. The authorities ruled out an accidental drowning because her body was wedged too tightly into the barrel; it seemed unlikely that, seeking a nightcap or a last sip of her home brewed nectar, that she could have slipped and accidently have wedged herself so tightly into the barrel. Suicide was ruled out for the same reason.

However, the authorities were never able to find a motive for the crime except a whimsical one of pique or graphic criticism by a disgruntled and ungrateful guest. Like so many other unexplained deaths by other than natural means, this case remains open today.

There is a quirk in my personality or character that drives me to write letters to the editor on almost any subject that you can imagine. I have done it as long as I can remember, not always with congenial results. You might think that buried in such a remote location, it would be easy for me to resist the temptation, but it wasn't.

This letter was triggered by an article I thought silly and ill-informed, that was published in a now long defunct men's magazine called *Blue Book*. The article I objected to described several methods for removing porcupine quills from a dog. The only method the author recommended that I agreed with was to take the poor animal to a veterinarian. The others he advocated were wrong.

Inspired by the purest of humanitarian motives, I wrote a letter to the editor describing a treatment I had discovered which was not covered in the author's discussion of the subject. Flamboyantly, and somewhat foolishly, I called the method the *Blue Tongue Treatment.*

We often saw porcupines. On two occasions, I even had to remove one from under the kitchen table. Both times, of course, the little beasts wound up in the stew pot. Like most wild meat, porcupine is gamey and tough but we weren't fussy. It was meat.

Evidently, the dogs felt the same way. We heard the ruckus out in the dog yard after we were in bed, but I merely assumed a wolverine or perhaps a lynx had wandered past the cabin and the dogs had gotten its scent.

The next morning, however, when I stepped outside the cabin and glanced at the dogs, my heart plummeted. The three animals sat subdued in their respective yards, their muzzles, faces, chests, legs, and feet bristling with new black whiskers. A dead, denuded, porcupine lay in front of Buck.

What could we do?

Unless the quills, especially those in their muzzles and noses were removed, there was a good chance that one of them would work its way into their brains. Whether the quills killed the dogs outright or slowly, with a hundred festering sores, the result was the same; unless we could devise a way of removing them, the humane thing would be to shoot the poor animals.

A vet wouldn't have had that problem. Just a simple anesthesia, and the animal would be out like a wedge. Then it would be child's play to extract the quills. But we didn't have any anesthetics to give.

As a general proposition, if you can't anesthetize an animal, you have to find a way to immobilize it. I think it's easier to control a big animal than a small one, because although big animals have much greater strength, it is easier to get hold of them. Also, they tend not to be as quick as smaller animals. I needed to find a way of immobilizing my sled dogs.

At first, mindful of my animal science courses at Bozeman, particularly the veterinary medicine labs, I tried to think how to design a canine equivalent of the traditional pole squeeze used when doctoring cattle. I quickly discarded that idea, as I did the idea of a muzzle, when I realized that I particularly needed access to the animal's heads, jaws, and mouths. None of the traditional restraints would work.

We finally hit on a draconian strategy. Partly inspired by

our experience with Frank Hiratsuka at Clarks Point, we decided to find a way of distracting the animal's attention by giving them something more serious to worry about. We had to do something. We were desperate.

We started with Buck. He was the oldest, and hopefully the least likely to maim one of us, should our strategy fail. We tied his hind legs tightly together, and secured them to a nearby alder tree. Then we tied his front legs together and after stretching him full on his side, on the ground, pulled that rope tight and tied it to another alder. Now, Buck was flat on his side, almost immobilized, but he was still capable of performing an operation on me if I got too close to his head and teeth, which is precisely where I needed to be.

We slipped a noose over his head and tightened it around his throat, cutting off his air. Jan was the anesthesiologist, controlling the noose. While poor Buck was focused on breathing, I gripped the quills, one at a time, with my pliers, and pulled them out of his feet and legs, his chest, and as he became more subdued, his nose and face, including one dangerously near an eye. His tongue, by now, was extended, and Jan watched it begin turning blue. She immediately relaxed her grip on the noose.

Poor Buck took several great gulps of air, while I began removing the quills from his lips and between his teeth. Then I reached inside his mouth and found five quills imbedded in his tongue. I removed them by pushing them on through. He even had a quill in the lining of his throat!

Satisfied that we had removed them all, we released him and repeated the process with Pan and Bill. I know the readers of my letter in *Blue Book*—at least those who bothered to write—thought I was a sadistic monster, but I knew of no alternative, especially when dealing with 80 pound sled dogs.

We had a variety of pets during those years, some wild, some domestic. Oren always had the girls in mind, and several times, when someone's cat at Iliamna had a litter of kittens, Oren would ask if the girls would like another kitten. In that way, over time, we acquired two or three cats. Lynnie's cat, an orange tabby that came late to us, was the most successful.

Trina, Debby and Lynnie

An earlier tomcat had seriously alienated us by spraying the sacks of flour and sugar stacked in the windbreak. Although Jan discarded the worst of the tainted flour and sugar, we couldn't afford to be squeamish about small quantities of yellow flour or sugar (even though much of it wound up as whiskey). No matter how much maple flavoring Jan used, our hotcakes often had more than a subtle hint of tomcat piss.

One of the girls had claimed the miserable animal for her own. We felt that the need the individual kids had for personal things outweighed the inconvenience of yellow hotcake batter, so although the cat, I'm happy to say, did not survive, I didn't dispose of it.

I don't know what happened to him. He simply disappeared. As oversexed as he was, I thought he might have been ambitious enough to try breeding a lynx, or a wolverine, perhaps. Whatever it was, it was fatal.

It probably served him right. It was too late to do him any good, but Jan's father, Lee, later showed me how to "fix" tomcats. His system was a variation of the Blue Tongue Treatment, only instead of a noose, he simply put the cat head first into a knee-high rubber boot.

The cat couldn't turn around, and no cat is going to back up when someone is doing unpleasant things to its rear end. Its entire impulse is to plow straight ahead, which is difficult in a rubber boot.

Macky was a small golden labrador. She liked to follow me when I put on the snow-shoes to go hunting. Once, on such an expedition, she had run ahead of me, probably to warn the game. I heard the excited bark she used to an-nounce treed game, then suddenly a horrified yelp, and shrieks of terror, as she bolt-ed out of the brush and ran to me. Safe between my legs,

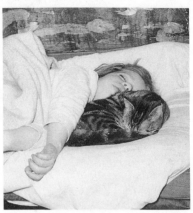
Trina and her pal

she turned to face whatever ferocious enemy was on her tail. Nothing emerged from the brush, although I half expected to see a hungry lynx bounding behind her.

Curious, I followed her trail. The story was plainly written in the fresh snow. My dumb little labrador had jumped a wolverine that was so startled it had lost its presence of mind and had scrambled up a nearby tree. That's when Macky had announced her treed quarry. On reflection, the wolverine must have felt silly. It was like Frankenstein being treed by Shirley Temple. From the wolverine's point of view, lunch was sitting at the bottom of the tree. It was when the wolver-ine reversed his course that Macky realized she had made a terrible mistake.

During the later years, after Buck began having difficulty working the kinks out of his old bones in the mornings, I bought a young Siberian husky. Buck and I trained him as a new leader. Then I retired Buck from active duty. Although he was off the chain, and free to run with the team if he

321

Lynnie and friend

chose, most often he and Macky laid in the sun and hung around the cabin.

They were always alert to the traffic out on the ice in front of the cabin, and considered it their sacred duty to regulate it. Quite regularly one or the other would spy a wolverine galloping clumsily, bear fashion, across the bay. Then all hell would break loose.

Roaring in full throated pursuit, Buck and Macky would go sprinting down the slope to the ice. The noise they made alerted the wolverine, of course, and it would respond by increasing its speed, sprinting for the cover of brush at the shore. Once it reached the shore, however, it would stop and turn, waiting for its pursuers to catch up.

They never did. The moment the wolverine stopped, so did the dogs. The dogs would immediately turn and, full of themselves, trot back to the cabin, tongues lolling and tails wagging, their duty done.

Wolverines are interesting animals. Members of the weasel family, wolverines, pound for pound, are among the most ferocious animals in the world, yet they were not difficult to trap. However, a wolverine set, like a wolf set, required the use of several traps so that when the animal was thrashing about after stepping on the first trap, it would almost unavoidably step in another, and possibly even a third trap. This prevented them from amputating the trapped leg, which they were quick to do.

Their hides were in demand because the fur would not frost; therefore, they made wonderful parka ruffs to be worn around the face. Also, the Fish and Wildlife Service offered a $35 bounty for their capture. This was an interesting example of bureaucratic schizophrenia, because their capture was lawful only during the general fur trapping season!

Our area was thickly populated with them, probably as a result of the rabbit explosion. Babe Alsworth had a photo of a neighbor at Port Alsworth actually having a tug-of-war with a wolverine over a dead goat. The doughty little animal, not much larger than a terrier, was dug in, squatting back on its haunches, the dead goat's head firmly

"Moosey"

clenched in its jaws. The animal's adversary, a tall, and I thought foolish, young man had an equally firm grip on the dead animal's hind legs. It made an interesting photograph, but knowing something about wolverines, I wouldn't have been surprised to see the animal climb right up that goat's carcass and seize the man by the throat. I wouldn't play those kind of games with a wolverine. It is too dangerous.

It reminded me of Joe Pendleton's untimely end. I never met the man, but the news story was a timely reminder to all of us living in bear country that poking sticks into bear dens in the spring is never a good idea, even if your motive is merely to present a trophy opportunity to your hunter/client. It was a perfectly legal spring bear hunt over on Montague Island, but the bear didn't know that. Irritated by the rude poking and jabbing, instead of coming politely out of the hole yawning, stretching and rubbing its eyes, the bear came right up the stick and destroyed poor Joe.

Federal game management was not much more sophisticated than the management of Alaska's salmon fisheries, except that there were no powerful economic interests pushing and pulling at the game regulator's elbow. Animals were seen as good or bad depending on their potential for successful competition with man. "Bad" animals, in true Western fashion, had a price on their head. Harbor seals, for example, commanded a bounty of $2, which was paid on presentation of the animal's "mask" or face skin. I've already mentioned the bounty for wolves ($50). Coyotes were bounty animals, as were wolverines, bald eagles (50¢ a claw), and Dolly Varden trout (2¢ a tail).

The year that Bob Walker and I built the bridge at Iliamna, an unusual pet was dumped, like a foundling at an orphanage, on our doorstep by some young fishery biologists. They had found the young, orphaned, moose calf shortly after their arrival the previous spring. They had kept it alive on evaporated milk, and eventually weaned it. But that fall, when their work was done, they thought the animal was still too young to survive by itself, so they had brought it to us.

It was a bull calf. I admit I flirted briefly with the idea of castrating and trying to domesticate it, since it was already tame, but I knew that unlike my still, it would be impossible to conceal the animal from the Eskimos, and that the game warden would take a very dim view of such a project.

I don't know what happened to it. It was still digging the stray potato we had missed when we had harvested the garden and engaging in mock combat with Mack and Buck, when I left for Iliamna with Bob Walker. It was gone when I came back from the hospital after Christmas.

14

A New Washing Machine

Although the DEW line, augmented by ground observers like ourselves communicating directly to the
Sadie Hawkins net, had come on line a year earlier, it
was evident to the Pentagon that holes existed which no
ground observer corps, no matter how vigilant or dedicated,
could fill.

Consequently, although the King Salmon unit was already
on line, it was decided to build another radar station at Big
Mountain on the southern shore of Lake Iliamna, midway
between Igiugig and Kakhonak during the summer of 1956.

When I learned of the project, I harnessed my dogs, and
drove 25 miles to the camp, where I met the superintendent.
Advance crews, supplied by airplanes landing on the lake ice,
were already at work building the construction camp.

After identifying myself, I said, "I don't know whether you
realize it, but President Eisenhower has declared this part of
Alaska a federal disaster area for the past three years because
of the poor salmon runs. Some men, myself included, have
just about given up on fishing if something better comes
along. What are the chances of local men finding work here?"

The superintendent said, "I've been told to hire as many
local men as I can get. Of course, you realize, we won't
begin work until the lake opens up and we begin
barging equipment down from Pile Bay."

Since Carl Williams had the only scow on the lake, I mentally congratulated him on his good fortune. Then I asked, "When do you think that will be?"

He pushed his cap back on his head, and peered at the calendar on the tent wall. "It's hard to say, exactly," he said, "but I'd guess somewhere between the end of May and the middle of June. We'll get in touch with you when it's time to come to work."

This was great news, and I told him so. We shook hands again, and I happily left. I stopped at the village on the way home, to share my good news with the Eskimos.

The spring passed very quickly. Anticipating that I would be employed at Big Mountain well into the fall, I began cutting next winter's firewood early. By the end of breakup, I had a good start on my fall chores, and was listening carefully to the radio, momentarily expecting a message from the construction camp. Days, then weeks, went by without the promised summons to work.

The Eskimos, smarter or more cynical than I, went fishing, while I clung to my childish faith in the fidelity of a Morrison–Knutsen superintendent. After everyone else had left for Bristol Bay, I could wait no longer. I drove my skiff down to the construction camp to learn when I should report for work.

I was very surprised when I beached the boat to see the high level of activity. I would imagine that several hundred men were at work carrying things, driving nails, building roads, fitting pipes, and unloading Carl's scow. The man I had met in April was no longer at the camp, and his successor had never heard of me. "I'm sorry," he said, "we get all our people out of Anchorage."

I know now what it feels like to be left at the alter. When I left the office shack, a workman wearing a badge that said "Shop Steward" stopped me. "You looking for work?" he asked, his eyes sympathetically flickering over my ragged appearance.

"I sure am," I said.

"Well, let me give you a tip," he said. "The only way you can get a job here is to go to Anchorage and join the union and sit in the hall, waiting to be called." He paused, then added, "Understand, that ain't no guarantee you'd get a job on this site. They might send you anywhere."

"But I live here!" I said. "Besides, I don't have the money to fly to Anchorage, or join the union, or live in Anchorage while I'm waiting to get a job. Don't get me wrong," I added hastily, "I'll be glad to join the union. It's just that I don't have the money. Come on, give me a break!"

The steward shook his head and told me to think it over. Then he turned away and I dispiritedly walked back to my boat. Things had happened too fast. Now what the hell was I going to do?

When I returned to the homestead with my sad news, Jan was supportive as always. "Something like this should be against the law," she said angrily.

Against the law? Perhaps it was. I didn't know much about the Taft-Hartley Act, but I had taken a course in labor economics when I was in college, and I seemed to remember that closed shops—the condition the steward at Big Mountain had described—were no longer legal. I wrote a letter to the district attorney in Anchorage describing what had happened, and promptly forgot the matter, because traveling to Anchorage was out of the question.

Meanwhile, the country was filling up. Bob and Doris Walker, and their children, from Kenai, staked a cabin site near the sawmill on the edge of our northwestern boundary that spring. Bob was busy cutting and peeling cabin logs, which we dragged to his building site behind the tractor.

Gene Pope had returned from Ohio, and married an

327

Eskimo girl named Madrona. The young couple was building a cabin on Copper River, about two miles away. The lumber business was good, and I spent a lot of time at the sawmill that summer.

Raising Bob Walker's cabin (Author is under the log.)

Late in the summer, the fishermen returned, flush with the earnings of a banner year. Meanwhile, Bob and I had bid a contract with the Territorial Department of Roads to furnish the materials for a vehicular bridge across a small stream at Iliamna, connecting the roadhouse with the village of Newhalen. We were to do the work as Territorial employees. That turned out to be a wise decision.

Bob and I cut the necessary timbers and planks on the mill, and rafted the timbers and piling behind Bob's cabin cruiser across the lake to Iliamna. We planned to do the actual building after freeze-up, because we knew it would be easier to build the bridge standing on ice than from a boat.

Late that fall, while Bob and I were running the sawmill, an airplane, a Grumman Goose, unexpectedly appeared from the direction of the roadhouse. It swooped low overhead, turned into the wind, and landed, taxiing up to the beach. The bow hatch opened, and a middle-aged man wearing a rumpled business suit, leaned out. "Is one of you fellows named Moore?" he shouted over the sound of the idling engines.

I stepped forward. "That's me," I said.

"Well, good," the man said. "My name is Latimer. I'm the

General Counsel for the National Labor Relations Board. We're having a hearing on your complaint tomorrow at Big Mountain. Climb aboard, and we'll be on our way."

Climb aboard? Just like that? "Hold on," I yelled back. "I've got to get my gear and tell my wife where I'm going. Wait a few minutes."

I rushed across the portage, and burst into the cabin. "Remember that letter I wrote last spring to the DA in Anchorage?" I asked. Not waiting for an answer, I continued, "An NLRB guy is over on the other side waiting to take me to Big Mountain for a hearing. I'll probably be back tomorrow night."

Grabbing a change of

A pensive Bob Walker.

clothes, I hurried out the door and back to the mill. Meanwhile, the pilot had swung the plane around so the door was out of the water. The door was open, and I climbed in.

After quickly shaking hands with Latimer, I settled back to enjoy the short flight to Big Mountain. A trip that required hours by dog sled now took only minutes. As if by magic, a new graveled airstrip already occupied by several parked cargo planes, appeared beneath our wings. I was surprised. I had no idea M–K would be this far along with the project.

The hearing was held the next day in a nearby Quonset hut. A driving rain storm caused lengthy delays because the noise of rain pounding on the tin roof made it difficult for the reporter to hear the proceedings. He frequently had to ask for clarifications and repetitions. We were stormbound at Big Mountain for three days.

Since I was the complainant, during the weeks and months following the hearing, I received copies of dozens of legal documents. Almost every mail contained one, sometimes several, pleadings prepared by one of the parties to the litigation; either the Construction Laborers and Hod Carriers Union local 341, Morrison–Knutsen Corp., or the NLRB.

When Oren resumed regular mail service after freezeup, Bob and I moved temporarily into our own construction camp at the roadhouse. We chopped holes in the ice and up-ended pile "bents"–prefabricated rows of piling–through those holes, standing them on the stream bottom. The blocking that held them in place was removed the following morning because the new ice that had formed overnight, closing the holes we made, held them firmly in place.

After the project was well begun, while Bob and I were slipping and sliding on the ice, using Swede hooks to drag a heavy log piling into position, my feet shot out from under me, and I fell sideways under the log. The log, then Bob, fell across my unstable right knee. It's hard to describe the sheet of nauseating agony that washed over my body! Tears stood in my eyes while I swallowed, trying not to vomit.

After resting for an hour or so, I hobbled painfully to the roadhouse. Irving, the project supervisor, was sitting at the kitchen table filling out time slips. When he saw my swollen knee, he said, "I think we'd better send you to Anchorage."

The next day, I checked into the 5005th USAF hospital as a VA patient. They tapped my knee, and drained the accumulated fluid. Then I spent two months in physical therapy, and was sent home shortly after Christmas.

While in the hospital, I was interviewed several times by a National Labor Relations Board investigator, who indicated that my complaint against M–K and the Laborer's Union was still being pursued.

A few weeks after I returned home, I received a $3,000

check from the Territorial Workman's Compensation Fund. I promptly ordered a 26-foot fishing skiff from Bryant's Marina in Seattle, to be delivered on the spring boat.

I also filed, that year, for a seat in the Territorial legislature. In Territorial days, legislative apportionment was based on the four judicial divisions in Alaska. Consequently, the urban candidates almost invariably won. Yet, since it cost only ten dollars to file, every once in a while, a quixotic soul like me would throw his or her hat in the ring.

This was my second venture into elective politics. I had resigned earlier from the commissionership so I could become a candidate for election to the Constitutional Convention in 1955. Unfortunately, I was defeated by a margin of two to one by Truman Emberg, of Dillingham.

Unlike that election, I had no expectation of winning this one. I merely filed because I wanted to participate in what was generally believed to be the last Territorial general election. We knew statehood was just around the corner. This was yet another manifestation of the romantic streak that led me to mark the end of the sailboat era by attempting to sail my fishing boat back to the cannery in 1953.

There were plenty of civic projects closer to home that needed my attention. For instance, since there were 12 school age children in Kakhonak (not counting my kids, who lived too far away), I had negotiated an agreement with the Territorial Department of Education that if the community would construct a suitable building, the Territory would provide a teacher and pay a modest rent to the community for the use of the building.

I persuaded the village elders to agree to building the school (with appended teacher's quarters). Then, I helped them design a building that met Territorial standards. Finally, after the villagers cut the logs and brought them to the mill, I turned them into lumber. No charge. The village elders used church money to pay for the things that had to be bought; roofing, nails, windows, and other building materials.

Remembering my experience with gas driven washing machines and Coleman lanterns at Clarks Point, I urged the villagers to go into the public utility business. I thought they could form a co-op, which is not that different from the basic Eskimo social structure, and sell electricity to the school. I thought they might electrify the village for practically nothing, and I even located a surplus 15 Kw diesel plant for them.

Little Joe bringing logs to the mill.

I got too far ahead of them in this instance. Instead, much to my surprise, they went into the telephone business. Evidently someone had seen an ad in *Popular Mechanics* for war surplus field telephones, and they ordered a dozen phones and a couple of spools of wire. The whole village was on a big party line.

At Clarks Point, we had occasionally seen the down side of somewhat corrupted Eskimo/Aleut customs. But when we moved to Lake Iliamna, living as intimately as we did with the people at Kakhonak, we gained a much deeper understanding and appreciation for their culture. It has enabled people to survive and prosper in one of the world's most hostile environments with nothing more than their collective wit and tools of their own manufacture.

They had a rigid code of sex specific social expectations. For instance, they were always mildly scandalized to see Jan splitting wood. When that happened, I was usually teased about it. Only later did I realize that the "teasing" was really a form of Eskimo social control. Women cooked, looked after the house, cared for the babies, and made clothes. Men were expected to do the outside work; hunting, splitting wood, and hauling water.

You saw those differences in adolescent children. The girls were always busy in the house, helping mother, looking after the baby, and so forth, while the teenage boys lolled around listening to the radio, playing the guitar, or, if the spirit moved them, possibly engaging in a voluntary outdoor activity. They were not expected to produce food,

Sawing lumber for schoolhouse

and in many cases, were not even required to cut firewood.

But even in that society, there was no free lunch. While most young couples paired off and married much as young people do elsewhere, when a girl became pregnant and no husband was at hand, the community had a ready, and I think rather neat, solution. Although I never heard this rationale articulated, it was clear that intuitively, the village elders knew how destabilizing single parenthood would be for the village.

Therefore, they would gather to review the list of eligible bachelors in the community. They made no attempt to determine paternity. Their purpose was simply to create another stable branch of the community/family, which was crucial to community survival. Consequently, the young man with the most wealth, however modest that might be, was usually selected to become the bridegroom.

It was almost unheard of for a bachelor to be selected, and to subsequently decline the honor. I never knew it to happen. If it did happen, the defaulting bachelor, at the very least,

333

would have been subjected to public ridicule, the same punishment I received for letting Jan split the wood, only on a much grander scale. He might even have been banished.

The pragmatism of these supposedly primitive people was astonishing. If the timing of the pregnancy allowed it, those nuptial decisions were made at the conclusion of the fishing season and after the post season gambling adjustments had been made. Consider the significance of that arrangement.

Eskimos love to gamble. If there was a pregnant, but unspoken for, lass in the village, the bachelors could be expected to play badly (to the joy of the married men), because the only way bachelors could retain their happy, carefree, existence was by divesting themselves of whatever wealth they might have accumulated. How could the village elders lose in a deal like that?

The purpose of this kind of social control, of course, was to enlarge the family. Eskimos know that the larger the family, the more secure each member in it becomes.

This concept probably underlies another striking characteristic of Eskimo village life. Mothers occasionally gave their babies to women without children. When children were old enough to toddle around the village, they sometimes chose new parents. In that way, the family was constantly expanding, since the child's new foster parents could now claim a kinship with the child's natural parents.

Similarly, Eskimos regarded food (but not personal possessions) as community property. A successful hunter fed the community, whether the prey was a duck or a whale.

Not so, the Indians. When I was in Nondalton—an Athabascan village—meeting with the village council in the chief's kitchen to discuss their food relief needs during the disaster years, the chief abruptly said something in Athabascan to his son. The boy obediently lifted the trap door to the cellar, jumped down, and began handing cans of food up to his father, who said, as he stacked the cans neatly on the table, "Now you see this can? This is peaches." Then, he reached for the next, saying, "This is real good ham. Do you see the picture on the label?"

After describing the contents of 25 or 30 cans to a hungry audience, he snapped, "This belongs to me! You guys got nothing!" Then, to the boy, he said, "Put it back."

The most frequently heard expression in an Eskimo village was *"nam-ee-geega."* This is a useful phrase meaning literally "I don't know." Often shortened to a simple *"nam-ee,"* it also meant "I know but I'm not going to tell you," or "I know but I'll forgive your bad manners for asking," or perhaps, bluntly, "it's none of your business." It depended on the speaker's inflection and the phrase's context.

To a newcomer, the English patois spoken in the upriver villages could be misleading. Simple declarative statements were frequently preceded by a tentative "maybe," as in "maybe he rain," while you and the speaker are being drenched in a downpour.

Eskimos live in a violent world. Perhaps that is why they were seldom violent, or even discourteous, toward each other. When men fought, which was rare, instead of punching one another, combatants would duel verbally, to the great delight and amusement of the assembled community. Even rarer, when their conflicts became physical—I saw physical combat between Eskimos only once—the men would attempt to tear each other's clothes, perhaps thereby demonstrating to the village the inferior quality of the opponent's wife's needle work.

When Eskimos like Carl Evon became outlaws or rogues, however, there was no limit to their brutality. Carl was the only rogue Eskimo I encountered, but Ole Wassenkari, Pinky Peterson, Butch Smith, and Henry Shade, remembered Klootuk, an Eskimo who terrorized the Mulchatna and upper

Nushagak in the 1920s. Seeking matches, salt, and ammunition, he murdered a dozen trappers in their lonely, isolated, cabins. He was captured twice by posses of trappers. Both times, heavily bound, incredibly, he escaped by murdering his heavily armed captors.

Klootuk was never brought to justice. In 1935, a human skeleton holding a rifle that some thought had belonged to Klootuk's victim was discovered in an abandoned trapper's cabin on the Hoholitna River in the Kuskokwim drainage, a short distance from the head waters of the Nushagak. Nobody could say definitely that the skeleton belonged to Klootuk, but he never struck again.

People other than rogue Eskimos disappeared from time to time. During my brief tenure as commissioner, two people vanished in the Iliamna Precinct. One was the Eskimo girl, Octrina Wassillie, whose family perished on the ice. The other was a reclusive trader named Jack Mack who had a store on an island in the mouth of the Kvichak immediately adjacent to Igiugig.

His disappearance occurred in the fall, shortly after I was appointed commissioner. There was nothing to suggest foul play. It was generally believed that he may have fallen through the ice and that his body had been swept downriver. There was no possibility that his body could have been recovered at that time of year, since travel was even more restricted during freeze-up on the river than it was on the lake. By the time breakup occurred six months later, his body would have disintegrated, and there would have been nothing to find. The moving river ice would have scattered his skeleton over a wide area.

Another mysterious, but better publicized, disappearance occurred the following year in the adjoining Naknek Precinct, a few miles down the Kvichak River from Jack Mack's place.

Ted Lambert was an Alaskan artist of the first rank. He

336

was a bitter man, who lived in an isolated little cabin on the Kvichak River, on a subsistence level, trading his exquisite paintings for food to avoid paying alimony to his ex-wife. He lived the life of an extremely reclusive hermit, discouraging nearly all visitors.

His only contacts were with Gren Collins, a local bush pilot whose wife owned the Alaska Treasure Shop in Anchorage, and his nearest neighbor, Ole Wassenkari. Collins provided his basic supplies, and Ole provided fresh vegetables in season and, if I knew Ole, all the moonshine Lambert cared to drink.

The new fishing skiff

Like Jack Mack, Ted Lambert simply disappeared, apparently, during freeze-up. People speculated that he might have died of a heart attack in a remote area behind his cabin. The foxes and other wild scavengers soon would have scattered his bones so that when the snow disappeared in the spring, there would have been little for searchers to find.

My big skiff arrived on schedule; it had been consigned to me in care of Nakeen cannery. I powered it with a 35-hp Evinrude; the biggest, meanest, outboard motor I ever owned. Although by most standards, the fishing season of 1957 was only fair, for me it was outstanding. For the first time since we had moved to Kokhanok, I came home at the end of the season with a boat load of groceries and a check for cash money in my pocket.

However, when Hermy Herrmann arrived six weeks later on the *Fajen,* my euphoric bubble burst. I had ordered eleven drums of gasoline—about 600 gallons—and Hermy showed up with only three drums. Where were the rest?

"Well," he said defensively, "they were out of gas at Igiugig, so I had to let 'em have some of yours. . ."

I was furious. My plans for a busy winter logging the islands in Intricate Bay suddenly collapsed. I was also confronted with another unexpected problem.

Jan had badly needed a washing machine to keep up with the needs of three daughters, a new baby, and an active husband. After lengthy debate the previous spring, remembering that sorry machine we had owned in Clarks Point, I talked her out of ordering another gasoline powered washer. Instead, since we now had a ten-hp aircooled engine, I convinced her that it was time we moved into the 20th century by beginning to use regular electricity. Consequently, we ordered an *electric* washing machine and a 3–Kw generator from Sears.

Now, as I stood on the beach, peering past the lowered bow gate and my trifling three drums of gas, I saw, tucked back in among other crates and barrels, a large crate. Gleaming white porcelain sparkled between its slats.

"I see the washing machine, Hermy," I said. "Where's the generator?"

Hermy looked puzzled. "There wasn't any generator for you on the ship," he said.

Oh, oh.

In the following mail, we received a notice that our generator had been back ordered, and would be shipped in 30 days. *"Sears serves Alaska best,"* all right. Some service.

I'll say this for Jan. She was a wonderfully good sport. At first, there was only a moderate amount of "won't you ever listen?" and "I told you so!" She could really have lowered the boom; lots of women would have.

However, in the days and weeks that followed, Jan grew increasingly unhappy as she stared at that pristine washing machine in the corner of the cabin while she rubbed dirty clothes on her worn wash board. The new washing machine became a never-ending topic of conversation.

A bedtime story.

I've already mentioned my unfortunate propensity for writing letters to the editor. There's another quirk in my psychological makeup that also causes bruises from time to time. It seems that my intuition is highly developed. Or perhaps I've learned to recognize and act on its promptings. Whatever it is, I gave Jan a new washboard for Christmas.

Sensible men reading this will cringe. How could I be so stupid? Ordinarily, they would be right. But the pressure that foolish gift generated was the spur I needed to write to NC Company in Anchorage, and order a generator to be flown out to us as soon as possible.

I won't argue that sensible people shouldn't need to torture themselves into doing the right thing. But crazy or not, the system worked for me, and Jan soon was happily plugging in the machine to wash our clothes.

As we had learned at Clarks Point, when you begin using washing machines, you are talking about serious quantities of water. Our primitive water system involving a neck yoke and two five gallon buckets was not equal to the task. That spring, as soon as weather conditions permitted, I put in a well.

This turned out to be a much more ambitious project than driving the well at Clarks Point, or even digging the well in Anchorage. Judging from the rock outcroppings in the path

Trina and Lynnie "driving" the family sled

leading down to the lake, the knoll we had selected as a building site was solid granite underlying a two or three foot layer of soil.

Here, I was going to have to drill through rock. Luckily, I had followed my father-in-law around the oilfields in northern Montana long enough to see what old-fashioned "cable" tools could do.

Cable drilling is the old fashioned well-drilling technique where a steel tool bit is continually raised and dropped, raised and dropped, in a wet hole. It requires great patience. Unlike a rotary drill, a drop tool doesn't cut a hole. It merely crushes whatever material it may encounter. The hole is lubricated with small quantities of water. The dust created by the tool bit combines with that water to make a slurry, which is occasionally bailed out.

Luckily, I had a big tool bar made of octagon steel that would serve as a miniature tool bit. It weighed around 30 pounds, and measured seven feet long by about two inches in diameter. One end was pointed; the other had a chisel shape. I sharpened the chisel end and opened the roof. Then I rigged a small tripod above the roof from which I hung a pulley and rope. My bailer was an empty orange juice concentrate can nailed to a long stick.

To concentrate the initial blows of my improvised tool bit, I dug a short piece of two and a half inch pipe down to bedrock through the dirt under the sink (about a foot). That became our well head.

A cup full of water went into the hole, and I grabbed the

rope and began the monotonous pull, drop; pull, drop; pull, drop. Hour after hour after tedious hour. I saw almost immediately that my drill, crude as it was, was going to work. The drop tool slowly chipped away at the rock. After a week of steady pounding, the well was down seven feet. The bailer stick became too short, so I began lashing extensions to it.

After two weeks, the well had reached 15 feet, and as we approached 18 feet in the third week, the bailer came up wet. We had a well.

Also that spring, the National Labor Relations Board in Washington, DC, handed down their verdict in Moore v. Morrison-Knutsen and Laborer's Local 341.

> *We find that the conduct of respondents Morrison-Knutsen and Laborer's Local 341 demonstrate such a fundamental antipathy to the intent and purposes of the Labor Management Relations Act that . . .jointly and severally, respondents must refund . . . all the fees and dues paid by all the laborers as a condition of their employment on all the White Alice sites in Alaska. In addition. . .*

M-K and the Union immediately appealed the decision to the federal 9th Circuit Court of Appeals in San Francisco, on the ground that the penalty was excessive; repayment of that sum might have bankrupted the union. Of course, this meant nothing to me since I was never a member of the union.

As a postscript, two years later, I enjoyed a somewhat embarrassing moment during the first state legislature, when Anchorage attorney and legislative committee chairman John Radar, mildly intoxicated, came to the table I was sharing with Henry Hedberg, business agent of the laborer's union, in the Bubble Room of the Baranof Hotel, and somewhat untactfully announced the circuit court's decision.

He slapped me on the shoulder and said loudly, "Here's the man who broke the Laborer's Union!"

Meanwhile, we had not given up the lodge idea; it's just

that we were still preoccupied with survival. Now, returning to our original plan, I thought that reindeer might attract visitors, and I began to think about reintroducing them.

Before the catastrophic Novarupta–Katmai volcanic eruption of 1912—one of the most violent in modern times—which occurred only about 85 miles away, hundreds—perhaps thousands—of reindeer had lived in the Kakhonak Bay area. This region was particularly suitable for reindeer, partly because there were no indigenous caribou to lure them away, and partly because the big peninsula immediately west of our homestead made a superb summer grazing ground.

The eruption blew off the summit of Mt. Novarupta, hurling an estimated 15 cubic *miles* of material into the atmosphere. Older Eskimos who remembered the eruption told me that the residual ash was more than two feet thick! It drifted before the wind like a snow that never melts, temporarily suspending most terrestrial life in the region. It's hard to imagine what must have been like.

The unfortunate reindeer and other grazing animals suffocated in the fine ash, or they starved, not being able to paw through it to reach the caribou moss. Other animals doubtless died of thirst because the water in the streams and along the lake shore had turned to thick mud.

Even today, nearly a century later, a compact two to three inch strata of pale brownish-gray clay, the residue of that ash, lies everywhere beneath the tundra around Lake Iliamna.

Reindeer are not indigenous to Alaska. Their presence is due largely to the persistence of an early-day Presbyterian missionary named Sheldon Jackson (for whom the boarding school in Sitka was named), and Congressional perception of an incipient famine in the newly developed Alaskan gold fields. Spasmodic importations of reindeer and their herders from Lapland began in the late 1800s. Those importations continued until the mid 1920s.

An aerial view of our homestead

Dock extends into the water lower right. Nearest building to the beach is the cabin. Next is the bunkhouse. Then the garage. Across the road is the chicken house. White object is weather bureau instrument shelter. Tall poles identify radio antenna. Intricate Bay is visible at the top, across the portage.

I had met one of those herders, Mike Sauri, and his family, at Clarks Point during the fishing season in 1948. He had come to Alaska in 1925, had married an Eskimo woman, and was the father of Helen, one of the most beautiful young women I ever met. He was a victim, as often seems inevitable, of the evolutionary process where small economic interests flow together to become large ones. The reindeer herds had been consolidated, and his services as a herder were no longer required.

Eventually, the Lomann Brothers came to dominate the thriving reindeer industry on the Bering Sea coast. Several slaughter houses and cold storage plants were built at key points, and large quantities of meat were shipped to Seattle aboard refrigerator ships.

The Depression killed the business. Who would buy reindeer meat when beef was ten cents a pound? By 1935, the market for reindeer products had collapsed.

The Lomann Brothers were ahead of their time. Handed lemons, they made lemonade. Stuck with that elaborate infrastructure and an estimated 600,000 head of reindeer, they persuaded Congress to buy the reindeer and hand them over to the Eskimos. Congress was in a giving mood in the mid-1930s, and the Reindeer Act of 1937 was the result.

The government bought 600,000 head of reindeer and turned them over, nilly-willy, to the delighted Eskimos who promptly went on a meat binge that lasted three years. By 1940, only 25,000 reindeer survived. Alarmed by the impending extermination of Alaskan reindeer, the Reindeer Service (another agency of the Interior Department) established a large reindeer reserve on Nunivak Island.

The Reindeer Act prohibited white people from owning reindeer. However, as far as I know, the underlying Constitutional issue was never litigated. Instead, the Reindeer Service simply refused to sell the animals to anyone.

I made a formal application for a foundation herd of 25 animals as a demonstration project, hoping to persuade the Interior Department to make a gift of the animals, and Northern Consolidated Airways to provide free transportation from Nunivak to Kokhanok.

The Reindeer Service sent an inspector from Juneau to examine our proposed reindeer range. He had formerly worked as a range specialist for the Bureau of Indian Affairs in Montana. When he learned that I had about two and a half years of Montana State College under my belt, and, more importantly, that Evan McRae, a major lessor of Crow Indian reservation lands, whom he knew well, was Jan's uncle, the deal was all set, except for one thing. While Northern Consolidated offered us a good price, they wouldn't fly the animals for the publicity in it. Unfortunately, publicity was all I had to offer, so the deal fizzled.

I was still smarting from Hermy's failure to deliver 11 drums of gas. After giving the matter a great deal of thought, I decided to design and build a barge. I needed one to carry the tractor to the islands and perform the many other tasks that required a boat bigger than my river boat or the old sailboat hull. Also, with my own barge, I would no longer be forced to rely on someone else for my freight. The barge would measure 15 feet wide by 30 feet long, big enough for my purposes.

Like so many of my projects, this one required a series of preliminary stages. Before I could build the barge, I needed to construct a level surface to use as a building base or "ways," and for winter storage. Since I wanted to avoid the inevitable ground heaving that occurs during the winter, I had to put the building ways on piling. I lacked a pile driver, but I remembered seeing a little drop hammer—roughly 1,000 pounds—in Carl William's junk pile.

After a short discussion with Carl over the radio, the hammer was mine in exchange for 2,000 board feet of lumber which he would pick up when he delivered the hammer. Carl gave me the hammer's dimensions. By the time he delivered it, the pile driver frame was ready, and the 30 foot marine ways were laid out in a series of parallel stakes driven into the ground where the piling were to be driven next to the sawmill.

Without an engine to lift the pile driver's hammer, I was forced to improvise. I hung the hammer between its "leads" in the frame by two cables. Both cables ran through pulleys

The homemade piledriver

at the top of the frame. One passed over a second pulley near the base of the frame, and to the tractor. The second cable ran through a pulley at the top of the frame, and dropped to the spool of a hand-powered winch mounted at a convenient height on the frame.

Jan raised the hammer by driving the tractor slowly forward, pulling on the first cable. While the hammer was slowly rising, I feverishly cranked the hand winch, taking slack from the second cable.

Then I would hold the friction brake on the winch with my left hand and remove the crank with my right, while Jan backed the tractor ten feet, and I would release the brake.

THUD!

The hammer would drive the piling another three inches into the ground. Crude? Definitely! Dangerous? Very. Slow? Like molasses.

It took all day to drive a single piling, but I was patient, and by the end of two weeks, the foundation for our marine ways was complete. A week later, I began framing the barge. I completed the framing by freeze-up. I planned to complete the barge the following summer. But, as happened so often, something else got in the way.

Shortly after breakup that year, by coincidence, two old ladies in the village—one was Feeny's mother, the other the wife of the chief—became seriously ill with respiratory infections. Jan called *Sadie Hawkins 68,* and after explaining the problem, was patched through to an Air Force doctor.

He asked how much penicillin she had. She told him. He prescribed two *million* units for one of the patients, and half that for the other. We slept that night on the floor. The old ladies were in our bed.

The next morning, an Air Force amphibian landed near the sawmill, and the two women were flown to the hospital in Anchorage. Just before he closed the door, the airman pulled a large cardboard box from the passenger compartment. "This is for you," he said.

The box contained supplies that Jan had only dreamed of possessing. The Air Force doctor had evidently raided his pharmacy and had prepared a "care" package, containing not only five million units of penicillin and other antibiotics, but scissors, dressings, adhesive tape, sulfa powder, sutures, Novocaine, the list ran on and on.

When the time came in the spring of 1958, to leave for Bristol Bay, the garden was planted and the barge was ready to be planked. We were out of debt, having paid off the SBA loan and Northern Commercial Company. We had a new crop of pullets in the chicken house, the homestead

The chief's wife

had been surveyed and our patent had been issued. Life was sweet.

Jan went to Anchorage while I was in Bristol Bay, and successfully gave birth to our fifth daughter, Jennifer Joyce.

Nakeen was closed in 1958, so I had made other arrangements for my fish. Since I would not be living in a bunkhouse, I had decided to build a semi-permanent tent frame in the setnet village on Naknek Point where we had camped four years earlier. Thus, when I loaded the skiff for my trip

347

downriver, in addition to the tent, I carried tools and the lumber necessary to build a tent frame, chairs and a table, and, of course, an outhouse.

I arrived in Naknek on June 15, and within two days had put up a nicely floored tent frame on the beach at the setnet village just inside the mouth of the Naknek River.

I had barely completed that pleasant chore when Gunnar Bergen and Father Endahl drove up in Gunnar's surplus four-wheel drive truck. As soon as I poured coffee, Gunnar came straight to the point. "Did you know dot Truman is in yail?" he asked in his heavy Norwegian accent.

"No," I said, surprised and faintly apprehensive. Truman Emberg, in my eyes, was a giant. A former trapper and commercial fisherman, almost singlehandedly, he had fashioned the Bristol Bay Fish Producer's Association (BBFPA) two years earlier, had enlisted nearly all the independent fishermen in Dillingham, and had made a good start on enrolling fishermen in the other rivers. Already, he had successfully negotiated two contracts with the industry.

As the director from Lake Iliamna, I had participated in some of those negotiations, and had learned to respect his negotiating skills.

Gunnar quickly explained that Truman had gotten crosswise with the law, and unfortunately, had made some foolish threats to the US marshal. It was universally conceded that Truman was a man of sterling character; therefore, when he said he planned to do something, the US marshal had every reason to regard those threats as promises, and Truman had been arrested and taken to jail in Anchorage.

"Ve t'ink you should take over 'til Truman gets out," Gunnar added.

15

Leaving Kokhanok

Accustomed as I was to Gunnar's bluntness, nevertheless, he had caught me by surprise. I was on unfamiliar ground, and I needed to catch up.

Father Endahl had remained silent, but seeing the uncertainty on my face, he added, "I realize it's an imposition, Denny, but who has taken a more active interest in the fishery? Or is better qualified? And after all, who knows how long Truman will be gone?"

In vain, I mentioned Kallenberg's name, and the names of three of four other people I knew on both rivers who I considered better qualified. I also mentioned problems that might rise because I lived nearly 150 miles upriver. If this dragged on, that would be a serious inconvenience.

It was obvious they had given this matter considerable thought. Patiently, they met each of my objections with counter arguments, and explained why the alternative solutions I suggested were less satisfactory.

We argued much of the afternoon, but in the end they appealed to my sense of duty, and I reluctantly agreed to become the acting manager of the fisherman's co-op, the Bristol Bay Fish Producer's Association.

My temporary appointment was not popular. Fishermen in Dillingham, Truman's home town, were the first to complain. Since there were more resident than nonresident fishermen on the Nushagak river, residents there had enjoyed much better relations with their canneries in recent times than we with ours. They had even avoided the problems we faced in 1954. Therefore, they assumed my appointment was merely another unpleasant manifestation of inter-Bay rivalry.

Nor was I Mr. Brindle's first choice. On hearing of my appointment, he was reported to have said, "Hell, no! I'm not going to deal with that God damned Moore!"

True to his word, he refused to negotiate or even meet with me. That was a major disappointment, because only Mr. Brindle's cannery, Red Salmon, and Alaska Packers cannery in South Naknek, opened their doors that year.

Making the sentiment unanimous, I wasn't happy about my new assignment, either. I only wanted to go fishing. Therefore, I concentrated at first on getting Truman out of jail.

Since I was involved in local politics, and having served for a time as US commissioner for the Iliamna Precinct, I was on a first name basis with the US marshal and the US attorney in Anchorage, and I spoke with both men several times trying to get Truman released.

Although the grand jury subsequently refused to indict him, he had been charged with obstructing justice. Each time I spoke to the US marshal, Fred Williamson, I got the same answer. "My deputy is a nice young man with a family, and we're afraid to turn Truman loose because he won't withdraw his threat against him!"

As the days went by, and it neared the first of July, I knew it was too late to worry about a contract for the current year. Old-timers like Gunnar were nervous about fishing without one, but the traumas of 1954 were safely behind us. Brindle had unilaterally set a price of 83¢ for independent fish and bought all the fish that was offered.

Still, he was adamant in his refusal to negotiate a contract

with me. I wasn't worried, because I still believed that my
role was merely to keep the chair warm until Truman's
problems were resolved. Gradually, however, knowing how
stubborn Truman could be, I began to realize that he would
probably remain in jail for the rest of the season, or at least
until someone blinked. It slowly dawned on me that it was up
to me to lay the groundwork for 1959.

I found that new responsibility almost terrifying. For
one thing, I knew nothing of
labor-management relations,
and lacked serious negotiating
experience. Moreover, I knew
I was dealing from a position
of weakness. Most of my 300
or so members were entirely
reliant on the good will of the
canneries, not only for their
boats and gear, but also, in
too many cases, for their win-

BBFPA members

ter grubstakes. Like Appalachian coal miners, they lived from
year to year on company credit.

Moreover, despite the 1955 FTC order, most of them still
thought they belonged to the ranks of organized labor. That
really didn't matter, because for us, labor's traditional
method of coercion—a strike—would have been as ineffective
as it was illegal. I rarely saw Mr. Brindle smile, but I'll bet a
strike notice from the BBFPA would have had him rolling on
the floor, holding his sides in laughter! Striking a company as
well armored with company boats as Mr. Brindle's, would
have been the wildest of follies. Talk about futility!

I knew intuitively from the beginning that we had to
become more aggressive. If we continued to maintain the
passive posture of a labor union in our dealings with the
industry, we would forever remain in a weak, subsidiary, role.

351

Consequently, I felt it was important, right at the beginning, to give Mr. Brindle cause to regret his decision not to negotiate with the BBFPA, regardless who its agent might be. The key was finding new buyers for our fish.

The canned salmon industry, which Mr. Brindle exemplified, had an almost phobic fear of competition. In a way, that was not surprising. Evolution, after all, is a two-way street. The industry had been so lulled for so long by consistently rich economic returns, insulated by the physical isolation of Bristol Bay, favored by tight political connections, coddled by warm friendships with their federal regulators, and protected in their cozy sweetheart deals with the union, that they had grown fat and careless. They had almost lost the vital ability to compete.

Having fished in Cook Inlet in 1952, I had learned how salmon fisheries were conducted in places where, unlike Bristol Bay, buyers actually bid for fish. Also, because I had worked for him, I knew Henry Emard, owner of the Emard Packing Company in Anchorage.

I flew into Anchorage and met with Mr. Emard, and the manager of a tiny, one horse airline that owned a surplus C-46. Two days later, I returned to the Bay with two contracts. One contained Henry Emard's promise to buy Bristol Bay red salmon from the BBFPA at $1.47 each, F.O.B. Anchorage International Airport. The other was with Martinaire Air Charter Corporation. It was a charter agreement where the carrier agreed to carry salmon from King Salmon airport to Anchorage for $500 per round trip. Given the carrying capacity of a C-46, that worked out to 38¢ per fish.

Brindle was always well informed. I imagine his first intimation that strange things were afoot was when he learned the BBFPA was receiving fish from boats by backing an old dump truck on the beach into the water. Later, he probably learned that the truck, loaded with about 1,500 fish, had been driven out to King Salmon. There it discharged its cargo into 400 pound cardboard flour barrels which were then lifted with a borrowed forklift into the plane's cargo door. The airplane had subsequently taken off in the direction of Anchorage.

I knew we had engaged his attention when we brought a second truckload of fish to the airport several hours later, and Northern Consolidated's station manager apologetically denied us the use of his forklift. I'm sure it was no coincidence that Mr. Brindle was a major stockholder in the National Bank of Alaska, the bank that held Northern Consolidated's paper. But it was only a minor inconvenience; two more planeloads of fish left that day.

In reality, of course, this operation was only a symbolic gesture, hardly worth Brindle's notice, but he went ballistic! One of McKernan's assistants, George Kaydas, later told me that Brindle had exploded into his office, as he put it, "spraying tobacco juice all over the walls," (Brindle was the only millionaire I knew who chewed tobacco and chopped his own firewood) demanding that the airlift be stopped; that somewhere there must be a law against it! Mr. Brindle's remarkably intemperate reaction to our modest project merely confirmed my suspicion about the industry's fear of competition.

From then on, I tried to make sure that the industry always faced competition. Sometimes the competitors were real; sometimes they were only illusory. But they were always there.

Meanwhile, however, much to my surprise and delight, our "fish-lift," as it was called, caught the eye of the media. Reporters and photographers came from Anchorage to cover the story, which even made the wire services. My mother happily sent clippings from the Seattle papers.

With the unexpected publicity, I'm sure additional pressures were brought on Mr. Brindle. While he, undoubtedly, was personally impervious to a bad press, he was no longer a free agent, because of the consolidations that had occurred. His new partners at Castle & Cook, Ltd. for instance, may have been concerned about a possible adverse fallout on other products of theirs. I hoped so. I mentioned Dole pineapple juice and Bumble Bee tuna at every opportunity during the several interviews I gave reporters.

A modern gillnetter
(compare with sailboat at p. 84)

The fishing season was dismally similar to 1955; by the Fourth of July, traditionally the midpoint of the season, the season was almost over. By the seventh of July, we fishermen weren't getting enough fish to eat. We ended the fish-lift because we could no longer fill the plane.

Following the 1955 debacle, the Interior Department had seen to it that the White Act (which I had invoked) was amended by revoking the escapement provisions of the earlier law. This now became the Fish and Wildlife Act of 1956. Thus, when I suggested to McKernan that an early closure might be in order, I had no way of forcing the issue.

However, I believe he gave my views serious consideration, not because of my questionable scientific acumen, but because he knew I was active in state politics, and also because under the Statehood Act, the State of Alaska was slated to take control of its fisheries in 1960. I was sure he didn't want to leave the legacy of a tarnished reputation and a ruined fishery behind when he withdrew in 1959.

The airline manager and I spent the evening of July eighth in Joe Hurd's bar with a dozen BBFPA members, celebrating the successful conclusion of our project. We hadn't flown a lot of fish, but I had scored an important point with Mr. Brindle about competition, and had demonstrated the advantages of competition to my members who had received 17¢ more for their fish through the co-op than Brindle was willing to pay.

The airline people were happy. They hadn't made a lot of money, but they had received a million dollars worth of highly favorable free publicity.

It was very late when I got to bed, and it seemed as if I had barely laid down when I was abruptly wakened by heavy pounding on the tent frame door. Reluctantly, I opened my eyes and yelled, "Wait a minute!" Crawling out of the bunk, I pulled a pair of pants over my long underwear. Then, squinting against the light, I opened the door.

Nakeen (Squaw Creek) dock

I was astonished to see McKernan standing there, sand running out of his shoes. "I hope I didn't wake you, Denny," he said with false sincerity, "but I couldn't wait to give you the good news!"

Straining to make the connection—what the hell was McKernan doing here?—I hesitated, actually wondering for a moment if I was still in bed dreaming this, before I found my manners and invited him in.

He shook his head, and blurted, "I drove the Bureau car to the end of the road and walked the rest of the way," he gestured toward the loose sand in his shoes, "because I knew you'd be as happy as I am." He paused.

"Garrett (John Garrett, then the Bureau of Commercial

355

Fisheries (BCF) Regional Director in Alaska) and I just flew the Kvichak," he said, adding, "in separate planes," to authenticate what was to follow. "And we each got the same count."

After a dramatic pause to let that information seep in, he continued, "We each saw **three million** fish in the clear water in the river below the towers!" McKernan was ecstatic. "You realize what this means, Denny. We have our escapement!"

At that moment I realized how very worried he must have been. I was slightly ashamed. My nagging couldn't have helped. But with a big slug of fish now headed for the spawning grounds, everything was suddenly wonderful. No wonder he was excited! I was excited, too.

It never occurred to me to wonder why the fish were eight days late—something that to my knowledge, had never happened before—or why we hadn't seen the vanguard of this run on our last fishing trip on the river.

Neighboring fishermen, realizing that the BCF boss was standing in front of my tent, gathered around. McKernan launched into a happy impromptu lecture on fish population dynamics, illustrating his talk by drawing figures in the sand with a long stick.

On the strength of those observations, we were given a 36 hour fishing period beginning the following morning. Before leaving, I happened to meet Chuck Meachem, the State area fishery supervisor, on the road, and I shared the good news with him.

When I put my net in the water the next morning, I knew something was wrong. There were no fish. If anything, there were fewer fish than there had been three days earlier. Those fish had to be somewhere. I ran all over the river, and worked like hell for the rest of the period, but I caught only a dozen fish or so. Meachem was waiting for me when I returned to Naknek. He was as excited as McKernan had been two days earlier.

"McKernan's 3,000,000 fish arrived at the towers yesterday," he said. "Guess how many fish there *really* were?"

I shrugged my shoulders.

"*One hundred sixty-five thousand,*" he shouted.

Good Lord! I thought. How could this be? I was sure it wasn't duplicity on his part. The only possible explanation was that McKernan wanted so badly to see fish, he had simply deceived himself into seeing fish that weren't there.

As a courtesy, before telephoning the Governor to ask for an early closure, I poked my head into the FWS office to give them advance warning. The place had a funeral air about it. George Kaydas was in his office.

"Yes," he said quietly, "I think McKernan's going to close the season anyway, but a phone call wouldn't hurt." I placed my call. Two hours later, the closure was announced.

Truman Emberg was released from jail near the end of the season, and returned to Dillingham. I saw him briefly that fall. For reasons I never understood, he was very angry, and responded to my greeting with a curt, "I have nothing to say to you, Moore, now or ever!" That was the last word either of us spoke to the other for nearly 30 years.

At the fall meeting of the BBFPA, the Board of Directors made my appointment as manager permanent. The pay of $100/week was minimal, but it was expected that I would continue my career as a commercial fisherman.

I felt as if I faced an impossible task. Moving fish out of Bristol Bay in war surplus airplanes to make a point in a poor year like 1958 was one thing, but trying to do it as a steady thing would have been folly. What could I do for an encore?

Shortly after I returned to the homestead that fall, while I was cutting firewood one evening, a full blown idea suddenly popped into my head. At first glance, it seemed a nearly flawless solution to our long range problem of serious competition. The root of that idea lay in the recent history of the Bristol Bay salmon fisheries.

Homestead cabin, seen from the rear. (Note the lean–to greenhouse)

After the Japanese Peace Treaty came into effect in 1952, desperate for foreign exchange, the Japanese had begun an intensive high seas salmon gillnet fishery 800 to 1,000 miles west of Bristol Bay.

Beginning in 1953, fish that bore partly healed net marks begun appearing in our fishery. Apart from those scarred salmon, however, there was no hard data concerning the numbers of fish involved in the Japanese fishery. They were fishing mixed Asian and North American stocks, so even their catch statistics, whatever you may think about their reliability, said nothing about the percentages of North American or Asian fish in the catch.

There was another unknown factor. The scarred fish we were catching (in 1957, nearly ten percent of the Bristol Bay catch bore those telltale marks) were the survivors. What about the unknown numbers of fish which might have washed out of the nets dead or escaped only to fall prey, in their weakened condition, to sharks and other predators, or which had simply succumbed to their wounds?

We were sure that high seas fishery was partly, perhaps mainly, responsible for the collapse of the Bristol Bay salmon fishery in the mid-1950s. The International North Pacific Fisheries Commission seemed unable to curb the Japanese appetite for Bristol Bay salmon, or force the Japanese fleets to move further west.

My idea was simple. Perhaps we should emulate other Alaskan businesses. Some were selling timber, others were selling coal, copper ore, and other natural resources to the Japanese. Why not go a step further and sell them the fish we apparently couldn't prevent them from catching?

My board of directors, at first, was uneasy about approaching the Japanese. However, they agreed with my basic idea that it was necessary to maintain pressure on the industry by stimulating competition for Mr. Brindle. Only the Japanese seemed to offer that essential potential.

Consequently, as manager of the BBFPA, I wrote a naive letter to the Consul General of Japan that became public knowledge and was to demonize me in the eyes of the industry for years. In it, I offered to sell raw fish to Japanese processors if they would provide suitable delivery platforms so we could make daily deliveries directly from our boats to them, *and if they would shift their high seas gillnet fishery ten degrees west (from 175°W to 175°E)*. They ignored the condition, of course, but responded enthusiastically to the first part of my proposal.

While that revolutionary idea percolated, I turned my attention to matters of more immediate concern. I had been active on the periphery of Republican politics for several years prior to my running as a candidate for the Territorial legislature in 1957. Kokhanok Precinct was the only precinct in Alaska that had consistently voted 100% Republican. Of course, our 18 votes scarcely tipped the scales, but it was the idea that counted.

District apportionment came with statehood, so I had decided to file as a candidate for the Bristol Bay seat in the House of Representatives in the special primary election that was held August 26, 1958. I won the primary handily, since I was the only candidate on either ticket. In my innocence, I thought it looked like a done deal in November.

Suddenly, however, I had two opponents. Jay Hammond of Naknek and Walter Noden of Dillingham each filed a petition as an Independent candidate. Ironically, it probably didn't matter that my fishing payday had been so poor that I couldn't afford to campaign. Both Walter and Jay had ties into the extended Eskimo family system that I lacked.

Walter's link was by blood, Jay's by marriage. I don't think Walter was a serious candidate. His candidacy merely reflected the Dillingham animosity my appointment as manager of the BBFPA had generated. I doubt whether he especially wanted to win; he just didn't want me to.

Jay, to my surprise, was a serious candidate. He had left the Fish and Wildlife Service, and had become a bush pilot and a registered guide. Although he and his family lived in Naknek, his wife, Bella, came from an old Dillingham family.

He told me later that his original motive for filing, like Walter's, had been pure patriotism. He saw it his civic duty to keep me out of public life. However, as the campaign unfolded, a lust for political office had gradually taken hold, and he had become a very aggressive campaigner.

He came to Kakhonak seeking votes. I'm afraid I was too complacent. I remembered the babies Jan had delivered, the old ladies she had treated, and the wounds she had sutured. I also remembered the struggles with the canneries in Bristol Bay, the schoolhouse we had built, and the Social Security forms I had filled out. But while I was looking back over my shoulder, my opponent was looking ahead. I had forgotten something that Jay knew intuitively. Gratitude always runs a poor second to future expectations.

When the votes in the Kokhanok Precinct were counted, I had six votes, Noden had four and Hammond had twelve. I was crushed literally and figuratively. The proportions, by the way, mirrored the final result. Noden received roughly twice the number of ballots cast for me, and Hammond received more than the two of us combined. But it was weeks before I knew definitely that I had lost the election.

Although I had anticipated what the letter would say, when I read it and knew that all hope was gone, I can't describe the wave of bitterness, disappointment, and depression that washed over me. Almost in tears, I walked across the portage with that letter burning my hand, and hiked up the road to Beaver Lake.

I sat on a snow-covered rock, staring at the ice for a long, long time. I searched for an explanation, and ultimately for a modicum of comfort. I read the letter a dozen times. Finally, I crumpled it into a tiny ball, and threw it away.

I promised myself that I was finished with elective politics. Ole Wassenkari had once remarked that I had a wonderful knack for making enemies. Obviously, he was right. It was foolish to waste my time and money seeking political office. Second, I was finally forced to realize that my grandiose plans for a hunting and fishing lodge had come to nothing. It was now time to think seriously about our future.

We had discussed the need to get the older children into a more urban setting. Knowing how to skin porcupines was a skill of doubtful advantage in the middle of the 20th century. The skills my girls really needed involved learning to socialize with other children, and in the not too distant future, learning about boys. But our planning had not gone beyond boarding the children with relatives living Outside.

There was now the more immediate problem caused by my sudden career change. Managing the day-to-day affairs of the BBFPA from a distance of 150 miles was wildly impractical. Also, even though elective office was now out of the question, I knew myself well enough to realize that I could not remain aloof from the opportunity to help shape Alaska's future resource management policies. Suddenly, the election results threw all these factors into sharp relief.

It was time to leave Kokhanok Bay. The winter passed quickly. Poor Jan had an increasingly tough time of it. Lynnie and Trina were in the second and fifth grades of their respective correspondence courses, and much of Jan's time was taken up helping them. Debby was five, and was taking the kindergarten course. Lizzy was a Terrible Two, and we had a brand new baby daughter.

Debby was precocious. Once, when she was asked to preform some minor chore—it may have been carrying in the evening stovewood—she solemnly looked up, her sparkling blue eyes serious for once.

Debby, the heavy-duty kid

"What do you think I am? Heavy duty?" she asked.

Another time, I returned from a trip to Anchorage with numerous packages, including a rare treat—a fresh leg of lamb—Debby insisted it was a ". . .leg of lamb moosemeat."

Almost as soon as I returned to the homestead after the fishing season, I had written letters to the heads of other Alaskan fishing unions and cooperatives, urging the need to organize a political action committee; a state-wide federation of fishermen and allied worker's organizations, to make sure that our views were known when the new state legislature began writing the appropriate resource legislation.

In common with thousands of other Alaskans, I was fed up with absentee fishery management, particularly as it was practiced by the federal government, because it was wrecking our fisheries. There was no accountability in the system; it was laden with favoritism, political cronies, and even on occasion, overt corruption.

I stressed that this would be a rare, perhaps unique,

opportunity to write on a clean slate; to devise a system for resource management that would be reasonably resistent to political pressure while remaining highly accessible to constituent recommendations and suggestions.

My letters were quickly answered. As I had hoped, my vision was shared by other industry leaders. We met in Anchorage in early December. Five of us, representing about half the licensed fishermen in Alaska, sat on beer cases in the basement of the old Montana Club and put together a strictly homegrown political action committee.

We decided to incorporate, and styled the committee the *Alaska Fishing Industry, Inc.* The group endorsed the fishermen's newsletter I was then cranking out at home on a mimeograph machine. I was elected Secretary–Treasurer, and at my urging, was appointed chief lobbyist, and instructed to promote our legislative agenda.

I knew, as every propagandist since Gutenberg has known, that the mere *appearance* of a neatly printed page (utterly without reference to its content), inevitably conveys a subliminal message of authenticity and authority. For that reason, I was very dissatisfied with our newsletter. I felt that to the average reader, it would look frivolous because of its amateurish appearance. Mimeographed materials, no matter how you dress them up, always seem to look like an announcement from the Ladies Missionary Society.

Months later, on my way to the legislature in Juneau, I detoured to Seattle. I wanted to spend time with mother, and call on a printing equipment dealer. Tentatively, I purchased a long list of printing equipment, including an antique drum cylinder press, several tons of newsprint and a shirt full of type. The dealer deemed that a basic outfit which would get us started in the newspaper business at a minimum price.

Don McKernan, by then director of the Interior Department's Bureau of Commercial Fisheries, was threatening a

total Bristol Bay closure in 1959 in response to the unrelenting pressures generated by the Japanese high seas gillnet
fishery. Such a closure would have been an economic
catastrophe for local residents.

I also visited several industry leaders in Seattle to lay the
groundwork for the upcoming 1959 negotiations, and gauge
the seriousness of the threat McKernan was making. I
reasoned that industry folks would know whether McKernan
was bluffing. Two days after my first contact with the industry
people, the phone in my mother's house began ringing. The
topic of conversation was the letter I had written earlier to
the Japanese Consul General.

The first was from Mr. Brindle. He came right to the point.
"What the hell is this I hear that you want to sell fish to the
Japs?" he demanded.

When I explained that as manager of the BBFPA I had a
duty to my employers to find markets for their fish and since
he had no interest in entering into a contract with us. . . he
cut me off.

"Listen, Moore. I fought those bastards on Adak, and I
sure as hell don't want to do business with them now."

Brindle was apparently unaware of my war record. I
couldn't resist telling him, "Well, Mr. Brindle, I picked up
two Purple Hearts from Iwo Jima, if you want to talk about
the war, but I'm in the business of selling fish. . ."

Again he cut me off, "You lay off those Japs, Moore. We
can take care of your fish." With that, he hung up.

Next, I received a phone call from Senator Bartlett, who
urged me to withdraw my offer. He brushed aside the point
that my offer had been conditioned on their willingness to
move their high seas salmon gillnet fleets ten degrees west
from their present position. "They'll never do that," he said.

The next day, Governor Egan called, also urging me to
withdraw my offer. I told him the same thing I had said to

Senator Bartlett. Unlike Senator Bartlett, he seemed more concerned about the precedent-setting aspect of my proposal than with the specifics of my letter. He was afraid fishermen in other districts might use Japanese buyers as leverage in their negotiations with domestic processors. In this, he was prescient; two years later, the fishermen in Prince William Sound did exactly that.

Nothing of direct consequence came of my quixotic letter to the Japanese, but wisps of that proposal colored nearly all my future relations with the industry. More immediately, however, I had serious political axes to grind.

When I arrived in Juneau, I discovered that although Bella had remained in Naknek because their children were in school, Jay had rented an apartment. Jay invited me to share it, and I was glad to move in for the company and to save some money. If he remembered the circumstances of our first meeting in 1952, he never mentioned it.

Although Jay had run as an Independent, it would have been foolish for him to remain uncommitted because Independents usually wind up on housekeeping committees.

We agreed about the desirability of his joining one of the caucuses. The question was, which? Of the 60 member Alaska legislature (20 senators and 40 house members) 54 members in that first legislature were Democrats, four were Republicans, and two (including Jay) were Independents.

As far as I knew, Jay had no strong ideological leanings. If he had decided to become a Democrat, he might have been just another pretty face in the crowd. As a Republican, however, he would have his pick of committee assignments. That was the basis of my argument, and while I may be wrong, I think that's why he became a Republican.

Jay was a delightful roommate. He was smart, and possessed an enviable sense of humor. The first State legislature was full of amateur politicians, unschooled in the art of compromise. Many times, I saw him rise to break an impasse or to soothe ruffled egos by reading a hastily drafted limerick satirizing the debated point, or bit of clever doggerel immortalizing it.

He was a natural master of the political arts, and quickly gained the respect of his fellows on both sides of the aisle. There is no doubt in my mind today whether the best man won. He served Alaska well, and I'm proud of my (accidental) role in making it happen.

Like myself, he was an ex-Marine. His service was far more glamorous than mine. He flew fighter planes in the South Pacific during the war, and was a captain when he was discharged from the Marine Corps.

I, on the other hand, was promoted to PFC after I had been in the service for a year and a half, during which time I was in two engagements, had received two Purple Hearts, and had spent six months in Naval hospitals. My second chevron was awarded three days before my medical survey. The second stripe was so grudgingly given that my discharge specifies my rank as a **"Corpoal"**.

Understandably, the first session of the legislature ran well into the spring, but I left Juneau soon after the bill that created the Alaska Department of Fish and Game was passed.

I returned to Kokhanok for a few weeks, then was on the move again, while Jan began making preparations for our departure. This time, I was involved in spring negotiations in Naknek with the industry. There, I stayed, as usual, with Gordon and Anisha McCormick.

I had met Gordon casually some years before. In 1955, Gordon, Anisha, and their oldest son, Jay, had flown to Kokhanok to spend a few days with us. That trip coincided with the awful Simeon Wassillie tragedy. Gordon gave me badly needed emotional support.

I'm one of those unfortunate people who do not easily

form lasting friendships, so it is significant that Gordon subsequently became one of the very few close friends I've had. God knows we didn't always agree. Although we were both Republicans, I was quite liberal, even then, in my social philosophy, while Gordon was intensely conservative. He lived in a rural community heavily populated by Democrats. He was a construction worker living in an isolated fishing community.

Gordon is smart, logical, and tough. In this respect we complemented one another. It was due largely to his encouragement and support that I was able to carry off the unusual and somewhat novel bargaining strategies I employed during those early years. For instance, when we were delivering fish to the airplane in 1958, the truck we used was a war surplus dump truck that Gordon owned and drove.

He kept his eyes open, and knew what was going on. When he learned of our plans to relocate, Gordon mentioned that the owner of a local bar had died intestate and without heirs. The building (but not the business) was for sale.

The property consisted only of a building containing one large bar room and a semi-finished loft. It was not known then where the title to the land resided; but it was generally believed that it belonged to the Russian Orthodox Church of North America. I submitted a bid of $2,500 for the building, which was accepted.

Meanwhile, Gene Pope, his wife, uncle, and by that time, several children, had settled at a place now called the Pope–Vanoy Landing on Copper River. Shortly before we left, he came to make an offer for our tractor and sawmill. "I can give you $4,000 cash for the whole works," he said. There was no haggling or argument.

Suddenly, I had the means to solve my newsletter dilemma. I would start a fisherman's newspaper. Resident fishermen throughout Alaska were facing serious challenges, and needed an authoritative voice. I sent a wire to Seattle confirming my purchase of the printing equipment.

Scarcely two weeks later, in June, 1959, after cramming everything we thought we might need in our new home in the big skiff and the old fish boat, we left Kokhanok Bay forever. I never looked back.

Jan, the children, and I rode in the skiff. We towed the old fish boat. We reached the Kvichak River shortly after noon, and camped for a few hours below Kaskanak Flats. We arrived at Naknek at five the next morning. After anchoring our little flotilla, the children and I walked up into the village so they could see what their new home looked like.

The first building we came to was Joe Hurd's Fishermen's Bar. A neon beer sign flickered in the window. Debby looked at it thoughtfully for a moment and said, "Somebody left their light plant on."

Farewell to Kokhanok. The road across the portage.
The nearest building on right is the garage; left, is the
Chicken coop. Bunkhouse and cabin barely visible in rear.

(Compare with photo on page 174)

16

Long John's Epitaph

*T*hroughout our married life, I think Jan must have been continually shocked by the conditions I imposed on her. I have no idea what she may have thought when we unlocked the door of the Anchor Inn, and she saw her new home for the first time.

In most respects, it looked exactly like what it was; a single room made into a rural bar. No frills. The room was dominated by a homemade bar that walled off the back third of the room. Behind it was a back bar. In front of it, several stools and some home-made booths cluttered the floor.

The thing that set it apart from all others, if you overlooked the photographic debris on the bar—crumpled film wrappers and burned out flashbulbs—was the large dried bloodstain in the middle of the floor.

The former owner, Henry Miller (no relation to the famous novelist), had died with his boots on. He had been shot twice. Some said Billy Nekeferoff had been trying to rob Henry—if you had known Henry, you'd have known what a joke that was—while others thought Billy had been upset about something. I'm more inclined to believe the latter; Billy was notorious for his tender sensibilities.

That explained, of course, why Billy had pulled the trigger twice. The first shot was simply the reflexive result of Billy's pique. He had fired the second

369

bullet into Henry's body, according to his trial testimony, for humanitarian reasons; simply to put poor Henry out of his misery. After I got to know Billy, I realized that he wasn't entirely sane, so I'd guess he was probably telling the truth.

Jan and I scrubbed the stain with bleach and covered it with a throw rug. Eventually, after I discovered my energetic and enterprising nine-year-old, Lynnie, lifting the rug to show the neighborhood kids for a fee what remained of poor Mr. Miller, I even sanded the floor.

Naknek reminded me of Clarks Point in many ways, because many of its inhabitants were similar to people we had known on the Nushagak. But the town itself was quite different. For one thing, it was a very sophisticated community considering that its population was only about three times greater than Clarks'. It had a four-teacher school, a hotel, an ice cream parlor, two churches, and until the demise of the Anchor Inn's former owner, *five* bars. It had a taxi business, a private public utility (of a sorts), a big company store, and a road that went somewhere.

I was very busy that summer. I divided the bar into three rooms; a combined living room/kitchen, a bedroom, and an office. The kids slept upstairs in the loft.

In several important ways, our standard of living hadn't improved at all. True, we used diesel oil as fuel, which saved countless hours of rustling and splitting wood, but municipal sanitation was based on old-fashioned outhouses. Since our drinking water came from a shallow well in the cellar, we concluded that our water was badly contaminated, and Jan faithfully boiled every drop that passed our lips.

Ike Jensen, the local cab driver, provided municipal power. His electrical generating equipment was an ancient 25-Kw, four-cylinder, Superior diesel/electric set fitted with a 110 volt, single phase generator. His distribution system was equally quaint.

He had acquired at least two hundred old sailboat masts from the Red Salmon cannery. Using them as poles, he had strung wires all over the village. It was said that consumers at the end of this Christmas tree-like distribution system had to strike a match to see if the light was on.

There were no meters. We paid Ike a flat $25 a month for enough power to provide lights and drive the washing machine and small appliances. We had been at least as well off at Kokhanok with our 12 volt windcharger for lights and the big light plant for use on wash days.

Unfortunately, some things are actually worse than they seem. Ike's electric generation equipment was like that. For months, his tired old diesel had limped along on three cylinders. To compensate for the loss of power, Ike had cranked the engine's throttle wide open. Considering the anemic character of the engine's output, few of his customers, certainly not me, thought it necessary to install fuse boxes.

However, one notable evening at supper time, when folks were listening to the evening news, or as in the case of the George Tibbets family, to a symphony on their new hi-fi system, the fourth cylinder abruptly cut in.

I have no idea what the voltage surge was that fried our radio and blew out the lights, cooked George Tibbets' hi-fi system, and affected everyone, but it was obviously substantial. It's a wonder it didn't set the village on fire. Ike was very embarrassed.

Meanwhile, much to my surprise, Mr. Brindle proved agreeable to early negotiations which were speedily concluded. Soon after, an intense, prematurely bald young man named Karl Sjoblom, came to see me. He was the owner of a Puget Sound salmon canning company, American Packing Corporation. He said he had heard about the letter I had written to the Japanese the previous fall, and he wanted to explore the possibility of building a new cannery in Naknek to utilize salmon caught by independent fishermen.

To get his feet wet in Bristol Bay, he had chartered a floating cannery, a war surplus LST named the *Kayak*, which was to arrive in Naknek shortly before the season opened.

I was secretly elated that at last, the potential for a truly competitive market for our fish seemed to be developing, but I was somewhat wary. I explained to Mr. Sjoblom that a contract with the co-op didn't guarantee fish or fishermen; it merely established the ground rules such as price, limits, and so forth, under which members would contract individually to deliver their fish.

However, I also explained that there was nothing to prevent him from offering *more* money than the contract stipulated. Sweetening the kitty was a sure way of attracting fishermen.

The contract price I had negotiated with Brindle was the same as the 1958 price, 83¢. Sjoblom quickly signed a contract, and promptly raised the ante to $1.00.

The *Kayak*, skippered by a tall, slender man named Jack Most, arrived on schedule. I fished for American Pack that year, but there wasn't much fishing to do. The Fish and Wildlife Service (now the Bureau of Commercial Fisheries) was playing it very safe. Alaska now had two senators and a congressman. Also, since this was the last year of federal management, there would be no future opportunity to rectify management errors or mistakes.

Although the initial purpose for which the *Alaska Fishing Industry, Inc.* was created—helping the first State legislature mold the Alaska Department of Fish and Game—had been accomplished, the other directors and I believed it was important to continue developing a legislative agenda.

We had learned during the hotly contested fight in the first session over H.B. 113, the Organic Act that organized the executive branch of the new state government, that the purity of our motives counted for very little. We quickly realized that our influence with the legislature was directly proportional to the perceived influence we had with the voters in the fishing districts of the new state.

Our printing machinery arrived on the summer ship. I had nearly completed the new print shop in our front yard, when suddenly, Hermy Herrmann's truck and small crane were on the street outside the Anchor Inn. The truck carried a huge crate containing the three-ton press, three smaller crates containing a folder, a stereotyper, and a 14-inch C&P platen press. In addition, there were several smaller boxes containing a printer's stone, a "brayer" to hand ink the galleys, several California cases, numerous fonts of movable type, composing sticks, galley trays, a planer, mallet, chases, quoins, press rollers, lead, five gallons of ink, and a grossly excessive quantity of cut newsprint.

I had known the press was coming, of course. I even had a vague idea how big it would be, but I was astounded and dismayed when I saw that huge chunk of complicated cast-iron machinery on Hermy's truck. *What have I done now?*

I had left part of the roof and one wall of the shop open, so it was convenient for Hermy to maneuver his crane, landing the press exactly where I wanted it.

I quickly learned that setting up a newspaper involved much more than the ego-stroking indulged by many editorial writers. No one in Naknek (including me) had ever *seen* a printing press before, let alone operate one. This one, an antique Babcock drum cylinder, had an interesting history. It was first erected in Puyallup, Washington, in about 1895. (I later saw one like it in the Smithsonian, and another in the Mystic Seaport Museum in Connecticut.)

I used to reflect on the headlines it must have printed over the years: "Battleship Maine Sunk in Havana Harbor,"

"Wright Brothers Fly," "Henry Ford Invents Automobile," "Marconi's Transatlantic Wireless Successful."

This type of flatbed press was sometimes called a "camel" because of its humped profile. The machine was about five feet wide by eight feet long, and stood about five feet high. The feed board on top of the machine was a conspicuous feature. It was a large, heavily varnished board tilted slightly down and forward, above and behind the top of the drum. This is where the operator fed the sheets of cut newsprint into the press.

After we learned how to run the press, we had to teach ourselves to set type, using a printer's "stick" and a California case. Hand-setting type is slow, tedious, exacting work.

One of the salesmen in Seattle had given me his apprentice's manual. That and Gordon McCormick's extensive mechanical savvy, a world of patience, and considerable trial and error, enabled us to produce the first issue of *The Alaska Fisherman* on August 5, 1959. True, it was only a single sheet, with widely spaced lines, but it was a *printed* sheet!

Mechanical printing is a mirror image process. Although type is set the way it reads, the letters are placed in the stick right to left and backwards, so the tops of the letters face toward you. I found, as most compositors do, that it's surprisingly easy to read type upside down and backwards.

It took two weeks, at first, to set the type for a single page. But with practice, I got that down to a week, then to about three days per page. Since *The Alaskan Fisherman* was a monthly newspaper, I spent a lot of time standing in front of the type cabinet.

However, I soon discovered other ways of filling that white space. Advertising agencies and public relations firms quickly found out about the embryonic *Alaska Fisherman.* We received many press releases, papier-mâché "mats," and even occasional engravings.

Bristol Bay Run Good; Other Areas Slow

The Alaska Fisherman

Vol. No. 11   Number 1   Published By The ALASKA FISHING INDUSTRY, INC.   August 5, 1959

..IE BIG GET BIGGER -

FOR SEVERAL WEEKS - since last winter , in fact, rumors have been rampant through the Industry that Alaska Packers were negotiating to buy indeed - did buy G. P. Halferty.

This, following hard on the heels of the formation of Columbia Ward last winter, has set off a wave of speculation about additional mergers in the future.

Most of the talk appears to center upon a possible New England - Pacific American marriage.

While such moves may result in increased efficiency and greater economies Alaskan fishermen cannot help but view such mergers with considerable misgivings, because in most areas they tend to reduce the number of competitive outlets available to the fisermen; and in some cases, remove all competition.

This is a problem which the next State legislature may want to study.

YOUR   MESSAGE

IN THIS SPACE

$3.00 PER ISSUE

AN OPEN LETTER

THIS is your paper; and whether it becomes a good paper - or a bad one will, to a very large extent depend on your interest and support. News items - a new boat or baby (with good sharp photographs) or, just drop us a line. Our address:

THE ALASKA FISHERMAN
NAKNEK, ALASKA

12.3 MILLION REDS IN

Bristol Bay - F.W.S Puzzled

Fishermen Are Delighted

ON THE BASIS OF EARLY REPORTS, THE BAY MAY PROVE STRONGER THAN ANY OTHER ALASKAN FISHERY AREA DESPITE EARLY PREDICTIONS.

One fact that was demonstrated again this year is this: the science of predicting is not very accurate. But still another lesson was pointed out: even a very poor year can be rewarding when the effort is held to a reasonable level.

The Nushagak system was outstanding and except for the loss of 25 per cent of the season because of a price dispute, 1959 would have been topped only by 1948. Even so, the boat average was well over 6,000 and the catch and escapement was 4,500,000.

Egegik and Naknek were not far behind. Catches in Egegik averaged nearly 10,000 reds, was the best run in ten years.

The Naknek River supported the entire Naknek - Kvichak fishery with a sustained run unparalleled in modern times. The boat catches ranged upward to more than 20,000. On the other hand, the Ugashik system, officially predicted good, proved very disappointing. The Kvichak washed out entirely.

But even with these flat spots, the pack was about on a par with 1958, while the escapements soared above '58 level.

Other than Bristol Bay, early reports have been discouraging with first pinks off over 60 per cent.

EDITORIAL----

LET'S FACE IT: A treaty is about to expire.

In 1953, a ten year contract between the United States, Canada and Japan was drawn as a part of the general Peace Treaty between those nations, in an attempt to regulate and control a pelagic fishery which even then cast a threatening shadow across the future of Alaska's salmon fishery.

Despite the enormous success the Japanese have had in developing this fishery, they complain bitterly about what they call 'the treaty which was signed with a gun in our back' and openly look toward Bristol Bay and other districts with covetous eyes, and talk of sharing our fish - IN OUR OWN WATERS!

The only reason they are not now in these waters is because of this - the treaty soon to expire.

Somebody pushed the panic button last winter. Somebody designed a program of embargo, boycott, and sanction to compel an almost total abstention of this fishery - in 1959. But the stakes in 1959 were not very high.

Alaskan fishermen should now ask the architects of this policy whether it will be equally effective in 1960? or '61? or '62?, - when the stakes will be far greater? And, even more important is this question: Is this program likely to create the necessary climate of mutual respect so vital to the successful voluntary give and take of negotiations between equals?

In other words, where do we go from here?

A. F. I. PRESS ARRIVES

Tackles sagged and lines creaked as the huge crate containing our three ton press swung ponderously up out of the Coastal Rambler's number three hatch and down into the waiting lighter Fajer to be brought ashore to its permanent home in Naknek.

Since then, we have been pretty busy, just putting up an all-weather and heated building, hand-set the type, and figure out how the press operates.

Meanwhile, we would like to ask our members and friends to overlook the missing June and July issues.

Bristol Bay Prices
Set New Highs

Besides the surprisingly good run, Bay fishermen enjoyed very substantial price increases over last year. This was generally contrary to the state - wide trend as the Industry successfully held to 1958 prices in most areas.

Despite the A. F. U.'s acceptance of the '58 prices - which historically sets the pattern - the B. B. F. P. A. found an independent processor who's offer of $1 which was a 15 cent increase stirred up a scramble for independent fish.

American Pack
Building New
Plant at Naknek

Karl V. Sjoblom, owner and manager of American Pack, announced last week that his company will enter the Bay picture next year with a shore cannery. When asked about his plans, Mr. Sjoblom said, "It's just plain good business for us as well as the fishermen for us to concentrate on local independents and their fish".

American Pack has a modern and highly efficient plant in Anacortes, Wn. which does a good share of the Puget Sound custom canning.

Replica of the first issue of The Alaska Fisherman.
—Courtesy of the Alaska State Library

I was especially grateful for the engravings because they filled that yawning white space without any additional effort on my part, saving me hours of labor. There was no money involved, of course, but who cared? The only problem with the engravings was that there weren't enough of them.

The papier-mâche mats had the potential to fill that same white space as the engravings, since they were three-dimensional molded impressions of steel engravings, but I couldn't figure out how to convert them into lead "slugs."

Our Seattle suppliers had furnished us with the proper equipment; but unfortunately, my 15-minute apprenticeship in Seattle had not covered stereotyping. I spent hours fooling with those mats, and wrote dozens of letters to my mentors in Seattle, and received a lot of advice, but without result.

Months later, when I was in Kodiak for a fisheries meeting, I paid a courtesy call on the publisher of the *Kodiak Mirror,* a local newspaper that used machinery similar to mine. While the publisher and I stood chatting in his print shop, I noticed his printer working on a papier-mâche mat. He was gluing small bits of sticky felt to the relieved parts of the mat, then, just before he inserted the mat into the hell box, he fastened an apron made of several layers of masking tape to the bottom of the mat, and after it was in place, he secured it with masking tape inside the box. I had just witnessed, for the first time, someone "packing and tailing" a mat.

That incident taught me something immensely important about communication. With the best intentions in the world, the printing people in Seattle and I had thought we were exchanging useful information, but in fact, since we were each proceeding from a different set of assumptions, our efforts to communicate had failed.

They had assumed I knew the basic stuff like packing and tailing mats. I had assumed they realized how ill-informed and unprepared I was. We were both wrong.

I often think about that incident. When I enter into a complicated discussion, especially of a technical nature, I sometimes begin the conversation by relating that little story. Watch out for those assumptions!

Another incident in the shop reinforced my skepticism about assumptions. Since the only electricity then available was the (approximately) 110 volt AC current from Ike's miserable little diesel/electric set, and since the motor that came with the press required 220 volts and was rated at five hp—a hopeless mismatch—we were obliged to drive the press with the same Briggs and Stratton air-cooled gas engine I had used on the homestead to drive the electric generator. There, however, the engine was operated in the open air.

Here, the engine was run inside a building as tightly sealed against fresh air as I could make it. Right away, we were in trouble. Everyone knows that you must never, **never** run an internal combustion engine inside a closed building. People get killed that way. We almost were. The engine was mounted on the floor next to the drive pulley on the press, which placed it awkwardly and inconveniently in the middle of the room. I attempted to vent the exhaust gases by feeding them into a 12 foot length of two inch galvanized pipe that extended outside through a notch cut in the door.

We continued to drive the press during the fall months with that makeshift arrangement, and had even begun to feel reasonably comfortable with it; as comfortable as possible, that is, considering that the roaring staccato bark of an air-cooled gas engine, over the rumbling, clanking, squeaking, noise of the press, was mind-deadening.

Jan and I were printing the second side of the newspaper late on a very cold night. She was standing on the step feeding the press, when she began complaining of a headache. Almost at the same moment, I smelled exhaust fumes.

I immediately shut down the engine, and, taking a long

screwdriver, slipped outside to see if some mysterious enemy had blocked the exhaust pipe.

It was blocked, but not by the hand of man. I hadn't realized how much water vapor gasoline engines emit in their exhaust fumes. The pipe was plugged with ice. You'd think after my experience with the kitchen still at Kokhanok Bay that I would have been alert to condensation problems. But as usual, I had to learn the hard way. After that experience, when we were running the press, I routinely checked the exhaust pipe for ice every hour or so.

Those night printing runs sometimes went on until two or three in the morning. In the early years, the press runs were small—300 or 400 copies. Since the press ran at about five revolutions per minute, in theory it shouldn't have taken more than an hour and a half to do the job. But, as every printer's devil knows, apart from the ever-present problem of static electricity, there were a myriad of problems created by the very complexity of the printing operation. If the ink was especially sticky, for example, it was always possible that as the bed ran under the ink rollers, a piece of loose type might be plucked out of the chase. The errant type would then rest on top of the other type, and would appear on the printed page as a rectangular blob. Unfortunately, you might not discover it until any number of sheets had been printed.

When the weather was cold and the air was especially dry, printing a single side could take all night. The reason was static electricity. I can't explain the physical laws involved, but I know that one sheet of newsprint sliding over another in dry air generates a hell of a lot of static electricity.

The moving parts in the press also seemed to generate electricity. Often, after they were printed, sheets of paper would cling to the drum, or they might cling together, causing the operator to miss the opened grippers, and we would print the packing on the drum instead.

We tried everything, including grounding the press by connecting it to a copper grounding rod driven deep into the ground under the press. We hung Christmas tree tinsel from the lower frame to the floor, and I kept a teakettle of water boiling on the Coleman stove under the press.

The folder presented the most serious static problems. We learned, eventually, to overprint the first run of four pages by 200 copies or more. On a bad static night, when we were printing the second side of the paper, the folding machine would eat that many sheets of paper.

That machine was driven by a linked chain that ran over a huge sprocket fastened to the press' drum. When the folder was attached, as it always was when we were printing the second side of the sheets, as the drum turned, so did the folder. There was no forgiveness in its drive system.

In a Rube Goldberg sort of way, the folder was a marvel of mechanical ingenuity. It was capable of converting a flat single sheet of paper into a neatly folded eight-page tabloid size newspaper. Narrow cloth tapes, about four inches apart, carried the sheets of newsprint through the machine. Those tapes ran over wooden spools that looked exactly like old-fashioned thread spools. The machine carried a name plate, the *Omaha Folding Machine Co.*, but no date of manufacture or serial number.

If the least little thing went wrong; if, for instance, instead of moving squarely into the maw of the machine, one of the sheets was slightly askew, it would jam, and silently block the sheets coming inexorably behind it. If I was working at the front of the press, adding more ink, say, and was away for five minutes, we could have a pileup of 25 or 30 useless crumpled papers.

That was on a good night. On a bad static electricity night, the papers would cling to the drum or the frame of the folder. They would stick to the folding knives, or refuse to be expelled from the machine. On a night like that, I was kept busy stopping and starting the press, and maintaining a constant watch over the papers as they filed through the machines.

Hermy delivering the Linotype.

Later, I solved my typesetting problems by investing in a re-built model 5 Linotype that had a four-digit serial number, and was built around 1910. Of course, that was after the Rural Electrification Administration (REA) had replaced Ike Jensen's home-made public utility by bringing 220 volts of reliable electricity to Naknek.

If the mind of man is capable of devising a more complicated piece of machinery than a Linotype, I can't imagine what it would be. Yet for all its quaint cast-iron parts and noisy, erratic movements, it performed almost flawlessly after we figured out how it worked.

Hermy delivered it as he had delivered the press. It filled a wooden crate roughly the size and shape of a small telephone booth. We removed the crate and the restraining packing that protected its fragile parts during shipment. Then he lifted it from the truck and placed it on the floor of the shop. Gordon and I began rolling it over by hand, watching the complicated interrelated movements of the various levers, arms, elevators, and so forth.

In theory, the Linotype utilized was a relatively simple concept, in which gravity played a major part. The operator faced a keyboard much like that of a typewriter. When a key was pressed, a tiny bar opened the gate to the appropriate slot in the matrix magazine and released a brass matrix bearing that key's imprint on its inside edge. Those matrices, and space bars as appropriate, were assembled, to form a line of type of a predetermined length. When the line was full, with the left hand, the operator pressed a handle.

A number of things then happened in quick sequence. When things worked right, a brand new, shiny slug or line of type was deposited neatly in the tray under the operator's left hand. When things went wrong, the operator often received another squirt of molten lead on the left hand.

Primitive though it was, that ancient Linotype was an enormous leap forward. It had taken all my time and physical resources to publish *The Alaska Fisherman* while we were hand setting the paper, but after I learned how to operate the Linotype, we decided to begin publishing a regular weekly newspaper. We continued to publish the *Fisherman*, but it was quickly overshadowed by the *Bristol Bay Digest.*

Naturally, with a weekly publication, we had to follow a much tighter schedule, since, except for our community correspondents and frequent help from Gordon and Anisha when we were running the press, Jan and I were the publishers, editors, advertising sales staff, compositors, typesetters, printers, circulation managers, and mailroom staff.

Our schedule required that the paper be delivered to the post office no later than eight o'clock each Thursday morning. We spent Wednesday nights and early Thursday mornings printing, wrapping, and addressing newspapers.

The *Digest* was successful almost from the beginning. Jan traveled to Bethel and Dillingham, arranging with local traders to sell the paper. However, more importantly, Jan sent copies of the paper to her relatives in the "Lower 48."

One was an aunt in Southern California who sent a copy

to a popular radio personality, Pat Buttram, who often read a country newspaper over the air to his national audience. He read ours, and we received a number of subscriptions from nearly every state in the Union. That, and a reprint in *Reader's Digest,* may have been responsible for the recognition we received by *The Publishers' Auxiliary* which named us Editors of the Week (July 14, 1962).

Meanwhile, I slowly established a network of community correspondents. My correspondents were a varied lot. Some, like a lady who submitted material from Togiak, an Eskimo village 75 miles west of Dillingham, reported on village rules (all dogs must be chained up) and occasionally submitted an Yupik fable as news. One I remember especially well, because it was reprinted, involved a dialogue between village children and a flock of passing ducks.

Others, like my big city correspondent from Dillingham, concentrated on the social scene. One of her contributions, describing the wedding of the year, got me into serious hot water with a prominent local family.

Her material had not arrived until Wednesday morning. I had known it was coming, and I had saved space for it on the front page. It was an important story. I opened her letter and sat at the Linotype where I began setting page after page of her handwritten material. She went into elaborate detail about the bride's gown, and the dresses worn by the bride's maids. She cataloged in exquisite detail the many wonderful gifts the blessed couple had received. She carefully listed the guests, and even provided a summary of the wedding sermon. There was only one thing she missed, and lousy editor that I was, I failed to see it until it was called to my attention by irate folks in Dillingham.

Nowhere in the article did she mention the groom's name.

Naknek had an official population, according to the 1960 census, of 271. You wouldn't think such a small population

State Historical Museum
Juneau, Alaska

Bristol Bay Digest

| Volumne I   Number 1 | Naknek, Alaska Wednesday,   December 13, 1961 | Price 10c per copy |

Dillingham News

The biggest news of the week in Dillingham is the celebration of Mr. and Mrs. Carl Nunn's 25th wedding anniversary. Carl attended the Central District Democratic Convention in Fairbanks, along with Mrs. Virginia Spears, David Harrison, Joe McGill and William R. Brandon. Friends of the popular Nunns are afraid that Carl won't make it back home in time for the anniversary party scheduled for Monday, Dec. 11th. Mrs. Nunn is making bets even up that he, will show.

A series of spectacular mishaps occurred Friday night, caused by our icy roads and treacherous travelling conditions. Bob Cummins ran off the road a bit and had to abandon his car; Trudy Ward, who was driving Frank Thomas' car, struck Cummin's car inflictin $1500.00 damage to Frank's vehicle. Olif Johnson happened along and also hit Bob's car, causing $500.00 damage to Ote's car. Cummins car was unmarred. Min. H. Springer, road commissioner, stated that the Dillingham drivers must learn to either put on chains or quit driving, because, Mr. Springer said, the Road Commission is not equipped to spread sand or gravel on the icy roads.

Peggy Keane of the P.U.D. is leaving Tuesday morning for a month's vacation in San Francisco. Her job in the office will be taken over by the petite 'Vi' Wendler until Peggy's return.

Fritz Kruse will be four years old on Tuesday, Dec. 13th. Happy Birthday, old man!!

The Koffee Klatch recieved a card from a former quaffer, Mrs. Donna (state trooper) Barber. She'll have her sev-
Please turn to page 8

This is your first issue of the BRISTOL BAY DIGEST, a new weekly newspaper designed to serve Southwestern Alaska. Look it over. Read our statement of editorial policy on page 2. This is your paper, about people you know.

This paper is just as close as your post-office. $3.50 (only 7c per week!) is all it costs. But don't put it off. Send the handy subscription blank today to:

BRISTOL BAY DIGEST
P.O. BOX 105
NAKNEK, ALASKA

To the Editor:
Yes, I'd like to subcribe to the BRISTOL BAY DIGEST and I am enclosing $3.50 which is the annual subscription rate (rates somewhat higher outside Alaska). Please send the BRISTOL BAY DIGEST to:

Name: ....

Address: ....

Bay Men Attend Demo Meeting

BRISTOL BAY was well represented at the recent Central Division Democratic Convention in Fairbanks. Dillingham sent Joe McGill, Carl Nunn, William Brandon, Dave Harrison, and Virginia Spears, while the Naknek-King Salmon group were represented by Rasmus Casperson, Norman Tibbetts and Arne Ohlmholt.

This gathering has special significance for all of the men interested in running for the office of governor in the upcoming primary election, and in additionto the two announced Democratic candidates, Warren Taylor of Fairbanks, and John Rader, of Anchorage, there are several hopefuls lining up support. Of particular interest to the Dillingham contingent was the fact that Robert Kallenberg, Jr. was chosen as a delegate to attend the State Convention in Nome early in 1962. Robert is living in College attending school.

THE WEATHER OUTLOOK Realizing that weather information is of extreme interest to Digest readers, as a regular feature, we will try to describe the general weather pattern so that readers may draw their own conclusions about the coming weather in each locality.

There is nothing very puzzling about the weather map tonight. Important to Bay residents are the two weakening low-pressure areas—one over the Chain and the other above Anchorage. Neither of these Please turn to page 5

Ice Forces Delay in Drilling Plans

HOPES THAT the Nushagak Peninsula would become the "Spindle Top" of Alaska were temporarily shelved this fall when the Pure Oil Co. drilling crew failed to land their equipment this fall.

This particular drill rig had been working all summer in the Canoe Bay area on the Alaska Peninsula. The Nushagak operation had been carefully planned so that the camp trailers, messhall and other furnishings would come out of Seattle on the barges all ready to be put in place at the drill site. The plan was that the tugs would stop in Canoe Bay to pick up the barge loaded with the drill rig and proceed on to Bristol Bay. They knew, of course, that the season was pretty late to be fooling around in the Bering Sea—and if they didn't the marine underwriters did—and as it turned out, it was entirely too late.

By the time the Donna Foss arrived off the beach with their four barges, the beach was choked with ice. Bernard Wamser had his 'M' boat Independence under charter to the oil company, but after fighting the weather and the ice and waiting for about ten days, they finally called off and the tugs left for Dutch Harbor.

This wasn't the end of it, however. Just as the Donna come abreast of Cape Leiskof, one of the barges broke loose and went hard aground. The tow-boats had no choice but to keep right on to Dutch where they left the three scows and then returned to the Cape to rescue the barge. Inspection of her showed, however, that four of her eight compartments were flooded, so a crew of men was flown to the barge Monday to begin the task of unloading her and hauling thecargo to winter storage at Port Moller, fifty miles away. It is hoped that after the cargo is removed that she will be light enough to float.

Asked about the company's plans, Mr. Posie replied, "As matters stand at present, we hope to be back in the Bay about May 1."

o—o
BBFPA MEETING THURSDAY NITE, Dec. 14, at 7:30
o—o

1962 COMMERCIAL FISHING RULES MADE BY F&G BOARD

THE BOARD of Fish and Game has set the regulations for 1962 except for a few loose ends such as HB 143 which is currently being studied by the Federal Court. This wound up one of the best fishery hearings ever conducted by this Board.

There was a great deal of fisherman participation — something not always seen in previous meetings — and the crowd which jam-packed the Loussac Library Auditorium both Saturday and Sunday was very impressive.

The 1962 rules for Bristol Bay pretty much follow last year's pattern. The minimum mesh size is again 5-¾". The Egegik District was closed to all drift netting, and the Naknek-Kvichak District was divided into two separate management districts with the provision that if drift fishing would not be permitted until the escapement appeared assured.

The first item on the agenda was the General Provisions and the reoccuring conflict over the fate of the "Perryville" District. Chuck Turner of Kodiak Fisheries suggested that the district be abolished. This was also the view of Alaska Packer's Don Cooper who urged that this area be combined with the Peninsula area. As might be expected, P.E. Harris' Bill Lilly took a dim view of any such move saying, "Turner keeps stretching his domain further west." Stieg Osman from PAF and NEFCO's superintendent both argued that there should be no change in the Areas. Several fishermen from Chignik also test'fed.

Attention was then focused on Bristol Bay as Mr. A. W. Brindle of Ward Cove. Columbia Ward and Red Salmon congratulated the Board and the Department staff for management which he felt was on the whole, very good, and he pointed to the good relations he enjoys throughout the State.

Mr. Brindle suggested that the Board was placing too much emphasis on methods of taking salmon and not enough thought was being given to the quality of the finished product. To illustrate his point, Brindle told the Board Please turn to page 4

that the chum ad pink quality were below par this year, and he said, "Salmon runs are actually unpredictable." He urged that the Department retain full flexibility so that the salmon runs can be fully utilized.

"Red" Tilden of Dillingham offered a motion by Floyd Curnutt concerning the powers of the Advisory Committee and criticized the April 15th deadline for gear registration.

As soon as all des'ring to be heard, Chairman Roy Selfridge of Ketchikan turned the spotlight on Bristol Bay and the Bay discussion by pro-

Bob Martin Passes Away

Word has just been received here that Bob Martin of the Board of Fish and Game suffered a fatal heart attack this evening and passed away at his brother's home in Seward.

He is survived by his wife, Alice, and several brothers in Seward.

Augie Alto, of Egegik, starting the first that a separate advisory committee be established in the Egegik District. He named five men who had been elected by the people of Egegik to serve on such a committee. He recommended that the outer boundaries be moved well inside the Egcik River, and that the fishery be confined to setnets only. He concluded his remarks by complimenting the Dep artment staff and the fishery particularly Member-Bob Martin for the manner in which the fishery has been managed.

Mr. John Gilbert of Bumble Bee Seafoods, had no objection in the division of the Naknek-Kvichak District but he did object to the provision restricting drift netting in the area. He said this would constitute an "exclusive right of fishery". He reviewed the data and said there was no justification from the viewpoint of the scientist, why the area should be reduced in would provide much news, but with our far flung correspondents and schoolteachers like Bob Veach, we never lacked things to put in the paper.

Veach taught the fifth and sixth grades. He was a fighter pilot during the war. Since Lynnie was one of his students, I received a nightly report on his teaching methods. They seemed unusual, but remembering my own unorthodox classroom behavior, I was very forgiving.

When Veach decided to perform a citizen's arrest on dump trucks carrying goods from a barge at Naknek Point to King Salmon, because they lacked valid Alaska license tags—he accomplished this by tying the front bumpers of the offending trucks to a nearby tree—I assumed he was demonstrating good citizenship to his students, and I printed the story as a straight news story, just as I had the fable about the children and the ducks.

But when Veach organized a Democratic caucus and filed in the primary election for the United States Senate against popular incumbent Ernest Gruening, a former governor, I began to wonder if he was playing with a full deck.

When he announced his candidacy, I printed a profile on him, which described these and other somewhat bizarre episodes. It was not complimentary or flattering.

Veach was a big man. When I saw him looming in the shop doorway after the paper came out, my first guilty thought was that he had come to horsewhip the editor.

Instead, he asked, "Could I buy a thousand copies of this issue?" He wanted to use those papers as campaign literature.

I gulped and sighed in relief. "Sure," I said. "It will take a little while. . ."

Bob broke in, "How about printing some of this in red, so it will really stand out?"

"I could try," I said, still trying to make sense out of his peculiar reaction. I overprinted a red box around the story, which suited Bob very well.

An odd thing was happening in the community. The Democratic caucus began meeting twice a week. Through his father-in-law, Gordon began hearing strange and uncomplimentary things about the half dozen people in town who were identified as Republicans. Gordon was the precinct committeeman, while I was a former Republican candidate. Then there was Jay Hammond, Harry Shawback, and Patsy Pierce, the Republican precinct committeewoman. Even my old friend, Gunnar Bergen, began looking the other way when we met on the street. Old friends quit talking to one another. This was serious.

Looking at the community through half-closed eyes was like looking at the world through an old-fashioned window pane. Things seemed slightly out of focus, mildly distorted, and unreal. It seemed as if the entire community was suffering a particularly malignant form of cabin fever.

I'm sure that if communities were capable of paranoia, Naknek would have been certifiable. We later learned, after he was hospitalized, that Bob was mildly psychotic. Based on my observation of Naknek that winter, I'm convinced there is such a phenomena as the Pied Piper syndrome. I watched a man who was more than slightly screwy lead a community of normally rational people right over the edge of a figurative cliff.

Even the penis splint joke lightened the mood of the community only briefly. I personally thought it was very funny, and I wish I could take credit for it, but I can't. Apparently a local wag had sent the name of every man in Naknek to an advertiser promoting penis splints.

I was in the post office when Gunnar Bergen received and opened his envelope containing the appliance's advertising. He silently studied the drawing and read its description.

385

Then he said to the room at large, "This reminds me of when Russian Alex took Moonface Nellie upriver. He said he had to lash a spoon on it!"

The community was so wrapped up in this bizarre set of circumstances that not even poor "Long" John Fielding's untimely death shortly before Christmas offered much of a distraction. His was a sad story.

Long John was a construction worker. He and his wife had come into the country the previous fall. Shortly before freeze-up, the couple decided to separate. Long John went to Ole Creek, planning to spend the winter with our old pal, Ole Wassenkari. However, he wasn't happy there, and shortly before Christmas, he returned to Naknek.

We hardly knew he was back in town before we heard a frantic knock at the door, and upon opening it, heard a man urgently say, "Come quick! Long John's shot hisself. He's on the other side o' Munson's place!"

Jan's services were always in demand. She grabbed the little emergency bag that she kept handy, and after pulling on our parkas, we rushed out into the frigid air. Other people were hurrying toward the Munson's place, and we followed, slipping and sliding on the packed snow.

John was still sitting, leaning against the house, but slumped over, his .22 rifle across his lap. His eyes were closed. You had to look close to see the wound in his right temple, but when Jan lifted his head, there was no mistaking the bulge of the bullet under the skin of his left temple.

He was barely alive. Jan stood up and looked around. Ike Jensen's house was just around the corner.

"Get a blanket," Jan said, "and carry him to Ike's house."

One of the men disappeared and in moments he returned with a blanket. As gently as possible, John was laid on the blanket. Then a dozen hands lifted it and carried him into Ike's living room where he was laid on the floor, and where he died a few minutes later.

Since Alaska was now a state, the old commissioner/coroner system had given way to a strict regimen requiring a state police inquiry whenever a death by shooting occurred. I think it was a good idea, but at times like this, it was clearly overdone.

The nearest state policeman was in Anchorage. We called the emergency number and were told that no policeman would be available until after New Year's Day.

I thought this was inconvenient, but as long as the weather remained cold, we had no problem, except we needed a place protected from foxes and weasels to store the corpse. The cannery store warehouse seemed a perfect solution.

I went down to the cannery store and explained our problem to the storekeeper. Not being superstitious myself, I'm slow to recognize it in others. I thought Gerrit seemed strangely reluctant, but I put that down to the fact that this was his first winter not only in the store, but in the United States. Gerrit was from The Netherlands.

He reluctantly consented. Soon, Gunnar backed his weapons carrier with its sad cargo up to the warehouse door, and we carried John's body inside. We put it in the corner and laid a sheet of plywood over it to conceal it from a casual visitor to the warehouse. Accidentally discovering a corpse could be traumatic.

Then we found out how very superstitious our Dutchman really was. The holidays traditionally feature much baking of cakes and cookies. The store ran out of flour and sugar. Too bad. There was no way the storekeeper was going into that warehouse as long as Long John lived there. We began trading staples back and forth. Some folks drove out to King Salmon for them because Gerrit wouldn't chance a face to face meeting with John.

It was almost two weeks before the policeman showed up.

387

Meanwhile, a coffin had been shipped in (the cannery carpenters no longer left three or four coffins behind when they left) and considering how frozen the ground was, we had dug the smallest grave imaginable. The empty box would just fit. As we chipped our way though that frozen earth, I was very much reminded of my "chain gang" at Clarks Point.

We led the policeman into the warehouse and lifted the plywood. When we had covered John, it was to protect the sensibilities of innocent passersby. We didn't think what it would do to John. But the sheet of plywood resting on his nose had distorted it. When he was alive, John wasn't a bad looking guy, but now he was just plain ugly. So ugly, in fact, that the policeman was visibly shaken. He glanced quickly at the bullet hole in John's temple and pressed his finger against the bullet's outline under the skin on the other side of John's head. "OK," he said, "you can bury him, now."

I really wish life were that simple. Long John's nickname was well earned. In life, he stood four inches over six feet. In death, he seemed to have grown a foot as we struggled to cram his rigidly frozen corpse into that box.

We knew, without discussing it, that it would have been futile to ask Gerrit if we could stand John quietly in a corner of the store until he thawed. To be fair about it, however, none of us volunteered our kitchens for that purpose, either.

Ultimately, our alternatives as amateur morticians were narrowed to three choices. We could get a bigger coffin and chip more frozen earth to enlarge the existing grave, or we could forget the coffin and simply bury John wrapped in the blanket he was lying on when he died, or we could adjust John to fit the box we had.

We decided to adjust John.

17

Smoke and Mirrors

As 1960 approached, I knew that we in the Bristol Bay Fish Producers Association were about to revisit that ancient axiom that you can go broke a lot faster with too much fish than you can with too little.

US observers with the Japanese high-seas gillnet fleets had begun reporting disproportionately large catches of very young red salmon in the summer of 1958. Those fish, from the 1956 year class (when those fish, as eggs, were deposited in their natal gravel) continued to dominate the 1959 Japanese high-seas catch. During the winter of 1959-1960, when scale samples from those fish were analyzed, scientists in the Bureau of Commercial Fisheries and the Fisheries Research Institute realized that an enormous flood of red salmon was poised in the North Pacific, ready to return to Bristol Bay in 1960 as mature spawners.

Just as the salmon packers courted independent fishermen in the poor years, so did they disdain them in years of anticipated high abundance, when cheaper "company" fish—fish caught by fishermen/employees fishing in company-owned boats—would meet their needs. I knew our need for new buyers would never be greater.

Unfortunately, the new American Packing Company cannery would not be ready. It was still under construction. Gordon McCormick, a highly skilled catskinner, had spent many hours on an old Caterpillar bulldozer the previous fall (with my uncertain assistance), carving a new cannery site out of a hillside.

Karl Sjoblom was confined to the production capacity of the *Kayak* in 1960, which wasn't great. Even with the *Arctic Maid* under charter as a back-up, I knew he could not handle the quantity of fish our boats, now numbering nearly 200 in the Kvichak River alone, were capable of producing. Therefore, I had continued my search for new buyers, at least for 1960.

I had contacted a small shipping company in New York which operated a specially equipped ship transporting tropical fruits from the Caribbean to New York. The ship had been fitted with a powerful compressor capable of generating liquid nitrogen, which was used to freeze the ship's exotic cargo. I easily pictured that ship freezing and hauling several million salmon from Bristol Bay to Japan. Unfortunately, the shipping line merged with American Export Lines before negotiations were completed.

However, while the deal was still on the table, we had tested the feasibility of the project by conducting a crude experiment using liquid nitrogen to freeze raw fresh salmon. Liquid nitrogen is unbelievably cold. The kettle of steaming liquid stood at an incredible $-310°F$. Our purpose was threefold. We wanted (a) to discover how quickly nitrogen would bring the fish's internal temperature to $0°F$, (b) whether fish frozen instantly by this method would have a higher market value than fish frozen by conventional methods, and (c) the quantity of nitrogen required to freeze a five pound fish.

The experiment was conducted at the *Linde Air Products* plant in Seattle. Our lawyer, Dave Weyer, had obtained the fish from the Indians on the Olympic Peninsula. Bill Lilly (then Vice President of Nick Bez's *Peninsula Packers*), arranged for the nitrogen. We placed a cast iron kettle filled with liquid nitrogen on a platform scale. I inserted a thermometer with a long probe into a whole fish, and dunked the fish into the kettle. Bill stood by with a stop watch. Dave held a note pad.

Only the second question was satisfactorily answered. The thermometer was too slow to answer the first question. Although the thermometer's needle still registered above freezing after a 15 second immersion, the fish was already brittle. Also, since the experimental vessel was an open kettle, continually venting gaseous nitrogen, and since we didn't know with certainty when the cold penetrated the fish's internal tissues, simple before and after readings on the platform scale gave us only a very rough approximation.

It appeared that it required at least a pound of nitrogen to freeze each fish.

We froze ten fish. Then we packed them in a cardboard box (accidentally dropping one, which shattered like glass) and took them to the Nordic Cold Storage plant where they were placed in ordinary cold storage for three months. Then Lilly had the fish removed and canned in ¼ pound cans.

When a can containing fish that was frozen by conventional methods prior to canning is opened, the pack often displays a white curd on top of the meat. This has no nutritional significance, but it detracts from the product's appearance. In a competitive market, it reduces the product's value. We wanted to know if our fish would display that curd.

Bill sent ten cans to the salmon lab in Seattle for analysis, telling the lab director that some of the cans were filled with previously frozen fish. He challenged the director to identify them, but he was unable to do so.

Bill Lilly was free to help us because he and his boss, Nick Bez, like ourselves, occupied a niche on the periphery of the mainline salmon packers such as Brindle and his billion-dollar cohorts. Bill Lilly was a genuine friend. I think his interest and limited participation in this project was only partly motivated by self-interest.

Nick Bez

Of course, he had every possible reason to be seriously interested in our experiments with new processing techniques. But beyond that, Bill had a wonderful sense of humor, and I know he derived much enjoyment at Brindle's continuing perplexity and discomfiture at our various negotiating strategies.

He and Bez would have done well in vaudeville. Bill Lilly was, in every conceivable respect, dissimilar to Bez. Where Bez was a big man, Lilly probably never weighed more than 140 pounds in his lifetime. Bez was flamboyant; Lilly was conservative. Bez was Machiavellian; Lilly was straightforward.

Bez was likely to go off on tangents. He served for a time as chairman of the finance committee of the National Democratic Committee. I believe Lilly was a Republican.

Bez's open admiration for Juan Tripp, former CEO of Pan–American Airlines, and his long-time friendship with Jimmy Doolittle, offer an explanation for his venture into the airline business (West Coast Airlines). Lilly, on the other hand, was strongly focused on the fish business to the exclusion of everything else. But that's where the dissimilarities ended. Both were strong, honest men, and they were exceedingly loyal to each other.

Although Nick Bez had lived in the United States since 1911, when he had left "Oustria" to avoid the draft, he always spoke with a heavy Slavonian accent. He sometimes promised more than he could deliver, but I liked him. It is commonly believed that Taylor Caldwell used him as a model for the villainous "Zeb" (Bez spelled backwards) in her Alaskan novel, *Ice Palace*. If she did, I think it was a bum rap.

Rumor had it that he had begun his fishing career in a small naphtha-powered seiner called the *Ruth* in Southeastern Alaska. He is said to have pioneered a peculiar sort of business arrangement which was termed "fish piracy" but in fact was an under-the-table business arrangement between himself, the fish trap watchmen, and the cannery superintendent. He would buy fish from the fish trap watchmen at a very low price and sell them back to the canneries, which owned the traps, at the seiner price. It was tacitly understood, of course, that the "pirate" would never sell the fish to a competing cannery.

There was also another form of piracy practiced on the fish traps. When I was a trap watchman in 1946, I declined to participate in the first sort of piracy, and was a victim of the second, which was out and out larceny, but I was able to help bring those pirates to justice.

Win Brindle, like Nick, was a self-made man, driven by powerful ambitions. In their way, each was a extraordinary personality. Legend had it that as a boy in Ketchikan (where his mother was a schoolteacher), Win was forcibly ejected from a Libby, McNeil, Libby cannery dock. If the story is true, it must have been a source of great satisfaction to him when, in 1957, Libby threw in the sponge and Win acquired their Alaskan properties.

Brindle was intelligent, tough, hard, and highly focused. In business, he was merciless. But with people, he was compassionate. He was also very human. In a perverse sort of way, I liked and admired the man, and have always regretted that the feeling was not reciprocated.

A. W. (Win) Brindle
—Photo Courtesy of ADF&G

When a house in Naknek caught fire, the Red Salmon fire truck, often with Win at the wheel, was always quick to respond. Similarly, when Dorothy Bergen, Gunnar's wife, was in the Anchorage hospital, Win not only visited her, but he also quietly paid her bill.

That both men were successful going head to head against huge *Fortune 500* corporations tells as much about corporate weaknesses as it does those men's strength. Except for Brindle and Bez (and later Sjoblom), all the superintendents were hired hands. Their time horizon extended no further than the next annual profit and loss statement and the Bristol Bay report, which compared the annual production of individual canneries. Woe to the superintendent whose percentage of the total production slipped. The fishermen weren't alone in competing against the "average."

That explains, of course, why the superintendents drove their fishermen and cannery workers so hard.

That's also why Bez and Brindle were so successful competing against them. Neither was worried about his job or concerned about a corporate bureaucracy. Unlike their corporate rivals, both men could make whatever mid-season adjustments seemed desirable, including bidding for additional fish if necessary. Moreover, the two independent operators were smarter and more aggressive than the average hired superintendent.

But where Brindle gained his objectives by a blunt show of strength, Bez was more inclined to rely on his personality and charm. He was much more devious. Although I fished for Nick, drank with him, and considered myself a friend, I was never really sure how he regarded me. Brindle never left me in any doubt.

As part of his charm, Bez was an accomplished raconteur. One evening, when he and I were attending a Fish and Game Board meeting in Kodiak, and were staying in adjoining rooms on the top floor of the old Kodiak Hotel, we spent an evening sharing a bottle of whiskey. He told me the following incredible story, which makes the point:

Where Brindle had bought his way into Bristol Bay by buying the Red Salmon cannery, Nick Bez had earlier forced his way into the fishery with an old wooden, bald-headed, schooner, named the *La Merced*. The year was 1936. Nick had scraped together enough money to buy the vessel, on which he installed a small one-line salmon cannery. He had also, through his connections with Columbia River Packing Corporation, obtained a half dozen sailboats. He was ready to begin operations in Bristol Bay. It goes almost without saying that the canned salmon people went nuts when they realized what Bez intended.

However, in an unrelated tragedy, they saw an opportunity to stop him. A year earlier, a cruise ship, the *Morro Castle*, had burned with a huge loss of life. Congress, in response, was revising the Maritime Code, stiffening safety requirements for merchant vessels. Salmon industry lobbyists made every effort to ensure that the proposed legislation was broad enough to include *La Merced*, reasoning that the old wooden schooner, with her cannery boilers, could never comply with the new marine fire prevention standards.

In desperation, Nick went to the chairman of the Maritime Commission, a gentleman by the name of Joseph P. Kennedy, who doubtless recognized a kindred spirit, and who listened sympathetically to his story.

Kennedy said, "The Japanese have floating processing plants they call mackerel schooners. There may be an exemption in their maritime code for such vessels. Congress might give you an exemption based on that precedent. Unfortunately, our relations with Japan at the moment are such that they are unlikely to give us anything. However, I suggest that perhaps the Yugoslav government could obtain them for you."

Bez went to the Yugoslav Embassy, and a formal request for the Code was sent to Tokyo via Belgrade. A year later, long after Bez had succeeded in carving an exemption for floating processing vessels like the *La Merced,* a package arrived from Tokyo, via Belgrade, via Washington. Nick never bothered to unwrap it. He simply put it on a closet shelf and forgot it until December 7, 1941.

Following Pearl Harbor, Nick immediately saw himself in an admiral's uniform, and went to Washington to offer his services to the Secretary of the Navy. Secretary Knox demurred, insisting that America needed experienced salmon processors far more desperately than it needed instant amateur admirals.

Nick had foreseen that reaction. With the instincts of an Alaskan fish pirate, he had brought trading stock. Specifically, he had the unopened package of books which had come from Tokyo four years earlier.

He put the package on Secretary Knox's desk. "I show you why I should be admiral," he said.

Knox summoned an aide who took the package to the intelligence unit for evaluation. In less than 15 minutes, a real admiral appeared, eyes wide with excitement.

It seems the Japanese clerk who had responded to the Yugoslav request had been careless. Instead of shipping the Japanese maritime code, he had shipped the coastal maritime *pilot* with the latest charts of Tokyo Bay. They were better than any charts we then had of that area, and were used by American submarines when they penetrated Japanese waters toward the end of the Pacific war.

Nick's naval ambitions were frustrated, but he was shrewd enough to share his moment of glory with old Joe Kennedy. Partly as a consequence, he became a power in the National Democratic Party. When President Truman visited Seattle in 1948, Nick Bez had the honor of rowing the Presidential skiff around Elliot Bay while President Truman (successfully) trolled for salmon.

I don't know whether Brindle knew of my limited experiment with liquid nitrogen, or of my discussions with Jacob Isbrandsen, or more importantly, of the fact those discussions were fruitless, but my efforts to open negotiations with him in 1960 were continually frustrated; he was too busy, or he had another appointment, or he would get back to me.

Brindle was acting as if he held all the cards, which, in fact, he did. Day after day dragged by. Without a contract, which was where we seemed to be headed, we faced two problems: First, while the canners would pay a "fair" price for independent fish, our idea and theirs of fair was miles apart.

Second, if a heavy run materialized, as seemed certain, and company fishermen were put on limit (restricted to a 2,000 fish per day catch), we feared that my members might not be able to continue fishing at all. Still, the consent decree of 1955 remained in force. Notwithstanding the fears of old timers like Gunnar, I thought the canners might be legally obliged to receive independent fish subject to the same restrictions imposed on company fishermen. But this was scant comfort. I wanted to focus on fishing, not on guard-house lawyering. Therefore, I wrote a letter to the Federal

Trade Commission, alerting that agency to the problems we feared might arise if we were compelled to fish without a contract that summer.

There were other possibilities. The industry remembered my naive letter to the Japanese Consul General. Well, why not capitalize on that?

I decided to try a bluff. It was late in the spring, less than three weeks before the season would begin, and my members were very worried. I called a general membership meeting in the Naknek fisherman's hall to consider our next move. The place was packed.

I described my efforts to meet with industry representatives, and expressed my suspicions concerning their motives. I concluded my remarks by saying, "For personal reasons you all know, this idea bothers me a good deal more than it may bother some of you, but since American Pack is still gearing up, and there are no other big buyers on the horizon, what would you think about selling fish to the Japanese this year?"

Knowing that some of the men had come straight to the meeting from Joe Hurd's bar, I had hoped, by that indirect reference to my war experiences, to head off a demagogic anti-Japanese outcry from the floor. I was prepared for almost anything *except* the outburst of enthusiasm and approval that I received. I hadn't expected that.

Knowing that Brindle would hear about the meeting almost immediately, I waited to hear from him. Nothing happened. It looked as if I had to raise the ante.

I had a secret weapon. I knew that one of the GIs working in the King Salmon Alaska Communications System (ACS) office seemed to be on the industry payroll, because copies of my telegrams and the gist of my telephone conversations became known very quickly to the industry people. Although I had been tempted to report the man, wisely, I had kept this bit of information to myself.

The next day I unobtrusively boarded Northern Consolidated's flight to Anchorage. The last time I had visited Anchorage, I had bought a new pair of pants in the men's department of the Northern Commercial Company store. One of the clerks, I remembered, appeared to be a Nisei (American born of Japanese parents).

On the flight into Anchorage I worked out a scenario. When we landed, I went to the store. Sure enough, there he was; a stocky middle-aged man with thick black hair and strong Japanese features. He was gravely waiting on a customer. When his customer left, I approached him.

"How'd you like to make an easy $200?" I asked.

He stared at me impassively. "What's the catch?" he asked.

"I need a Japanese actor," I said. "Let me buy your lunch and I'll explain."

On his lunch hour, we sat in a booth drinking coffee, and I explained what I had in mind; that he was to be a Mr. Iturbe, representing a Japanese fishing company arranging with me to buy salmon from fishermen in Bristol Bay.

After he listened to my proposal, he solemnly nodded. "OK," he said, "I'll do it. Just tell me what to say."

We arranged for my newly minted Mr. Iturbe to receive a telephone call from me at ten o'clock in the employee's lounge, two days hence. I handed him a slip of paper with an outline of the conversation I wanted to hold.

Another thought occurred to me. "How's your Japanese accent?" I asked.

"Ah so, Moah-san," he replied with a grin and a slight nod of his head.

Perfect.

At precisely ten o'clock, two days later, I placed a call to Mr. Iturbe through the long distance facilities of the Alaska Communications System at King Salmon.

The phone rang, and was answered, "Hearo?"

"Is this Mr. Iturbe?"

"Yesss," came the sibilant response.

"This is Mr. Moore. I'm the manager of the Bristol Bay Fish Producer's Association."

"Ah so, Meesta Moah. We are happy to hear yo'."

God, I thought, *I hope he's not overdoing it!* Aloud, I said, "Has the letter of credit arrived?"

"Ah so, Meesta Moah. Two mirron dollah, jus rike we promise."

"Would you like to meet some of your fishermen?" I asked.

"Ah, yesss, Meesta Moah."

I quickly arranged for our new "buyer" to arrive on the flight from Anchorage the following morning. After we hung up, I drove back to Naknek and posted a notice for a meeting the following evening.

The next morning, the King Salmon air strip was teeming with activity. It appeared that every superintendent in Bristol Bay had found a reason to meet NCL's flight five from Anchorage. I parked near the edge of the field and joined the others as we silently watched the silvery, high wing, twin engine Fokker F-27 circle the field and land.

The plane rolled into the parking area, and the pilot turned the plane slightly, then shut down the engines. The door swung down and passengers clutching the hands of small children or luggage, or both, began filing down. The last person straggled off the ramp, and my heart sank. No Mr. Iturbe.

But suddenly, there he was, framed in the doorway. His timing was superb. Looking out the window, he had seen the score of solemn faced men standing together, and correctly guessed they were there to witness his arrival. Therefore, he had made his entry as dramatic as possible.

Mr. Iturbe paused under the wing, a bit uncertain, and I rushed forward, hand outstretched. Before accepting my hand, Mr. Iturbe bowed.

It was wonderful. Mentally, I promised him a $50 bonus.

I gently steered him to the passenger seat in my jeep. As I was walking around the car a cannery representative sidled up to me and whispered coarsely, "Who in the hell is that guy, anyway?"

I was surprised at his boldness. "Just a friend, Pinky," I said as I climbed into the jeep and started the engine.

On the drive to Naknek, I reminded my pseudo fish buyer that my membership thought he was real; everyone expected to be delivering their fish to Japanese buyers that summer. Only three people knew differently, and he was one of them.

We drove down the beach that afternoon. Mr. Iturbe had a wonderful conversation with Gunnar Bergen. Gunnar was earnestly protesting the high-seas fleets' inroads on our salmon. Mr. Iturbe had no idea what he was talking about, and merely thickened his accent and feigned difficulty with Gunnar's Norwegian/English. Gunnar couldn't understand him. I had a tough time keeping a straight face as I listened to the two men.

That evening, Mr. Iturbe took questions from the members at the fishermen's meeting. I answered most of them for him after pretending to consult with him. Then we went to Joe Hurd's Fishermen's Bar, where we had a drink. Then I took him to the hotel. The next morning, I took him back to King Salmon and gently put him on the plane for Anchorage.

An hour later, Brindle's dusty station wagon roared into my yard. I answered the loud banging on the door. Mr. Brindle was standing there, cloth cap square on his head. He looked me sternly in the eye. "Moore," he said, "we're getting close to the season. When are we going to sit down and work out an agreement?"

Before he left my home that afternoon, we had a contract which covered all members of the BBFPA, and awarded them a seven cent (per fish) increase. We still weren't getting $1 per fish except from the fringe operators like Sjoblom, but we were getting closer.

Some people later considered my tactics shabby. I can only say that we were desperate. Brindle could have called my bluff merely by telephoning the US Fisheries Attaché in Tokyo, but he didn't. Considering everything that had transpired between us during the previous few years, I was shocked when, two years later, when we discussed this episode, Mr. Brindle confided in me that he honestly believed I was trying to put him out of business. In actual fact, the literal opposite was true.

Feeling against Mr. Brindle and Red Salmon ran so high in Naknek's bars, that once in 1954, and again in 1958, Bob Martin, an outspoken BBFPA director who prematurely died of a massive heart attack a year later, and I stopped a half drunken mob bent on setting Red Salmon cannery afire.

As if my plate wasn't already overflowing, Gordon Mc-Cormick and I decided that 1960 was the year that we ought to go into the cannery business. I had thought Gordon was crazy when he first proposed the idea during the summer of 1959, but it was something he had been thinking about and planning for a long time.

Cannery sites had three primary prerequisites. They had to be adjacent to the fishing grounds, they had to be accessible from the water at some stage of the tide, and they had to have access to an abundant supply of fresh water. As I have already mentioned, the earliest cannery operators had surveyed and purchased every potential cannery site they found, whether they intended to use them or not. Sometimes, however, their surveyors were a bit sloppy. Gordon knew of such a case. Thus was born Mormac Corporation.

It was a simple case of shoddy survey work. Gordon had found a small fresh water stream, bracketed by survey stakes some 75 feet apart. We filed a trade and manufacturing site claim between Alaska Packer's Association ground to the west and Bristol Bay Packers' claim on the east.

Red Salmon cannery at Naknek
—Photo Courtesy of ADF&G

The site Gordon had found was on the beach around Naknek Point, about two miles away from Naknek across the tundra, but it was accessible that way only during the winter. During the summer months, to reach it, we had to drive roughly twice as far around the beach.

Bill Ritter of Pan-Alaska Fisheries advanced our start-up capital, and during the 1959-1960 winter, using the same truck we had used to carry fish to King Salmon during our famous "fish lift" two years earlier, we transported four surplus Quonset huts from the air base at King Salmon through Naknek and across the tundra to our building site. After our lumber arrived on the spring boat, we constructed what may have been the longest Quonset hut (138 feet) in the world. Then we installed the canning machinery.

Neither of us knew beans about canning fish, so we hired an expert, Eugene Sheerer, from Everett, Washington. Gene brought his son and an assistant along to help.

Most red salmon was then canned in the familiar one-pound tall can. Half-pound cans were gaining in popularity, and little quarter-pound cans had just been introduced to the

403

American market, although the Japanese had been selling them in England for several years.

Anisha McCormick (left) fills a 4-pound can at the packing table while author slices fish. Note the retort and canning machinery in background.

We went in the opposite direction. We packed fish in four-pound cans for the institutional market. The fish came from family nets and we provided the labor.

Gordon, Anisha, Jan, and I took turns butchering fish, and cutting them to the proper length. We also spent many weary hours standing at the packing table fitting pieces of salmon together and stuffing them into those cans.

Each can was individually weighed before it went on the endless belt to the closing machine, which pulled a vacuum in the can as it sealed the lid in place. The cans then went into the retort where they were cooked for three and a half hours under ten pounds of steam. You could hear those cans in the cooling shed hours later: "Ping!" "Ping–ping–ping."

Our initial pack was flawed. The vacuum machine had pulled only four inches of vacuum. While that had no adverse effect on the quality of the pack, it obliged our broker, Bill Ritter, to ship the pack to our East Coast buyer through the Panama Canal rather than by train, because at a 10,000 foot elevation in a Rocky Mountain pass, some cans might have bulged. Nevertheless, we nearly paid for the cannery that first year. It was the next year that we got into trouble.

The escapement in 1960 was about 12 million fish, largely because the canners lacked the ability to can more fish than they did. True to tradition, the canners approached 1961 as if it would be a replay of 1960, which, of course, it was not.

It was the same story, although not as bad, as 1953. Too much gear; not enough fish. Unlike the earlier years, however, the independent fishermen were infinitely better off than they had been.

Mormac Corporation, in the meanwhile, suffered what eventually amounted to a fatal attack of ambition. We decided, in 1961, to break out of our strictly family oriented mode, and get serious. On paper, the idea was wonderful. Unfortunately, as they say, the devil was in the details.

We decided to pack both quarter-pound and four-pound cans, depending on the abundance of fish. When fish was plentiful, we'd pack only the big cans, but when fish was scarce, we'd maximize our return by packing the little cans as a specialty product, with added oil, for the British market. Unfortunately, we didn't know enough about the British market before we jumped into it.

Jack Most, skipper of the *Kayak*, brought a considerable amount of freight north for us that spring. He had loaded 10,000 cases of quarter pound cans and an ancient closing machine for our quarter pound "line."

We filled most of the cans, spot checking their weights as we would for the US market, and shipped them to England. That's when we discovered what we didn't know earlier about the British market.

In the more tolerant US market, the weights of the fill in the product are OK if they *average* the required weight. In England, however, the fill of *every* can had to make the weight. When the British inspector found a short weight can (less than a three and three-quarter ounce fill), the whole pack was condemned and had to be relabeled at three and a half ounces. Then, it was sold as distressed merchandise. Instead of making two dollars a case, we lost two dollars a case. Ouch.

The year following Mr. Iturbe's propitious visit, I opened negotiations on behalf of the co-op with Bud Day, a high level representative from California Packers, (now Del Monte), one of the world's major food corporations. Bud taught me something new about high-level corporate mores.

The co-op represented both boat and beach fishermen. Both groups caught red salmon, but the boat catch was usually diluted by about ten percent of much lower valued chum (or dog) salmon. Beach fishermen almost never caught a chum salmon because that species favored deep water. On the other hand, some drift net (boat) fishermen targeted that species late in the season.

Freshly caught reds and chums closely resemble each other. For convenience, both were counted as reds when they were delivered to the cannery. The fish were separated in the fish house and were packed separately. After the cases of each species were counted at the end of the season, it was known which percentage of the catch was composed of red salmon and which was chum salmon. Then the chum percentage was calculated, and each fisherman's pay check was adjusted downward accordingly.

The beach fishermen (setnetters) insisted that since they never caught chum salmon, they should be exempted from the chum percentage. That seemed reasonable. When negotiations began, that was one of our initial demands.

In negotiations like this, you always pay for your demands. When the Cal Pack negotiators, Bud and Norm Rockness, realized this particular demand was important to me, they agreed to it only after extracting concessions elsewhere. Why not? It didn't cost them anything. It amounted only to a changed bookkeeping procedure on their part.

Three weeks later, Mr. Day, who bore a startling resemblance to the late Telly Savalas, and his pilot, found me hanging a net in the American Pack net loft.

Mr. Day indicated the stack of papers in his assistant's arms. "These are the contracts, Denny," he said. "They've just come back from San Francisco. There are 37 copies here. We need 35, and I made two for you."

I looked at the stack of papers. It was a formidable pile of paper. Each copy was about 45 pages long. Tentatively, I lifted one from the pile and began leafing through it.

Mr. Day interrupted me. "We're in a hurry, Denny," he said. "George, here," he nodded toward his pilot, "landed on the beach, and we've got to get back before the tide turns."

I looked him in the eye. "Is this what we agreed to Bud?"

He returned my stare. "Every word is exactly what we agreed to," he said. Shrugging, I accepted his pen and signed the contracts, thereby making a terrible mistake.

I didn't find out about it until after the season, when a distraught Gunnar Bergen came storming into my office. "Dot crook Brindle, he took de dog percentage oot of me payday!" he said.

I studied his pay slip. There it was, in neat, bookkeeper's handwriting, the deduction of $624 for "chum percentage." Even before I said it, I knew I was whistling past the graveyard. "There must be a mistake, Gunnar. Let's take a look at the agreement." I opened the agreement, but I knew the pertinent clause had to be missing. Brindle didn't make mistakes like this. No wonder Bud had been in such a hurry!

I felt terrible. I had difficulty meeting Gunnar's outraged stare, and I cursed myself for being foolish enough to sign that agreement without reading it. We were all going to pay a price for my bad judgment.

I shrugged. "I guess we'll have to go talk to Brindle," I said. I didn't think it would do much good, but I had to try.

We drove out to the Red Salmon cannery, and found Mr. Brindle in the cannery office.

"We need to talk to you about Gunnar's payday," I said.

Brindle nodded solemnly, and invited us into his private office. "Now, what's this about Gunnar's payday?" he asked.

"I guess you didn't know that setnetters are exempt from the dog percentage. . ." I began, but he interrupted me.

He opened a file drawer and searched through it for our contract. He found one of the copies I had signed that fateful day and opened it. He pretended to search through it, then handed it to me. "Could you point that exemption out? I can't seem to find it," he said, still as solemn as a deacon with a collection plate.

This had gone far enough. "Look, Win," I said, "we both know the clause isn't there, but it should be. It was negotiated in good faith but someone—my guess is that it was you—objected, so it was deleted and I was tricked into signing the agreement without reading it."

Brindle stood quietly behind his desk listening. I went on, "I doubt whether I'll ever understand you, Win. We've had our differences, but I always considered you an honest and honorable man. This is a fraud, and we both know it. How you, a man with more money than you'll ever be able to spend, can gain satisfaction by cheating poor Gunnar here out of a lousy $600 is more than I can understand! If it was me, I'd have a hell of a time sleeping tonight."

There was nothing more to be said. We turned and left the office. That night, shortly after dark, Brindle drove his station wagon to Gunnar's house and presented him with a check for $624. Of course, the other canneries quickly fell into line. In 1961, setnetters were not penalized for the dog percentage.

Our problems were not confined to perpetual warfare with the industry. We also found some aspects of state fisheries management troublesome. Gone were the days when a Mahaffy could dance circles around a somewhat confused Albert Davy, trying fish and game violation cases backwards. Unfortunately, there were sharp edges around the state's new management philosophy. It seemed as if the pendulum had swung too fast, too far.

One of those sharp edges was an overly zealous—almost unreasonable—level of fisheries enforcement coupled with a formal take-no-prisoners, good guy-bad guy prosecutorial style pressed by young lawyers and judges who were sent from Anchorage to try fishery violation cases.

The Naknek–Kvichak fishing district physically resembled a huge funnel about 20 miles long and 15 miles wide at its widest point. The outer limit line was anchored at its southern end near the elongated crest of Johnson Hill. It then invisibly crossed the Kvichak estuary in a northwesterly direction, ending at a wooden marker 15 miles away on a flat, nondescript beach, near Dead Man Sands. *(See chart on page 244.)*

In sailboat days, you could fish as far out as you wished. The only restriction was the captain's sense of self preservation and fear that the wind might die before the boat could return to the river. Now, with power, boats were confined to a much smaller area. It was illegal to fish west of the outer line. Since salmon normally entered the fishery on a flooding tide, fishermen often tried to meet the first of the flood as close to that line as possible. Unfortunately, the tide tables lacked precision. You never knew definitely when the tide had changed direction.

Instead, the boats would tend to congregate on or near the line. Newcomers would attempt to block or "cork" the fishermen who already had nets in the water, by setting between them and the incoming fish. So it went at the beginning of almost every flood, fishermen leapfrogging each other, vying for the incoming fish.

If the tide was flooding strongly, it usually didn't matter. Even if a fishermen set his nets in the closed area, within minutes the tide would carry him into legal waters. But when the tide stubbornly continued to ebb for an hour after the book said it had turned, an alert game warden could really earn his pay.

Enforcement was like shooting fish. The game warden merely flew over the Johnson Hill marker, and set a course by his compass heading for the marker across the river. Any boat visible from his left window was in the closed area. After noting the boats and their relative positions while making his initial pass, within ten minutes or so, the game warden would return and fly low over each offending boat, noting the boat's license number painted in large numbers on the cabin trunk.

On the tenth of July, the game warden flew over the grounds and found 173 boats fishing over the line. About half belonged to BBFPA members.

As part of my compact with the Association, I was always available to help members in court after they had been cited by the game warden. In the old commissioner's court in Territorial days, such lay representation was almost the norm. About the only time Mahaffy behaved himself was when Brindle was defending one of his Italian fishermen.

However, when I attempted to defend my members in the new state court, I ran into an unexpected problem. "Are you admitted to practice law in Alaska, Mr. Moore?" the magistrate, a somewhat snotty, recent law school graduate, asked.

Of course, I wasn't. I slunk back to my seat and watched justice being served. I didn't wait long.

The next defendants were a pair of Eskimo fishermen. They spoke no English. I almost pitied the poor judge and prosecutor as they looked helplessly around the hall.

Then the prosecutor leaned over and had a short conference with the magistrate. They stared at me. The judge
motioned me to step forward.

"Can you speak Eskimo, Mr. Moore?" the judge asked.

"Only a few phrases, your honor," I replied.

"Is there anyone here who could interpret?" he asked.

I pretended to look around the room. My old friend Feeny
Andrew was on a bench in the back. "Yes sir," I said. I
pointed at Feeny. "He lives in my village upriver," I added.

"Will he interpret for us?" the judge asked.

I shook my head doubtfully. "Some of these upriver
Eskimos are pretty shy," I said.

A long discussion between the judge and the prosecutor
ensued. Finally the prosecutor turned to me. "Would you be
willing to represent these defendants?" he asked.

"Only if I can represent *all* the defendants," I said.

The judge sighed. "Well, it's highly irregular," he said, "but
ask the interpreter to step forward and be sworn."

I didn't realize then, but if I had kept my mouth shut, I
doubt whether those defendants could even have been tried.
Also, I didn't then realize that we had a hanging judge—one
predisposed to harsh penalties. But, I suppose I sacrificed
those poor Eskimo defendants in order to gain standing in
the court. And in the long run, it was well that I did.

The facts were simple. The game warden flying along the
coast from Egegik to Naknek, claimed to have observed the
defendants fishing in the closed area, whereupon, he had
flown low over their boat and taken down the numbers.

As it happened, the line had been shifted temporarily on
the day in question, so the marker on the beach was not
relevant. A company power scow had been anchored to mark
the temporary location of the line.

After the warden gave his direct testimony, I attempted to

411

cross examine him. Knowing that the captains of power scows often anchored just over the line to be close to their boats, I asked, "Were other scows anchored near the marker scow?"

"I don't remember."

"What color was the marker scow?"

"I don't remember."

"How do you know that scow was the marker scow?"

"I just know."

"How far was the marker scow you can't identify to the regular marker?"

"I don't know."

"All you really know is that you saw a scow and you saw the defendant's boat. Isn't that right?"

"I saw them in the closed area."

"But how do you know they were in the closed area?"

"I know what I saw."

The magistrate brought his gavel down. "Guilty as charged. The fine is $500."

Each case was similar to the others. The judge had imposed a $750 fine on a half dozen of my members when I finally asked permission to address the court.

"Your Honor," I said, "I'm afraid there's something wrong here." I had his attention. He motioned me to continue.

"The area where these cases were made," I continued, "is like a strange city with regulated intersections but without stop signs. The area is unmarked, the tides are uncertain, and there are no landmarks. I have fished in Bristol Bay since 1947, yet when I'm in near that line, I can't tell you where I am within a margin, give or take, of two or three miles!"

Suddenly, I was inspired: "To make the point, your Honor," I continued, "let me arrange an expedition to the line tomorrow. The wardens can come along and tell us where to anchor. Then we could summon Dick Jensen, who would fly the line and verify our position with respect to it."

The game warden was unhappy. For him, this was a no-win situation, but when the judge accepted my invitation, he and his assistant felt obligated to come along.

The next morning, we boarded a boat belonging to a BBFPA member, and headed downriver. The skipper followed the shore until we came abreast of the marker at the base of Johnson Hill, then he turned and headed straight out into the river, presumably following the invisible line.

The game wardens were as prepared as possible. They had charts, two compasses, and even a pelorus.

After running half an hour, we reached a point some five miles offshore. Johnson Hill was still above the horizon; but we couldn't see the marker. The northern horizon showed only sky. We decided to anchor and call the bush pilot.

I went forward to drop the anchor. As soon as it caught, I tied off the anchor rode and returned to the cockpit. The boat swung into the tide. The skipper turned off the engine, and the current noisily burbled alongside.

"Well, where are we?" I challenged the game wardens.

They looked at me, then at the judge. The older one was cagy. "Where do *you* think we are?" he asked.

I smiled and shook my head. "It's like I said in court. I can't tell where I am within three miles when I'm out here. You can go ten miles up and down the coast before Johnson Hill appears to change at all."

The two wardens looked at each other. "I'm probably wrong," the senior one said slowly and reluctantly, "but I'd say we were right about here," as he pointed to a spot on the chart immediately south of the line. He didn't know where we were. He just thought he was playing it safe.

We called the bush pilot's office on the radio and asked his wife to send the plane out to verify our position. She promised he would be there in 20 minutes.

We waited and waited and waited. No plane. After an hour, we called again. She said he was out looking for us.

They should never have let me anchor that boat!

The game wardens began looking uncomfortably at each other. Apparently we were nowhere near the line. Finally, after another hour of waiting for the flight that never came, I pulled up the anchor, and we made our way back to the dock in the Naknek River.

The pilot, Dick Jensen, met us at the dock and reported that the only boat he had seen was a test boat fishing about 30 miles north of Egegik, or about ten miles below the line. Only there was no test boat out there. The boat he had seen was us. Even I was surprised that we had gone so far.

The next day, the judge stated in court what he had seen. I thought he should have dismissed the cases, but he cut the fines in half. Later, he wrote a report excoriating the Alaska Department of Fish and Game for failing to mark the line.

The following year, the line was marked with a series of buoys. Unfortunately, the fishermen soon discovered that if enough boats were tied to them, they could be dragged out to sea on a strong ebb.

18

Starting Over

A n honest description of the social and economic
conditions prevailing in Bristol Bay during the
decade preceding statehood cannot avoid the acri-
mony which erupted from time to time between the folks
living in Dillingham toward the Kvichak communities,
primarily Naknek. While my appointment as manager of the
fishermen's cooperative was the focal point for much of it, I
don't believe it was the cause. As a former editor of the
Bristol Bay Digest, I believe the root causes are embedded in
the unique history of each community.

The fisheries on the Nushagak River (Dillingham) side of
Bristol Bay were developed a full generation earlier than
those of the Kvichak (Naknek), partly because the Nushagak
River was deeper, hence more navigable. That was an
important consideration when cannery crews and supplies
arrived aboard sailing ships, which lacked the maneuverability
of steamships. Those ships remained at anchor throughout
the season. When the salmon pack was loaded aboard at the
end of the season, the fishermen sailed the ship back to San
Francisco.

Another important reason was that the abundance of
salmon on the Nushagak was smaller and therefore more
manageable, considering the primitive fishing and
canning methods then available.

The earliest canneries were built adjacent to

preexisting communities for the same reasons those sites had attracted their earliest settlers. Nushagak Point was the site of the Russian–American Fur Trading Company store and fort. Across the river was the Eskimo village of Koggiung (which later became Snag Point). Both sites offered essential physical attributes. Both had abundant fresh water, easy access to the fishing grounds, and sheltered anchorages for cannery ships.

Almost every year, from the very beginning of the Bristol Bay fisheries, some fishermen elected to remain behind in Alaska when their ship left in the fall. Some may have had a more personal interest in avoiding an early return to civilization. They might have left San Francisco one jump ahead of an unhappy wife, their creditors, or even the sheriff. Others, accustomed to the industrial hardships (such as the sailboat fisheries) of the early 20th century, found the harsh but free life of a fur trapper relatively congenial. However they came into the country, or for whatever reason, many of these early settlers married Eskimo women, and some founded large families.

Between the two world wars, the government built a hospital, school, jail, federal offices and housing in what was then called Dillingham, but which reverted to its Yupik name of Kanakanak after the post office migrated to Snag Point.

A second wave of immigration occurred when Seventh Day Adventists built a community 30 miles up the Wood River near the lower end of Lake Aleknagik. As a consequence of these developments, Dillingham became an insular, self-sufficient, family-oriented community.

Meanwhile, a full generation after the Nushagak fisheries had been developed, the salmon packing companies began exploiting first the Naknek and later, the Kvichak River fisheries. The canners encountered enormous logistical problems. Since the Kvichak is much shallower than the Nushagak, instead of anchoring directly in front of the canneries, here, their ships were obliged to anchor in open roadsteads, miles from the canneries they supported.

Moreover, the small, flat bottomed dories ("flatties," as the fishermen called them) used originally in the Nushagak River were unsuited to the Kvichak, partly because of the volume of fish the fishermen encountered, but also because the fishing grounds were more exposed to the often severe Bristol Bay weather.

Before a suitable method for harvesting Kvichak salmon evolved, processors fruitlessly experimented with salmon traps. However, by the mid-1920s, the trap experiments had been abandoned. The Carlisle boat was derived by crossing a classic whaleboat with the fishing sailboats used in the Sacramento, Columbia, and Fraser river fisheries. Just as the Conestoga (covered) wagon made possible settlement of the West, these boats, capable of fishing in bad weather and carrying at least twice the load of "flatties," made possible the development of the Kvichak fishery. That was the standard 28 foot sailboat in common use when I entered the fishery.

As the Kvichak fishery developed, a few hardy fishermen elected to remain behind each fall when their ship sailed south. But these men were fewer and more scattered than the original settlers in the Nushagak had been.

Things abruptly changed, however, with the War Department's decision to build an Army air base near Naknek during the war. That development tended to isolate the Nushagak district, but propelled the Kvichak region suddenly into the 20th century. Although Alaska Packers still owned the SS Chirikof, the last cannery steamer, in 1947, the Naknek Air Base quickly rendered the traditional cannery fleets obsolete, and caused the Naknek–Kvichak region to become the transportation hub of Bristol Bay.

Meanwhile, although residents on the Kvichak were still a small minority when the turbulent decade of the 1950s opened, Nushagak resident fishermen virtually dominated their fishery. Consequently, the fishermen on the Nushagak were spared much of the bitter conflict Kvichak fishermen experienced, which marked the transition from sail to powered fishing vessels in the larger fishery.

It was understandable, therefore, why people in Dillingham failed to understand or fully appreciate the consequences of the lockout in 1954, or the collapse of the Naknek–Kvichak fishery in 1955, or the struggles Naknek fishermen had to gain bargaining acceptance in 1958, because they took these things for granted.

Also, they failed to fully appreciate the bitter conflicts that persisted between resident and non-resident fishermen as a result of the jurisdictional strike in 1951, echoes of which still reverberated in Joe Hurd's bar as late as 1966, fifteen years later. That battle was not fought in the Nushagak; it was fought in the Kvichak, and the Kvichak fishermen carried that burden for many years.

There may be an additional contributing factor. Although Naknek, South Naknek and Levelock, like Dillingham, were home to several large families for whom commercial fishing was a primary occupation, Naknek lacked the focus on fisheries found in Dillingham.

Dillingham's economy, in other words, was community based and fisheries oriented, while Naknek still relied on outside payrolls. The annual influx of nonresident fishermen *and* workers from the Naknek Air Base, people like Long John Fielding, and institutions like the Air Force, the Federal Aviation Administration, Fish and Wildlife Service (later, the Alaska Department of Fish and Game), the Alaska Communications System, and eventually the White Alice people, supported the community and tended to dilute community interest in fisheries. So did the later community preoccupation with local politics when the *Bristol Bay Borough* was formed.

Thus, while even forty years ago, consumers in Dillingham had several stores to chose from, the folks in Naknek, like the people at Clarks Point, were obliged to trade at the company store. Conversely, if you wanted to buy a drink in Dillingham forty years ago, you had to go to the Willow Tree, almost out of town for it, but Naknek was home to five bars.

Possibly because of the greater proportion of transients in the population, Naknek seemed to be a more violent community. The winter of 1958-59 was a bad one, even for Naknek. There was one homicide, one accidental freezing death, and a death which might have been accidental, but was more likely to have been homicide. That was the year Billy Nekeferoff murdered Henry Miller. Billy was a strange bird.

A year after we had moved to Naknek, two years after Henry's death, I answered a knock on the door. When I opened it, I was startled to see Billy standing there.

Although I had never met him, the description I had been given was unmistakable, and I recognized him immediately. To cover my temporary embarrassment—what is the protocol when you first meet the murderer of your home's former owner?—I invited him in, and we sat on a wooden bench in the front room. I was acutely aware that we were only about ten feet from Henry Miller's indelible blood stain hidden under the rug, as I studied my strange guest.

Billy was a small man, one of those odd people who seem never to age. Had I not already known his history and that he was at least 40—possibly 50—years old, I might have thought he was only 16. He had a small, almost a pug nose. His blue eyes were wide and utterly candid. His skin was almost unnaturally white and pink—a natural result, I suppose, of two years spent in a federal penitentiary. His face was unlined, and he had a full head of light brown hair. Our meeting was innocuous. He had come to the door, thinking the *Anchor Inn* was open under new management.

Billy and "Deefy" Swanson were cut off the same piece of leather, only Deefy was more direct, and less homicidal. When I knew him, Deefy was probably in his early 60s. A small man like Billy, Deefy loved to fight. More accurately, I think he lived for the rush of adrenaline in his veins. As his nickname implied, he was, to use the popular cant, hearing impaired. He wore a hearing aid to rectify the problem, but when he was in his cups, and thirsting for blood, he would turn his hearing aid off, lower his head to signify he wanted to be left alone, and lay in wait for his quarry.

There seemed to be no possibility of winning a fight with Deefy. Like Billy, he was a veritable human wolverine. I saw him bleed, but I never saw him flinch. I once saw him whip a truckload of seismic engineers; men half his age and twice as big.

The fight started in Joe Hurd's bar on a Saturday night. I don't know what provoked it; where Deefy was concerned, it never took much. Possibly one of the engineers had rudely attempted to communicate with him—even local children knew that when he turned off his hearing aid, it was a signal that he wanted to be left alone.

Deefy suddenly, and without warning, leaped on the astonished man. It took four of his victim's companions to rescue the hapless stranger. But that wasn't the end of it.

The strangers retreated to their table, marveling at local folkways. Soon, the seismic crew left the bar. Deefy followed them. Suddenly, we heard shouts and screams and the truck's horn from the parking lot. Then silence.

We rushed outside to see what had happened. It was not clear whether his victim had stopped the truck and climbed down to correct Deefy's manners, or whether Deefy had attacked the truck. Whichever it was, climbing out of that truck was perhaps the most serious mistake the young man ever made. By the time the bar crowd reached the field of honor, five young engineers were gathering their wits and beginning to stir and sit up, while a grimly satisfied Deefy, a man who might have been old enough to be the grandfather of the youngest of them, stood to one side, reflectively smiling and rubbing his rock-like knuckles.

The accidental freezing death occurred on a cold, dark winter's night when an unfortunate Aleut, three sheets in the wind, stopped in a shed housing a power plant, to warm himself on his journey from Jenny's bar to the Fishermen's Bar. That's where his body was found the next morning. The poor man was apparently too drunk to realize that the plant wasn't running.

The third death might have been scripted by Agatha Christie. Six friends had gathered on a cold, windy, wintery night, when no sensible person would be wandering about, to enjoy a private New Year's Eve party in a lonely, out of the way place. During the evening, the hostess' boy friend got drunk and became abusive. After several warnings, the other men put him outside. Later, when the party broke up, the departing couples saw the deceased, then still alive, lying at the bottom of the steps in the snow. Fearing that he was waiting to strike with his feet if they came within range, they gave him a wide berth, climbed into their cars and left.

The next morning, the man's body was found *on the other side* of the steps, his skull crushed. The marshal later told me that the victim had been struck so hard that his skull was literally broken in two. The marshal was certain it was impossible for that injury to have been self-inflicted.

If anyone had been wandering around the neighborhood on foot, drifting snow soon obliterated any telltale foot prints. After a thorough police investigation, including a voluntary polygraph examination of the survivors, the people at the party were exonerated. The case remains open to this day. No one was ever charged in the murder of Joe Anders.

While Naknek was much larger than Clarks Point, and infinitely more sophisticated, the old timers who lived in both places shared many characteristics.

For one thing, they looked after each other. The late Patsy Pierce, Republican precinct committeewoman, and founder of Patsy's Bar (which passed to Jenny Nelson when Patsy died), was an active and aggressive caretaker of the older, mostly retired, fishermen who lived in Naknek, eking a minimal living on their Social Security retirement. She always had light chores available around her place to keep them busy. I remember commenting once on the four or five old pensioners raking her yard when I stopped in for a midafternoon beer.

Patsy laughed. "It's only right," she said. "They took care of me when I was young, now it's fair that I look after them when they are not so young."

You had to know Patsy's history before that remark made much sense. She had come to Alaska when the gold fields in Nome opened in 1911, and had worked as a whore on the "line" for several years, before she got a stake together and went into the bar business. She used to boast that she knew most of the early Alaskan upper crust—judges, lawyers, businessmen, and the like, but she only recognized them when they had their pants off.

Patsy wasn't shy, but some of old sourdoughs were. I remember Charlie Wolfe in particular. He was an aging bachelor who lived alone in Combine Slough above Creek cannery near Clarks Point. Charlie was a likeable person who lived frugally on a diet limited to the cheapest food the cannery store offered. The cheapest food, that is, that his ill-fitting teeth (which he usually wore in a shirt pocket) could handle. Charlie gummed (rather than chewed) his snoose. I vividly remember his delight when he discovered an over-looked carton of freezer burned pig tails in the back of the cannery freezer that he bought for 25¢ a pound.

Charlie's frugality had a purpose. Once every two or three years, he treated himself to a wild trip to Anchorage; a trip that always included a monumental binge, and usually a visit to one (or several) of the several "B" joints that flourished around Anchorage's periphery.

I remember his vivid description of one such encounter. He us told how this friendly taxi driver had delivered him to the Green Lantern—a place I knew from personal experience to be one of the more sleazy of a tarnished breed—where one of the B-girls took him to a private corner and gently separated him from his little hoard of $100 bills, as he manfully bought bottle after bottle of wine for his new friend. As he later recounted the adventure, he always ended by wistfully remarking, "I bet I could have kissed her, too."

A poor judge of character. Bill Stroh, Charlie's Naknek counterpart, was not much better. Another reclusive sourdough bachelor in late middle age, Bill was the only year-around inhabitant on the beach at the setnet village. He owned the little saltery—where fresh caught salmon were cleaned and preserved in barrels filled with salt.

Bill's was the only permanent building in this tiny settlement. The other structures were temporary buildings and a half dozen tent frames belonging to summer residents.

Bill was more worldly and sophisticated than Charlie, and certainly had his share of lady friends, but like Charlie, he was a poor judge of character. I met him when he and his partner were on trial for fishing in the closed area. Bill wanted to plead guilty, but he was terrified of his partner, a paroled felon named "Mexican" Frank Corroso. Frank had been convicted of assault and mayhem following a barroom knife fight, and feared that a misdemeanor conviction meant the revocation of his parole.

When the commissioner, a former Army master sergeant who had succeeded Albert Davy, realized what Frank was attempting to do, he accepted Bill's plea, and convened a jury to try Mexican Frank. The jury didn't even adjourn from the room to reach a guilty verdict.

Frank might have gotten off with a fine, but when the commissioner asked him if he had anything to say before passing sentence, Frank foolishly said what was on his mind, threatening the commissioner, the jury, and Bill. When last seen, he was in handcuffs on his way back to prison to complete his original sentence.

That verdict seemed sensible in the circumstances, but commissioner's juries sometimes returned strange verdicts. Sid Morgan, Mahaffy's former partner, used to tell about the jury that tried a winter watchman in Egegik on a misdemeanor theft charge. The cannery for which the man had worked had charged him with stealing company tools. Tools bearing the initials "APA" had been found in the defendant's tool shed. The jury deliberated for a few minutes, then returned the following verdict: "We find the defendant not guilty, but we recommend he return the tools."

Bill Stroh must have been guided by the same logic when he got into a shotgun duel with another crusty old-timer, Cliff Johnson, who lived across the river in South Naknek. Bill's skiff had gone adrift. He borrowed a boat and went looking for it.

Late in the afternoon, he found it across the river pulled up above the tide on the beach in front of Cliff's house. As he struggled to push it back into the water, Cliff came sliding and scrambling down the bank, a shotgun under his arm.

"What the hell do you think you're doing with my boat?" Cliff demanded.

"What do you mean, *your* boat?" Bill countered.

"I salvaged it," Cliff said. "That means it's mine."

"It is like hell," Bill rejoined. But wisely, he decided not to press the issue while Cliff was pointing his gun at him.

Instead, he pushed his borrowed boat back into the stream and went home for *his* shotgun.

Soon he returned. Cliff, of course, had been watching for him, and according to Bill, Cliff fired at him as he landed.

We don't know whether Cliff fired in the air, hoping to frighten Bill off, or if, in fact, he fired at all. Bill said he did, but if he did, it was a clean miss.

Bill then went on the offensive. He ran across the open beach, and gained the shelter of the low overhanging bluff.

Nothing happened. He cautiously climbed to the top of the bluff, careful to stay low. Cliff came around the corner of a building, and a volley was exchanged.

This time, however, Cliff cried out in pain. Bill scurried back to the beach, and hastily pushed his boat into the water. Then he tied it to the borrowed boat, and returned to his saltery in the setnet village.

There was a considerable amount of traffic on the beach in front of Bill's place, as fishermen and their families trekked back and forth to their nets. Twice that afternoon, Bill stopped people going past and told them he had killed Cliff Johnson, and that he wouldn't be taken alive.

I knew nothing about this when I went into Bob Hadfield's hotel bar that afternoon. But when the second person came in almost on my heels to deliver Bill's ultimatum, Bob told me that the state trooper in Dillingham had already been sent for. Bob was worried. He told me that Bill was mistaken. Cliff had gotten off lucky; he had only a half dozen shotgun pellets in his rump.

Bob was afraid that a strange policeman, not realizing that Bill was only frightened and not dangerous, might shoot first and ask questions afterwards. This seemed entirely plausible. I decided to see if I could disarm Bill and possibly prevent a needless tragedy.

I drove down to the beach and parked my jeep. Then I walked through the sand, approaching the saltery. The weathered and rusty corrugated iron sides of the building seemed innocuous, but I knew a frightened man with a loaded shotgun was hiding in there. The last thing I wanted to do was surprise him.

Stopping in the middle of the beach, well out of shotgun range, I cupped my hands around my mouth. "Hello, Bill!" I shouted. "Can you hear me?"

There was no response.

I waited for several minutes. Unless Bill had suddenly gone deaf, I knew he must have heard me. We had been on friendly terms since Mexican Frank had been sent back to prison, and I wanted to give him ample opportunity to review his options. I was obviously unarmed, and I didn't think he would shoot me.

"This is Denny. I'm coming to see you, Bill," I yelled.

"Stay back," his voice was muffled, coming from inside the building.

"I can't do that, Bill," I shouted back. "There's a trooper on the way. I'm your friend, and I don't want to see you to get in any more trouble than you already are."

Bill's voice sounded desperate. "I killed Cliff, Denny. Nobody's going to take me alive!"

"Cliff's sitting on a cushion," I replied. "He only got five or six pellets in the ass."

"You're lying," Bill said. "Stay back."

I had slowly but steadily been moving forward, and by now I was well within shotgun range.

I said, loudly enough for him to hear, "Bill, there's no reason for me to lie to you. Cliff is as alive as you or me. Now I want you to come out here and give me your shotgun. You might as well, because I'm not going away until you do.

Then we'll go up to the hotel and have a drink while we wait for the trooper. How does that sound?"

By that time, I was only about 50 feet from the saltery. I stood patiently while Bill thought it over.

"Are you sure about Cliff?" Bill asked.

"Absolutely. He's like a wounded bear. He's madder'n hell, and I wouldn't want to be in your shoes when he comes over on this side of the river, but you just annoyed him."

"OK," Bill said. "I'm coming out."

He stepped around the corner of the building, his shotgun under his arm. I was relieved to see the muzzle pointing down toward the sand.

Bill handed his shotgun over and stuck out his hand. "I'm taking a chance on you, Denny. Did you tell me the truth about Cliff?"

I accepted the gun and shook his hand. "I didn't lie, Bill," I said. "Cliff's alive and kicking. Bob and I were scared that you and some trigger-happy trooper would get into a pissing contest. That's why I came down here."

Bill climbed into the jeep with me, and we drove back to the hotel. Bill and I were enjoying our second drink (Bob was setting them up) when a nervous young state trooper came into the bar, inquiring after Bill Stroh. I introduced him to Bill. Cliff failed to press charges. After spending a week in the Dillingham jail, Bill was released and returned to Naknek.

I was incredibly busy those days. In the fall of 1960, Hermy Herrmann made a trip down to False Pass in the *Fagen* for a load of fish trap piling made suddenly obsolete by statehood and a flat prohibition against fish traps.

I spent many hours at American Pack the following spring, setting up and running a worn-out Frick 00 sawmill (with a 54 inch IP blade), that Sjoblom had bought, sawing those piling into planking and dock timbers. In some ways, the mill was a refreshing change from the smaller mill I had operated at Kokhanok. Instead of a 28-hp gas engine, this mill was powered by a 175hp, GMC diesel engine. Instead of an endless flat belt, power was delivered to the saw by a pulley carrying 27 V-belts. Some of the piling fairly bristled with spikes and staples. The tin roof under which I worked soon looked like a star filled sky from the hundreds of tooth holders and "points" from the saw that went flying into the air when the tooth, traveling 10,000 feet per minute, struck a piece of iron embedded in the wood.

Like many Alaskans, especially those living in outlying communities, I wore several hats. I was still manager of the Bristol Bay Fish Producers Association. I was also a commercial fisherman. Gordon and I were still struggling to get Mormac Corporation on a solid footing. I was publishing two newspapers. I held an insurance broker's license, and wrote a general line of life and property insurance.

Also, as spokesman for the state-wide fishermen's PAC (*The Alaska Fishing Industry, Inc*), I shuttled back and forth to the legislature in Juneau on a variety of fish related issues. I had received a panicky phone call the previous week that the legislature, which was still in session, was going to plunder the Fisherman's Fund—a state administered workman's compensation fund for independent fishermen—financed by commercial fishing license fees.

As soon as the next issue of the *Bristol Bay Digest* was delivered to the post office, instead of going to bed, I had quickly put on my city clothes. Ike Jensen then drove me out to King Salmon so I could catch the plane to Anchorage.

I spent the night in Anchorage, because my connecting flight to Juneau didn't leave until eight the next morning. Therefore, I had made a few calls when I arrived at Anchorage International, and was joyfully greeted by friends willing to accept any excuse to party.

Friday morning, unrested and bleary eyed, I crawled aboard the Juneau flight, arriving at the state capitol in the early afternoon. After checking into the hotel, I went to the capitol building, and talked to several key legislators.

That evening, after an overly rich dinner, I went to the Bubble Room in the Baranof Hotel where the legislators I particularly wanted to see were loading up for the weekend. I sat and drank with them, and other lobbyists, again urging the key players to respect the fund they had their eyes on.

I didn't get to bed until after midnight, but I was up at six because the Anchorage flight left Juneau at 8:30.

It was Saturday noon when I returned to Anchorage. I napped much of the afternoon. That evening, I tried to keep up with my friends, but at midnight, I gave it up and went to bed. The flight to Naknek left at eight the next morning.

I still had my tie on when I arrived back in King Salmon, but I took it off while Ike drove me to Naknek. When he let me out of the cab, I went straight to the print shop, and began to set type. I was three days behind on a weekly schedule that had no slack whatsoever.

That evening, I had my "heart attack" while we were having supper. I had just filled my plate and passed the serving dish to Trina, when my left arm suddenly went numb and a piercing pain shot through my chest. I nearly fainted. As I hovered on the edge of consciousness, I thought instantly of Bob Martin, a dear friend not much older than I, who had succumbed to a massive heart attack less than six months earlier. I wondered if I was about to die. Jan saw the distress in my face, and led me to our adjoining bedroom. Then she sent Trina for the Public Health nurse.

The pain had moderated by the time Betsy arrived. She discovered what Jan had already found; that I was manifesting a variety of classic symptoms of a heart attack. As if to confirm their diagnosis, Betsy gave me a nitro capsule which quickly eased my chest pain.

The next morning, George Tibbets flew me to Dillingham. A cab delivered me to Dr. Libby's office, and wasting no time, the doctor quickly put me on the examining table and after a preliminary examination, hooked up his electrocardiograph. Never before had I had an EKG examination, and I was fascinated by the elaborate way I was connected to the machine, and by the tracing paper, marked with jagged spikes, that came out of the machine.

Dr. Libby studied the tracing, gravely pursing his lips, while I studied his face, searching for a clue concerning my life expectancy. Finally, he looked up. "Sit up," he said, "I want to listen to your heart again." I sat up, and he listened to my chest, to my back, and to the big blood vessels in my neck.

Finally, he said, "I can't find anything wrong."

I was genuinely shocked. "What do you mean, 'there's nothing wrong?'" I demanded. "What about my chest pain?"

He stuck to his guns. "I wasn't there, last night, when this episode occurred," he said. "So I don't know what to say about that. But I can tell you that the EKG seldom lies, and it thinks your heart is perfectly healthy. Everything I hear sounds normal. I don't think there is anything wrong."

There wasn't much more to say. He advised me to cut down on my smoking, and to take it easy for a day or two. He also told me to continue taking the nitro capsules if they eased the chest pain I was still experiencing.

Tibbets flew me back to Naknek, and I reported to Jan and Betsy what Dr. Libby had said. I thought that Dr. Libby, in this case, was wrong. Frankly, I wasn't surprised.

He had an excellent reputation as the sort of frontier doctor you might hope to find if you needed a splint or a suture. He had delivered two of my children, the most recent my son, Harry, the previous year. The problem, frankly, was that I knew he was a Seventh Day Adventist.

One of the things I remembered from the lectures that Dean Paddock had given me—Dean, you'll remember, was the fisheries biologist with whom I had traveled to the upper reaches of the Iliamna watershed—was that the earth was only 6,000 years old. I'm surprised they don't also insist that the earth is flat. Some religious people do.

I assumed Dr. Libby shared the 6,000 year view of history. I suppose that's acceptable if you view the practice of medicine as an art rather than a science. Skill at mending broken bones and delivering babies is an art. But working with a machine like an electrocardiograph seemed to me to be more of a scientific activity.

Quite frankly, I find it difficult to work up much confidence in a scientist who thinks the world is only 6,000 years old. In other words, I didn't believe the doctor's diagnosis. I often wonder how things might have turned out if I had believed him, but that's water under the bridge. A later, very thorough examination in Seattle, confirmed Dr. Libby's original diagnosis.

I was smart enough at the time to realize, whether I had a heart attack or not, that Nature had just given me a warning tap on the shoulder. Something had to give.

I let two issues of the *Digest* slide while I rested. The pain in my chest did not abate. That fact, alone, seemed to us to be a clear and continuing warning that I had better slow down, or else. Jan and I spent many hours coming to grips with this new reality.

Naturally, I didn't like it, but the memory of Bob Martin in his coffin painfully reminded me that I was as mortal as the next guy; a proposition I have not always accepted. Like me, Bob had survived a particularly harrowing war, and had tended to think of himself as invincible.

Clearly, changes had to be made. I knew myself well enough to realize that simply shedding one or two of the several responsibilities I had accumulated wouldn't get the job done. We had to consider a major change in our lifestyle.

If I did have a bad heart, then I had to find a physically less demanding way of earning a living. That suggested returning to school. To become what?

My grandfather had been a lawyer, as had an uncle. I had enjoyed my work as commissioner, and since I had been involved with the state legislature for the past four years, I knew something about the legislative processes.

Moreover, my experience with the North Pacific Fisheries Commission had convinced me that a new era in international fisheries management was emerging that would require the services of lawyers rather than biologists. I wanted to be a part of that process. I decided to go to law school.

We found a buyer for the newspaper and our home, and arranged to fly our little Volvo to Anchorage.

In the autumn of 1962, we retraced our steps over the Alcan Highway. Instead of six horses and a truck, however, this time we were accompanied by six children in a little car. This trip marked the end of a long, complicated trail. I was looking at something entirely new. It was time to start over.

A family portrait by the Volvo on the Alcan Highway
(L to R) Jan, Jenny & Harry, Lizzy, Debby, Trina and Lynn

The End

Index

435